MOVING OUT OF POVERTY, VOLUME 1

Cross-Disciplinary Perspectives on Mobility

Moving
Out of
Poverty

VOLUME 1
Cross-Disciplinary Perspectives
on Mobility

Deepa Narayan *and* Patti Petesch, *editors*

A COPUBLICATION OF PALGRAVE MACMILLAN
AND THE WORLD BANK

1 2 3 4 :: 10 09 08 07

A copublication of The World Bank and Palgrave Macmillan.

Palgrave Macmillan
Houndmills, Basingstoke, Hampshire RG21 6XS and
175 Fifth Avenue, New York, N. Y. 10010
Companies and representatives throughout the world

Palgrave Macmillan is the global academic imprint of the Palgrave Macmillan division of St. Martin's
Press, LLC and of Palgrave Macmillan Ltd.

Macmillan® is a registered trademark in the United States, United Kingdom and other countries.
Palgrave® is a registered trademark in the European Union and other countries.

Cover photo: Arne Hoel/World Bank
Cover design by Drew Fasick

ISBN : 978-0-8213-6991-3 *(softcover)*
ISBN : 978-0-8213-7111-4 *(hardcover)*
eISBN : 978-0-8213-6992-0 *(softcover)*
DOI : 10.1596/978-0-8213-6991-3

Library of Congress Cataloging-in-Publication Data has been applied for.

Contents

Tables

Figures

Boxes

Case Studies

Foreword

This volume brings together multidisciplinary perspectives on poor people's mobility, a dynamic approach that hopefully will add to our understanding of how and why people move into and out of poverty. The contributors' findings about mobility patterns, factors, and processes are rich, insightful, and important.

The chapters draw on the latest longitudinal micro data to present a moving picture of poverty that is rather different from what one can see in single snapshots, the staple of traditional poverty analysis. The book is also important because the contributors' distinct disciplinary perspectives demonstrate clearly why it is critical to draw on diverse information to improve our understanding about how to reduce poverty.

The economic findings reinforce what we have known for some time: fast economic growth underpins poverty reduction, but the speed of declines in poverty is greatly affected by social and political factors. The economic panels also show that the people mired in chronic poverty around the world are actually fewer in number than the people moving in and out of poverty. Static studies do not capture this dynamic quality of poverty and vulnerability.

Of particular interest are the chapters clarifying interactions between the local social, political, and economic factors that underlie persistent poverty, vulnerability, and inequality. They point to the need to draw from different disciplines as we turn to the task of reaching the bottom poor trapped in poverty and those churning in and out of poverty.

By exploring the pathways out of poverty as well as the roadblocks caused by economic and social exclusion, as this volume does, we hope to expand our understanding and strengthen our poverty reduction efforts.

> Danny M. Leipziger
> Vice President and Head of Network
> Poverty Reduction and Economic Management
> The World Bank

Preface

Moving Out of Poverty is a bottom-up study that was designed to learn about mobility directly from the experiences of people across the developing world. The research program builds on many lessons from our earlier cross-country poverty work, *Voices of the Poor*. From the start, we wanted to engage meaningfully with a broad network of experts across disciplines who could contribute to the quality of the study. We wanted to make sure that the study benefited from the latest thinking about mobility.

When we began designing the research, we had little notion of how difficult it would be to work across disciplines. Complicating the challenges of framing the research were the deep tensions between, on one hand, the more standardized and accepted economic concepts and tools for mobility analysis in the development economics field, and on the other hand, the more interdisciplinary frameworks and wider range of quantitative and qualitative data collection methods used by sociologists, anthropologists, and other social scientists examining mobility. The latter approach presented both promise and risk.

The background papers for this research project were important in shaping our thinking, and they form the chapters of this book. As the papers rolled in one by one, we were struck by the authors' abilities to bring new perspectives to the question of poor people's mobility while usefully synthesizing a substantial volume of earlier literature. We are deeply grateful to each of them for their contributions.

In addition to the authors, we extend our appreciation to the anonymous peer reviewers who provided thoughtful and constructive reflections. To Ravi Kanbur, Michael Woolcock, and Arjan de Haan, we say a special thank you for pushing us to take our own overview chapter to the next level.

We also thank the World Bank for support during this study program, especially Danny Leipziger, vice president for the Poverty Reduction and Economic Management network (PREM); Luca Barbone, director of the Poverty Reduction Group; and Louise Cord, sector manager, Poverty Reduction Group. We also thank Gobind Nankani, former vice president of PREM, and John Page, former director of the Poverty Group, under whose able guidance the study was formulated and launched. Financial support was provided by the governments of Finland, Luxembourg, Norway, Sweden, Thailand, the Netherlands, and the United Kingdom, as well as by various departments in the World Bank. The Global Development Network also provided financial and organizational support through its networks and yearly capacity-building workshops.

We are indebted to Cathy Sunshine for her superb and scrupulous editing. Pat Katayama and Mark Ingebretsen in the World Bank's Office of the Publisher provided indispensable oversight for getting this to publication. We also thank Sumeet Bhatt, Mohini Datt, Kyla Hayford, Soumya Kapoor, Divya Nambiar, Elizabeth Radin, Nithya Rajagopalan, Sibel Selcuk, Rahul Shaikh, Sarah Sullivan, and Sunita Varada for coordination and research support in different phases of the book project.

Deepa Narayan *and* Patti Petesch

Acronyms

AIDS	acquired immune deficiency syndrome
BNS	Bangladesh Nutrition Survey
BPS	Statistics Indonesia
CASEN	National Socioeconomic Characterization (Chile)
CILSS	Côte d'Ivoire Living Standards Survey
CNEF	Cross-National Equivalent Files
CONGUATE	Coalition of Guatemalan Immigrants
CONIC	National Indigenous and Campesino Coordinating Committee
ECHP	European Community Household Panel
EHM	Household Sample Survey (Venezuela)
EIHS	Egypt Integrated Household Survey
ENAHO	National Household Survey (Peru)
ENEU	National Survey of Urban Employment (Mexico)
EPH	Permanent Household Survey (Argentina)
ERHS	Ethiopia Rural Household Survey
EU	European Union
EU-15	pre-2004 members of the European Union
EUHS	Ethiopia Urban Household Survey
FENACOAC	Federación Nacional de Cooperativas de Ahorro y Crédito (Guatemala)
FMHS	Farm Management and Household Survey (Côte d'Ivoire)
FODIGUA	El Fondo de Desarrollo Indígena de Guatemala
GDP	gross domestic product
GUATENET	National Congress of Guatemalan Organizations in the United States
HBS	Household Budget Survey (Poland)
HDI	Human Development Index
HHP	Hungarian Household Panel
HIES	Household Income and Expenditure Survey (Bangladesh)
HIV	human immunodeficiency virus
HTA	hometown association
ICRISAT	International Crops Research Institute for the Semi-Arid Tropics
IDB	Inter-American Development Bank
IETS	Instituto de Estudos do Trabalho e Sociedade (Brazil)

IFAD	International Fund for Agricultural Development
IFLS	Indonesia Family Life Survey
IFPRI	International Food Policy Research Institute
IHS	Integrated Household Survey (Uganda)
INS	Immigration and Naturalization Service (United States)
IOM	International Organization for Migration
IRCA	Immigration Reform and Control Act (United States)
IRNet	International Remittance Network
KHDS	Kagera Health and Development Study (Tanzania)
KICS	Kenyan Ideational Change Survey
KIDS	KwaZulu-Natal Income Dynamics Study (South Africa)
LAC	Latin America and the Caribbean
LSMS	Living Standard Measurement Survey
MFI	microfinance institution
MIF	Multilateral Investment Fund (of the IDB)
NCAER	National Council of Applied Economic Research (India)
NGO	nongovernmental organization
OECD	Organisation for Economic Co-operation and Development
OI	original interviewee
OLS	ordinary least squares
PDS	Public Distribution System (India)
PIDI	Integrated Child Development Project (Bolivia)
PSID	Panel Study of Income Dynamics
Q	quetzal
REDS	Rural Economic Development Survey (India)
RHS	Rural Household Survey (China)
RIMCU	Research Institute for Mindanao Culture (Philippines)
RLMS	Russian Longitudinal Monitoring Survey
Rs	rupees
SC	scheduled caste
SES	socioeconomic status
SLID	Canadian Survey of Labour and Income Dynamics
ST	scheduled tribe
TAMPA	Tegemeo Agricultural Monitoring and Policy Analysis Project (Kenya)
TPDS	Targeted Public Distribution System (India)
UNDP	United Nations Development Programme
UNHS	Uganda National Household Survey
USAID	U.S. Agency for International Development
VLSS	Vietnam Living Standards Survey
WMS	Welfare Monitoring Survey (Kenya)
WOCCU	World Council of Credit Unions

Contributors

Shelton H. Davis is a senior fellow at the Center for Latin American Studies in the Edmund A. Walsh School of Foreign Service at Georgetown University in Washington, DC. He previously served at the World Bank, first as principal sociologist in the Social Development Department and later as sector manager for social development in the Environmentally and Socially Sustainable Development Department of the Latin America and Caribbean Region. Dr. Davis has conducted research on the history of Mayan communities in Guatemala, focusing on the social effects of the political violence that took place in Guatemala in the early 1980s. His current research interests include migration of Mayan refugees to the United States and effects of the Guatemalan peace accords on cultural and other policies relating to indigenous peoples in Guatemala.

Stefan Dercon is professor of development economics at the University of Oxford, a member of the European Development Network, and a research fellow of the Centre for Economic Policy Research in London. He is also poverty research director of the Young Lives project at the University of Oxford, a 15-year cohort study of children in Ethiopia, India, Peru, and Vietnam. His recent work focuses on wealth dynamics and the role of risk, based on long-term panel data collected in Ethiopia, India, and Tanzania. Other interests include land tenure rights, education, health, child development, technological innovation, and conceptual work on chronic poverty and vulnerability. He is the editor of *Insurance Against Poverty* (Oxford University Press, 2004).

T. Scarlett Epstein OBE is a retired research professor from the University of Sussex and a pioneer in the field of development anthropology, with a focus on Africa, Asia, and the Pacific. She started her socioeconomic action-oriented studies of South Indian villages in 1954 and continues this type of research today, encouraging a young generation of students to follow her example. She also pioneered the conduct of large action-oriented cross-cultural research projects in which she involved developing-country doctoral students as her researchers. Her 19 graduate students have each published two research papers in their names before going on to obtain their doctorates. Dr. Epstein is the author of 14 books and numerous articles.

Robert Erikson is professor of sociology at the Swedish Institute for Social Research, Stockholm University. His research interests include social stratification, education, family, and health, especially the study of individual change over the life cycle and how it can be understood with regard to individual and structural conditions. He is a fellow of the Royal Swedish Academy of Sciences, the British Academy, and Academia Europaea, and an honorary fellow of Nuffield College, Oxford. His recent books include *The Constant Flux: A Study of Class Mobility in Industrial Societies* (with J. Goldthorpe, Clarendon, 1992) and *Can Education Be Equalized: The Swedish Case in Comparative Perspective* (co-edited with J. Jonsson, Westview, 1996). His recent articles deal with social selection in education and social class differences in mortality.

Xavier Godinot is director of the Research and Training Institute of Mouvement International ATD Quart Monde (International Movement ATD Fourth World) near Paris. He is the author of numerous books and articles, including *On Voudrait Connaître le Secret du Travail* (Editions Quart Monde, 1995). He has worked closely with international institutions and is co-editor of the World Bank working paper *Participatory Approaches to Attacking Extreme Poverty: Case Studies Led by the International Movement ATD Fourth World* (with Q. Wodon, World Bank, 2006).

Anthony Hall teaches social policy and planning at the London School of Economics. His main areas of research interest are social safety nets, international migration, and conservation and development. His recent books include *Global Impact, Local Action: New Environmental Policy in Latin America* (Institute for Study of the Americas, University of London, 2005); *Social Policy for Development* (with J. Midgley, Sage, 2004); *Amazonia at the Crossroads: The Challenge of Sustainable Development* (Institute of Latin American Studies, University of London, 2000); and *Sustaining Amazonia: Grassroots Action for Productive Conservation* (Manchester University Press, 1997).

Claude and Patricia Heyberger have worked for International Movement ATD Fourth World for more than 25 years. They have been involved in different projects with families living in poverty in Europe, notably in Germany, Alsace (France), and Luxembourg. In 1994 they joined the ATD Fourth World team in Burkina Faso, working with children living on the streets of Ouagadougou. They are currently based in Bangkok as part of the ATD Fourth World coordination team for the Asian region.

Anirudh Krishna teaches public policy and political science at Duke University and is a researcher with Duke's Sanford Institute of Public Policy. He has been tracking movements into and out of poverty of over 25,000 households in India, Kenya, Uganda, Peru, and North Carolina, USA. An article from this research, published in *Journal of Development Studies,* won the Dudley Seers Memorial Prize in 2005. Recent books include *Active Social Capital: Tracing the Roots of Development and Democracy* (Columbia University Press, 2002); *Changing Policy and Practice from Below: Community Experiences in Poverty Reduction* (United Nations Press, 2000); and *Reasons for Success: Learning from Instructive Experiences in Rural Development* (Kumarian Press, 1998). Before turning to academia, Dr. Krishna worked for 14 years in the Indian Administrative Service on projects related to rural and urban development.

Deepa Narayan is senior adviser in the office of the vice president of the Poverty Reduction and Economic Management Network of the World Bank. She is currently leading the 15-country study entitled Moving Out of Poverty: Understanding Freedom, Democracy and Growth from the Bottom Up, aimed at finding out how people create wealth to escape poverty. She was team leader for the multicountry Voices of the Poor project and is lead author of the three-volume series *Voices of the Poor* (Oxford University Press, 2000–02). Her recent edited volumes include *Empowerment and Poverty Reduction: A Sourcebook* (World Bank, 2002); *Measuring Empowerment: Cross-Disciplinary Perspectives* (World Bank, 2005; Oxford University Press, 2006); and *Ending Poverty in South Asia: Ideas that Work* (with Elena Glinskaya, World Bank, 2007).

Brian Nolan is professor of public policy in the School of Applied Social Science, University College Dublin. He worked for many years in the Economic and Social Research Institute, Dublin. An economist, he has published widely on income inequality, poverty, public economics, social policy, and health economics.

Janice E. Perlman is president of Mega-Cities Project, a nonprofit organization that seeks innovative solutions to urban problems. Before founding Mega-Cities, she was professor of city and regional planning at the University of California, Berkeley; coordinator of President Carter's Neighborhood Task Force on National Urban Policy; and director of strategic planning for the New York City Partnership. She won the C. Wright Mills Award for *The Myth of Marginality: Urban Poverty and Politics in Rio de Janeiro* (University of California Press, 1976). Her chapter "Fighting Poverty and Environmental Injustice" concludes Worldwatch Institute's *2007 State of the World*. With awards from Guggenheim and Fulbright and support from the World Bank, she is completing a new book based on her multigenerational research in the favelas of Rio de Janeiro.

Patti Petesch, a specialist in qualitative poverty analysis, freelances for international development organizations and U.S. and European foundations and think tanks. She served as coordinator for the World Bank's Voices of the Poor and Moving Out of Poverty studies. With colleagues, she has developed a conceptual model for measuring changes in poor people's empowerment. Her recent publications include "Evaluating Empowerment: A Framework with Cases from Latin America" (with C. Smulovitz and M. Walton, in *Measuring Empowerment: Cross-Disciplinary Perspectives,* World Bank, 2005) and *Voices of the Poor from Colombia: Strengthening Livelihoods, Families and Communities* (with J. Arboleda and J. Blackburn, World Bank, 2004).

Joseph S. Shapiro is a PhD candidate in the Department of Economics at the Massachusetts Institute of Technology. He is co-author of "Redistributing Income to the Poor and the Rich: Public Transfers in Latin America and the Caribbean" (with K. Lindert and E. Skoufias, World Bank, 2006) and has published papers on the economics of education and health in developing countries. He has served as a Junior Professional Associate at the World Bank and as chief editor of the *Stanford Journal of International Relations*.

Charles Tilly is Joseph L. Buttenwieser Professor of Social Science at Columbia University. He earlier taught at the universities of Delaware, Toronto, and Michigan, at Harvard University, and at the New School for Social Research. He works mainly on large-scale political and social change, small-scale interpersonal processes, inequality, and the logic of social analysis, drawing especially on European and North American experience since 1500. Dr. Tilly is the author, co-author, editor, or co-editor of about 50 books and monographs, most recently the *Oxford Handbook of Contextual Political Analysis* (co-edited with R. Goodin, Oxford University Press, 2006); *Why?* (Princeton University Press, 2006); *Contentious Politics* (with S. Tarrow, Paradigm, 2006); *Regimes and Repertoires* (University of Chicago Press, 2006); and *Democracy* (Cambridge University Press, 2007).

Marco and Rosario Ugarte have been active members of International Movement ATD Fourth World since 1987, and in 1991 they founded the ATD Fourth World association in Peru. They currently work at the international center of ATD Fourth World in France. Marco Ugarte is a former professor of anthropology at the National University of San Antonio Abad del Cusco in Peru. Rosario Ugarte has worked in business administration and social services, including running a services-based center for young people.

1

Agency, Opportunity Structure, and Poverty Escapes

Deepa Narayan and Patti Petesch

The theory and empirics of why someone moves out of poverty and stays out of poverty, while others remain in chronic poverty, are still in their infancy. Debates rage about how many people are poor, how to measure poverty over time, and what causes poverty. This book is about these debates and their consequences for policy.

A stylized debate particularly spins around where to place the poverty line.[1] If you elect to define poverty as surviving on about a $1 per day or less—a defi- nition used by the World Bank—you would find an important decline in the numbers of poor people globally, from 1.5 billion to 1 billion over the nearly 25-year period from 1981 to 2004.[2] But if you judge a $1 poverty threshold to be quite low for this day and age, you might opt instead to set a higher pov- erty line, say at a daily rate of $2. At this higher level, you would then have to conclude that much hard work remains: in 1981 the world's poor population amounted to 2.5 billion and rose to 2.6 billion a quarter century later.

Just 15 percent of the world was still poor in 2004 with a lower poverty line, compared to 40 percent with the higher one. Other economists make compelling arguments for considering far higher poverty thresholds (Pritch- ett 2003).

In the specialized area of measuring economic mobility, there is even more controversy. According to noted labor economist Gary Fields, "The mobility literature is plagued by people talking past one another because one person's idea of mobility is not another's" (2000, 103). Furthermore, few of the large longitudinal studies conducted in developing countries provide causal analy- sis of mobility factors. Hence their usefulness for policy is limited.

Still other experts, especially from the fields of sociology and anthro- pology, find all the attention to dollars, poverty lines, and individual head counts to be a fundamentally misdirected way to understand poverty and the challenge of what to do about it. Lack of money is just one of many disadvantages of being poor and one of the many obstacles to escaping a life of impoverishment. The United Nations Development Programme's Human Development Index makes progress in correcting for this bias by integrating other dimensions of human capabilities.

Yet economic paradigms continue to dominate the analysis informing poverty policies. Some consider this persistent focus on individual—and principally economic—characteristics associated with poverty to be a reflection of disciplinary tensions and institutional weaknesses in the international poverty research and policy community (Kanbur and Shaffer 2007; Hulme 2007; Rao and Woolcock 2007). Others make a case that the narrow focus is an attempt to depoliticize the problem of global poverty by disregarding social class and power structures (Harriss 2006).

The conceptual, measurement, and political debates about poverty and mobility analysis are important because what we measure becomes the center of policy attention and policy intervention. Yet there is little consensus on the underlying causes of poverty and the mechanisms and processes that determine access to economic opportunity and mobility.

This introductory chapter opens by introducing the Moving Out of Poverty series and framing the different disciplinary approaches to analyzing poor people's mobility. It then makes a case for applying an empowerment framework that focuses on power asymmetries within institutions and on social structures to understand underlying causes and processes of exclusion of poor people in an unequal world. It argues that these inequalities are both reflected in and perpetuated by the dominant social structures and values and norms that determine the opportunity structure poor people face. Given these barriers, poor people's own efforts to move themselves out of poverty are often unsuccessful.

We review the rich and diverse evidence presented by the contributors to this volume in relation to the central concepts of the empowerment framework, namely opportunity structure and agency. We conclude with some reflections on the policy and research implications of an empowerment approach to supporting poor people's mobility.

The Global Research Initiative

The Moving Out of Poverty study is a follow-up to Voices of the Poor, which was a multidimensional study of poverty from the perspective of poor women and men in 60 countries of the developing world.[3] This new cross-country research similarly seeks to learn directly from people on the ground, but rather than asking what it's like to *live in* poverty, the study asks how and why people *move out* of poverty. Research teams have traveled to more than 500 communities across 17 countries to learn from people who have either moved out of poverty or stayed in chronic poverty over the last decade. The volumes to follow in the Moving Out of Poverty series will present these "bottom-up" findings. This first book offers some of the latest thinking about mobility from experts across disciplines.

The authors of the following nine chapters are leading development practitioners and scholars from the fields of anthropology, economics, sociology, and political science. They not only critically examine the literature about poverty and mobility from their disciplines but also contribute new conceptual models and evidence, based on their own investigations into how and why some people manage to escape poverty while many others stay trapped.

There are several analytic traditions for examining mobility, however, and the next sections provide background for navigating this very rich but sometimes technical literature. At the broadest level, the economists explain life chances mainly from the attributes of individuals and their preferences, while the sociologists and anthropologists ground their work in a society's social structures and culture. From such different perceptions of causal processes emerge distinct conceptual maps and measurement tools.[4] In recent years there has been healthy cross-fertilization among the disciplines, but less so in the area of mobility analysis concerned with poverty transitions in the developing world. This field has mostly been dominated by economic assumptions and methods, and so we turn to this approach first.

An Economic Perspective on Mobility

Key assumptions in the discipline of economics are that welfare is an expression of individual choices and preferences and these can be captured adequately along a distribution that is most often scaled in absolute monetary terms. In a "welfarist" approach, living standards are typically determined by aggregating "expenditures on all goods and services consumed, valued at appropriate prices, and including consumption from own production" (Ravallion 1992, 7). Poverty is seen as an individual's inability to consume enough to fulfill basic preferences or needs.

Kanbur and Shaffer (2007, 185) describe poverty concepts in the welfare economics tradition as "an amalgam of two variants of utility theory, revealed preference theory and money metric utility, and nutrition science." The absolute poverty line is typically calculated as the food expenditure necessary to meet dietary recommendations, supplemented by a small allowance for nonfood goods (Ravallion 1992, 26). But quite different means for setting a poverty line are also available to economists, as discussed below.[5]

The study of economic mobility extends the basic assumptions for calculating living standards at one point in time to examining changes in welfare over time. These types of analyses frequently measure the probability that individuals or households will shift across a standardized distributional scale, again often derived from some form of monetary metric. Bob Baulch and John Hoddinott (2000, 1) usefully identify three key dimensions of analyses of economic mobility: (a) the metric with which changes in welfare are measured, (b) the time frame for the analysis, and (c) the method used to summarize these measures for the population under study.

A difficult aspect of this literature is that the welfare metric used affects results and varies from one study to the next. An absolute line might be used, which is tied to a level of purchasing power considered necessary to be just out of poverty. Alternatively, the poverty line could be a relative share of the distribution (such as the bottom decile or quintile) or a share of median incomes (say 40 or 50 percent of the median). But other measures of welfare might be applied, such as an asset, occupational, or educational index.

In addition to the poverty metric, the time span covered and the number of observations will also vary across studies, and these will affect both the type of analysis that can be conducted and the results obtained. A mobility study can cover a period ranging from one or two years to much longer periods that involve intergenerational change. For short observation periods, typically three years or less, the transition groups of interest for poverty dynamics are often simply identified as (a) those who are persistently poor in all of observation periods, and (b) those who are transiently poor, or poor in at least one but not all of the observation periods. A panel with a longer observation period can expand the transition groups to include those who experience permanent poverty escapes and descents as well as those who never cross above or below the poverty threshold.

Another key feature of longitudinal survey research is its specialized sample. A representative sample is selected in the baseline year of the survey and the same "panel" of individuals or households are systematically resurveyed. Panel studies have more explanatory power than do cross-sectional surveys with fresh samples because they eliminate the effects caused by inherent time-invariant differences between people (such as intelligence). However, an important challenge for panels, which Stefan Dercon and Joseph Shapiro address at length in chapter 3 of this volume, is that the samples can lose their representativity as the periods of observation lengthen and households change composition.

Gary Fields (2000) describes five basic approaches to conceiving of income mobility, each of which provides a valuable perspective depending on the purpose and focus of a particular study. Each also gives rise to its own summary measures for describing mobility outcomes.

- *Time dependence* measures the extent to which one's current position is determined by one's position in the past.
- *Positional movement* measures changes to an individual's position in the income distribution, which could be scaled, for example, as quintiles or deciles.
- *Share movement* measures an individual's change in income relative to everyone else's, or changing share of income.
- *Symmetric income movement* measures the magnitude but not the direction of movements across the distribution.
- *Directional income movement* measures fraction of upward and downward movers and the average amount gained by the winners and lost by the losers.

Positional movement is the most widely used approach to analyzing mobility. But even within this common framework, there seem to be countless approaches for designing panel studies and measuring mobility. The two chapters in this volume that review the developing-country and industrial-country panel literature stress that the results are sensitive to the summary measures chosen and to the observation frequencies and intervals in the panels. In chapter 3 Dercon and Shapiro highlight problems of measurement bias, including potentially substantial distortions due to errors with welfare measures and with attrition in the sample. Brian Nolan and Robert Erikson vary the poverty lines or observation periods in different sections of chapter 4, both to provide a cross-check on results and to illustrate the measurement dilemmas.

The economics mobility literature also examines factors driving mobility. Typically, however, a quite limited set of factors are considered. Studies can be concerned with intergenerational questions, such as the influence of a father's education or occupation on a son's welfare. They may also look at intragenerational questions concerning the influence on mobility outcomes of an individual's initial (or change in) characteristics related to age, gender of household head, education, occupation, and earnings. Nolan and Erikson review recent works on causal factors in industrial societies. But in their review of 50 developing-country panel studies over the past five years, Dercon and Shapiro find that only a third of them cover a long enough period for causal analysis. Most of these provide only descriptive statistics of mobility correlates rather than examinations of causation.

More recent panel studies have considered a wider range of mobility factors, including structural dimensions, asset-based approaches, and social group inequalities.[6] Inspired by earlier sociological works, for instance, studies are relating people's mobility to changes in the wider economy as well as to their individual attributes (Morgan 2006). Michael Carter, Christopher Barrett, and others use more multidimensional asset-based frameworks in their analysis of panels and find social capital, in addition to other assets, to be important for resilience to shocks as well as for mobility (Carter and Barrett 2006; Adato, Carter, and May 2006; Carter and May 1999, 2001). In addition, social group inequalities such as those structured by caste have provided key organizing concepts for a small number of economic mobility analyses (see, for example, Drèze, Lanjouw and Sharma 1998).

While there are notable exceptions, relatively few developing-country mobility studies examine causal factors influencing life chances, and those that do most often consider a relatively limited set of economic, demographic, and human development dimensions. These limitations, as explored below, reflect wider gaps in the international development research community. "It would be fair to conclude," notes leading development economist Ravi Kanbur, "that concerns with multidimensionality have not to date penetrated into the mainstream of poverty analysis among economists" (Grusky and Kanbur 2006, 7).

Sociological Perspectives on Mobility

There is an enormous literature on sociological and anthropological accounts of mobility. In this tradition, one's chances for a good life are shown to result primarily, although not exclusively, from affiliation with an advantaged social group rather than from particular individual attributes. And society's prevailing values and norms, for instance about sources of prestige and authority, are seen to underpin and reinforce unequal social structures and the resulting inequalities in life chances that endure from one generation to the next (see, for instance, Smelser and Lipset 1966).

In one form or another, social structures and social relations are key analytical categories for sociologists seeking to explain sources of inequality.

Social structures can be broad social classes or social groups. Social structures reflect patterns of social interaction ordered by norms and values. There is consensus on the importance of social structures, their functions, and the role of individual agency, but sociologists disagree on the relative importance of these factors and on the nature of the interactions between them (Durkheim 1982; Weber 1968; Giddens 1984). A sociological inquiry seeks to understand and explain the underlying institutional processes, the hows and whys of observed social differentiation, discrimination, and deprivation, and the meanings assigned by social actors to their actions and social reality.

Patterned social relations and social structures are maintained by superficial and deep value structures. A location within a social category defines the status identity of a person and his or her honor, prestige, taste, stigma, roles, expectations, rights, and duties.

Social class provides a central organizing concept for the discipline. According to Grusky and Kanbur, social class frameworks are grounded in

> the presumption that the social location of individuals is determined principally by their employment status and job characteristics (esp. occupation), the former determining the strength of their commitment to the formal labor force, and the latter revealing the market power and life chances of those with substantial commitment to the labor force. (2006, 8)

Weber (1948) considered status—from having honor, prestige, or a religious affiliation—and political ties to be important axes for stratification in addition to class. Pierre Bourdieu (1977) focuses on *habitus*, a set of acquired patterns of thought, behavior, and taste that produce and reproduce the practices of class or class fraction. This perspective allows for a cultural approach to structural inequality and hence a focus on agency. Family (box 1.1) and community life also feature in this literature as central transmission mechanisms for cultural influences.[7]

In chapter 2, Charles Tilly posits an "interactive" theory of social inequality that is grounded in the presence of social group differences and the unequal power relations between groups (see also C. Tilly 1999). He draws special attention to the presence of frequently paired and highly uneven social groupings such as "male–female" and "black–white." The norms and behaviors that surround these pairings do the organizational work to maintain a society's unequal structures, including by giving rise to interactions between the pairings that routinely favor the dominant social group. Tilly acknowledges other types of social interactions based on individual attributes such as a person's skills, credentials, and merit. These types of processes, referred to as

BOX 1.1
The Family as a Unit of Analysis

An area of socioeconomic research that provides a useful perspective on mobility channels centers on the family and kinship relations as a key arena of decision making. There is also an important related body of work on the very deep gender inequalities within families and communities.

A focus on family arenas recognizes that individuals frequently act as members of a household whose productive capacity is greater than the sum of its parts. Ideally, they maximize collective utility through "family adaptive strategies" that "respond to, rework and reframe external constraints and opportunities" (Moen and Wethington 1992, 234).

Exemplifying this school, economist Gary Becker develops economic models that predict family behavior through explanations that are sensitive to the increasing returns derived from family strategies involving specialization of human capital and division of labor "even among basically identical persons" (1981, 57). This theory explains not only the traditional division of labor across married couples but also the frequent division of labor among siblings.[8]

While rationalist models resonate with commonly observed family strategies, another branch of the literature draws attention to social and cultural factors that also affect decision making (see, for example, Lewis 1961, 1966, 1970; Harevan 1991; J. Scott and Tilly 1975; L. Tilly 1979; L. Tilly and Scott 1978). Louise Tilly and Joan Scott, in particular, note that cultural norms and practices may constrain or prevent optimal rational choice (see also Moen and Wethington 1992, 237). For example, while Becker's (1981) theory would predict that a family will invest in the education of the best-endowed child, the family may not do so if that child is a girl and their culture frowns upon women leaving the house unaccompanied.

Similarly, local norms surrounding women's domestic and economic roles can be extremely important in determining women's agency and household mobility (Agarwal 1997). Naila Kabeer (2003) argues that household poverty determines and is determined by poor women's highly unequal role in the labor market. Female labor force participation is highest among the poorest households in countries such as India, Pakistan, and Bangladesh, where social norms mainly constrain women to very insecure and poorly paid work in the informal sector. Karen Mason's five-country study finds that "the country and community of residence predict women's reported domestic empowerment better than their personal socioeconomic and demographic traits" (2005, 91).

queuing, are much less common phenomena throughout history, however, because they require more sophisticated institutional mechanisms for reproducing social structures (for instance, through college entrance tests, professional licensing, or workplace promotions). "In particular," explains Tilly, "a view of inequality and poverty as outcomes of individual-by-individual competition according to widely shared standards of merit, worthiness, or privilege obscures the significance of organized distinctions and interactions among members of different social categories."

Within sociology there is a strong tradition of large-N surveys measuring the importance to mobility of occupational status, wages, education, structural changes in society, and other factors. In his recent summary of the field of mobility studies, Morgan describes two basic schools of work with large panel datasets. In one, "mobility is modeled by accounting for movement between aggregated groupings of occupational titles, generally labeled social classes." In the other, "the levels of social mobility are measured by intergenerational correlations of socioeconomic status" and "focus on the causes and consequences of differences in socioeconomic status." Morgan (2006, 4–5) indicates that a "main triumph" of the field has been to distinguish mobility due to structural changes such as growth in higher-status occupations from mobility due to "exchange" factors.

Seemingly quite separate from the quantitative studies is a large literature that relies on analytic narratives and small-n case study approaches. These undertake more holistic inquiries into the role of social structures, agency, and values in mobility processes, and they can engage researchers in visiting and revisiting their study communities for months or years. Some of the best-known work of this type was done by Oscar Lewis, whose research in Puerto Rico began in 1963 and was still ongoing in 1970 just a few days before his death (Lewis 1966). Susan Rigdon (2003, 51) explains that Lewis generated highly reliable data by using multiple questionnaires and repeating the same questions with different family members and during different visits, as he "rarely trusted first response." Caroline Moser's longitudinal work with 56 families in a slum community of Guayaquil, Ecuador involved numerous revisits to capture changes in family asset portfolios and mobility experiences over three decades (Moser 1997; Moser and Felton 2006). She traced family members who moved not only across the city but all the way to Barcelona, Spain because of the importance of this path for mobility.

In chapter 6 of this volume, Scarlett Epstein employs a mix of quantitative and qualitative methods to provide a 50-year account of how and why members of scheduled castes from two villages of South India became increasingly impoverished even as area farms modernized and flourished and markets diversified. She provides insights into the processes that generated widening inequality by relating the villages' very rigid caste structures to the surrounding economic transformations. Epstein's analytic approach draws on relational explanations of poverty and inequality that explicitly examine the use of power by more advantaged social groups to secure and extend their privileged positions.

Despite its explanatory power, in-depth case study research has enjoyed less attention than quantitative studies from the poverty research and policy community. Some social scientists have endeavored to address this by arguing for qualitative research designs that more closely mirror quantitative techniques, such as by increasing sample sizes and using more standardized data collection instruments.[9] Among other concerns, such recommendations seek to address perceptions that "small picture" studies do not provide a sufficient evidence basis for informing policies. Other critiques focus on problems of validity and researcher bias stemming from reliance on narrative information as opposed to survey-based evidence that can better stand tests of "intersubjective observability."

Brady and Collier (2004, 8) provide a thoughtful response to a range of critiques of qualitative research approaches, arguing, for instance, that "increasing the N may push scholars toward an untenable level of generality and loss of contextual knowledge." For sociologists such as Weber, moreover, sociology is fundamentally about being able to interpret social life in a way that can uncover the motivations and desires behind human actions as a means to understand the causes of such actions. From this perspective, only deep and extended engagement with study contexts can enable investigators to meaningfully grasp and trace processes of change and the relationships between different factors that lead to those changes.

Cross-Disciplinary Approaches: An Uneasy Marriage

There is a small but growing literature that integrates qualitative methods of data collection with panel surveys. These studies attempt to push the frontier of knowledge by building on the strengths of the contextual understandings from sociology and the breadth and statistical rigor of survey-based economics. Such works often provide a more multidimensional picture of the factors and mechanisms associated with poverty persistence and escapes than do more conventional economic mobility studies.[10] Combining methods in their examination of poverty transitions in Uganda, for instance, Lawson,

McKay, and Okidi (2006, 31) discover the importance of social and political concerns mainly through their qualitative work, including factors related to "poor governance, excessive local taxation, a culture of excessive drinking and pervasive insecurity."

Mixed-methods initiatives in the mobility field grow out of a larger poverty literature derived from "Q-squared" methods. Yet, in arguably the most influential arenas for international poverty research—namely the World Bank and leading U.S. universities—these approaches have only "shallow roots" (Hulme 2007, 4). There is an important discourse underway precisely about the causes impeding greater collaboration across disciplines on international poverty research (see Hulme 2007; Hulme and Toye 2006; Kanbur and Shaffer 2007; Bebbington et al. 2006; Rao and Woolcock 2007). Here we flag two hurdles related to institutional disparities and intellectual tensions.

Michael Woolcock, drawing on his sociological expertise, argues that "noneconomic" approaches are routinely disregarded in the World Bank because economic frameworks "inherently square more neatly with the imperatives of large modernist bureaucracies for universal and quantifiable metrics" (personal communication, March 2007). Given the stranglehold by economists on the ideas that get research and policy attention, Rao and Woolcock warn that "development policy at the Bank tends to reflect the fads, fashions, controversies and debates of one discipline" (Rao and Woolcock 2007, 2).[11]

Others look within academia, focusing on the diverse philosophical paths and normative orientations of the different social sciences to better understand the hurdles to greater cooperation. Drawing on epistemology and normative theory, Kanbur and Shaffer (2007, 192) shed valuable light on significant theoretical and methodological tensions, particularly with respect to their very different approaches to establishing validity and the real "tradeoffs between retaining the comprehensiveness and richness of people's perceptions of well-being on the one hand and meeting the requirements of standardization to make consistent interpersonal comparisons of well-being, on the other." Hulme and Toye also point to problems of "incommensurate" intellectual orientations and to different cultural norms within the different "knowledge communities," among a range of other factors. These norms seem to make economics a better training ground for interacting with powerful policy makers; anthropologists and sociologists, note Hulme and Toye, are "more likely to mix and relate well to the less powerful and even the powerless and marginalized" (2006, 22). We return to these important struggles in the conclusion.

Revisiting the Empowerment Framework

While it is essential to refine measurement instruments, we are interested not only in measuring mobility but also—and more importantly—in understanding processes and causes underlying observed differences in mobility outcomes. To examine these processes we return to our earlier conceptual work for measuring empowerment.

Empowerment is fundamentally about enlarging the freedom of poor and marginalized people to make choices and take actions to shape their lives. The outcome we focus on here in applying the framework is escaping poverty. We fully recognize that poor people have greater aspirations for their lives, but moving out of poverty can enlarge an individual's freedom to fulfill these other dreams, whatever they may be. As Amartya Sen notes:

> It so happens that the enhancement of human capabilities also tends to go with an expansion of productivities and earning power. That connection establishes an important indirect linkage through which capability improvement helps both directly and indirectly in enriching human lives and in making human deprivations more rare and less acute. (2000, 92)

The analytic model (figure 1.1) consists of interaction between two sets of factors: (a) changes in the *opportunity structure*, consisting of the dominant institutional climate and social structures within which disadvantaged actors must work to advance their interests, and (b) changes in the capabilities of poor individuals or groups to take purposeful actions, that is, to exercise *agency*.[12] The framework has been slightly refined from earlier versions to highlight the role of families in the exercise of agency.

The empowerment framework is informed by concepts of social exclusion, which focus on the "nature and causes of deprivation, in a way that takes context dependence as one of its key starting points" (de Haan and Dubey 2004, 5).[13] Throughout the Voices of the Poor series people vividly describe multiple, interlocking sets of disadvantages that leave them powerless to get ahead:

> Experiences of illbeing include material lack and want (of food, housing and shelter, livelihood, assets and money); hunger, pain and discomfort; exhaustion and poverty of time; exclusion, rejection, isolation and loneliness; bad relations with others, including bad relations within the family; insecurity, vulnerability, worry, fear and low self-confidence; and powerlessness, helplessness, frustration and anger. (Narayan, Chambers, et al. 2000, 21)

The recurrent findings about the multidimensionality of powerlessness point to the presence of processes that create and sustain inequality over very long periods (C. Tilly 1999; see also Tilly's chapter 2 in this volume). More recently, the concept of "inequality traps" has been developed to refer to pervasive inequalities in economic, political, and social opportunities that combine and persist over time to keep people poor (World Bank 2005; Bebbington et al. forthcoming). When states, for instance, serve only very narrow interests and are characterized by a "culture of corruption, clientelism, exclusion, and discrimination," even the best-designed policies and programs to reform institutions, address inequalities, or meet most other public-good objectives will struggle for effectiveness (Narayan 2002, 16). The empowerment framework is designed to shed light on these processes that reinforce social exclusion and inequality as a means to identify policy actions that can support poverty escapes on a much wider scale.

Opportunity structure

The left-hand side of the framework is about the hidden and visible battlegrounds where poor people strive to realize their aspirations. These battles take place both in the real world of public, market, civic, and family life and in the more hidden or symbolic world of competing values and norms that shape what people believe and do not believe and what they perceive they can and cannot do.

In figure 1.1, the top box on *institutional climate* highlights four areas that can heighten the bargaining power of poor and disadvantaged groups: *information, inclusion/participation, accountability,* and *local organization capacity.*[14] An array of societal values, norms, rules, rights, and other institutional arrangements—broadly referred to as culture—affect these four areas.

Formal and informal rules and institutions, or "institutional blueprints," give structure to organizational life, but they do not necessarily control it (Portes 2006, 241).[15] This is because prevailing values, norms, and informal practices routinely subvert formal rules. For example, many developing countries now have laws that provide for widows to inherit property, but these laws are routinely disregarded by deceased husbands' fathers, mothers, brothers, and other relatives who immediately disenfranchise the widow of her property rights. In many countries, despite legal rights, a husband's death can leave widows and children homeless and destitute, with little practical recourse.

The opportunities for poor people to express and realize their interests can blossom where incentives are in place to support their access to information, their political inclusion, their ability to hold their leaders accountable, and their capacity for local organizing. Conversely, where information is closely guarded, local power structures are excluding and unaccountable, and poor people lack basic freedoms of association and collective action, the possibilities for their empowerment and economic mobility narrow considerably.

The lower box on the opportunity structure side focuses on *dominant social structures* and highlights the importance of openness, competition, and conflict.[16] Examinations of social structures recognize that all societies are heterogeneous and stratified, some much more than others. Closed caste systems that confer extensive hereditary privileges on upper castes are one extreme. But there are many other contexts, local as well as global, where elites are relatively small in number, hold similar political, economic, or other strategic interests, and can easily collude to resist challenges; in such circumstances the possibilities for disadvantaged groups to have voice are also greatly reduced. Conflict is more likely to occur in these restricted contexts, especially where ethnic lines are sharply drawn (Bates 1999; Varshney 2003; Weiner 2001). In environments where the interests of dominant groups are not closely aligned, or where there is greater elite competition for political or market power, there should also be greater chances for disadvantaged groups to find allies (who may be in search of a power base) and make claims.

Examinations of social structures are explicitly concerned with "the deliberate actions and inaction" of the more powerful groups (Moncrieffe 2004, 9). In chapter 2 of this volume Tilly specifies the diverse resources and mechanisms that allow dominant groups to exercise control in their interactions with less powerful groups. Analyses of power relations sometimes trace processes around defining moments in the exercise of power. Epstein illustrates this approach in chapter 6 by recounting the devastating consequences of an attempt by a lower-caste person in an Indian village to be served inside an upper-caste coffee shop.

The growing social capital literature offers additional tools for examining the openness of dominant social structures to poor and disadvantaged groups. Social capital refers to the norms and networks that enable collective action, but the "basic idea . . . is that one's family, friends and associates constitute an important asset, one that can be called upon in crisis, enjoyed for its own sake, and/or leveraged for material gain" (Woolcock and Narayan 2000, 236). Empirical work across countries repeatedly finds that the influence of social capital on more inclusive development "is most profound when relationships are among heterogeneous groups" (Narayan and Cassidy 2001, 60). But poor people very often find themselves excluded from such linking networks and their valuable connections, information, and resources. In addition, there are forms of associational life that actively work against inclusion, including "communities or networks which are isolated, parochial, or working at cross-purposes to society's collective interests (e.g., gangs, drug cartels)" (Woolcock and Narayan 2000, 229).

Poor people's agency

Agency, shown on the right-hand side of figure 1.1, is about people's ability to act individually or collectively to further their own interests. In this discussion, it is about men and women having the means to envision and make choices that *can* lead to their escaping poverty. The term "can" is stressed because the likelihood or chance of this outcome will be a product of two broad forces: incentives and structures in the wider society, discussed above, *plus* the assets and capabilities—both individual and collective—that poor and disadvantaged people can marshal in pursuit of their goals.

FIGURE 1.1
Overview of the Empowerment Conceptual Framework

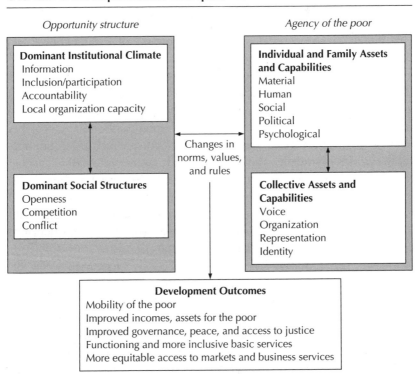

Source: Adapted from Narayan, D., "Conceptual Framework and Methodological Challenges," in Narayan 2005.

Individual and family assets and capabilities, in the top box, encompass the material assets and human capabilities that are available to poor men and women individually and to a family as a unit. They influence what a person is able to do or be. There are five dimensions:

- *Material:* land, housing, livestock, savings, and jewelry
- *Human:* good health, education, skills
- *Social:* social belonging, leadership, relations of trust, a sense of identity, a belief in values that bring meaning to life, and the capacity to organize
- *Political:* capacity to pursue rights, represent oneself or others, make claims, access information, form associations, and participate in the political life of a community or country
- *Psychological:* self-esteem, self-confidence, and ability to imagine and aspire to a better future

With scarce assets and capabilities, poor people are greatly constrained from having choices, from weathering shocks, and from fighting for better deals for themselves. Most studies of empowerment have focused on changes in material assets and human capabilities because these data are more available. But growing evidence points to the importance of social, political, and psychological influences on agency.

Psychological dimensions are one of the least studied areas, although there is now a great deal of empirical work on the importance to agency of aspirations and belief in one's own efficacy and power.[17] In a study conducted with groups of junior high school students in rural north India, stereotypes about caste greatly affected their performance on solving mazes—but only for the groups of students who had been made aware of caste differences in the composition of the groups doing the mazes. The completion rates for the mazes were no different for the groups, both high- and low-caste, that had not been told of their caste status in relation to that of other groups. But 25 percent fewer mazes were completed on average by the groups informed of their lower caste status (Hoff and Pandey 2004).

While arguments related to the "culture of poverty" have been widely dismissed, some sociologists have examined the attitudes and behaviors of poor people to illuminate mechanisms that may work to reduce agency and reinforce inequalities. Several of these works have focused on poor communities and have spotlighted the harmful influences of fatalism, preference for manual jobs over higher-status occupations, and lack of discipline and regularity (Lewis 1961; Willis 1977; Wilson 1996). To varying extents, sociologists have linked these factors to broad structural trends. For Wilson, for instance, the pathologies among

African American men living in ghettos result from structural changes in the wider economy that generate urban unemployment and poverty; the pathologies are not the cause of the men's poverty. But a concern in some of this literature has been the adoption by children and youth of subculture behaviors and attitudes that then contribute to intergenerational poverty traps.

As noted above, poor people's empowerment and mobility are also influenced by the assets and capabilities available to the wider family and by intrafamily inequalities in status and power, particularly between males and females. Inclusive and cohesive family relations can provide a powerful resource for accumulating assets and capabilities and exercising agency. But where family bonds are disrupted or fraught with gaping inequalities or conflict, the consequences can be very pervasive and damaging for attempts to move out of poverty.

Collective assets and capabilities, in the lower box, enable poor people to organize and mobilize to be recognized on their own terms, to be represented, and to make their voices heard. As explained in *Measuring Empowerment,* the importance of poor people's organizations in poverty reduction strategies is only gradually coming to be understood:

> Given their lack of voice and power, and given the deeply entrenched social barriers that exist even in many formal democracies, poor people are often unable to take advantage of opportunities to effectively utilize or expand their assets or exercise their individual rights. To overcome problems of marginalization in society, poor people critically depend on their *collective* capability to organize and mobilize so as to be recognized on their own terms, to be represented, and to make their voices heard. These aspects of voice, representation, collective identity, solidarity, and terms of recognition help overcome the deep external social and psychological barriers that are usually internalized by poor people. (Narayan 2005, 11)

Interactions between opportunity structure and agency

Given that empowerment, like mobility, is a dynamic process, the model is designed to be applied over time to examine change processes. For example, the success of a policy reform requiring participation of women in local councils will be influenced by the norms, values, and institutional rules associated with local political structures and gender relations. In contexts that are marked by sharp political inequalities and norms of exclusion of women from decisions on important community affairs, the possibilities for such reforms to foster empowering processes will be less than in contexts with more favorable opportunity structures. Over time, even in very excluding contexts, such reforms can enlarge women's individual and collective capacities for voice, representation, and agency, and this in turn can feed back to affect the opportunity structure.

On the agency side, poor people's self-help groups can be quite effective for increasing assets, solidarity, and self-confidence among their members. As groups consolidate and federate and gain in numbers, they achieve recognition and political clout in the wider society. These capabilities in turn can increase their access to new economic and political opportunities (Narayan and Kapoor 2005).

Confronting Opportunity Structures

In this section we use the empowerment framework to examine some of the mobility concepts and findings in this book. The section begins with large panel studies that provide a society-wide analysis of an individual's chances of escaping poverty. It then shifts to subnational levels and more multidimensional examinations of what may help or hinder movements out of poverty. We argue that analyses that capture the role of prevailing norms and values and of dominant groups contribute importantly to understanding how opportunity structures shape mobility. This understanding can then inform strategies for supporting transitions out of poverty on a larger scale.

Mixed chances for poverty escapes

Four important findings emerge from comparative panel data studies. First, the opportunity structure for poverty escapes varies greatly from one country to the next, and some analysis suggests that levels of poverty significantly affect rates of poverty escapes. Second, most poor people are constantly churning in and out of poverty, creating a murkiness about the numbers who are truly not poor; this challenges the reliability of poverty rates derived from cross-sectional data. Third, the variation in mobility outcomes extends down to the local level, with significant geographic differences in poverty transition patterns even among communities in close proximity. Fourth, education invariably emerges as important to economic mobility.

With panel data covering three years and a relative poverty line of 50 percent of median income, Nolan and Erikson find that the industrial countries with higher rates of poverty also have fewer poverty escapes (chapter 4). The share and immobility of the poor is highest in the United States and lowest in Denmark. However, they also present a study by Ayala and Sastre (2004) that uses a five-year window and a relative poverty line set at the bottom 30 percent of the distribution. This finds levels of poverty persistence in the United States comparable to those in five major European Union countries. Nolan and Erikson make a case for their measurement approach but recognize that each of the different measures provides relevant information.

Dercon and Shapiro (chapter 3) review results from 50 panel studies in developing countries, and table 3.1 highlights the large range in rates of transitory poverty among the countries. Just 11 percent were "sometimes poor" in one of the Vietnam panels, compared with 80 percent in an Ethiopian panel wave. The authors point out that two-thirds of the studies were less than five years in duration and are therefore of more limited use in conveying mobility patterns. Even in the longer studies, however, results are very sensitive to the number of survey rounds and the time elapsed between them. They illustrate this measurement difficulty with 1994–2004 rural panel data from Ethiopia: 80 percent of the population fell below the poverty line at least once if six panel rounds are examined, but the rate of transient poor drops to nearly half that if just the first and last rounds are compared.

Both chapters, reviewing the shorter-term panels, describe income poverty as "fluid" and as characterized by extensive churning above and below the poverty line. And they suggest that short-term studies likely overstate the extent of movements out of poverty. As Nolan and Erikson note,

> the typical year in poverty is lived by someone who experiences multiple years in poverty and whose long-term income is below the income poverty threshold on average. . . . [T]here is more persistence than just looking at the length of individual spells in poverty would suggest.

These two chapters also provide results from studies that examine how broad macro forces interact with micro influences, yielding insights into factors that influence mobility. Nolan and Erikson cite a study by Valletta (2004) that predicts that a child in a family with a single head, low education, and no workers would spend 3.5 years in poverty in Canada and 7.0 years in the United States. But a child with parents of prime working age and medium education would spend only half a year in poverty in Canada and just over a year in the United States. Work by Dercon (2002, 2006) in Ethiopia concludes that food market liberalization affected households differently depending on whether they were in food surplus or food deficit regions and also whether the household was a surplus farm household or not.

Anirudh Krishna examines mobility in three states in India (chapter 5). A central finding is the significant village-level variation in mobility patterns.

To illustrate, he contrasts two villages from the same district of Andhra Pradesh. In one, about a third of the villagers are currently poor and almost half escaped poverty during the 25-year study period; in the other, 85 percent of the villagers are poor and more than half fell into poverty during the same period. Results demonstrating high levels of short-term churning in and out of poverty and the uneven geography of poverty transitions draw attention to the benefits of more periodic and disaggregated poverty analyses, as well as to the need for more decentralized development strategies that can be sensitive to this variation.

The grip of norms and values

Norms of behavior matter intensely, whether one is at the bottom or the top of the social scale. They prescribe the dos and don'ts of whom to treat well, whom to exclude, and whom to mistreat, what brings prestige and what ruins it, and ways to meet one's obligations or bring shame. A display of the "correct" behaviors and attitudes reaffirms a person's social position and negotiating power in relation to all others around. Chapters 6, 7, and 8, which present in-depth case study work, emphasize the critical role that norms play and their potential to derail the best-intentioned policies. These and other chapters also describe successful efforts to challenge prevailing social norms that perpetuate poverty (see box 1.2 for two illustrations).

From a slum in Rio de Janeiro to the streets of Ouagadougou to a village in Karnataka, the axes of social differentiation, rank, and exclusion vary enormously. Xavier Godinot and his colleagues find that the stigma and exclusion associated with extreme poverty drive the recurring disadvantages facing the Rojas-Paucar family of Cusco, Peru (chapter 8). While it took the family two years to pay for their daughter Laura's school uniform bought on credit, even more difficult was the cruelty from teachers and classmates who taunted the girl for muddy shoes and other telltale signs of poverty. Her shoes were muddied as she walked to school from her steep hillside barrio that lacked paved streets.

Indeed, the places where poor people live very often bring stigma and exclusion. Epstein explains that scheduled caste children in her study villages in India learn at a very young age that they cannot enter a peasant caste neighborhood or play with peasant caste children (chapter 6).

Janice Perlman's 25-year panel study of three favelas of Rio de Janeiro found that residence in a favela presented more of a barrier to mobility than did race (chapter 7). The data collection began in 1969 with a baseline sample of 750 households and later involved teams in tracing original household

BOX 1.2
Campaigning for Institutional Change

Changes to the institutional climate can make a great difference to poor people. Two chapters in this volume refer to awareness-raising campaigns in India that helped modify particular attitudes and behaviors that have disadvantaged the poor.

The first was a campaign in rural Andhra Pradesh that sought to restore food preferences for more nutritious and less costly sorghum over rice (chapter 6). It was designed to ease nutrition problems that had emerged when many poor households switched to rice, which was identified with higher-status consumption. The second was the dowry-rejection campaign in the state of Rajasthan, which helped poor families resist heavy indebtedness incurred when marrying a daughter (chapter 5). The campaign's success was evident in Krishna's findings that dowry had a dramatically lower importance for descents into poverty in Rajasthan compared to the study villages in Andhra Pradesh and Gujarat.

It is interesting that these campaigns did not target the poor specifically. Of the pro-sorghum effort, Epstein argues that this lack of targeting helps explain the campaign's success in light of sensitivities to "prestige concerns" that often cut across social structures.

members across Rio to resurvey more than 2,000 of the original household members. Those who remained in favelas experienced the lowest mobility.

It is common practice for a favela dweller to use the address of a friend or relative from a "good" neighborhood when applying for a job, rather than be stigmatized by residence in a community rife with drug gangs and other criminal activity. Perlman stresses that the favelas continue to be excluded places despite large gains in overall socioeconomic levels, access to services, and quality of housing. Her earliest work on the favelas argued that the slum dwellers of Rio are not marginal to society but are marginalized by it. Such processes begin to shed light on the common finding from the larger urban economic longitudinal work that location and access to particular types of jobs appear to matter (see chapter 3 by Dercon and Shapiro).

Yet the boundaries of social differences very often do not receive treatment in the mobility literature. Political scientist Anirudh Krishna applies a "Stages of Progress" methodology that engages groups of villagers in identifying expenditures associated with different levels of well-being and then uses these levels to determine poverty transitions of the village households (chapter 5). With an

expenditure lens, it is understandable that caste differences and other noneconomic dimensions would not emerge in the results, but Krishna nevertheless
asserts that "social recognition matters as much as economic conditions in
defining the shared understandings of poverty."[18]

If one examines his data from an empowerment perspective, however, it
might appear that social recognition matters more for understanding mobility
processes. Table 5.5 reveals that ill health and health-related expenses are the
number one reason for falling into poverty in the villages he studied. But if
one combines the social obligations of dowry (Krishna's second most important reason for descent) and death feasts (the third), these factors become more
significant than health in explaining downward slides. And their significance
would grow even more if these two were combined with debt (the fourth reason), which is frequently the result of expenditures on dowry and death feasts.

Across cultures, relationships of indebtedness can be an enduring disadvantage for poor people. However, the in-depth case studies in the volume
also reveal that debt has different meanings in different cultural contexts. The
youngest members of Perlman's sample, the grandchildren of the original
migrants who moved into the favelas, considered their indebtedness to be an
important source of satisfaction, along with a title to their house. As Perlman
notes, in this case the debt is consumer credit and "consumption is a badge
of prestige for the young" (chapter 7). In India, by contrast, debt entails very
high costs and diminished prestige and control—but it is accepted that large
debts must be incurred to cover a daughter's wedding or a husband's death.
And Epstein unexpectedly finds that for scheduled caste members, it is the
shame of being unable to celebrate children's weddings "in our accustomed
style" that is the greatest hardship of their deepening poverty (chapter 6).

Confronting dominant social structures

A consistent finding from the chapters in this volume, and a central message
in Voices of the Poor, is that the formal institutions of the state and private
sector are very often inaccessible or outright unhelpful to the poor.

Employment by the private or even the public sector appears to play
only a minor role in poverty transitions. From Epstein's fine-grained analysis,
we see how patron-client relationships in a caste system are critical for success in local labor markets and serve to virtually exclude lower castes from
all good jobs, whether public or private. As the upper peasant castes held
exclusive control of management positions in the area factories, for example,
none of the scheduled castes could obtain these unskilled jobs for which they
were otherwise qualified. Moreover, many scheduled caste children could not

attend school to improve their employability because they were working in bonded labor arrangements in the homes of moneylenders to whom their parents were indebted (chapter 6).

Perlman reports that unemployment in Rio nearly doubled over the study period as the city's economy lost factory and public sector jobs to other Brazilian cities. Although they have much higher levels of education, fewer than 40 percent of the children and grandchildren of the original interviewees were able to obtain better jobs than their parents. Those living in the favelas had the highest unemployment rates and the lowest share of nonmanual jobs (chapter 7). In the Indian context, Krishna finds that just 7 percent and 11 percent of poverty escapes resulted from private and public sector employment respectively in Andhra Pradesh and Rajasthan (chapter 5).[19]

In addition to difficulties accessing formal jobs, the chapters also highlight poor people's exclusion from public services, with health issues standing out as a leading hardship. As noted, Krishna finds ill health and high health care costs to be the top cause for descents into poverty across his 107-village study. Dercon and Shapiro present a panel study from South Africa (Booysen 2003) that compares the mobility outcomes of HIV/AIDS-affected households with nonaffected ones, finding that the former are more likely to fall into and remain in chronic poverty

Godinot et al. (chapter 8) describe the Rojas-Paucar family's devastating interactions with the health care system in Cusco, Peru, that led to family indebtedness and humiliation. The family endured financial and emotional trauma when their older daughter Margarita needed a costly Cesarean delivery for her first child. The nurses verbally abused her and threatened to take the baby and give him up for adoption if the family didn't pay. When Margarita's second child was born, the family had to use money saved for school enrollment to pay the hospital costs, putting the children's education in jeopardy.

The support that poor people obtain from formal safety nets appears limited in the developing-country contexts reported here. In industrial countries, on the other hand, studies find that the size and character of the welfare regime influences the degree of income inequality. Nolan and Erikson (chapter 4) examine the relationship between welfare regime types and patterns of poverty transitions. They only find a good fit for the outlier cases: the "liberal regime" (which confines the state to a residual welfare role) is associated with very high rates of poverty persistence in the United States and Canada, and a social democratic regime (which assigns the state a substantial redistributive role) is associated with the highest rates of poverty escapes in Denmark and the Netherlands. The welfare regime lens become much less useful when examining countries with less distinctive mobility patterns among the poor: the United Kingdom and Ireland, with their liberal regimes, have mobility trends similar to those of countries with regimes that play a very active welfare role. The authors suggest that different attitudes and beliefs regarding the role of the public sector in reducing poverty and insecurity perhaps help to explain the mixed reach and effectiveness of these programs.

The wide prevalence of health shocks as a trigger for descent provides an important indication that public safety nets often do not help poor people cope with health crises. Furthermore, there is little evidence that public assistance and programs run by nongovernmental organizations (NGOs) help people move out of poverty. Krishna finds that public and NGO poverty programs are associated with relatively few escapes, ranging from 14 percent in Andhra Pradesh to 6 percent in Gujarat and less than 4 percent in Uganda and Kenya (chapter 5). More hopeful news can be found in C. Scott's (2000) nearly 20-year panel study of eight rural communities in Chile, which documents declining agricultural incomes and finds safety net programs to be critical supports for security and mobility.

Even for safety net programs with strong community participation, it seems that reaching the poor remains a challenge due to local norms and power structures that can easily subvert formal rules. Chapter 8 describes how Alicia was excluded from the "Glass of Milk" food subsidy program in Cusco, Peru. Though she could not afford the entry fee, she was not offered the opportunity to help serve the meals as another means to become eligible—a humiliating exclusion. Chapter 7 describes the life of Edson, who lives in a precarious two-room shack in Rio. Edson explains that the local Pentecostal church that distributes the *cesta básica* (basket of food staples) in his community denies him the food if he does not attend their services. He becomes ineligible for the *bolsa escola* stipend for the families of schoolchildren if his child misses even a day of school.

The overlaps between social, economic, and political elites help shed light on the mechanisms of exclusion. In Wangala, one of the two villages of Karnataka that Epstein studied, upper-caste villagers easily flouted government efforts to transfer lands to scheduled castes. Despite rules requiring that at least half of newly released government lands be made available for purchase by lower castes at below-market rates, customary patron–client ties, relationships of heavy indebtedness, as well as a legacy of lower-caste exclusion from land ownership made it relatively easy for the upper peasant castes to take over all the new lands. In a visit to Wangala in 1996, Epstein found that the village had benefited greatly from having one of its own rise to prominence in the government bureaucracy. This patron helped the village become designated as a group panchayat headquarters and obtain piped water, a health center, a veterinary clinic, a bank, a school complex, and other services. Epstein nevertheless found that these improvements made little dent in the gaping socioeconomic divide between the castes (chapter 6).

There is relatively little evidence from these chapters that democratic governance greatly improves poor people's capacities to confront dominant structures and access jobs and services. Democracies, Tilly explains, can enfranchise poor workers and lead to larger safety nets, especially in good times when firms are eager for peaceful and productive workers. But the capacity of states to affect poverty transitions on a large scale appears very uneven—especially for the vast majority of poor people who lack formal jobs and the entitlements they provide. More generally, Tilly (chapter 2) is not sanguine about the possibilities for governments to reduce inequalities, and he elaborates on the considerable means available to states for maintaining inequalities. From Perlman's longitudinal data emerges the ironic finding that those who lived through the Brazilian dictatorship report feeling more politically excluded now than before the restoration of democracy some 20 years ago.

Poor People's Agency: Individuals and Families Reaching Up

Most economic accounts of mobility consider a limited set of resources that poor people need to resist and escape poverty. The importance of material assets, work, education, and good health is well documented, but the extent to which social, political, and psychological factors are also captured seems to be a function of the methods used. These latter aspects feature more prominently in studies with open-ended methods, although survey questions on all of these factors have been available for years if not decades.[20]

The known world: Material and human assets and capabilities

Chapters 3, 4, and 5 present findings from large datasets on the individual and household characteristics that influence poverty transitions. It is difficult to compare and draw conclusions across these works as the studies vary greatly in their designs. Nolan and Erikson provide econometric findings from North America and Europe indicating that "the age, gender, and educational attainment of the household head, the number of workers in the household at the outset, and family composition all have a substantial impact both on poverty exits and on the likelihood of being persistently poor." The education of the household head is most important for escapes,[21] and the number of household workers for descents (chapter 4).

Dercon and Shapiro's review of the developing-country panels cautiously concludes that education and household assets correlate with mobility across a wide number of studies. They also acknowledge that the developing-country panel literature is limited both in its inclusion of non-economic factors and in examining causality even among the narrow range of factors that are considered. They ask, "Is it education that makes people move out of poverty, or is it that families who manage to offer education to their children are also able to offer their children other opportunities—ones that may be unobservable to the researcher but that are important in climbing out of poverty?" (chapter 3).

Throughout Krishna's study, villagers identify income diversification as by far the most important reason for climbing up.[22] He finds, moreover, that these livelihood bundles can vary widely from one region to the next. In the Rajasthan villages, these activities include rearing goats, making charcoal, and doing day labor in mining, transport, and agriculture. In Andhra Pradesh, tiny businesses and diversification into nontraditional crops are noted. In both states migration to cities also provides a key pathway (chapter 5).

The less-known world: Social, psychological, and political assets and capabilities

Perlman uncovers a wide range of factors as significant for upward mobility in her 25-year panel of the three favelas of Rio de Janeiro (chapter 7). The quantitative data reveal that mobility is highest among individuals who are male, young, with smaller families, raised in favelas closer to the upscale neighborhoods of the city, and with bridging social networks.[23] She also finds that a sense of agency, optimism, perseverance, and aspirations significantly correlated with different measures of successful outcomes, including higher socioeconomic status and income, exit from favelas, political participation, and self-reported satisfaction. The author points in particular to optimism as an invaluable psychological resource for agency and future transitions out of poverty. By contrast, a sense of fatalism was associated with negative outcomes.

It is in Perlman's qualitative work, however, where the importance of family bonds, social networks, and psychological factors such as drive, optimism, and self-confidence emerges most strongly. Hélio's story of upward mobility is based on soccer prowess, tremendous hard work, and advantageous political connections that helped him land a job, but his determination and optimism clearly played an important role. "Whatever sort of work came my way, I always grabbed it. . . . Success is having luck provide an opportunity and then acting on it. . . . I had health, friendship, and soccer, and I made the rest happen." Hélio is also proud of his daughter, who has earned professional degrees in accounting and law. But as Perlman indicates, "being well educated, hard-working, persistent, and highly motivated" are traits also found in some of those who did not escape poverty. Agency alone does not make for movement out of poverty, and the opportunity structure for those living in favelas is very limited.

Family and other kinship and community ties and the relationships of nurturing, support, and reciprocity they provide are the central themes explored by Godinot and his team (chapter 8). The first of two in-depth monographs in the chapter describes the life of Paul, a 15-year-old who spent four years on the streets of Ouagadougou, Burkina Faso. Paul got along by doing odd jobs for a pittance and by stealing, using drugs, and sleeping in gutters. Volunteers from ATD Fourth World, the international NGO to which the chapter authors belong, befriended Paul and helped him reestablish ties with his family and natal village. There his father and uncles guided him toward productive work, including selling gasoline, vegetable gardening and other farming, hawking clothing and chickens, making bricks, and raising animals. The monograph shows how Paul's reconnection with his family and village, although both were quite poor in material terms, brought him affiliation, identity, education, protection, and sharing of responsibility that he lacked as a youth on the city streets.

The critical importance of political and social capabilities runs through the chapter's second monograph, which tracks the Rojas-Paucar family of Cusco, Peru. The father, Benigno Rojas, works as a night watchman and represents his neighborhood in meetings in exchange for housing. This desperately needed work-for-housing opportunity arose from Benigno's friendship with a community leader. Similarly, after repeated failure to navigate the health care maze, the family was finally able to capitalize on their relationship with the director of the comprehensive health system to obtain urgently needed medical treatment for their son Miguel.

Within the family there are often acute gender differences. Epstein describes how men in one Indian village have resorted to drinking and gambling, which then triggers violence against women. Yet no organization in the village speaks up for the women. While legislation requiring reserved seats for women in the panchayat has led to more women councilors being elected, Epstein reports that in her study villages they tend to remain "the mouthpiece of their male sponsors" (chapter 6). Again, in such closed and unequal opportunity structures, rule changes alone may not be sufficient to enlarge agency and empowerment.

Defying Boundaries: Collective Agency and Poverty Escapes

Remittances from migrants working outside their native countries provided nearly $150 billion dollars to developing countries in 2004 (Page and Plaza 2006, 248). In addition to this flow of cash, the flow of people generates new relationships and networks that span urban-rural and international borders as well as conventional social, economic, and political divides. Migration is about individual aspirations, family strategies, and social networks. And it is about defying real and hidden boundaries of all sorts. The importance of migration to mobility is evident across the chapters in the book. These examinations, moreover, provide especially rich material for bringing together both sides of the agency–opportunity structure framework to examine how their interaction can facilitate empowerment and poverty escapes.

A panel study of the effects of HIV/AIDS on families in Kagera, Tanzania cited by Dercon and Shapiro finds especially high poverty reduction among those who left the remote region. In fact, the 10 percent of the panel sample that migrated outside Kagera saw their poverty fall by 23 percentage points, compared to a fall of just 4 points for those who never moved. Despite an extensive questionnaire, however, the study does not explain why the migration led to greater movement out of poverty (chapter 3).

Simply moving to less remote communities even within remote regions can also have high payoffs. An eight-village Moving Out of Poverty study of Kagera, which was drawn from the panel sample, found larger gains in household mobility in communities with good roads and markets compared with households in isolated communities. Using regression analysis, the study determined that a household's initial assets mattered more to mobility in remote villages than in accessible villages. The qualitative data reveal that poor households in high-access areas had much more freedom and livelihood choices from "exposure . . . the right friends, traveling and getting ideas" (de Weerdt 2006, 17).

Yet inequalities are not left behind when people migrate. The most successful migrants to Bangalore from Epstein's two study villages in Karnataka are young, healthy, educated, English-speaking men from the dominant caste who can call on a powerful patron. By contrast, all but one of the scheduled caste migrants in her sample who venture to the city lack the connections to find adequate work; they remain trapped in grinding poverty, unable to send anything back to their families. Many just give up and return to their village (chapter 6).

By conservative estimates, international migrants numbered 175 million in 2000 (Page and Plaza 2006, 261). These numbers, however, hide many border-crossing deaths as well as the pain, discrimination, and family dissolution that many migrants face. Shelton Davis tells the story of indigenous Maya who venture from the remote Western Highlands of Guatemala to the United States (chapter 10). While the migrants must confront difficulties with housing, work, legal status, and language, among other barriers, they still manage to send substantial amounts of money back to their families. Each municipality in the Western Highlands annually receives nearly $2 million in remittances, more than double the budget allocated by the government for each town's public works. This is a striking display of the agency made possible by family and community bonds.

Davis focuses on the collective action story of migrants coming together to form hometown associations (HTAs). HTAs began springing up in U.S. cities in the 1980s to provide legal services for newly arrived migrants and to sponsor religious, cultural, and youth programs that reaffirm Mayan culture and heritage. Over time, these groups have taken on economic development activities both for their members in the United States and for their communities of origin in Guatemala. With support from U.S.-based Catholic networks, the Guatemalan HTAs are connecting with each other. They are also beginning to reach out to international NGOs and donors as well as the government of Guatemala to explore partnerships in aiding their hometown communities. These ties are only incipient but are, in Davis's view, promising. He also highlights the work of U.S. and Guatemalan networks of cooperative banks and credit unions to ease access to remittances and provide other financial services in remote areas of Guatemala.

While Davis is optimistic about the development potential of migrant resources and networks, Anthony Hall cautions against assumptions that remittances can easily be directed to local economic development (chapter 9). Noting that remittances are a mainstay of family support in many Latin American communities, he contends that there is limited scope for shifting these cash flows to more directly productive activities. And the difficult political and investment climate in these countries raises additional barriers to channeling remittances away from family needs. Nonetheless, like Davis, Hall acknowledges the promise of new economic and political relationships that are forming around the migrant networks. For instance, both the federal and state governments in Mexico are actively encouraging HTA investments with matching investment programs. He also mentions new commercial ventures funded by wealthy overseas Mexicans, as well as stronger political relationships between the migrants (who recently obtained absentee voting rights) and state politicians.

Another way of conceiving why migration paths can be so effective is that migrants get to exit their current opportunity structure for an entirely new one that may offer greater promise. But examinations of how migration contributes to mobility will likely fall short if they leave out the norms and structures that shape family obligations, social networks, and aspirations. Interventions can work to build on and strengthen key individual and collective assets and capabilities that enable migrants to take advantage of new opportunities. They can also seek to make the institutional climate more supportive of migration and to facilitate access to remittances and the productive savings and investment they can generate.

Power and Poor People's Mobility: Implications for Policy and Future Inquiries

In this final section we summarize key findings from the different disciplinary approaches and highlight some of their policy implications for accelerating poverty escapes. We also draw attention to important gaps in our understanding about mobility processes. Statistics consume research and policy attention, while the factors that interact to get people out of poverty or keep them stuck there remain a black box. Indeed, of the hundreds upon thousands of developing-country poverty studies, only a small fraction look at causes of poverty and mobility. Most others present correlates of poverty from which we extrapolate policies with the intention of making the poor look like the rich. We therefore close with suggestions for improving poverty and mobility diagnostics as a critical means of identifying and enabling more effective actions to reduce poverty.

Panel data: What we can learn and act upon

Panel studies are irreplaceable for their data on changes in welfare and inequality over time across a society and among different societies, and for their analyses of the factors associated with or influencing these changes in welfare. Panel sampling frames and standardized distributions and poverty lines make such analyses possible. But while panel work may be considered the gold standard for examining poverty transitions, important limitations should be recognized: results are acutely sensitive to different welfare measures and periods of observation, and very often only a limited set of factors is considered.

From the panel data, nevertheless, five important policy messages stand out. The first concerns the importance to poverty escapes of the macro context. There is little doubt that an economy's size and growth are central forces behind mobility. In the industrial countries, however, mobility of the poor is lower in countries with higher poverty when measured with metrics that are sensitive to differences in inequality. As many studies have concluded, growth alone is not enough—especially when inequalities are large (Besley and Cord 2007; Kraay 2004).

A second finding arises from the numerous panel studies that demonstrate very high rates of short-term churning in and out of poverty. A third, closely related, is the importance of illness to poverty descents. Together these findings point to the potential for improved safety nets to bring about large increases in poverty escapes, especially safety nets that give high priority to helping poor people access health care and health and life insurance. Most workers in the developing world are in the informal economy, while the attention of policy makers and the design of safety nets are most often focused on the tiny share of developing-country populations with formal jobs. This is a reflection of both the blindness of policy makers and the powerlessness of poor people.

Individual and household attributes clearly matter, and a fourth strong message from the panel literature is the significance of education to intergenerational poverty escapes. However, it is important to recognize that the returns on education are affected by the macroeconomic environment and by the microeconomic and microsocial environment. These create the opportunity structure within which people seek employment. Perlman reports that greatly improved education levels among Rio's favela dwellers have not yet been accompanied by commensurate access to better jobs. The macro environment clearly plays a role in opening up opportunities for a more educated labor force; however, in the case of Rio's job market, college education is increasingly needed. And the stigma of having a favela address further reduces access to employment, even for the educated.

A fifth policy message from the panel literature is the need for more disaggregated poverty analyses and policies, as evidenced by strong geographic variations in the patterns of and reasons for poverty escapes and descents. The literature also indicates that mobility factors relate not only to particular attributes of households and communities but also to how these varied attributes interact with wider economic forces. Again, Dercon illustrates these relationships with his comparative work showing that food market liberalization affected Ethiopian households and communities differently depending on whether they were in food deficit or food surplus regions, and in food deficit or food surplus households.

Sociological inquiries: What we can learn and act upon

The more sociological literature makes clear that the disadvantages faced by poor women and men are multiple, and that they very often combine to reinforce marginality and circumscribe agency. These interlinkages trace back to inequality in underlying social structures and social relations that are reproduced in state and market institutions.

State institutions in many developing countries have a very poor track record of contributing to poverty escapes on a large scale, even when this is part of their mandate. There is an expanding literature on carrots and sticks available for improving public sector performance and making local governments and frontline service providers more responsive and accountable to the poor (World Bank 2004; Fox 1995; Ackerman 2003; D'Cruz and Satterthwaite 2005). Some of these approaches are not quick technical fixes but focus on enabling processes for broad-based and informed dialogue, problem solving, and recourse mechanisms should plans go awry (Woolcock 2007b). This "software" of transparent, inclusive, and accountable development planning and operations should be given much greater priority.

Many researchers have addressed the synergies between widely shared economic growth and democracy (see, for example, Friedman 2005), but the empirical evidence is still weak on the linkages.[24] The lack of a clear relationship between democracy and poverty reduction is primarily due to the complex interactions among economic, social, and political factors. Where democracy fails to contribute to reduced poverty, Diamond (2003, 9) argues that the weaknesses do not derive "from the intrinsic limitations of democracy as a political system, but rather from the fact that democracy functions in a limited, shallow and illiberal fashion." Varshney (2005, 387) usefully examines relationships between ethnicity, class, and voting power to explain democracy's weak impact on poverty: "If the poor belong to very different ethnic groups . . . and no ethnic group is large enough to constitute a significant voting bloc, the pressure on the political elite to ease poverty decreases significantly."

From a micro perspective, it is people's values and the power dynamics of their relationships with their families and friends and with the surrounding market, public, and civic institutions that give meaning and direction to their lives. For this reason, a cause for discrimination and mistrust in one context may bring prestige in another, and a poverty program's success or failure may hinge critically on the difference. Similarly, initiatives to transfer material assets to the poor or to enlarge women's political representation may take off in one environment but be wholly ineffective in another. Attitudes and behaviors related to prestige concerns, social obligations, highly unequal patron–client dealings, or deeply ingrained gender discrimination all weigh heavily but in very different ways in the mobility experiences across different localities.

On the agency side, it is important for policies to be sensitive not only to variations in material and human asset endowments but also to a wider set of social, psychological, and political assets and capabilities that also shape the effectiveness of poverty policies and programs. Research by Brook and colleagues (1998, 1999) in Colombia finds that family counseling services can be an efficient investment for reducing the probability of drug use, criminal involvement, and other hardships facing poor youth. Indeed, in a participatory poverty study in Colombia, local people identified support for better family relations as a key entry point for reducing poverty and violence in their households and communities (Arboleda, Petesch, and Blackburn 2004).

Poor people do not automatically form groups, but when they do, interventions can support these efforts by linking the groups to influential policy champions who will support their agendas. While the role of collective assets and capabilities is increasingly recognized, the lessons from these approaches are still rarely reflected in poverty policies.

Typical economic analyses of migration, for example, do not single out hometown associations as holding promise for addressing migrant hardships in receiving countries or local poverty in migrant-sending countries. When people migrate, however, success or failure can turn on social connections. The HTAs help poor migrants by increasing access to housing, jobs, and legal services and by reaffirming cultural identity and social belonging. They also address social and economic needs in the migrants' home communities, and this in turn is helping to make migrants more visible to policy makers in their home countries. These political and economic relationships may also offer promise for more development-friendly and equitable migration policies in both migrant-sending and migrant-receiving countries.[25]

New research and policy mindsets

There is little doubt that panel studies provide valuable insights into mobility patterns. But it is dangerous to allow the analysis and debate to stop there.

We need a better understanding of the underlying causes of poverty. We need to wrestle with the deep influences of power relations and social norms. This calls for new mindsets that can effectively address the disciplinary and institutional biases that currently distort our knowledge of and action on poverty.

A study comparing per capita consumption of lower-caste households and others in Uttar Pradesh, India, found that half the difference could be attributed to assets and the other half to differences in returns to those assets. The differences are not only in the assets themselves, then, but in *how* they can be used. "For many poor people," the authors explain, "low-caste status and gender operate as social barriers that exclude them from many realms of social and economic opportunity" (Kozel and Parker 2003, 389). Without an understanding of context and power relations, most survey-based analyses simply miss the importance of caste and gender inequalities to poverty transitions. Without a grasp of these key barriers, how can policies possibly relate to them?

Institutions are made in the image of the powerful. The same empowerment framework used in this chapter to examine the mobility literature and the factors that perpetuate poverty could be equally applied to the most influential arenas of the international poverty analysis industry.

At this juncture, the disciplinary battle lines within the World Bank appear more sharply drawn than ever. After a period of flirting across disciplines from the 1990s to the early 2000s—and a stream of high-profile reports and policy statements about the significance of participation, social capital, empowerment, and culture—trust across fields has been shattered. Throughout those years most new participatory and qualitative poverty assessments sat largely ignored and were not reflected in policy advice.

No matter the sample size, methods used, robustness of findings, or author credentials, explanations that draw on concepts of power, social structures, cultural values, and behaviors are often labeled "small picture" or "emotive" and summarily dismissed as inappropriate for informing broader policy actions. As discussed earlier, these types of responses reflect the economists' grip over leading arenas for poverty research and policy making as well as large differences in how the different disciplines approach research questions. Economists search for objectivity and universal results. Sociologists accept the value of the subjective meanings that people attach to their lives and the context-specificity of findings. The latter also acknowledge the influence of the researcher's place in time and space in the understanding and interpretation of social life.

The choice of concepts and methods really depends on the purpose of the research and on whom it is trying to influence. Most policy makers like numbers (de Haan and Dubey 2004). And if the research question is about how widely a particular phenomenon is distributed in a society or set of societies, then a survey will be appropriate. But if the research question is about the nature and causes of a phenomenon, then historical work that examines social relations and norms and values will be indispensable to uncover and understand the hows and whys. Not all social relations and norms can be translated into survey instruments, but many findings can be tested later for their significance in well-framed representative and comparative case study works.

Longitudinal investigations of any kind, nevertheless, raise sensitive ethical dilemmas concerning the relationship between research and action and between researcher and subject. This work provides an ongoing catalogue of poor people's hunger, illness, powerlessness, grief, exploitation, humiliation, and frustration. How should the research team respond? Households and communities that are repeatedly asked to contribute their experiences and understandings have a right to expect something concrete in return. This onus is particularly heavy for research and learning partnerships that extend over long periods. Concerns about contaminating samples and results simply cannot hold.

Ultimately, we are agnostic if the issues raised by empowerment concepts seem to favor more sociologically inspired research concepts and designs. The landscape of poor people's empowerment and mobility does not lend itself readily to approaches that single out economic factors and explicitly remove context:

> Within sociology, the implicit critique, then, of income-based approaches rests not so much on the argument that the income distribution is just one of many distributions of interest (i.e., multidimensionalism), but rather on the argument that measurement strategies based on income distribution alone impose an excessively abstract, analytical and statistical lens on a social world that has much institutionalized structure to it. (Grusky and Kanbur 2006, 9)

After a half century, it is well past time to move beyond describing poverty outcomes to explaining how they came to be. Economic opportunities are shaped by the rules, norms, and values that make up the institutional climate, by social structures, and by the possibilities for exercising individual and collective agency. An empowerment approach provides a tool for understanding this broader set of underlying factors and their interactions. It is time to open up this black box.

Notes

1. For a useful, not-too-technical presentation of some of the key debates among economists over poverty and inequality measures, see Ravallion (2003).
2. All poverty data presented here are from Chen and Ravallion (2007). The poverty lines are actually $1.08 and $2.15 per day at 1993 purchasing power parity, and the analysis assumes that no poor people fell below these levels in the industrial countries. See Chen and Ravallion for other technical assumptions and helpful analysis of the weight of China in overall outcomes as well as significant regional differences in head count and poverty gap trends and in urban–rural poverty distributions and changes over time.
3. The research was published in three volumes: *Voices of the Poor: Can Anyone Hear Us?* (Narayan, Patel, et al. 2000), *Voices of the Poor: Crying Out for Change* (Narayan, Chambers, et al. 2000), and *Voices of the Poor: From Many Lands* (Narayan and Petesch 2002).
4. Moser (2003) and Baulch and Scott (2006) provide useful background on conceptual and methodological concerns about longitudinal research, drawing from both disciplines. For more technical discussions that focus on panel work in the respective disciplines, see Morgan, Grusky, and Fields (2006) and useful chapters in part 2 of Birdsall and Graham (2000). Although the measurement of mobility is not a focus, Grusky and Kanbur (2006) provide a particularly useful discussion of advances and challenges within the two disciplines with respect to conceiving and measuring poverty and inequality.
5. See Ravallion (1992) for a technical discussion of how to compute poverty lines and the strengths and weaknesses of the different approaches for specific research questions.
6. There is more evidence of economists measuring beyond "the usual suspects" with cross-sectional studies. For instance, *World Development Report 2006*, which focuses on equity and development, highlights the significance of gender, ethnicity, religion, and other social group identities as influences on economic welfare and inequality outcomes (World Bank 2005).
7. A classic case is Whyte's (1955) study contrasting gang members and college students in a poor Italian immigrant neighborhood of Boston.
8. Becker (1981) also develops an economic model of the dilemma that families face in investing scarce resources in their children. "If the same amount were invested in each child, marginal rates of return would be higher for better-endowed children, while marginal utility would be higher for the worse-endowed. More human capital would be invested in the better-endowed only if differences in rates of return exceeded differences in marginal utilities" (190).
9. The important work of King, Keohane, and Verba (1994) especially stands out in this regard. See Kanbur and Shaffer (2007) for a more recent work calling for use

of more standardized data collection methods to strengthen the intersubjective reliability in qualitative work.

10. For an introduction to the strengths and weaknesses of each approach, see Kanbur (2003). Examples of Q-squared poverty work in developing countries are provided by the Centre for International Studies at the University of Toronto (http://www.q-squared.ca/papers.html) and by the Chronic Poverty Research Centre at the University of Manchester (http://www.chronicpoverty.org/). Da Silva (2006) provides an annotated bibliography of recent Q-squared literature.

11. In addition to Rao and Woolcock (2007), see Bebbington et al. (2006) for perspectives from sociologists on their struggles to advance more multidimensional understandings of poverty and cross-disciplinary work within the World Bank. For a view on diverse barriers facing anthropologists working inside the Bank, see Mosse (2006).

12. For a fuller explanation of the framework presented here, see chapters 1 (Narayan 2005) and 2 (Petesch, Smulovitz, and Walton 2005) in *Measuring Empowerment: Cross-Disciplinary Perspectives*.

13. For a thoughtful discussion of social exclusion concepts and the importance of moving beyond descriptions of poverty, see de Haan and Dubey (2004).

14. See Narayan (2002) for more discussion of the rationale and practical illustrations of these four dimensions.

15. Portes (2006) provides a useful critique of recent work in the area of institutional economics and argues that this work has suffered from conflating concepts of norms, values, and institutions. The article also offers helpful definitions and an analytic framework for understanding "social life" and varied processes for institutional and organizational change.

16. See Petesch, Smulovitz, and Walton (2005, 45–53) for a discussion of factors and mechanisms that are important for understanding political opportunity structures.

17. See Appadurai (2004) for concepts relating to culture's key forward-looking "navigational" role but the very unequal distribution of the "capacity to aspire" in societies. For further discussion of psychological dimensions, see Narayan (2005, 20–21) and Diener and Biswas-Diener (2005).

18. To illustrate, he gives examples of determinants of higher levels of well-being (the fifth and sixth stages respectively) in Gujarat. These include fixing leaky roofs and renting small tracts of land, because individuals at these higher levels "do not have leaky roofs" and can afford upfront rental fees.

19. The public and private sectors play greater roles in Gujarat, but Krishna qualifies these findings by stating that they reflect a one-time increase in teaching positions and greater industrial growth in this state. He goes on to indicate that half of the residents in his sample of Gujarat villages remain poor, as much of this industrial work is being carried out by migrants from elsewhere who are more willing to take the low-quality, short-term work offered by the factories.

20. A few examples include the World Values Survey and the Afrobarometer and Latinobarómetro surveys. For measures of democracy, governance, and rule of law, see Munck (2003). For measures of social capital see the Social Capital

Assessment Tool at http://go.worldbank.org/LHI4AYZEF0. For survey questions on happiness and other dimensions of subjective well-being, see Ed Diener's Web site at http://www.psych.uiuc.edu/~ediener/faq.htm.

21. See Erikson and Goldthorpe (2002) for useful review of cross-country sociological panel literature on intergenerational mobility. While they conclude that educational status is "probably *the* major" mediating factor in explaining the importance of social class origins to mobility, they recognize a need to examine a wider range of individual attributes to better understand the processes at play.

22. Grootaert, Kanbur, and Oh (1995) also find income diversification to be important for mobility in a Côte d'Ivoire panel study, but physical capital, especially land and farm equipment, proved even more important for rural mobility there.

23. Perlman defines bridging networks as having important friends and family members living outside the community.

24. Studies find negative or ambiguous relationships as well as positive relationships. For studies demonstrating a negative or ambiguous relationship between democracy and growth, see Barro (1997), Helliwell (1994), Rodrik (1997), and Tavares and Wacziarg (2001). Studies finding a positive relationship include those by Feng (1997), Kaufmann and Kraay (2002), Londregan and Poole (1996), Rivera-Batiz (2002), and Roll and Talbott (2003).

25. See Pritchett (2006) for a creative set of recommendations to address migration pressures and enlarge the economic and social benefits of migration. Suggested measures include scaling up (but also tightening enforcement of) temporary work programs and reaching special agreements with the poor countries most in need of the financial flows that migration brings.

References

Ackerman, J. 2003. "State-Society Synergy for Accountability: Lessons for the World Bank." Civil Society Team, Latin America and the Caribbean Region, World Bank. siteresources.worldbank.org/EXTECAREGTOPSOCDEV/Resources/Ackerman_Paper_FINAL_08-20-03.doc.

Agarwal, B. 1997. "'Bargaining' and Gender Relations: Within and Beyond the Household." *Feminist Economics* 3 (1): 1–51.

Adato, M., M. R. Carter, and J. May. 2006. "Exploring Poverty Traps and Social Exclusion in South Africa using Qualitative and Quantitative Data." *Journal of Development Studies* 42 (2): 226–47.

Appadurai, A. 2004. "The Capacity to Aspire: Culture and Terms of Recognition." In *Culture and Public Action*, ed. V. Rao and M. Walton, 59–84. Stanford, CA: Stanford University Press.

Arboleda, J., P. Petesch, and J. Blackburn. 2004. *Voices of the Poor in Colombia: Strengthening Livelihoods, Families, and Communities.* Washington, DC: World Bank.

Ayala, L., and M. Sastre. 2004. "Europe Versus the United States: Is There a Trade-Off between Mobility and Inequality?" *Journal of Income Distribution* 13 (1–2): 56–75.

Barro, R. J. 1997. *Determinants of Economic Growth: A Cross-Country Empirical Study*. Cambridge, MA: MIT Press.

Bates, R. H. 1999. "Ethnicity, Capital Formation and Conflict." Working Paper 27, Center for International Development, Harvard University, Cambridge, MA.

Baulch, B., and J. Hoddinott, eds. 2000. *Economic Mobility and Poverty Dynamics in Developing Countries*. London: Frank Cass. Special issue, *Journal of Development Studies* 36 (6).

Baulch, B., and L. Scott, eds. 2006. "Report on CPRC Workshop on Panel Surveys and Life History Methods." Chronic Poverty Research Centre, University of Manchester, UK.

Bebbington, A., A. Dani, A. de Haan, and M. Walton. Forthcoming. "Equity, Inequality Traps and Institutions: Cross-Disciplinary Views." In *Institutional Pathways to Equity: Addressing Inequality Traps*, ed. A. Bebbington, A. Dani, A. de Haan, and M. Walton. Washington, DC: World Bank.

Bebbington, A., M. Woolcock, S. Guggenheim, and E. A. Olsen, eds. 2006. *The Search for Empowerment: Social Capital as Idea and Practice at the World Bank*. Bloomfield, CT: Kumarian Press.

Becker, G. S. 1981. *A Treatise on the Family*. Cambridge, MA: Harvard University Press.

Besley, T., and L. J. Cord, eds. 2007. *Delivering on the Promise of Pro-Poor Growth: Insights and Lessons from Country Experiences*. Washington, DC: World Bank; Basingstoke, UK: Palgrave Macmillan.

Birdsall, N., and C. Graham, eds. 2000. *New Markets, New Opportunities? Economic and Social Mobility in a Changing World*. Washington, DC: Brookings Institution and Carnegie Endowment for International Peace.

Booysen, F. le R. 2003. "Chronic and Transitory Poverty in the Face of HIV/AIDS-Related Morbidity and Mortality: Evidence from South Africa." Presented at conference, "Staying Poor: Chronic Poverty and Development Policy," University of Manchester, UK, April 7–9.

Bourdieu, P. 1977. *Outline of a Theory of Practice*. Cambridge: Cambridge University Press.

Brady, H. E., and D. Collier, eds. 2004. *Rethinking Social Inquiry: Diverse Tools, Shared Standards*. Lanham, MD: Rowman and Littlefield.

Brook, J. S., D. W. Brook, M. De La Rosa, L. E. Duque, E. Rodrigez, I. D. Montoya, and M. Whiteman. 1998. "Pathways to Marijuana Use among Adolescents: Cultural/Ecological, Family, Peer and Personality Influences." *Journal of American Academy of Child and Adolescent Psychiatry* 37 (7): 759–66.

Brook, J. S., D. W. Brook, M. De La Rosa, M. Whiteman, and I. D. Montoya. 1999. "The Role of Parents in Protecting Colombian Adolescents from Delinquency and Marijuana Use." *Archive of Pediatric and Adolescent Medicine* 153: 457–68.

Carter, M. R., and C. Barrett. 2006. "The Economics of Poverty Traps and Persistent Poverty: An Asset-based Approach." *Journal of Development Studies* 42 (2): 178–99.

Carter, M. R., and J. May. 1999. "Poverty, Livelihood and Class in Rural South Africa." *World Development* 27 (1): 1–20.

————. 2001. "One Kind of Freedom: Poverty Dynamics in Post-apartheid South Africa." *World Development* 29 (12): 1987–2006.

Chen, S., and M. Ravallion. 2007. "Absolute Poverty Measures for the Developing World, 1981–2004." Policy Research Working Paper 4211, World Bank, Washington, DC.

D'Cruz, C., and D. Satterthwaite. 2005. "Building Homes, Changing Official Approaches: The Work of Urban Poor Organizations and Their Federations and Their Contributions to Meeting the Millennium Development Goals in Urban Areas." Working Paper on Poverty Reduction in Urban Areas 16, International Institute for Environment and Development, London.

Da Silva, J. 2006. "Annotated Bibliography of Recent Q^2 Analyses of Poverty." Q-Squared Working Paper 30, Centre for International Studies, University of Toronto.

de Haan, A., and A. Dubey. 2004. "Conceptualizing Social Exclusion in the Context of India's Poorest Regions." Paper presented at conference, "Q-Squared in Practice: Experiences of Combining Qualitative and Quantitative Methods in Poverty Appraisal," Centre for International Studies, University of Toronto, May 15–16.

de Weerdt, J. 2006. "Moving Out of Poverty in Tanzania's Kagera Region." Prepared for the World Bank's Moving Out of Poverty study. Economic Development Initiatives (EDI), Bukoba, Tanzania. http://www.edi-africa.com/.

Dercon, S. 2002. *The Impact of Economic Reform on Rural Households in Ethiopia.* Washington, DC: World Bank.

————. 2006. "Economic Reform, Growth and the Poor: Evidence from Rural Ethiopia." *Journal of Development Economics* 81 (1): 1–24.

Diamond, L. 2003. "Building a System of Comprehensive Accountability to Control Corruption." Comparative Democratization Project, Hoover Institution, Stanford University, Stanford, CA. http://www.stanford.edu/~ldiamond/papers/Horiz_Acct.pdf.

Diener, E., and R. Biswas-Diener. 2005. "Psychological Empowerment and Subjective Well-Being." In Narayan 2005, 125–40.

Drèze, J., P. Lanjouw, and N. Sharma. 1998. "Economic Development in Palanpur, 1957–93." In *Economic Development in Palanpur over Five Decades*, ed. P. Lanjouw and N. Stern, 114–239. New York: Clarendon Press.

Durkheim, E. 1982. *The Rules of Sociological Method.* New York: Free Press. Orig. pub. 1895.

Erikson, R., and J. Goldthorpe. 2002. "Intergenerational Inequality: A Sociological Perspective." *Journal of Economic Perspectives* 16 (3): 31–44.

Fields, G. S. 2000. "Income Mobility: Concepts and Measures." In Birdsall and Graham 2000, 101–32.

Feng, Y. 1997. "Democracy, Political Stability and Economic Growth." *British Journal of Political Science* 27 (3): 391–418.

Fox, J. A. 1995. "Governance and Development in Rural Mexico: State Intervention and Public Accountability." *Journal of Development Studies* 32 (1): 1–30. Paper CGIRS-Reprint-1995-1, Center for Global, International and Regional Studies, University of California, Santa Cruz. http://repositories.cdlib.org/cgirs/reprint/CGIRS-Reprint-1995-1.

Friedman, B. M. 2005. *The Moral Consequences of Economic Growth*. New York: Knopf.

Giddens, A. 1984. *The Constitution of Society*. Cambridge: Policy Press.

Grootaert, C., R. Kanbur, and G. T. Oh. 1995. "The Dynamics of Poverty: Why Some People Escape from Poverty and Others Don't." Policy Research Working Paper 1499, World Bank, Washington, DC.

Grusky, D., and R. Kanbur. 2006. "Conceptual Ferment in Poverty and Inequality Measurement: The View from Economics and Sociology." Q-Squared Working Paper 21, Centre for International Studies, University of Toronto.

Harevan, T. 1991. "The History of the Family and the Complexity of Social Change." *American History Review* 96: 95–124.

Harriss, J. 2006. "Why Understanding Social Relations Matters More for Policy on Chronic Poverty than Measurement." Paper presented at workshop, "Concepts and Methods for Analysing Poverty Dynamics and Chronic Poverty," Chronic Poverty Research Centre, University of Manchester, UK, October 23–25. http://www.chronicpoverty.org/news_events/ConceptsWorkshop-Oct2006.htm.

Helliwell, J. F. 1994. "Empirical Linkages between Democracy and Economic Growth." *British Journal of Political Science* 24: 225–48.

Hoff, K., and P. Pandey. 2004. "Belief Systems and Durable Inequalities: An Experimental Investigation of Indian Caste." Policy Research Working Paper 3351, World Bank, Washington, DC.

Hulme, D. 2007. "Integrating Quantitative and Qualitative Research for Country Case Studies of Development." GPRG Working Paper 63, Global Poverty Research Group, University of Manchester and University of Oxford, UK. http://www.gprg.org/pubs/workingpapers/pdfs/gprg-wps-063.pdf.

Hulme, D., and J. Toye. 2006. "The Case for Cross-Disciplinary Social Science Research on Poverty, Inequality and Well-being." Q-Squared Working Paper 19, Centre for International Studies, University of Toronto.

Kabeer, N. 2003. *Gender Mainstreaming in Poverty Eradication and the Millennium Development Goals: A Handbook for Policy Makers and Other Stakeholders*. London: Commonwealth Secretariat/IDRC/CIDA.

Kanbur, R., ed. 2003. *Q-Squared: Combining Qualitative and Quantitative Methods in Poverty Appraisal*. New Delhi: Permanent Black.

Kanbur, R., and P. Shaffer. 2007. "Epistemology, Normative Theory and Poverty Analysis: Implications for Q-Squared in Practice." *World Development* 52 (2): 183–96.

Kaufmann, D., and A. Kraay. 2002. "Growth Without Governance." Policy Research Working Paper 2928, World Bank, Washington, DC.

King, G., R. O. Keohane, and S. Verba. 1994. *Designing Social Inquiry: Scientific Inference in Qualitative Research*. Princeton, NJ: Princeton University Press.

Kozel, V., and B. Parker. 2003. "A Profile and Diagnostic of Poverty in Uttar Pradesh." *Economic and Political Weekly* (Mumbai), January 25, 385–403.

Kraay, A. 2004. "When Is Growth Pro-Poor? Cross-country Evidence." Policy Research Working Paper 3225, World Bank, Washington, DC.

Lawson, D, A. McKay, and J. Okidi. 2006. "Poverty Persistence and Transitions in Uganda: Combined Qualitative and Quantitative Analysis." Q-Squared Working Paper 23, Centre for International Studies, University of Toronto.

Lewis, O. 1961. *The Children of Sanchez*. New York: Random House.

————. 1966. *La Vida: A Puerto Rican Family in the Culture of Poverty—San Juan and New York.* New York: Random House.

————. 1970. *Anthropological Essays.* New York: Random House.

Londregan, J. B., and K. T. Poole. 1996. "Does High Income Promote Democracy?" *World Politics* 49: 1–30.

Mason, K. O. 2005. "Measuring Women's Empowerment: Learning from Cross-National Research." In Narayan 2005, 89–102.

Moen, P., and E. Wethington. 1992. "The Concept of Family Adaptive Strategies." *Annual Review of Sociology* 18: 233–51.

Moncrieffe, J. M. 2004. "Power Relations, Inequality and Poverty." Concept paper prepared for Empowerment Team, Poverty Reduction Group, World Bank, Washington, DC.

Morgan, S. 2006. "Past Themes and Future Prospects for Research on Social and Economic Mobility." In Morgan, Grusky, and Fields, 3–20.

Morgan, S. L., D. B. Grusky, and G. S. Fields, eds. 2006. *Mobility and Inequality: Frontiers of Research from Sociology and Economics.* Stanford, CA: Stanford University Press.

Moser, C. 1997. *Household Responses to Poverty and Vulnerability.* Vol. 1, *Confronting Crisis in Cisne Dos, Guayaquil, Ecuador.* Urban Management Program Policy Paper 21. Washington, DC: World Bank.

————. 2003. "Urban Longitudinal Research Methodology: Objectives, Contents and Summary of Issues Raised at the Joint DPU-ODI-World Bank-DFID Workshop." DPU Working Paper 124, Development Planning Unit, University College London.

Moser, C., and A. Felton. 2006. "Intergenerational Asset Accumulation and Poverty Reduction in Guayaquil, Ecuador (1978–2004)." Brookings Institution, Washington, DC. http://www.brookings.edu/views/papers/200611moser.pdf.

Mosse, D. 2006. "Localized Cosmopolitans: Anthropologists at the World Bank." Paper presented at Association of Social Anthropologists conference, "Cosmopolitanism and Development," Keele University, Staffordshire, UK, April 10–13.

Munck, G. L. 2003. "Measures of Democracy, Governance and Rule of Law: An Overview of Cross-National Data Sets." Paper presented at World Bank workshop, "Understanding Growth and Freedom from the Bottom Up," Washington, DC, July 15–17. http://lnweb18.worldbank.org/ESSD/sdvext.nsf/68ByDocName/Munck/$FILE/Munck+Paper.pdf.

Narayan, D., ed. 2002. *Empowerment and Poverty Reduction: A Sourcebook.* Washington, DC: World Bank.

————, ed. 2005. *Measuring Empowerment: Cross-Disciplinary Perspectives.* Washington, DC: World Bank.

Narayan, D., and M. F. Cassidy 2001. "A Dimensional Approach to Measuring Social Capital: Development and Validation of a Social Capital Inventory." *Current Sociology* 49 (2): 59–102.

Narayan, D., R. Chambers, M. K. Shah, and P. Petesch. 2000. *Voices of the Poor: Crying Out for Change.* New York: Oxford University Press for the World Bank.

Narayan, D., and S. Kapoor. 2005. "Beyond Ideologies: Creating Wealth for the Poor." Paper presented at conference sponsored by the World Bank in collaboration with DFID, Finland, Norway, and Sida, "New Frontiers of Social Policy," Arusha, Tanzania, December 12–15.

Narayan, D., with R. Patel, K. Schafft, A. Rademacher, and S. Koch-Schulte. 2000. *Voices of the Poor: Can Anyone Hear Us?* New York: Oxford University Press for the World Bank.

Narayan, D., and P. Petesch, eds. 2002. *Voices of the Poor: From Many Lands.* New York: Oxford University Press for the World Bank.

Page, J., and S. Plaza. 2006. "Migration, Remittances and Development: A Review of Global Evidence." *Journal of African Economies* 15 (2): 245–336.

Petesch, P., C. Smulovitz, and M. Walton. 2005. "Evaluating Empowerment: A Framework with Cases from Latin America." In Narayan 2005, 3–38.

Portes, A. 2006. "Institutions and Development: A Conceptual Reanalysis." *Population and Development Review* 32 (2): 233–62.

Pritchett, L. 2003. "Who Is Not Poor? Proposing a Higher International Standard for Poverty." Working Paper 33, Center for Global Development, Washington, DC.

———. 2006. *Let Their People Come: Breaking the Gridlock on Global Labor Mobility.* Washington, DC: Center for Global Development.

Rao, V., and M. Woolcock. 2007. "Disciplinary Monopolies in Development Research: A Response to the Research Evaluation Process." Development Economics Department, World Bank, Washington, DC.

Ravallion, M. 1992. "Poverty Comparisons: A Guide to Concepts and Methods." Living Standards Measurement Study Working Paper 88, World Bank, Washington, DC.

———. 2003. "The Debate on Globalization, Poverty and Inequality: Why Measurement Matters." *International Affairs* 79 (4): 739–53.

Rigdon, S. M. 2003. "Identifying Causes of Long-Term Poverty within Families: Experimental Use of an Anthropological Data Base." In Moser 2003, 48–57.

Rivera-Batiz, F. L. 2002. "Democracy, Governance and Economic Growth: Theory and Evidence." *Review of Development Economics* 6 (2): 225–47.

Rodrik, D. 1997. "Democracy and Economic Performance." Paper presented at conference, "Democratization and Economic Reform," Cape Town, January 16–19.

Roll, R., and J. Talbott. 2003. "Political Freedom, Economic Liberty and Prosperity." *Journal of Democracy* 14 (3): 75–89.

Scott, J., and L. Tilly. 1975. "Women's Work and Family in Nineteenth-Century Europe." *Comparative Studies in Social History* 17: 319–23.

Scott, C. 2000. "Mixed Fortunes: A Study of Poverty Mobility among Small Farm Households in Chile, 1968–86." *Journal of Development Studies* 36 (6): 155–81.

Sen, A. 2000. *Development as Freedom.* New York: Anchor.

Smelser, N. J., and S. M. Lipset, eds. 1966. *Social Structure and Mobility in Economic Development.* Chicago, IL: Aldine.

Tavares, J., and R. Wacziarg. 2001. "How Democracy Affects Growth." *European Economic Review* 45 (8): 1341–78.

Tilly, C. 1999. *Durable Inequality.* Berkeley: University of California Press.

Tilly, L. 1979. "Individual Lives and Family Strategies in the French Proletariat." *Journal of Family History* 4: 137–52.

Tilly, L., and J. Scott. 1978. *Women, Work and Family.* New York: Holt, Rinehart Winston.

Valletta, R. G. 2004. "The Ins and Outs of Poverty in Advanced Economies: Poverty Dynamics in Canada, Germany, Great Britain, and the United States." Working Papers in Applied Economic Theory 2004–18, Federal Reserve Bank of San Francisco.

Varshney, A. 2003. *Ethnic Conflict and Civic Life: Hindus and Muslims in India.* New Haven, CT: Yale University Press.

———. 2005. "Democracy and Poverty." In Narayan 2005, 383–401.

Weber, M. 1948. "Class, Status and Party." In *Essays from Max Weber,* ed. H. Gerth and C. W. Mills. London: Routledge and Kegan Paul. Orig. pub. 1924.

———. 1968. *Economy and Society: An Outline of Interpretive Sociology.* Trans. G. Roth and G. Wittich. New York: Bedminster Press. Orig. pub. 1922 as *Wirtschaft und Gesellschaft.*

Weiner, M. 2001. "The Struggle for Equality: Caste in Indian Politics." In *The Success of India's Democracy,* ed. A. Kohli, 193–225. Cambridge: Cambridge University Press.

Whyte, W. F. 1955. *Street Corner Society.* Chicago: Chicago University Press.

Willis, P. 1977. *Learning to Labour.* Farnborough, UK: Saxon House.

Wilson, W. J. 1996. *When Work Disappears: The World of the New Urban Poor.* New York: Knopf.

Woolcock, M. 2007a. Personal correspondence.

Woolcock, M. 2007b. "Toward an Economic Sociology of Chronic Poverty: Enhancing the Rigor and Relevance of Social Theory." Chronic Poverty Research Centre, University of Manchester, UK.

Woolcock, M., and D. Narayan. 2000. "Social Capital: Implications for Development Theory." *World Bank Research Observer* 15 (2): 225–51.

World Bank. 2004. *World Development Report 2004: Making Services Work for Poor People.* New York: Oxford University Press.

———. 2005. *World Development Report 2006: Equity and Development.* New York: Oxford University Press.

2

Poverty and the Politics
of Exclusion

Charles Tilly

A mong the many vivid vignettes of poor people's lives recorded in the World Bank's sweeping survey *Voices of the Poor*, listen to one of the more hopeful stories:

> Mahood Rab was destitute when he arrived at the slum of Chittagong City [Bangladesh] with his wife at the age of 18. He left his village after his father died, and his family had become impoverished covering medical expenses. When Mahood arrived in the city, he worked as a rickshaw puller, and his wife took jobs as a maidservant in several homes. Through hard work, and with his own and his wife's savings, he was finally able to buy a rickshaw. Within a year, he owned four. Today, at age 50, Mahood owns eight rickshaws, but does not rely just on this business. He took out a loan from Proshika (a national NGO) and rents five houses he built in another slum area. Mahood shared with the researchers that due to his wealth everyone knows him, and he is among those who are respected and take part in the major decisions of the neighborhood. (Narayan, Chambers, et al. 2000, 52; see also Narayan, Patel, et al. 2000)

Thirty-two years after Mahood's arrival in Bastuhara, a Chittagong slum, his story reads like a free enterprise morality tale: take risks, work hard, accumulate capital, invest wisely, and you will escape from poverty. According to the Voices of the Poor study of Bastuhara, the slum houses a number of migrants who have moved up through saving, investing, and working hard; new factories and microcredit schemes backed by nongovernmental organizations facilitated their rise (Narayan and Petesch 2002, 124). Mahood Rab's story also appears to illustrate the importance of crucial assets and capabilities of poor people shown on the checklist reproduced in box 2.1.

Although the tasks of defining and measuring poverty pose perplexing problems for experts, the checklist will serve this chapter's purposes well. "Poor" here means lacking most or all of these assets and capabilities. As

BOX 2.1
Crucial Assets and Capabilities of Poor People

Material assets
Bodily health
Bodily integrity
Emotional integrity
Respect and dignity
Social belonging
Cultural identity
Imagination, information, and education
Organizational capacity
Political representation and accountability

Source: Narayan and Petesch 2002, 463.

Amartya Sen (1995) puts it, *poverty* means capability deprivation. Relative poverty refers to a comparison with the bulk of a local, regional, or national population, while *absolute poverty* refers to a comparison with a worldwide standard. The once-destitute Mahood Rab, in these terms, left both absolute and relative poverty behind.

The vignette does not tell us to what extent Mahood capitalized on emotional integrity, imagination, information, education, or political representation and accountability. But he clearly benefited from other assets on the checklist. He deployed some of them during his exit from poverty, then enjoyed others as a result of his exit. Even this brief sketch shows him enjoying material assets, respect, dignity, and social belonging.

What we don't know, however, is whether he already belonged to some social category that facilitated his exit and whether he used previously existing connections on his way to Chittagong. Most likely he benefited from both social connections and membership in a favorable social category. After all, a landmark study of poverty in the northern Indian village of Palanpur, Uttar Pradesh, indicates that connections and categories matter greatly to South Asian exits from poverty (Lanjouw and Stern 2003). Cultural identities such as gender and caste enormously affect mobility chances in Uttar Pradesh and elsewhere. So do connections with patron-client networks.

Many poor people, however, lack helpful connections and membership. Indeed, while affirming the value of cultural identity to poor people, Narayan and Petesch emphasize that cultural practices can also be exclusionary:

In Nigeria the poorest of the poor are excluded from social events and ceremonies. In India women are excluded from many community and religious rituals conducted by men. In Ughoton, Nigeria, it is taboo for women to enter the Court Hall because it is regarded as a sacred place. Women may sit outside, where they can only listen while important decisions are made. In Adaboya, Ghana, the churches are perceived to sow seeds of disunity by engaging in competition between denominations. (Narayan and Petesch 2002, 468)

A broader look at the case studies in the World Bank's portfolios therefore suggests two qualifications to any straightforward inference from the Mahood Rab story that "virtue × effort = success." First, very few of the poor people surveyed for Voices of the Poor actually accomplished anything like Mahood Rab's spectacular family exit from poverty. In the study's detailed analysis of Bangladesh, for example, some of the "social poor" had connections to draw on, but the "helpless poor" did not, and the "hated poor" clearly belonged to the wrong categories for any such assistance (Narayan and Petesch 2002, 121). Most of the Bangladeshi poor apparently lack favorable categorical memberships and interpersonal connections.

Second, whether or not social connections and membership in a favorably situated social category facilitated Mahood's ascent, in general both of these circumstances affected mobility or immobility a great deal more than did individual pluck or luck. Most of the world's very poor people, it seems likely, lack favorable categorical memberships and helpful connections. If so, their exits from poverty—if they happen at all—would result from either (a) their acquisition of new categorical memberships and/or connections, or (b) political–economic changes that subvert the usual effects of categories and connections. Socially organized patterns of exclusion set formidable barriers to mobility in the way of most poor individuals and households (Munck 2005). The Mahood Rab story, in short, misleads us in two fundamental ways. It suggests that the main thing analysts of poverty reduction must explain is individual-by-individual exits from poverty, and it implies that the main causes of poverty reduction involve individual characteristics and behavior.

On the contrary, the real-life availability of most assets and capabilities on the comprehensive Narayan-Petesch checklist results from economic, organizational, and political processes over which the typical poor individual or household exercises precious little control. Those processes produce and maintain the crucial categorical memberships and social connections. They thereby cause differential exclusion of poor individuals and households. In order to explain how politics affects individual and collective exits from poverty, we must look directly at the impact of politics on organized exclusion from benefits.

The analysis that follows concentrates on causal links among four elements: social exclusion, poverty, exits from poverty, and overall processes that generate inequality among social categories. I argue that social exclusion lies at the heart of inequality-generating processes, that exclusion itself promotes poverty, and that exits from poverty therefore depend on eliminating or bypassing the usual effects of social exclusion.

Exclusion and Exits from Poverty

The World Bank's Moving Out of Poverty study intersects with this chapter's themes when it deals with inclusion and exclusion. The study operates at three levels:

1. *The local community level.* Evidence comes from a general analysis of community characteristics, observations of female and male focus group discussions, ladders of life produced by those focus groups, placements of local households on those ladders for both past and present (likewise done by focus groups), and household histories from a limited number of interviews.
2. *The national level.* National syntheses are based on combinations of data from multiple communities, with general observations on the countries.
3. *The international level.* The study's central staff is working to analyze variation, change, and common elements across all the countries in the study.

The study therefore embodies an obvious tension between hoped-for conclusions (international patterns of factors promoting or inhibiting exits from poverty across countries) and systematic evidence (detailed observations within single communities). It compounds the tension by insisting on identification of local standards of poverty or wealth instead of adopting putatively uniform standards such as nutritional sufficiency or income equivalents. Those tensions, paradoxically, give the study its peculiar strength: the possibility of connecting local processes of mobility, immobility, and inequality with worldwide patterns.

For all its strengths, the Moving Out of Poverty study design obscures the processes on which this paper concentrates: the politics of exclusion and the political production or reproduction of poverty. It obscures those processes in two unavoidable ways. First, it relies on local holders of power for access to the community. Second, its research design diverts attention from all sorts of political connections between the community and its individual households, on one side, and holders of power outside the community, on the other. The analysis that follows can therefore help the final synthesis of the study's findings both by identifying hidden influences on exits from poverty and by suggesting plausible supplementary explanations of differences between communities and between countries.

Toward that end, this chapter presents (a) a general sketch of exclusionary social processes that generate inequality in assets, capabilities, and social connections among different categories of the population and thereby produce poverty among the excluded; (b) an equally general review of the political underpinnings of inequality and its changes; and (c) a summary of policy implications following from that analysis.

To focus on these aims, the chapter deliberately neglects a whole series of relevant questions. It does *not* spell out its arguments' implications for change and variation in national configurations of material inequality among individuals or households as measured by such devices as the Gini coefficient. It does *not* propose a typology of countries or regions that differ significantly with regard to either their overall patterns of material inequality or the processes that generate material inequality. It does *not*, finally, assess existing or possible poverty reduction strategies in terms of the likelihood that they will actually reduce poverty and/or facilitate poor people's exits from poverty. In such a brief analysis, taking up any one of these crucial questions would enormously complicate the argument and very likely obscure its main elements.

Nor does the chapter offer a comprehensive account of all the factors causing poverty around the world. Many factors other than social exclusion produce poverty, most notably the overall character of economic activity within a given region. Many factors other than politics in any large sense of the word promote social exclusion, for example the salience of religious, ethnic, racial, and gender divisions within a population. Finally, any poverty-affecting political intervention (for instance, massive redistribution of income by means of progressive taxation) yields effects well outside of poor people's lives. Such an intervention may turn out to be impractical because of those other effects rather than because of its impact on poverty.

Yet without general pictures of inequality-producing processes and their connections with politics at large, we are likely to draw mistaken conclusions about relations between poverty and the politics of exclusion. The chapter's general discussions of inequality and politics therefore set the backdrop for its narrower treatment of political impacts on escapes from exclusion-induced poverty.

Individualistic Explanations of Inequality

Prevailing views of inequality's production and maintenance make it difficult to grasp the processes by which exclusion generates inequality and inequality causes poverty among excluded populations. In particular, a view of inequality and poverty as outcomes of individual-by-individual competition according to widely shared standards of merit, worthiness, or privilege obscures the significance of organized distinctions and interactions among members of different social categories. Since my main argument concerns categorical distinctions and interactions, it should help to first sketch the common view the argument rejects.

Compare two very different perspectives on the processes that produce inequality: *individual* and *interaction*. In an individual perspective, a person's attributes and behavior locate that person within one or more hierarchies. Individual accounts differ greatly with regard to personal agency: At one extreme, a person's performance determines where he or she ends up within this or that hierarchy. At the other extreme, holders of power decide which attributes to punish or reward, thus placing people with different attributes at different positions within hierarchies (for surveys of competing individual views, see Grusky 2001 and Romero and Margolis 2005).

To be sure, most individual accounts of inequality recognize that previous social experience strongly affects individual attributes and behavior. Still, the perspective's organizing ideas stress that inequality emerges from the sorting of individuals according to their attributes and behavior. In the Mahood Rab story with which we began, Mahood's individual attributes (his "crucial assets and capabilities," in Voices of the Poor terms) and his individual behavior (for example, his extraordinary entrepreneurship) caused his ascent from destitution to wealth.

In the individual perspective, how do hierarchies work? Imagine a rectilinear space with social rank defining its vertical axis, and various social sites along its horizontal axis. In the individual view, inequality consists of differential location within such a space. We can follow current fashion by making the vertical axis represent monetary income or wealth, but nothing in principle keeps us from adding or substituting criteria such as power, fame, prestige, and overall well-being. Any array of social units—individuals, groups, categories, jobs, or other positions—is unequal to the extent that its members occupy different positions along that space's vertical dimension.

The idea lends itself easily to the notion of a single hierarchy within which every individual has a defined place. The hierarchy may, of course, rank individuals according to income, wealth, power, prestige, or some combination of these advantages. The perspective also articulates neatly with the notion of social mobility as movement of individuals from step to step within such a hierarchy. Aggregate inequality thus conceived refers to distributions: in static terms, the extent to which higher-ranking individuals enjoy greater advantages than lower-ranking individuals. In dynamic terms, it concerns the extent to which the average individual and that individual's offspring stay in the same inferior or superior location throughout careers, lifetimes, or generations. A highly unequal system, in these terms, concentrates advantages at its hierarchy's top and fixes individuals or social units at their positions within the hierarchy.

A popular version of the individual perspective portrays the selection process within such hierarchies as a queue. In today's Western analyses of inequality, indeed, queuing images prevail. A queue, in this view, lines up individuals to pass a checkpoint where a monitor scans them; matches their various attributes and performances with well-established templates; and then shunts them into different channels, where they join other people having similar attributes and performances. In a queue, inclusion or exclusion operates one person at a time, even if categorical attributes of individuals such as race, gender, or religion affect an individual's inclusion or exclusion.

The best-known version of the queue employs one main template: human capital. In this scenario, the monitor is a market or its human agents. The monitor scans each individual for human capital, then matches the detected human capital with a position in which it will produce a net return for the market as well as for the individual. In competing versions of the queue, the monitor selects for gender, race, fame, estimated commitment, or other attributes instead of—or in addition to—human capital. Thus the manager of a fast-food restaurant hires, fires, assigns, pays, and promotes counter workers on the basis of a personal preference schedule, but does so in implicit competition with other potential employers of the same workers.

More complex accounts in the same vein allow for additional effects of effort, inheritance, social connections, and learning, with the individual passing multiple checkpoints over a career. Still, the central image shows us one person at a time passing a checkpoint and moving on to differential rewards as a consequence of attributes or performances registered at that checkpoint.

Cumulatively, such a process generates distributions of individuals and positions differing significantly in current rewards and accumulations of past rewards as a function of their relationship to criteria built into the monitor. If the process centers on human capital, then the unequal distribution of human capital across the population generates unequal rank and unequal mobility as well.

Inequality-producing queues do exist. Law firms vie vigorously for high-ranking graduates of prestigious law schools, as graduates compete for positions in high-ranking firms. Competitive tryouts for ballet corps, football teams, and Rhodes Scholarships produce sharp divisions between winners and losers. First-past-the-post elections cumulate individual votes into a monitor, having fateful consequences for politicians in parliamentary democracies. A knack for answering questions on what my colleague Nicholas Lemann (1999) calls the "Big Test," an early equivalent of the Scholastic Aptitude Test, helped me become the first member of my large, recently immigrated kin network to attend college.

That examination emphatically established a queue—a queue into elite American colleges. The question, then, is not whether inequality, immobility, and mobility ever result from queuing processes, but whether we can reasonably take the queue as a general model for the production of inequality. Later I will give reasons for thinking that, on the contrary, the inequality-generating queue constitutes an exceptional case that only works under special institutional conditions.

Scholars have reached little consensus on causes of long-term transformations over whole inequality spaces. The prevailing economic account, however, expands queuing mechanisms to a national or even an international scale. Markets, in that account, serve as monitors, sorting out individuals according to the marginal increases in productivity caused by incremental inputs of the resources they embody or control.

Thus, in general, resources currently in short supply that make large contributions to productivity command greater rewards than those in excess supply and/or without significant impacts on productivity. The relative supply and significance of such resources as land, labor power, knowledge, information, machines, and financial capital shift massively over time as a function of interactions between their own transformation, on one side, and the changing organization of production, on the other.

With lags due to the accumulation of wealth, in such a view, basic inequalities shift from dependence on control of one kind of resource (say land) to another (say capital). Explanation of inequalities therefore requires identifying forms of production and the resources whose possession those forms reward. People who control the crucial resources will, according to the argument, reap disproportionate gains. While raising doubts about the generality of queuing processes as causes of inequality, I will borrow that important insight from queuing approaches later on.

Interactional Explanations of Inequality

What about interaction as a source of inequality? As an inequality-generating process, an interaction looks quite different from a queue, indeed from any set of arrangements that sort individuals one by one according to their attributes and behavior. In the individual perspective, markets sort individuals by the attributes (e.g., human capital) and behavior (e.g., hard work) that they bring to exchanges such as those between bosses and workers. Turning the market back into a dynamic set of social relations, however, reduces the difference between individual and interactive perspectives. Recognizing relations within a Middle Eastern bazaar, relations within a stock exchange, and relations within a local bake sale as different manifestations of markets makes it easier to conceive of markets in general as interactions (White 2002).

Assuming that market operations play a part in creating inequality, then, we have a choice between (a) imagining the market as an impersonal sensor that sorts persons, performances, and objects according to unchanging general criteria and (b) including dynamic, negotiated, interactive social relations in our picture of the market (Zelizer 2005). To the extent that we take the second option, we move away from strict individualism.

For a strong analogy, think about a crucial form of interaction: conversation. Conversation provides an illuminating example and model of social life because it so blatantly contradicts portrayals of social life as driven by individual interests (Tilly 1998b). Participants in conversation obviously build on previous experience and follow known scripts. Yet they also improvise incessantly, and they collectively produce new outcomes that affect their subsequent interchanges. In the most elementary conversation, only two parties engage in negotiated communication. Although the parties begin with at least partially shared definitions of their identities and relationship, both identities and relationship modify as a result of the colloquy. In the course of their exchange, each party deploys available resources in efforts to influence the other party and to shape the collective output of their talk. Many conversations operate asymmetrically, producing a net flow of advantage to one party or the other. Those conversations alter relationships between interlocutors.

In the analysis of inequality, the best-known interactive image represents the relationship between the parties as joint participation in material production. Here we see one party imposing controls and restrictions on the other such that the two parties leave their interchange with unequal gains or losses. Marxist models of inequality generally fit that image, but so do a number of non-Marxist and semi-Marxist materialist accounts (see, for example, Bowles 2006; Bowles and Gintis 1976, 1993; Earle 1997; Granovetter and Tilly 1988; Kalb 1997; Midlarsky 1999; Tilly and Tilly 1998). They usually argue that the organization of material production creates unequal categories of participants in productive processes and their rewards. They therefore build into their accounts of inequality exclusion from control of production and from its benefits.

Competing interactive explanations of inequality—especially inequality by gender, race, ethnicity, nationality, and other criteria that are not *ipso facto* economic—stress guile, coercion, mystification, and rhetoric as bases of unequal exchange. The elementary two-person model has its uses as a starting point. Yet interactive explanations of inequality gain in value when they incorporate three or more participants, when categorical boundaries separate at least two of the parties, and when the residues of previous interactions among the parties shape their current interchange.

In the interactive view, inequality is a relation between persons or sets of persons in which interaction generates greater advantages for one than for another. At a small scale, we might trace out the unequal relations that characterize a shop, a household, or a neighborhood. At a large scale, multiple relations of this kind compound into vast connected webs of inequality. At either scale, the interpersonal networks involved approximate single hierarchies only under extraordinary circumstances—for example, when some powerful institution such as an army, a corporation, or a church clumps people into distinct levels. We cannot easily locate most such webs in the sorts of abstract inequality spaces (according to income, wealth, or prestige) commonly associated with queuing models. Yet the weblike structure poses no fundamental barrier to assessing aggregate inequality. It simply requires shifting from examination of static stocks to study of dynamic flows (see, for example, Brudner and White 1997).

Just as we can detect the world's dominant economies by tracing international trade flows, dominant firms by tracing interlocking directorates, and dominant universities by tracing movements of scientists among institutions, we can identify dominant clusters within larger interpersonal webs by tracing net flows of advantages among social locations. Analyses of black–white differentials in wealth and well-being in the United States (e.g., Oliver and Shapiro 1997; Conley 1999) indicate, for example, that even at similar levels of current income, parent-child transfers of wealth give U.S. whites, on average, great advantages over U.S. blacks. Racial endogamy probably reinforces those differences. Social mobility, in interactive perspective, does not consist of individual movement up and down an abstract hierarchy. It involves concrete flows of persons among clusters, especially clusters that differ significantly in dominance.

Long-run changes in inequality, in this view, depend on regrouping of relations among participants. Like their neoclassical counterparts, Marxists emphasize control over productive resources in explaining major shifts in inequality. Classic Marxist explanations differ dramatically from neoclassical formulations, however, in two regards. First, they deny that markets do the crucial adjudicating, insisting instead on the generation of inequality within relations of production. Exploitation—unequal sharing of value added by effort in socially organized production—thus forms unequal social classes. (Some Marxists also make concessions to unequal exchange, but that remains a secondary current within Marxism.)

Second, Marxists differentiate between a medium run and a long run. In the medium run, interaction within modes of production creates changes in the degree, but not the type, of inequality. For the capitalist medium run, Marxist theories predict ever-increasing polarization between capital and labor. In the long run, coercion in the form of conquest, colonization, or revolution creates shifts from one mode of production to another. The two time spans correspond to contrasting styles of interaction: grudging collaboration in the medium run, shouting confrontation in the long run.

At best, the Marxist historical account only explains the evolution of class differences. It lacks a plausible explanation of differences by gender, race, ethnicity, age, nationality, religion, and other categorical principles insofar as those principles operate in partial independence of class. The lack has led a number of Marxist theorists either to argue that inequalities among such nonclass categories ultimately derive from class inequalities or to search for ways in which their existence serves the interests of dominant classes (see, for example, Leiman 1993).

An Interactive Theory of Inequality

While drawing considerable inspiration from Marxist accounts, I have taken a different tack, investigating the interplay of categorical distinctions with various forms of exploitation and opportunity hoarding. To give it a full, cumbersome label, we might call my line of argument an "interactive resource control theory of material inequality generation." Here is how the argument runs:

- Material inequality results from unequal control over value-producing resources. (Example: Some wildcatters strike oil, while others drill dry wells.)
- Paired and unequal categories such as male–female or white–black consist of asymmetrical relations across a socially recognized (and usually incomplete) boundary between interpersonal networks. Such categorical pairs recur in a wide variety of situations, with the usual effect being unequal exclusion of each network from resources controlled by the other. (Example: In U.S. urban ghettos, immigrant merchants often make their livings by selling mainly to black people, but never simply integrate into the black community. For all their mutual influence, the networks of immigrant merchants and local black populations remain largely separate.)
- An inequality-generating mechanism we may call *exploitation* occurs when persons who control a resource (a) enlist the effort of others in the production of value by means of that resource but (b) exclude the others from the full value added by their effort. (Example: Before 1848, citizens of several Swiss cantons drew substantial revenues in rents and taxes from noncitizen residents of adjacent tributary territories who produced agricultural and craft goods under control of the cantons' landlords and merchants.)
- Another inequality-generating mechanism we may call *opportunity hoarding* consists of confining disposition of a value-producing resource to members of an in-group. (Example: Southeast Asian spice merchants from a particular ethnic–religious category dominate the distribution and sale of their product, while excluding members of other ethnic–religious categories from the trade.)
- Two further mechanisms reinforce the effects of exploitation and opportunity hoarding: *emulation* and *adaptation*. Emulation occurs when those who control an inequality-generating set of social relations import categorical distinctions (e.g., by gender or caste) that bring with them readily available practices and meanings. (Example: Early 20th-century operators of South African gold and diamond mines built the distinction between "Europeans" and "natives" directly into the workforce, with white workers enjoying supervisory positions and enormously higher

pay.) Adaptation occurs when subordinates adjust their behavior so as to incorporate and ultimately reinforce the social arrangements generating inequality. (Example: Factory workers meet their production quotas through speedups and collaboration in order to create time for sociable leisure with their workmates, but by that very effort commit themselves to management-imposed quotas.)

- Both exploitation and opportunity hoarding generally incorporate paired and unequal categories at boundaries between greater and lesser beneficiaries of value added by effort committed to controlled resources. (Example: The distinction between professionals and nonprofessionals— registered nurses and nurses' aides, scientists and laboratory assistants, optometrists and optical clerks, architects and architectural drafters, and so on—often marks just such boundaries.)
- Local categorical distinctions gain strength and operate at lower cost when matched with widely available paired, unequal categories so that their boundaries coincide. (Example: Hiring women as workers and men as bosses reinforces organizational hierarchy with gender hierarchy.)
- Over a wide range of circumstances, mobility across boundaries does not in itself change the production of inequality but alters who benefits from inequality. (Example: So long as college degrees remain essential for engineering jobs, acquisition of those degrees by immigrants reinforces the exclusion of nondegree holders, even among immigrants.)
- Inequalities produced in these ways become more durable and effective to the extent that recipients of the surplus generated by exploitation and/ or opportunity hoarding commit a portion of that surplus to reproducing (a) boundaries separating themselves from excluded categories of the population and (b) unequal relations across those boundaries. (Example: Landlords devote some of their available wage-labor to building fences and chasing off squatters.)

Those are the theory's bare bones (for more sustained treatments, see Tilly 1998a, 2005). Taken in these terms, it provides no direct explanations for individual-by-individual variation in success and failure or for change and variation in the overall distribution of a country's wealth and income. Yet the theory has direct implications for exclusion and poverty. It centers on exclusion (complete or partial) from benefits generated by control of resources. Both exploitation and opportunity hoarding exclude members of subordinate categories from benefits. If the argument is correct, that exclusion usually produces categorical boundaries between ins and outs.

Exclusion relates differently to relative and absolute poverty. It inevitably produces relative poverty for the excluded. But whether excluded people experience absolute poverty depends on the extent of exclusion, the availability of alternative resources to excluded people, and the absolute size of the shares coming to subordinate categories. As advocates of "trickle down" economics often argue, at least sometimes exploitation and opportunity hoarding generate increasing returns that benefit the excluded as well. In those cases, a rising tide lifts all ships.

Exclusion most emphatically and directly produces poverty, according to such a theory, if the crucial value-producing resources affect the livelihood of most or all people within the population under analysis. In an essentially agricultural region, for example, sharp differences in access to land increase the likelihood that landless households will suffer absolute poverty. Similarly, to the extent that an economy attaches benefits exclusively to employment in capital-intensive firms, categories of the population that systematically lack access to employment suffer absolute poverty. As the United Kingdom's Department for International Development puts it:

> Social exclusion matters because it denies some people the same rights and
> opportunities that are afforded to others in their society. Simply because
> of *who they are*, certain groups cannot fulfill their potential, nor can they
> participate equally in society. An estimated 891 million people in the
> world experience discrimination on the basis of their ethnic, linguistic or
> religious identities alone. (DFID 2005, 5)

The report goes on to specify that exclusion causes poverty in two complementary ways: by excluding individuals from opportunities available to members of other categories, and by underusing an economy's productive potential. These effects become more powerful to the extent that one or a few value-producing resources dominate the economy. As we will soon see, most economies do center on a limited range of value-producing resources. Hence most economies harbor the potential for generating absolute poverty through exclusion of whole categories of people from access to those resources.

We can, of course, invert the theory. For example,

- For a given level of control, segmentation or multiplication of value-producing resources—such as prospectors' discovery of new deposits in an existing gold field—weakens exploitation and opportunity hoarding, thereby reducing exclusion and impoverishment.
- Collective action by members of excluded categories, if successful, induces greater sharing of benefits and thus undermines exploitation or

opportunity hoarding; relevant collective action ranges from strikes to revolutions.

- Discovery or creation of new value-producing resources by members of previously excluded populations may well introduce new sites of exploitation and opportunity hoarding, but it at least facilitates the escape of excluded populations from earlier subordination.
- Subversion of boundaries between the privileged and the excluded (for example, by affirmative action on behalf of talented members of excluded minorities) weakens control over value-producing resources.

For whatever reasons they occur, declines in the range and effectiveness of exploitation, opportunity hoarding, emulation, and adaptation reduce exclusion. The reduction of exclusion in turn promotes individual and collective escapes from poverty.

The theory has some interesting extensions that likewise bear on exclusion and poverty. Within strong systems of exploitation, segments of excluded populations sometimes practice opportunity hoarding and thus mitigate the poverty and inequality-producing effects of exploitation. Most obviously, subordinate population segments create niches that exclude others from their benefits: jobs that go only to members of a specific gender, ethnic category, or migration stream; crafts monopolized by a single connected population; trading diasporas; and so on. Niche formation often benefits members of the hoarding category, but the fact that it excludes others from opportunities means it rarely reduces poverty in the aggregate. It sometimes even promotes aggregate poverty in two very different ways: (a) by blocking access of more productive workers to hoarded niches and (b) by locking into the niche members of the hoarding population who could actually produce and gain more outside the niche (Hoff and Sen 2006).

If exploitation and opportunity hoarding are the basic mechanisms behind inequality, while emulation and adaptation simply reinforce the two main mechanisms, then queuing is simply one of several differentiating mechanisms by which exploitation and opportunity hoarding produce their effects. Queuing requires unusual special conditions: individual-by-individual selection rather than collective incorporation of categories; centralization of monitoring rather than multiple, diverse points of entry; crisp and visible selection criteria; and relatively extensive divisions both among candidates and among positions to be allocated.

While these conditions commonly occurred in 20th-century schools and firms—hence the recent popularity of queuing models—they have rarely appeared together in history. They rest, in fact, on extensive organizational infrastructure. Human beings working in concert organize the queuing, the monitoring, the assignment to positions, and the allocation of rewards to occupants of those positions. In the more general case, collective (rather than individual) selection occurs, monitoring operates in a dispersed fashion, and criteria vary from situation to situation as the numbers of categories and positions remain limited. Even within contemporary capitalist firms, for example, mutual recruitment to jobs within channels marked by common origin—migration stream, schooling, race, or ethnicity—still plays a large part in hiring. Such practices do not conform to simple queuing models. Queues are special cases.

Describing and Explaining Systems of Inequality

In any particular setting, whether or not queues figure prominently in the production of inequality, other inequality-generating factors such as exploitation, opportunity hoarding, emulation, and adaptation always set crucial barriers in place. Understanding the basic mechanisms allows us to construct a questionnaire for the analysis of escapes from poverty. But a first take on inequality in any setting begins with specification of the value-generating resources on which exploitation and opportunity hoarding are operating. Box 2.2 lists the main classes of resources whose control has supported large-scale systems of inequality over the last 5,000 years (Tilly 2005).

All of these resources lend themselves to production of benefits for some recipients by means of coordinated effort. When they are in short supply and relatively easy to circumscribe, they all lend themselves to exploitation and opportunity hoarding, hence to the generation of inequality. Coercive means, for example, have underlain many systems of inequality for thousands of years, and they still play at least some part in the maintenance of inequality throughout the world despite the rising importance of later items on the list. Only much more recently, in contrast, has control over scientific–technical knowledge become a major basis of inequality around the world.

It may be obvious that early items on the list—coercive means, labor, animals, and land—lend themselves to punishing, poverty-inducing exclusion. Civil wars, for example, always involve huge disparities in access to lethal arms and almost always leave impoverished populations in their wake. More slowly, less visibly, but no less powerfully, monopolization of land in agrarian regions regularly produces acute poverty among the landless. But it is equally true that where employment in firms—capitalist, socialist, or otherwise—provides the chief source of material benefits, in the absence of extensive social insurance, unemployment and barriers to employability also generate acute poverty.

BOX 2.2
Historically Prominent Inequality-Generating Resources

Coercive means, including weapons, jails, and organized specialists in
     violence
Labor, especially skilled and/or effectively coordinated labor
Animals, especially domesticated food-producing and/or work animals
Land, including natural resources located in and upon it
Commitment-maintaining institutions such as religious sects, kinship
     systems, and trade diasporas
Machines, especially machines that convert raw materials, produce goods
     or services, and transport persons, goods, services, or information
Financial capital—transferable and fungible means of acquiring property
     rights
Information, especially information that facilitates profitable, safe, or
     coordinated action
Media that disseminate such information
Scientific-technical knowledge, especially knowledge that facilitates
     intervention—for good or evil—in human welfare

Of course, these value-producing resources operate in combination. Once
settled agriculture began to prevail in Eurasia 5,000 or so years ago, those who
controlled land and animals on a large scale usually also controlled coercive means. They acted either to contain, to displace, or to co-opt those who
deployed coercive means locally. Until recent centuries, the early items on
the list—coercive means, labor, animals, land, and commitment-maintaining
institutions—predominated in the world's production of categorical inequality. Even today, they probably account for the bulk of the world's inequality
at the local and regional levels. Local reports in the Voices of the Poor study
suggest that exclusion from control of coercive means, labor, animals, land,
and/or commitment-maintaining institutions is still the proximate cause of
deep poverty in poorer parts of the world.

Between the 18th century and the recent past, however, control over
machines gained ever-increasing prominence as a base of exploitation and
opportunity hoarding. Then, during the later 20th century, the last four items
on the list—financial capital, information, media, and scientific-technical
knowledge—began in their turn to displace control over machines as worldwide bases of inequality.

The prevalence of one combination of inequality-sustaining resources
or another strongly affects patterns of individual and collective mobility,

hence escapes from and descents into poverty. Where coercive means prevail, individuals and groups that acquire arms and warriors gain crucial mobility advantages. In agrarian systems, acquisition or loss of land (which often occurs, to be sure, through someone's use of coercive force) makes the great difference. Only in recent eras of wage labor and extensive commerce has it been widely possible for workers to save money from wages, then invest it in such small enterprises as craft production and retail trade.

By themselves, prevailing resources strongly differentiate systems of inequality, hence channels of individual or collective escape from poverty. Across the contemporary world, for example, the great prominence of land plus coercive means in the inequality of such countries as Sudan and Cambodia contrasts sharply with the inequality based on financial capital and scientific–technical knowledge that occurs in France or Japan. Brazil is moving from a system of inequality based chiefly on enormous differences in control over land to another system—no less unequal—based much more heavily on control over financial capital and scientific knowledge (Telles 2004).

For analysts interested in understanding mobility, then, box 2.2 provides a convenient checklist of resources that figure prominently in the forms of inequality prevailing in a given community or country. It also suggests some crude hypotheses for analysis of the evidence gathered by the Moving Out of Poverty Study. We might, for example, reasonably expect ladders of life produced by local focus groups to differ significantly following the extent to which control over land, labor, animals, or machines sustains local systems of exclusion. We might expect local ladders to stress household capacities and obligations in regions of subsistence agriculture and to focus much more heavily on income and wealth in highly commercialized locales.

Once they have identified the fundamental resources involved in the production of inequality, analysts must still figure out how processes based on those resources actually work. Box 2.3 provides an all-purpose questionnaire for identification of the crucial processes.

The questionnaire simply translates my earlier arguments into a series of operations applying to any inequality-generating system anywhere. It describes a search for value-producing resources, exploitation, opportunity hoarding, boundaries, and the rest of the apparatus that generates inequality. In so doing, it shifts attention away from conventional concerns with queues, individual mobility, income distributions, and aggregate flows of persons or resources within an economic system. It directs attention toward the processes that produce, reproduce, and transform inequality. It asserts that categorical exclusion from benefits lies at the heart of inequality. It also

BOX 2.3
An All-Purpose Questionnaire for Analyzing Escapes from Poverty

What major resources do exploiters control—land, labor, capital, knowledge, something else?

What major resources do opportunity hoarders control?

What boundaries separate exploiters and opportunity hoarders from the rest of the population?

To what extent do those boundaries correspond to other divisions such as gender, caste, religion, ethnicity, or citizenship?

What controls and constraints maintain individual and collective locations on either side of prevailing boundaries?

To what extent and how do beneficiaries of surpluses from exploitation and opportunity hoarding apply those surpluses to reproduce exclusionary boundaries and unequal relations across them?

How frequently do people cross those boundaries in either direction?

To what extent is boundary crossing, when it occurs, individual or collective?

What processes facilitate and inhibit boundary crossing, whether individual or collective?

Through what channels—kinship, religious affiliation, political connections including government employment, underground economies, occupational mobility, or educational achievement—do local people most regularly move out of poverty?

At what pace, and in what ways, are these arrangements changing?

---

asserts that categorically organized channels, rather than those that operate at a purely individual level, most often facilitate escapes from poverty when such channels actually form.

To identify such channels, analysts should look especially at the use of six kinds of connections in mobility: kinship, religious affiliation, political connections including government employment, underground economies, occupational mobility, and educational achievement. (One might add long-distance migration to the list, but substantial migration streams almost always operate within one or more of the six types of channels.) Occupational and educational mobility may well operate individually, although they too often involve sponsorship and categorical rather than individual advancement. But the first four—kinship, religious affiliation, political connections, and underground economies—more frequently engage whole categories of people and their internal connections.

Political Underpinnings of Inequality and Its Changes

Our all-purpose questionnaire serves an unexpected purpose. It specifies the pressure points through which political processes affect inequality and its changes. Politics sometimes enters the production, reproduction, and transformation of inequality through all 11 items on the list: control over resources for exploitation and opportunity hoarding, installation of crucial boundaries between controllers of resources and others, correspondence of those boundaries to gender or caste, and so on. Rather than a tedious item-by-item recitation of political influences, let us review them more generally.

Politics includes all exercises of power to which governments are parties, whether primary parties (as in military conscription) or secondary parties (as in legal enforcement of private contracts). Governments specialize in controlling concentrated means of coercion. Indeed, we commonly identify governments by looking for organizations that control the greatest concentrations of coercive means—for example, troops, police, jails, and means of imposing humiliation—within their operating territories. Control of such means gives governments great initial influence over the allocation of other resources.

Governments produce, maintain, and transform inequality both directly and indirectly. Directly, all governments operate systems of exploitation and opportunity hoarding. Via taxation and expropriation, they use their coercive means to organize the production of collective goods, whether or not individual citizens would contribute willingly without coercion. Sometimes they engage in wars—civil or international—that destroy productive resources and thereby increase inequality between the protected few and the damaged many. In the Voices of the Poor study, the impact of Bosnia-Herzegovina's civil war on poverty rivals the impact of Bangladesh's devastating floods (Narayan and Petesch 2002).

Outside of war, governments coordinate exploitation of value-producing resources such as minerals and water so that major categories of the population contributing their effort receive less than the proportionate value they have added. Taxation of wages for governmental projects provides the obvious example, but military conscription and forced nonmilitary labor operate in similar ways (Levi 1997; Tilly 1992). Of course, rulers commonly claim that their coordination of crucial resources adds so much value that everyone benefits in the long run. To say the least, real governments vary enormously in the extent to which they do add value, as opposed to operating essentially as protection rackets or simply seeking rents to benefit rulers (Tilly 1985).

Governments regularly engage in opportunity hoarding. They do so when they monopolize such resources as oil or diamonds and restrict benefits realized from those resources to members of the ruling group. Similarly, in poorer countries, holding governmental office often offers an escape from poverty. Despite meager salaries at all but the highest levels, government jobs offer more secure and remunerative employment than work in the private sector. They also frequently provide opportunities for bribes, service fees, and other payoffs (Bayart 1993; Fatton 1992; Migdal 2004; Roitman 2005; Rotberg 2004; Varese 2000; World Bank 1997).

Much more broadly, all governments provide more protection for their own property rights—for example, rights to armed force, public land, minerals, waterways, and national currencies—than for those of the general population. Distinctions between citizens and noncitizens likewise establish unequal protections for a wide variety of rights, including property rights (Ngai 2004). Those protections, too, involve opportunity hoarding.

Indirectly, but no less powerfully, all governments back up exploitation and opportunity hoarding on the part of their major supporters. To be sure, authoritarian regimes usually concentrate their support on the enterprises of much narrower elites than democracies do. We recognize a democracy precisely by the fact that a large share of the population has some control over how the government behaves and receives a degree of protection for its daily activity, including its pursuit of gain. But all historically known democracies have also favored the property rights, value-producing enterprises, and legal advantages of their dominant classes over those of ordinary people (Bermeo 2003; Tilly 2004).

Well before 19th-century welfare systems came into being, some governments installed protections against famine, disease, and disaster or their worst consequences. Chinese empires worked on authoritarian principles but regularly stockpiled and distributed grain to palliate the effects of famine (Lee and Campbell 1997; Will and Wong 1991; Wong 1997). Until the Black Death struck Europe and the Middle East during the 14th century, England and Egypt roughly equaled each other in wealth and productivity. But Egypt's economy took centuries to recover from the pandemic, while England moved back to its previous economic level quite rapidly. Contrasting systems of rule involving very different forms of land ownership made the difference (Borsch 2005).

Since the 14th century, governments west and east have repeatedly intervened to promote one form of economic activity or another and have thus affected patterns and intensities of exits from poverty. For better or worse, socialism's state-run enterprises drew on centuries of experience in governmental intervention (Verdery 1996). Well short of state socialism, governments have regularly protected and regulated industries on behalf of one national interest or another. Each such intervention affects who wins, who loses, and who suffers exclusion (Verdery 2003).

Since 1800, most countries have also used some of their top-down power to redistribute income and create some measure of security for vulnerable workers. Looking at a large number of countries, Peter Lindert has established that economic expansion has led regularly to formation of redistributive systems for social spending, especially as ordinary workers acquire political voice. Since the 18th century, he remarks,

> the rise of tax-based social spending has been at the heart of government growth. It was social spending, not national defense, public transportation, or government enterprises, that accounted for most of the rise in governments' taxing and spending as a share of GDP over the last two centuries. (Lindert 2004, 1:20)

As wage-labor became more central to economies, first in the West and then across the world, redistributive social spending skyrocketed.

Most of that increase has occurred recently. Before the 20th century, social spending never sufficed to maintain poor people in idleness, much less to entice them away from viable employment. Conservative criticisms notwithstanding, Lindert challenges the view that welfare benefits sap initiative. He concludes, indeed, that social spending stabilized the labor force and increased its productive capacity. Because it did so, even very high levels of welfare expenditure occurred at little or no net cost to the whole economy. To that extent, governmental activity (like economic growth in general) produced aggregate exits from poverty. Thus some political initiatives do promote collective escapes from economic exclusion.

In recent years, both governments and international organizations have often targeted particular political interventions to the reduction of poverty, seeking to include previously excluded segments of the population in opportunities for economic improvement. World Bank chief economist Nicholas Stern has warned, however, that investment-led economic growth alone will not mitigate poverty. "We should not," he declares,

> think only in terms of economic growth when we try to understand poverty reduction. It is vital that we work to empower poor people to participate in the process. And poverty occurs in many more dimensions than income. Hence, we must also recognize a second pillar in the fight for poverty reduction: empowerment. Empowering poor people so that they can participate in economic growth requires investments in health, in edu-

cation, and in social protection as well as building institutions that enable them to participate in decisions that shape their lives. (Stern 2003, xvii; see also Alsop, Bertelsen, and Holland 2006)

The prescription immediately raises a question: Whom would an effective poverty-reduction program empower, and how? My argument implies an answer: Without neglecting programs that make everyone richer, concentrate on empowering poor people to destroy, undermine, bypass, or create alternatives to the categorical barriers that exclude them from enriching opportunities. Do so by attacking the barriers directly, but also by offering poor people the means to destroy, undermine, bypass, or create alternatives on their own.

Direct political intervention obviously has a central part to play in either effort. Existing public programs to reduce exclusion and poverty range from investment in infrastructure to microfinance schemes to direct promotion of employment. In such programs, international institutions including the World Bank, national governments, and nongovernmental organizations all play significant parts. The enormous current concentration of microfinance in Asia surely results in part from the fact that the Grameen Bank and similar lending organizations made their most visible and successful start as public programs in South Asia with the endorsement, however reluctant, of national governments (Gibbons and Meehan 2002).

Political effects on escapes from economic exclusion and poverty, then, cover the entire range of inequality-generating processes: which resources support exploitation and opportunity hoarding, which boundaries separate beneficiaries of exploitation and opportunity hoarding from nonbeneficiaries, to what extent those boundaries correspond to other socially consequential boundaries such as gender or religion, what inhibits or facilitates movement across the boundaries, and the degree to which boundary crossing occurs individually or collectively. Our survey has, in fact, identified some rather different sorts of escapes from poverty.

Figure 2.1 schematizes the possibilities. It distinguishes two dimensions: how much transformation of inequality's overall patterns the particular escape entails, and the extent to which escapes are individual or collective. The five stylized types named in the figure merely indicate the range of possibilities, without by any means exhausting them.

Let us circumnavigate the named possibilities:

Individual passing refers to individual movement across a boundary through a change of identity, for example by acquiring a college degree or suppressing information about ethnic origins. Passing produces no significant

FIGURE 2.1
A Crude Typology of Escapes from Poverty

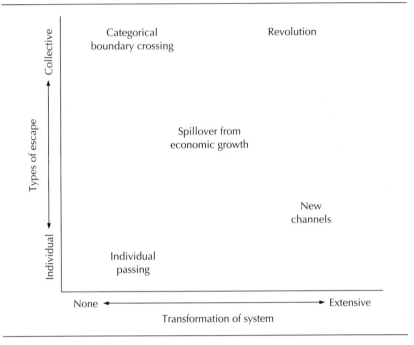

transformation of the system. It often reinforces existing inequalities by confirming the value of credentials and committing successful boundary crossers to maintenance of the boundary. To the extent that it drains away potential leaders, indeed, the promotion of individual passing aggravates poverty for remaining members of the impoverished category.

Categorical boundary crossing generally produces more change in the system, partly because movement of a whole category into the territory of privilege sets a visible challenge and precedent for other unprivileged categories, and partly because categorical movement brings new forms of culture and social ties into the privileged zone. The net movement of America's Chinese immigrants from stigmatized labor during the 19th century to entrepreneurship and professional standing during the 20th did not make a new American revolution. But it did change the connection between Chinese migration networks and American centers of wealth (McKeown 2001).

Revolutions continue to occur in our own time. In addition to the East European revolutions of 1989, Jeffrey Goodwin's short list of revolutions during the latter half of the 20th century includes Vietnam, China, Bolivia, Cuba, Algeria, Ethiopia, Angola, Mozambique, Cambodia, South Vietnam, Iran, Nicaragua, and Grenada (Goodwin 2001, 4; see also Goodwin 2005). Since they include displacement of a ruling class, revolutions simultaneously transform whole systems of inequality and produce substantial movements across existing boundaries of privilege. (As the painful experience of Russia since 1991 should remind us, however, revolutionary transfers of power do not necessarily reduce poverty across whole populations.)

Formation of *new channels* of mobility in systems of inequality transforms them over the long run by such means as connecting opportunities with new migration streams, moving people from agriculture to manufacturing or services, establishing new patron-client chains, creating new entrepreneurial networks, and destroying barriers that block whole categories of the population from existing mobility channels. If no significant economic growth occurs in the process, however, new channels produce turnover without net exits from poverty. One migrant stream or patron-client network simply displaces another.

Finally, *spillover from economic growth* does generate escapes from poverty to the extent that it opens new economic opportunities for the previously poor and/or involves redistribution of new benefits. Here political change or its absence makes a tremendous difference. On one side (as Lindert's historical comparisons document), redistributive social spending can generate mass exits from poverty as well as further economic growth. On the other side (as the cases of oil-rich authoritarian countries such as Sudan indicate), if a narrow elite hoards the returns from economic growth, poverty often grows more prevalent.

These types are necessarily abstract. But they become quite concrete in migration systems across the world. Migrants who move in chains and establish remittance systems commonly balance and mediate between advantages gained at the destination and reinvestment in mobility at the origin (Amuedo-Dorantes and Pozo 2005; Borges 2003; Chimhowu, Piesse, and Pinder 2005; Gold 2005; Kurien 2002; Proudfoot and Hall 2005; Roberts and Morris 2003; Singh 2005; Smith 2005; Tilly 2000). They frequently do so by locating niches (such as retail trade) at the destination within which they then practice low-level opportunity hoarding despite frequently becoming objects of exploitation. Long-distance migrants demonstrate the possibility of individual and collective escapes from poverty through combinations of passing, categorical boundary crossing, new channels, and spillover from economic growth. Similarly, microcredits allow sufficient initiative to budding entrepreneurs that they can, in principle, facilitate individual and collective escapes from poverty through paths that circumvent the barriers built into existing political and economic systems (Daley-Harris 2002).

My overall approach to poverty and the politics of exclusion, then, centers on an interactive understanding of inequality-generating processes. Material inequality, according to this view, results from unequal control over value-producing resources. Exploitation and opportunity hoarding, reinforced by emulation and adaptation, characterize the interactions around value-producing resources that produce material inequality, especially inequality between paired categories of people. The range of resources on which people have built systems of unequal economic interaction has run historically from coercive means to scientific-technical knowledge. To the extent that division with respect to control of these resources cuts across an entire economy, categorical inequality becomes more severe, and the likelihood that whole segments of a population will remain in poverty increases.

Political arrangements that support exclusive control of value-producing resources and/or reinforce exploitation, opportunity hoarding, emulation, and adaptation promote both inequality and poverty. Passing, categorical boundary crossing, revolution, creation of new mobility channels, and spillover from economic growth often mitigate or even destroy previously existing mainstays of inequality and poverty. Political interventions to reduce inequality can therefore fruitfully aim at one or more of these pressure points.

Implications

Despite these hints, no one should read promising poverty-reduction policies directly from my extremely general analysis of poverty and the politics of exclusion. At best, the analysis identifies elements that any worldwide program of poverty reduction must take into account lest it produce perverse consequences. I have not taken the obvious next step: to construct a typology of national inequality regimes that would permit distinctions among different settings requiring differing approaches to policy reduction. We can hope that the World Bank's Moving Out of Poverty study will lend itself to construction of just such a typology.

In the meantime, here are some implications of the analysis that bear on possible policy interventions to facilitate exits from poverty:

1. Although overall investments in economic growth may well produce collective exits from poverty, the social, economic, and political organization of exclusion makes it likely that very poor people will benefit least and last from broad interventions.

2. In the short and medium runs, broad investment programs that succeed will commonly increase inequality and therefore the relative deprivation of the very poor.

3. In particular, membership in stigmatized categories and lack of facilitating interpersonal connections regularly combine to exclude very poor people from mobility opportunities.

4. Existing political arrangements, furthermore, usually reinforce those forms of exclusion.

5. Any wide-ranging and effective intervention to reduce inequality and poverty will therefore harm some existing political interests and will require a political program to attack, subvert, bypass, or buy off those interests.

6. Individual exits from poverty can occur through deliberate facilitation of poor people's crossing of previously effective exclusionary boundaries, especially boundaries separating poor people from those who control crucial resources and benefit from them by means of exploitation and opportunity hoarding.

7. With greater difficulty but larger consequences for existing political arrangements, collective exits from poverty can also occur through facilitated movement of whole categories across boundaries from exclusion to inclusion.

8. New systems of production in which previously poor people acquire collective control over newly productive resources are likely to benefit whole categories of poor people more directly and rapidly than facilitated crossing of existing boundaries.

All of these changes involve transformation of existing systems of inequality and the political arrangements that support them. All of them together would amount to a quiet revolution across the whole world.

Note

Eric Calderoni, Andreas Koller, John Krinsky, Roy Licklider, Deepa Narayan, Rolf Scjhwarz, Nicholas Toloudis, Cecelia Walsh-Russo, Viviana Zelizer, Elke Zuern, and anonymous World Bank critics provided helpful critiques of this paper's earlier versions.

References

Alsop, R., M. Bertelsen, and J. Holland. 2006. *Empowerment in Practice: From Analysis to Implementation*. Washington, DC: World Bank.

Amuedo-Dorantes, C., and S. Pozo. 2005. "On the Use of Differing Money Transmission Methods by Mexican Immigrants." *International Migration Review* 39: 554–76.

Bayart, J. F. 1993. *The State in Africa: The Politics of the Belly*. London: Longman.

Bermeo, N. 2003. *Ordinary People in Extraordinary Times: The Citizenry and the Breakdown of Democracy*. Princeton, NJ: Princeton University Press.

Borges, M. J. 2003. "Network Migration, Marriage Patterns, and Adaptation in Rural Portugal and Among Portuguese Immigrants in Argentina, 1870–1980." *History of the Family* 8: 445–79.

Borsch, S. 2005. *The Black Death in Egypt and England: A Comparative Study*. Austin: University of Texas Press.

Bowles, S. 2006. "Institutional Poverty Traps." In *Poverty Traps*, ed. S. Bowles, S. N. Durlauf, and K. Hoff, 116–38. New York: Russell Sage Foundation; Princeton, NJ: Princeton University Press.

Bowles, S., and H. Gintis. 1976. *Schooling in Capitalist America: Educational Reform and the Contradictions of Economic Life*. New York: Basic Books.

———. 1993. "The Revenge of Homo Economicus: Contested Exchange and the Revival of Political Economy." *Journal of Economic Perspectives* 7: 83–114.

Brudner, L., and D. R. White. 1997. "Class, Property, and Structural Endogamy: Visualizing Networked Histories." *Theory and Society* 26: 161–208.

Chimhowu, A., J. Piesse, and C. Pinder. 2005. "The Socioeconomic Impact of Remittances on Poverty Reduction." In *Remittances: Development Impact and Future Prospects*, ed. S. M. Maimbo and D. Ratha, 83–102. Washington, DC: World Bank.

Conley, D. 1999. *Being Black, Living in the Red*. Berkeley: University of California Press.

Daley-Harris, S., ed. 2002. *Pathways Out of Poverty: Innovations in Microfinance for the Poorest Families*. Bloomfield, CT: Kumarian Press.

DFID (UK Department for International Development). 2005. *Reducing Poverty by Tackling Social Exclusion*. London: DFID.

Earle, T. 1997. *How Chiefs Come to Power: The Political Economy in Prehistory*. Stanford, CA: Stanford University Press.

Fatton, R. 1992. *Predatory Rule: State and Civil Society in Africa*. Boulder, CO: Lynne Rienner.

Gibbons, D. S., and J. W. Meehan. 2002. "Financing Microfinance for Poverty Reduction." In Daley-Harris 2002, 229–62.

Gold, S. J. 2005. "Migrant Networks: A Summary and Critique of Relational Approaches to International Migration." In Romero and Margolis 2005, 257–85.

Goodwin, J. 2001. *No Other Way Out: States and Revolutionary Movements, 1945–1991*. Cambridge: Cambridge University Press.

———. 2005. "Revolutions and Revolutionary Movements." In *Handbook of Political Sociology: States, Civil Societies, and Globalization*, ed. T. Janoski, R. R. Alford, A. M. Hicks, and M. A. Schwartz, 404–22. Cambridge: Cambridge University Press.

Granovetter, M., and C. Tilly. 1988. "Inequality and Labor Processes." In *Handbook of Sociology*, ed. N. J. Smelser, 175–222. Newbury Park, CA: Sage.

Grusky, D. B., ed. 2001. *Social Stratification: Class, Race, and Gender in Sociological Perspective.* Boulder, CO: Westview.

Hoff, K., and A. Sen. 2006. "The Kin System as a Poverty Trap?" In *Poverty Traps*, ed. S. Bowles, S. N. Durlauf, and K. Hoff, 95–115. New York: Russell Sage Foundation; Princeton, NJ: Princeton University Press.

Kalb, D. 1997. *Expanding Class: Power and Everyday Politics in Industrial Communities: The Netherlands, 1850–1950.* Durham, NC: Duke University Press.

Kurien, P. A. 2002. *Kaleidoscopic Ethnicity: International Migration and the Reconstruction of Community Identities in India.* New Brunswick, NJ: Rutgers University Press.

Lanjouw, P., and N. Stern. 2003. "Opportunities Off the Farm as a Springboard Out of Rural Poverty: Five Decades of Development in an Indian Village." In *Pathways Out of Poverty: Private Firms and Economic Mobility in Developing Countries*, ed. G. S. Fields and G. Pfefferman, 123–54. Boston: Kluwer.

Lee, J. Z., and C. D. Campbell. 1997. *Fate and Fortune in Rural China: Social Organization and Population Behavior in Liaoning, 1774–1873.* Cambridge: Cambridge University Press.

Leiman, M. N. 1993. *The Political Economy of Racism.* London: Pluto Press.

Lemann, N. 1999. *The Big Test: The Secret History of the American Meritocracy.* New York: Farrar, Straus and Giroux.

Levi, M. 1997. *Consent, Dissent, and Patriotism.* Cambridge: Cambridge University Press.

Lindert, P. H. 2004. *Growing Public: Social Spending and Economic Growth since the Eighteenth Century.* 2 vols. Cambridge: Cambridge University Press.

McKeown, A. 2001. *Chinese Migrant Networks and Cultural Change: Peru, Chicago, Hawaii, 1900–1936.* Chicago: University of Chicago Press.

Midlarsky, M. I. 1999. *The Evolution of Inequality: War, State Survival, and Democracy in Comparative Perspective.* Cambridge, MA: Harvard University Press.

Migdal, J. S. 2004. "State Building and the Non-Nation-State." *Journal of International Affairs* 58: 17–46.

Munck, R. 2005. "Social Exclusion: New Inequality Paradigm for the Era of Globalization?" In Romero and Margolis 2005, 31–49.

Narayan, D., R. Chambers, M. K. Shah, and P. Petesch. 2000. *Voices of the Poor: Crying Out for Change.* New York: Oxford University Press for the World Bank.

Narayan, D., with R. Patel, K. Schafft, A. Rademacher, and S. Koch-Schulte. 2000. *Voices of the Poor: Can Anyone Hear Us?* New York: Oxford University Press for the World Bank.

Narayan, D., and P. Petesch, eds. 2002. *Voices of the Poor: From Many Lands.* New York: Oxford University Press for the World Bank.

Ngai, M. M. 2004. *Impossible Subjects: Illegal Aliens and the Making of Modern America.* Princeton, NJ: Princeton University Press.

Oliver, M. L., and T. M. Shapiro. 1997. *Black Wealth/White Wealth: A New Perspective on Racial Inequality.* New York: Routledge.

Proudfoot, L., and D. Hall. 2005. "Points of Departure: Remittance Emigration from South-West Ulster to New South Wales in the Later Nineteenth Century." *International Review of Social History* 50: 241–78.

Roberts, K. D., and M. D. S. Morris. 2003. "Fortune, Risk, and Remittances: An Application of Option Theory to Participation in Village-Based Migration Networks." *International Migration Review* 37: 1252–81.

Roitman, J. 2005. *Fiscal Disobedience: An Anthropology of Economic Regulation in Central Africa.* Princeton, NJ: Princeton University Press.

Romero, M., and E. Margolis, eds. 2005. *The Blackwell Companion to Social Inequalities.* Oxford: Blackwell.

Rotberg, R. I., ed. 2004. *When States Fail: Causes and Consequences.* Princeton, NJ: Princeton University Press.

Sen, A. 1995. "The Political Economy of Targeting." In *Public Spending and the Poor: Theory and Evidence,* ed. D. van de Walle and K. Nead, 11–24. Baltimore: Johns Hopkins University Press.

Singh, S. 2005. "Sending Money Home: Money and Family in the Indian Diaspora." Paper presented at the Institute for International Integration Studies Seminar, Trinity College, Dublin, April 13. http://mams.rmit.edu.au/e0eneunbp2w.pdf.

Smith, R. C. 2005. *Mexican New York: Transnational Worlds of New Immigrants.* Berkeley: University of California Press.

Stern, N. 2003. Foreword to *Pathways Out of Poverty: Private Firms and Economic Mobility in Developing Countries,* ed. G. S. Fields and G. Pfefferman. Boston: Kluwer.

Telles, E. E. 2004. *Race in Another America: The Significance of Skin Color in Brazil.* Princeton, NJ: Princeton University Press.

Tilly, C. 1985. "War Making and State Making as Organized Crime." In *Bringing the State Back In,* ed. P. Evans, D. Rueschemeyer, and T. Skocpol, 169–91. Cambridge: Cambridge University Press.

———. 1992. *Coercion, Capital, and European States, AD 990–1992.* Rev. ed. Oxford: Blackwell.

———. 1998a. *Durable Inequality.* Berkeley: University of California Press.

———. 1998b. "Contentious Conversation." *Social Research* 65: 491–510.

———. 2000. "Chain Migration and Opportunity Hoarding." In *Governance of Cultural Diversity,* ed. J. W. Dacyl and C. Westin, 62–86. Stockholm: Centre for Research in International Migration and Ethnic Relations (CEIFO).

———. 2004. *Contention and Democracy in Europe, 1650–2000.* Cambridge: Cambridge University Press.

———. 2005. "Historical Perspectives on Inequality." In Romero and Margolis 2005, 15–30.

Tilly, C., and C. Tilly. 1998. *Work Under Capitalism.* Boulder, CO: Westview.

Varese, F. 2000. "Pervasive Corruption." In *Economic Crime in Russia,* ed. A. Ledeneva and M. Kurkchiyan, 99–111. The Hague: Kluwer Law International.

Verdery, K. 1996. *What Was Socialism, and What Comes Next?* Princeton, NJ: Princeton University Press.

———. 2003. *The Vanishing Hectare: Property and Value in Postsocialist Transylvania.* Ithaca, NY: Cornell University Press.

White, H. 2002. *Markets from Networks: Socioeconomic Models of Production.* Princeton, NJ: Princeton University Press.

Will, P.-É., and R. B. Wong. 1991. *Nourish the People: The State Civilian Granary System in China, 1650–1850.* Ann Arbor: University of Michigan Press.

Wong, R. B. 1997. *China Transformed: Historical Change and the Limits of European Experience.* Ithaca, NY: Cornell University Press.

World Bank. 1997. *The State in a Changing World: World Development Report 1997.* New York: Oxford University Press.

Zelizer, V. A. 2005. *The Purchase of Intimacy.* Princeton, NJ: Princeton University Press.

3

Moving On, Staying Behind, Getting Lost: Lessons on Poverty Mobility from Longitudinal Data

Stefan Dercon and Joseph S. Shapiro

Most studies on economic development offer statements on the evolution of poverty over time. It is surprising, then, that only recently have more systematic efforts started to use quantitative data to document this process of changing poverty in developing countries. This chapter surveys what has been learned from these efforts, focusing on the evidence gathered using longitudinal data in developing countries.

Extensive resources have been invested in carrying out large representative surveys with detailed data on different welfare indicators. A notable example is the World Bank's Living Standards Measurement Study (LSMS) program. While much insight can be gained from these datasets, in virtually all cases these surveys are cross-sectional (or, occasionally, consist of two-wave panel datasets). The problem is that by effectively interviewing different people in each period, surveys provide only limited information on the individual and household trajectories of poverty or living standards over time. While pseudo-panel techniques are possible and can be used effectively (e.g., Deaton and Paxson 1994), the attraction and use of panel data for illuminating the dynamic processes of poverty has become apparent in recent years.

Many conceptual issues related to measuring poverty trends remain unresolved. In this chapter, we stay away from these issues and limit ourselves to examining the type of analysis that is generally common in this literature: reporting poverty levels in different periods and providing some analysis of the evolution of these indicators over time, at the individual or household level. Such studies analyze the factors that are correlated with welfare outcomes and usually offer a causal explanation. We refer to this literature as the poverty mobility literature, even though no specific measures of mobility (such as income mobility measures) are usually used (Fields 2002).

Much research since 2000 has explored the short- and long-term dynamics of poverty. The Chronic Poverty Research Centre, a United Kingdom-funded partnership of universities, research institutes, and nongovernmental organizations, has sponsored several journal issues and numerous working papers on chronic poverty in various countries. The Pathways from Poverty study has also published initial reports from a number of countries.[1] The Indonesia Family Life Survey (IFLS), South Africa's KwaZulu-Natal Income Dynamics Study (KIDS), and the Ethiopia Rural Household Survey (ERHS) have each inspired numerous papers. An increasing number of studies use instrumental variables or pseudo-panels to estimate the bias that measurement error or panel attrition introduce.

In assessing the types of data that have been available for this kind of work, we summarize post-2000 research on income mobility that uses consumption or income data from a panel of individuals, households, or cohorts. We exclude studies that present region-level poverty indexes at two points in time, and we emphasize empirical rather than theoretical results.[2] This review did not revisit the raw data of these studies, but rather relies on the evidence reported in other papers.

The chapter is structured around three key questions. First, what are the findings on the extent to which people move in and out of poverty, and who escapes poverty and who stays behind? Although studies show a large degree of poverty mobility, there are marked differences across settings. There are also concerns about measurement error. Thus it is difficult to draw general conclusions on this point.

Second, what correlates are identified as linked with changes in poverty? We focus particularly on data from rural Ethiopia to discuss the typical emerging evidence. The main finding is that particular household and community endowments matter, although the context appears to determine the specific factors that are most influential. Further evidence is presented on the role of risk in keeping people poor or allowing them to fall into poverty.

Third, what are some of the problems with existing evidence? A number of issues are discussed, including the nature of the samples, attrition bias, and the problems with measurement error. In some cases problems with specific studies are highlighted, but this review is not meant to be mainly critical. The type of evidence that can be gathered from this work is discussed using examples from ongoing work in Ethiopia and Tanzania.

A number of recent overview articles have pursued related objectives, including Baulch and Hoddinott (2000) and McKay and Lawson (2002).[3]

While updating these reviews, we also emphasize some of the remaining challenges related to finding robust evidence for poverty mobility as well as issues such as attrition. In particular, it is our sense that crucial methodological lessons have to be drawn from many of the current studies on mobility. Much of the quantitative work on poverty mobility appears to miss opportunities. For one thing, these studies have not paid enough attention to the underlying problems in these datasets, specifically the methods used to sustain the panel and causal interpretations of attrition. Furthermore, poverty mobility is often also correlated with spatial mobility, yet most panel datasets underlying poverty mobility work limit themselves to tracing households residing in the original localities, missing a potentially crucial part of the analysis of poverty mobility.

In light of these problems, and drawing especially on ongoing work in Tanzania, we call for an increasing focus on individual mobility rather than just household mobility. It is an approach that implies intricate and time-consuming tracking and data collection but one that will pay off, we believe, in a deeper understanding of how and why some people escape poverty.

Selected Evidence from Recent Panel Data Surveys: Descriptive Statistics

The chapter annex presents a brief overview and update on useful panel data surveys and their coverage, based on rounds and versions of these surveys used in recent studies (see annex table 3.B at the end of this chapter). The evidence from nearly 50 panel data surveys was collated. Five of these surveys are rotating panels. Two-thirds of the panel data surveys are short, covering five years or less.

Rotating panels or relatively short panels are notoriously difficult to use for clear inference on poverty dynamics. In particular, they make it hard to disentangle phenomena such as poverty fluctuations (many people facing variable living standards, as measured by income or consumption) and measurement error (variables that are difficult to measure accurately for making statements on the standard of living) from genuine poverty mobility. In the latter, people move out of poverty into a persistently better standard of living or fall into a persistent state of poverty.

It would be an impossible task to summarize all the studies that used these panel data surveys, not least from the point of view of poverty mobility. Many studies present basic descriptive statistics and then continue to the analysis of specific questions. Only a subset of studies undertook an analysis of changes in poverty over time. Furthermore, methods for basic poverty analysis vary widely, and in many cases it would be hard to argue that the state of the art in basic poverty analysis has been followed. As a consequence, this chapter must generalize about the evidence brought forward. As do most studies on poverty mobility, we focus on monetary measures of poverty—that is, measures based on consumption or income aggregates, so other dimensions of poverty are ignored. Probably most problematic for careful analysis, we generally base our discussion on head count figures—in line with much of the reported analysis but deeply flawed as a full portrayal of poverty.

How Likely Are People to Fall into or Escape Poverty?

We can simply describe poverty persistence according to the portion of households that are always, sometimes, or never poor across a survey's waves. Loosely speaking, this tends to be interpreted as suggestive evidence for people who are facing "transient" poverty processes, while other people are "always," and therefore "chronically," poor. This dichotomy is close to concepts of chronic and transient poverty as introduced (more carefully) by Jalan and Ravallion (2002), but most of the empirical work tends to focus on poverty status only, that is, on the head count. Nevertheless, one should be cautious in interpreting these concepts (for a critique based on the analysis of risk and poverty, see Dercon 2005).

Different surveys have different numbers of waves, and different welfare measures (including sometimes income and at other times consumption-based measures); they cover different populations and use different poverty lines, so their results are imperfectly comparable. Even given different methodologies, table 3.1 allows the generalization that in most countries more than half the people whom a cross-section may identify as poor are in fact transiently poor, and only a minority are chronically poor. A transiently poor person in this context is someone who is not poor in all periods but only in some periods considered, while a chronically poor person is poor throughout the data period. The estimates vary by country and study: two studies using Ugandan data find that the ratio of households poor in only some of the waves to households poor in every wave is 68 and 70 percent, two very similar estimates. But for South Africa's KIDS study, estimates of this ratio are in the range of 27 to 66 percent.

While this updates the evidence from Baulch and Hoddinott (2000), it does not find different answers to their questions. Just as in their paper, caution is required in interpreting these results. First, the results will depend on the number of rounds: the more data rounds are used, the more likely someone is to be classified as "sometimes" poor, that is, transiently poor. For example, in the Ethiopian rural data presented by one of the studies in table 3.1, when all six rounds are used, we find that 80 percent of households have a consumption level below the poverty line in at least one but not more than five of the six rounds. When only the first and last rounds are compared, however, transient poverty is only 43 percent. Similarly, it will matter how far apart different rounds are.

While such poverty indexes reflect absolute mobility, transition matrices offer a more detailed picture of relative mobility (table 3.2). Across nine papers that include transition matrices, between 32 percent (Free State, South Africa) and 59 percent (Chile) of the poorest quintile of a country stays as the poorest quintile over two time periods. Less mobility appears for other quintiles: of all households, between 12 percent (Ethiopia) and 63 percent (Tehran, Iran) of households remain in the same income or consumption quintile across two time periods.

The overwhelming finding from these studies is that there is a considerable degree of poverty mobility. Many people move in and out of poverty. There are noticeable differences in country-by-country experience, but given that many of the surveys are not representative surveys of the country, interpreting these differences is difficult. Furthermore, there is a concern about measurement error. Poverty indicators, by documenting what happens to the lower end of the consumption or income distribution, do not explicitly distinguish measurement error but consider all data as an accurate representation of reality. If there is substantial (even if random) measurement error, then poverty mobility is likely to appear higher than it really is. Consumption and income data are always bound to be tainted by measurement error, but this error is also not likely to be the same across different settings. As a result, it is very difficult to learn about moving out of poverty and falling into poverty from these patterns across different settings, even when such movements are transitory. This issue is discussed further below.

Finally, some research has also expanded on nonmonetary measures of poverty, and a few researchers measure mobility in terms of education and nutrition (table 3.1). Baulch and Masset (2003) present mobility estimates from Vietnam's LSMS panel using education and malnutrition, and find different transition matrices. They find that monetary poverty is less persistent than poverty by most other measures—an intuitive result given the irreversibility of education and the long-run effects of malnutrition. Consumption and income poverty data effectively measure flows, while education and stunting are stock variables that change more slowly than flow variables.

TABLE 3.1
Proportion of Households That Are Always, Sometimes, or Never Poor
(percentages)

Country and period	Always poor	Sometimes poor	Never poor	Sometimes poor as % of ever poor[a]	Source
Income or consumption panel data					
Argentina 1995–2002	14.0	29.0	57.1	67	Cruces and Wodon 2003b[b]
Bangladesh 1987–2000	31.4	43.5	25.1	58	Sen 2003
Bangladesh 1994–2001	11.7	30.6	57.8	72	Kabeer 2004
Chile 1996–2001	10.1	21.1	68.8	68	Contreras et al. 2004
China (Sichuan) 1991–95	5.8	38.2	56.0	87	McCulloch and Calandrino 2003
Egypt 1997–99	19.0	20.4	60.6	52	Haddad and Ahmed 2003
Ethiopia (urban)	21.5	36.2	42.2	63	Kedir and McKay 2005
Ethiopia 1994–97 (rural)	7.0	63.0	30.0	90	Bigsten et al. 2003
Ethiopia 1994–97 (urban)	13.0	46.0	41.0	78	Bigsten et al. 2003
Ethiopia 1994–2004 (rural, 6 rounds)	6.0	79.0	15.0	93	Authors' calculations
Ethiopia 1994–2004 (rural, 2 rounds)	20.0	43.0	37.0	68	Authors' calculations
Indonesia 1998–99	17.5	40.3	42.2	70	Suryahadi, Widyanti, and Sumarto 2003
Iran 1992–95	4.9	43.3	51.8	90	Salehi-Isfahani 2003
Kenya and Madagascar 1993–95	70.8	22.5	6.8	24	Barrett et al. 2006
Nicaragua	27.0	22.0	52.0	45	Davis and Stampini 2002

(continued)

TABLE 3.1
(continued)

Country and period	Always poor	Sometimes poor	Never poor	Sometimes poor as % of ever poor[a]	Source
Poland 1993–96	5.9	31.6	62.5	84	Luttmer 2001
Russia 1994–98	3.4	41.9	54.7	92	Luttmer 2001
South Africa 1997–2001	35.9	58.3	5.8	62	Stevens 2003
South Africa KIDS	17.7	34.0	48.3	66	Carter and May 2001
South Africa KIDS	62.2	23.3	14.5	27	Cichello, Fields, and Liebbrandt 2005
South Africa KIDS	22.4	31.6	46.1	59	May et al. 2000
Uganda 1992–99	18.9	39.4	41.7	68	Lawson 2004
Uganda 1992–99	12.8	29.9	57.3	70	Lawson, McKay, and Okidi 2003
Vietnam 1992–98	6.1	18.6	75.3	75	Baulch and Masset 2003
Nutrition and education panel data					
Vietnam 1992–98 (stunting)	35.9	28.8	35.3	45	Baulch and Masset 2003
Vietnam 1992–98 (malnutrition)	23.5	18.0	58.6	43	Baulch and Masset 2003
Vietnam 1992–98 (primary education)[c]	3.1	11.1	86.8	78	Baulch and Masset 2003
Vietnam 1992–98 (lower secondary education)[c]	29.0	31.0	40.0	52	Baulch and Masset 2003

Note: For papers that report both expenditure and income poverty statistics, this table reports expenditure only; for papers that report only one welfare aggregate, this table reports that aggregate. Similarly, for papers that report both equivilized and per capita welfare aggregates, this table reports the equivilized aggregate, but for papers that report only one of these statistics, this table reports that number.

a. "Sometimes poor" as a percentage of "ever poor" is the ratio of those poor in some waves only to those poor in any wave (including those always poor).

b. The data from Cruces and Wodon 2003b are based on the mean across quarterly data.

c. The data refer to children of relevant age groups that are "always enrolled," "sometimes enrolled," and "never enrolled."

TABLE 3.2
Estimates of Poverty Movements in Transition Matrices
(percentages)

Country	All households			Households in bottom quintile			Source
	Remain on diagonal	Move up by one quintile	Move up by more than one quintile	Remain on diagonal	Move up by one quintile	Move up by more than one quintile	
Argentina[a]	46.5	19.9	9.6	45.8	25.3	28.8	Albornoz and Menéndez 2003
Chile	23.6	15.0	23.8	59.4	25.7	14.9	Contreras et al. 2004
Ethiopia	11.9	9.8	31.4	34.5	45.0	21.5	Block and Webb 2001
Indonesia[b]	39.6	19.4	10.3	49.7	26.5	23.8	Suryahadi, Widyanti, and Sumarto 2003
Iran (Tehran)	62.8	19.8	12.4	45.0	32.2	22.8	Salehi-Isfahani 2003 (Tehran)
South Africa	31.3	18.0	15.4	36.5	26.0	37.5	Woolard and Klasen 2005
South Africa (Free State)	20.0	19.9	14.4	32.4	29.4	38.2	Booysen 2003
South Africa KIDS	26.0	17.1	23.0	43.0	31.5	24.5	Keswell 2001
Vietnam	41.1	39.9	10.5	50.7	26.6	23.2	Glewwe and Nguyen 2002

Note: Based on income or consumption panel data.

a. Argentina is the 1991–95 quarterly mean.

b. Indonesia is the August 1998–December 1998 comparison.

Why Do Some Households Escape Poverty?

The standard approach to investigating the correlates and causes of poverty tends to start with a descriptive profile of poverty dynamics. What are the characteristics of those who moved out of poverty relative to other groups? Subsequently, many studies use simple regression analysis with per capita real household consumption or its natural logarithm as an outcome and explanatory household and community variables. Most also estimate a logit or probit for the probability of escaping or falling into poverty over a time period, rarely addressing Ravallion's (1996) critique of some of the implied assumptions. A number of studies estimate multinomial logits with different outcomes for the time periods during which a household was poor. Alternatively, some have looked at hazard models (e.g., Baulch and McCulloch 2003) or some form of ordered logits and probits, although they all suffer from Ravallion's critique that they reduce a useful continuous variable into a discrete variable.

Studies of this nature are not easily interpreted. For example, although the contexts and data differ, a common finding is that education helps people escape poverty. But interpretation is very difficult. Is it education that makes people move out of poverty, or is it that families who manage to offer education to their children are also able to offer their children other opportunities—ones that may be unobservable to the researcher but that are important in climbing out of poverty? Or, to put it differently, in a long-term dynamic view of poverty changes, education may have to be seen as endogenous to long-term wealth and poverty changes as well. This illustrates a more fundamental problem in this literature. Most of the analyses of the determinants of changing poverty over time have used frameworks that effectively only give (bivariate or multivariate) correlates of poverty changes, and causal analysis is limited. Nevertheless, we discuss below some of the findings in the literature, using data from Ethiopia as a specific example of moving beyond correlations to causal analysis.

Identifying the correlates linked to poverty mobility: An example

The standard approach starts with a profile of the characteristics linked to poverty mobility. An example is given in table 3.3, based on an analysis of Ethiopian rural data (see Dercon 2002). This is within the context of a subsample of the Ethiopia Rural Household Survey, for which data were available for 1989, as well as the regular rounds subsequently. This was a period of decreasing poverty in these villages, with poverty falling from about 61

TABLE 3.3

Household Characteristics by Poverty Transition in Rural Ethiopia

Category	Characteristic	Always poor	Fell into poverty (nonpoor in 1989, poor in 1994)	Moved out of poverty (poor in 1989, nonpoor in 1994)	Always nonpoor	Overall mean
Livestock	Value of livestock per adult in 1989 (birr)	155.32	550.92	344.72	828.89	418.60
Land	Land per adult in 1989 (hectares)	0.34	0.55	0.42	0.66	0.46
Export crops	Chat grown now	0.07	0.08	0.16	0.26	0.14
	Coffee grown now	0.35	0.15	0.02	0.05	0.17
Fertilizer	Fertilizer used in 1994	0.57	0.53	0.48	0.60	0.55
	Used more modern inputs in 1994 than in 1989	0.11	0.19	0.27	0.29	0.20
Demographics	Male adults (above 15 years) in 1989	1.34	1.25	1.41	1.32	1.34
	Adult equivalent units in household in 1989	5.56	4.65	5.42	4.29	5.08
	Male-headed household	0.83	0.83	0.88	0.81	0.84
Education	Head completed primary school	0.02	0.00	0.07	0.02	0.03
	Average years education of male adults in 1994	0.33	0.43	0.55	0.32	0.40
Location	Distance to nearest town by road (kilometers)	15.40	13.84	12.46	12.46	13.71
	All-weather road through village	0.05	0.27	0.36	0.62	0.29
Prices	Percentage change in real producer prices for crops between 1989 and 1994	19.86	28.27	37.70	23.26	26.69
Shocks	Any serious adult illness episodes between 1989 and 1994	0.71	0.70	0.51	0.55	0.62
	Number of adult illness episodes per adult in family	0.34	0.27	0.21	0.32	0.29
	Short-run rainfall experience (1994 minus 1989)[a]	−0.28	−0.20	−0.11	−0.08	−0.18
	Long-run rainfall experience (1994 minus 1989)[b]	−0.02	−0.02	0.06	0.02	0.01

Note: n = 354. Values are in 1994 prices. Birr is the local currency (6 birr in 1994 = approximately US$1).

a. Difference in percentage deviation from mean in 1994 and 1989. Deviation relative to long-term mean for main season preceding the 1994 survey was relative to the last mean season preceding the 1989 survey round.

b. Difference in percentage deviation from long-term mean in 1994 and 1989. Rainfall of last five years relative to long-term mean. Measure of how good the last main season preceding the 1994 survey round. Measure of how good the last five years were relative to the previous five years.

percent to 51 percent. There was also substantial mobility: 35 percent of households were poor in both periods, but 27 percent moved out of poverty and 16 percent moved into poverty. It was also a period of liberalization in food markets, so that large relative price changes occurred; depending on whether rural households were living in surplus or deficit areas, relative prices moved in opposite directions. These changes may also have had different effects depending on whether the household was a surplus farm household or not, as was subsequently confirmed in the analysis. For more on this see Dercon (2002, 2006).

It is noticeable that the characteristic profiles of those moving in and out of poverty are different from those of the other groups, at least in terms of descriptive statistics. These differences are also statistically significant in many cases. For example, relative to those who stayed poor (the "always poor" category), those who moved out of poverty had significantly better endowments in terms of land and livestock in 1989. They also had significantly more educated heads of household, but the levels of education in 1989 were still surprisingly low. They also had better roads and better rainfall, and they benefited in terms of better producer prices for the crops they were selling. Relative to those who fell into poverty, they also had a somewhat better household male labor supply. In sum, these data illustrate a more general finding: those moving out of poverty tend to be able to rely on good endowments, in terms of assets such as land and livestock, human capital, and infrastructure. However, one should not forget that these data were collected in a period of changing incentives in the economy that rewarded those whose assets gave them productive potential: in other words, economic liberalization is likely to have increased returns to these endowments.

Multivariate analysis can improve on this type of analysis, since it can help to establish the quantitative contribution of each factor to the observed changes in poverty, as well as establishing the marginal contribution of each factor to potential changes in consumption or poverty. Table 3.4 shows this for the same data presented in table 3.3, drawing on Dercon (2006), where details on the specification can be found. The left-hand side is the log of food consumption (total consumption data were not available for both periods, but in 1994 food still constituted about 80 percent of total consumption). The broad patterns discussed before show up here as well: increases in food consumption are correlated with having more land to start with (and gaining some land—on this, see Dercon 2006). The other significant factor is the change in producer prices faced by the household: the effect is positive for all, but larger for surplus farmers. Finally, good weather and access to

TABLE 3.4
Linear Regression: Explaining Changes in Consumption in Ethiopia

	Coefficient	t-value
Constant	0.185	(1.43)
Ln (land in hectares in 1989 + 0.1)	0.211	(2.07)
Δ ln (land in hectares + 0.1)	0.239	(3.24)
Ln (adults in 1989)	−0.090	(−1.23)
Δ ln (adults)	0.287	(1.18)
Ln (years adult education +1)	0.016	(0.07)
Ln (number of adult serious illnesses +1)	−0.205	(−0.92)
Δ (% real price changes)	0.371	(3.67)
Δ (% real price changes) squared	0.642	(3.28)
Surplus farmer *Δ (% real price changes)	0.664	(3.50)
Δ ln (rain last season)	0.826	(4.12)
Ln (distance to town)[a]	−0.223	(−2.18)
Road infrastructure?[b]	0.205	(2.36)
Adjusted R-squared		0.09

Source: Dercon 2006.

Note: n = 354. Dependent variable: change in log food consumption between 1989 and 1994 (mean 0.3733). Ordinary least squares (OLS) regression with robust standard errors corrected for village cluster effects.

a. The distance variable is the distance in kilometers to the nearest town scaled relative to the mean distance in the sample.

b. Road infrastructure refers to whether the road linking the village to the nearest town is accessible in all seasons.

nearby towns and good roads matter significantly as well. Table 3.4 uses food consumption as the dependent variable. Other studies (e.g., Lawson, McKay, and Okidi 2003) use poverty status as the dependent variable. While there are good methodological reasons for preferring to use consumption as the left-hand side variable (see Ravallion 1996), in this particular case the results are very similar.

Finding significant correlates and sizeable marginal effects is not quite the same as showing which factors matter most for the observed changes. For example, in table 3.4, an increased return to land size is shown, but given the relatively small landholdings, the contribution of this increase is only small. Dercon (2006) simulated the contribution of different factors to the observed changes in consumption by poverty status, in particular for those moving out of poverty in this period. It was found that the combined effects of increases in relative producer prices, returns to roads, and returns to location explained virtually the entire change in consumption for those moving out of poverty, with all the other factors only marginally affecting the overall change. To be clear, this means only that these factors were most relevant in this period, and not that this will always be the case.

Using the full sample, Dercon et al. (2006) have shown that the development of rural roads in the survey area of the Ethiopia Rural Household Survey has had considerable effects on consumption and poverty in later years as well, up to 2004. Indeed, from a policy point of view, it has been found to be a very robust and strong impact. In particular, the extensive work on the econometric specification and robustness of these results in this recent paper gives some confidence in the causal link between infrastructure and poverty in rural Ethiopia (see also Dercon 2004a).

Identifying the correlates linked to poverty mobility: Other evidence

Several other studies are reviewed below, but it is not possible to fully assess the statistical validity of the analysis in each case. In particular, most studies do not provide the detailed statistical analysis that would allow one to move from a descriptive set of correlates to a more causal analysis. Nevertheless, the results are interesting.

Table 3.5 gives some details of particular studies; the brief discussion cannot do full justice to them.[4] Education and/or the nature of jobs one has access to (which may at least correlate with education) appears to matter regularly, especially in the more urban settings. In rural settings in South Africa and Egypt, possession of livestock and land facilitates moving out of poverty. Location variables appear to matter as well. For example, in Ethiopia, residence in the capital city is a factor in escaping poverty. It is hard to generalize from these different studies—in fact, the two studies using urban Ethiopian data are not entirely consistent in their conclusions. In any case, not *all* standard characteristics reflecting better assets and human capital show up as significant factors, but typically a subset does. In other words, it is too simple to state that all endowments matter equally, but endowments do matter nevertheless. Which endowments matter most is likely to depend on the context, including the overall economic and policy climate, since this will largely determine the opportunities available to poor people. The rural Ethiopia data reported before are striking in this respect: roads clearly became more important in allowing people to escape poverty in the 1990s than they were in the 1980s. This may be because economic liberalization in the 1990s created

90

TABLE 3.5
Estimated Determinants of Escaping or Falling into Poverty from Selected Studies

Source	Locality	Estimation method	Factors significant for escaping poverty	Factors significant for falling into poverty
Contreras et al. 2004	Chile	Logit for escaping poverty, logit for falling into poverty	Owning own home; household head working in formal sector; technical education	Young household head; household head had health problems
Fields et al. 2003b	Indonesia	OLS for change in per capita income	Region; household head getting a job, particularly in formal sector	
Haddad and Ahmed 2003	Egypt	Quantile regression (0.7) for staying poor and changing poverty status separately	Significant negative association with chronic poverty: value of livestock assets; owning more land; head schooling; work in manufacturing; community and recreation, and other nonfarm sectors; old head	Significant positive association with chronic poverty: large household
Kedir and McKay 2005	Ethiopia	OLS for change in consumption	Location in capital city; household head working as wage employee	
Bigsten et al. 2003	Ethiopia (urban)	(1) Probit for falling into poverty; (2) probit for escaping poverty; (3) multinomial logit for always poor, sometimes poor, or never poor	Urban areas: education of household head and spouse; self-employed workers; living in regional capital	
Woolard and Klasen 2005	South Africa	OLS for change in expenditure, income, and predicted income, separately rural/urban	Owning more physical assets (including land, livestock, and other assets)	Large household; female-headed household; low initial employment access; poor initial asset endowment; low education
Herrera 1999	Lima, Peru	OLS for change in expenditure	Head of household with better education; female-headed household	Household with more children

trading opportunities that could be accessed by road, while civil war in the 1980s meant that access to roads was not necessarily beneficial for the poor, because war restricted the movement of goods and people considerably.

Risk and limited poverty mobility

One factor that has received relatively limited attention in most studies is the role of risk in causing poverty mobility. For example, in table 3.5, only Contreras et al. (2004) find some evidence for this, in particular that health problems are correlated with falling into poverty. The effect is also well documented in the Ethiopian rural data reported earlier, including in table 3.3. Dercon and Krishnan (2000) show that the risk factor is an important reason for the poverty fluctuations observed in 1994–95 in these data. In most other studies, its omission is largely due to the fact that no data are available on shocks experienced by households, even though the data turn up in many narratives of poverty mobility in more qualitative studies.

However, the relevance of risk goes beyond causing short-term fluctuations in outcomes. There is increasing evidence that it is an important factor in the lack of upward mobility of some households—that is, risk keeps them poor. For a detailed discussion, see Dercon (2005). This process is relatively well documented for nutritional shocks that lead to stunting in young children. Alderman, Hoddinott, and Kinsey (2006) document this for Zimbabwe; they found that young children of about 1 to 2 years of age who were seriously affected by a drought episode never quite recovered and stayed stunted. This led not just to effects on body height but also to lower educational attainment and lower lifetime earnings.

In this respect, HIV/AIDS represents a slow but devastating shock, and Booysen (2003) reports that it deepens and lengthens poverty spells. He uses panel data from the Free State of South Africa to compare the mobility of AIDS-affected households to that of a nonaffected group. Affected households are more likely to fall into poverty and to remain in chronic poverty. Predictably, morbidity and mortality worsen the disease's socioeconomic effects. The study's comparison group includes neighbors of AIDS-affected households that in the baseline period did not have individuals knowingly infected with HIV or suffering from related diseases, like tuberculosis or pneumonia, that serve as markers for likely HIV infection. The paper's estimates may depend heavily on the significant differences in characteristics between the HIV/AIDS and comparison groups rather than on the effects of the disease itself. Nonetheless, in the absence of good instruments or experimental evidence, this gives reason to believe that AIDS depresses mobility.

More evidence on this can be found in Beegle, De Weerdt, and Dercon (2006b), linking adult mortality in a region in Tanzania to consumption growth over 10 years. This area is one of the most severely affected by HIV/AIDS in the Lake Region of Central Africa. The authors find that losing an adult in the household has a strong negative impact, even though the effect does not persist beyond about four to five years. They find this effect by exploiting variation across split-offs over time, thus accounting for any initial fixed effects stemming from the original household's characteristics and, to a considerable extent, controlling for the unobserved heterogeneity. In another paper, Beegle, De Weerdt, and Dercon (2006a) find that adult mortality shocks have long-term implications for children losing a parent, resulting in stunting and lower educational attainment at adulthood.

Several theoretical studies argue that a one-time negative shock to income may permanently decrease income, and Lokshin and Ravallion (2004) test this proposition using six- and four-observation panels from Hungary and Russia. They assume that different households adjust similarly but to different equilibria. The data come from the mid-1990s in two transition economies, settings in which many households had faced recent shocks and hence possibly moved away from their long-run equilibrium incomes. The 50 percent attrition of observations over a short four- to-six-year observation period should inspire concern as to the extent of a poverty trap that these data could capture. The researchers estimate that following loss of half a household's income, in both Hungary and Russia, household income returns to 80 percent of its original level within three years. In both countries, however, shocks have longer-lasting effects for poor people. In Hungary, a household at the 25th percentile of the distribution will recover only 75 percent of its original income within three years, while a household at the 75th percentile will recover 90 percent of its original income within three years. While these results show the long effect of a shock, they do not suggest the existence of shock-induced poverty traps.

Dercon (2004a) finds even longer-lasting impact of shocks. This paper uses data from rural Ethiopia and finds that Ethiopia's 1984–85 famine had measurable effects on household consumption a decade later, in 1995. His main results come from fixed effects regressions, so that unobserved fixed heterogeneity in growth is accounted for, though he also estimates instrumental variables resembling those of Jalan and Ravallion (2002). Two of the factors with the clearest positive effect on consumption growth are rainfall and roads: having nearby roads increased consumption growth by 15 percent. Elbers, Gunning, and Kinsey (2002) build a model of the long-run effects of shocks and use generation-long panel data from a sample of resettled Zimbabwean households to monitor the persistence of shocks. They find that shocks changed income and capital accumulation and had surprisingly long-lasting effects.

An interesting dataset from rural Ethiopia, part direct measurement, part recall, confirms the importance of rainfall shocks but measures resistance to droughts as a function of herd size. Lybbert et al. (2004) use a 17-year panel of 55 pastoral households covering a time period with two major droughts. They suggest that the self-insurance of having a large herd of 45–75 cattle at the beginning of a drought helps smooth consumption and ensure a reasonable herd size after a drought, but that having fewer than 45 cattle may constitute a poverty trap wherein households cannot diversify income sources but remain vulnerable to shocks. McPeak and Barrett (2001) use the same data and compare with ongoing panel surveys of herders and farmers in Kenya. They emphasize the distressing frequency of income shocks in rural East Africa and note that increasing security in rangeland may improve mobility: at present much good land goes undeveloped because landowners fear threats from armed raiders.

Conclusions regarding the correlates of poverty mobility

In general, the intuitive notion that household and community endowments affect people's ability to escape poverty appears to be confirmed by most evidence. But it is clear that which endowments matter depends on the particular setting that is investigated. The general context, including the economic circumstances and opportunities, may well help to determine whether particular endowments matter. Furthermore, risk and shocks are a factor that hinders people from escaping poverty or even pushes them into poverty. The evidence on the assets and characteristics determining poverty mobility is nevertheless not always entirely convincing, since observing correlations is not the same as providing causal evidence. Much more work is clearly needed.

Some Problems with the Evidence

Beyond the caution regarding causal interpretation, there are further and possibly even more serious problems with most of the evidence. We focus on two issues. First, do we trust the data? Or, more precisely, does the fact that we know poverty is measured with error give us any reason to be concerned about inference regarding poverty mobility? Second, and most importantly, is attrition in panel datasets a serious issue for inference? This will lead us to a brief final section, largely focusing on evidence from one particular study that may provide a lesson for how to do this kind of work in the future.

How does measurement error affect estimates of mobility?

A first estimation problem arises when welfare aggregates inaccurately measure true income or consumption. Error can take four forms: surveys can elicit inaccurate or incomplete measures of consumption or income; price deflation over time and space can inaccurately reflect real prices; adult equivalency scales can inappropriately estimate per capita welfare; and survey cleaning can mismatch households in different survey waves (Baulch and Hoddinott 2000; Kamanou and Morduch 2002). Most literature focuses on the first type of error—survey responses that differ from a respondent's true income or consumption. In practice, the second and third types of error have a similar result: they increase the variance of welfare measures without increasing the variance of welfare, thereby erroneously inflating estimates of mobility. Causes of misreported consumption or income can include recall error, nonresponse, and inaccurate imputation of missing values (McKay and Lawson 2002). Misestimated consumption aggregates can arise from failure to address any of the issues outlined in Deaton and Zaidi (2002), particularly treatment of lumpy purchases like durables or bulk commodities—a point that Salehi-Isfahani (2003) emphasizes for grain purchases in rural Iran. Studies use two responses: quantifying measurement error and trying to eliminate it. In the rest of this subsection, we offer an (unavoidably more technical) discussion of some approaches in the literature.

Simulating measurement errors offers a direct way to approximate the effects of measurement error on mobility inference. Ligon and Schechter (2004) compare the bias and precision of various mobility indices in the presence of measurement error and find that some indices perform better than others. Chesher and Schluter (2002) derive methods to simulate the effect of measurement error on various poverty and inequality indices. They use a cross-section of data from Indonesia's 1993 National Socioeconomic Survey (SUSENAS) and show that larger errors generate increasingly imprecise poverty measures. Muller (2003) applies this technique to 1982–83 quarterly panel data from Rwanda to argue that only very large measurement error would affect his results.

Another simulation comes from comparing consumption, income, and income predicted from an earnings function. Woolard and Klasen (2005) report all results for consumption and income, since surveys tend to measure consumption more accurately than they measure income (Deaton 1997). These researchers find that the difference between the levels and change of income and consumption was greater in urban than in rural areas, but that estimates of inequality and mobility have similar magnitude for income and consumption. But it is difficult to discern the extent to which any differences in income and consumption measures reflect measurement error and the extent to which they reflect poor households' purposeful smoothing of consumption (Skoufias and Quisumbing 2005). Luttmer (2001) also compares income and consumption, as do Baulch and McCulloch (2003). Woolard and Klasen (2005) and Fields et al. (2003b) use predicted income in addition to reported income.

Others compare several welfare measures, an approach that links to multidimensional poverty literature. Scott (2001) compares transitory income of Chilean farmers to changes in the household's harvest, livestock production, and wealth. Albornoz and Menéndez (2003) use income predicted by household assets with the idea that it may have less error than reported income would. Gong, Van Soest, and Villagomez (2004) use Mexico's urban employment rotating panel to measure mobility between formal employment, informal employment, and unemployment. They argue that Mexico has far higher mobility between these sectors than most industrial countries do. In two papers, Munshi and Rosenzweig (2005, 2006) argue that caste continues to limit mobility in India, especially through mechanisms of school, marriage, and informal within-caste lending.[5]

Proxy reports may be another source of measurement error. Rosenzweig (2003) reports a correlation of 0.86 between self-reported and family-reported levels of schooling, a level near the 0.9 correlation for twins living apart in the United States (Behrman, Rosenzweig, and Taubman 1994). But for landholding, he finds correlation between self- and family reports of only 0.4. Although he offers no corroboration of income data, the individuals interviewed in surveys may cause additional error. As solutions for measurement error, dropping outliers from earnings functions, as Woolard and Klaasen (2005) do, may exclude the most egregious measurement errors but may also bias the remaining sample. Muller (2003), following Jalan and Ravallion (2002), also uses quantile regressions, partly to avoid sensitivity to income outliers.

Kamanou and Morduch (2002) emphasize that per capita consumption discontinuously changes when a family has a new baby. They estimate that up to a fourth of the variance in per capita consumption arises from changes in household size. Baulch and Masset (2003) show that equivalized and per capita expenditure give different pictures of mobility for Vietnam. Fields et al. (2003b) show that changes in log-income rather than household size account for at least half of the total income change they measure for 84 percent of households in Indonesia, 73 percent in South Africa, and 88 percent in Venezuela.

Instrumental variables offer a more common solution. If the instrument predicts true consumption but error in measuring the instrument is uncorrelated with error in measuring consumption, then the instrument can give reliable inference on mobility. Studies use rainfall, nutrition or weight, education, household size, assets, once- or twice-lagged income and their squares, dwelling materials, and subjective living standards ("How would you rate the general material situation of your household?") as instruments for current consumption or income (Luttmer 2001; Glewwe and Nguyen 2002; Fields et al. 2003b; Dercon 2004a ; Lokshin and Ravallion 2004; Antman and McKenzie 2005; Newhouse 2005). Glewwe and Nguyen (2002) estimate that half of mobility estimated by simple means is simply measurement error. Luttmer (2001) finds that measurement error may account for 30–60 percent of cross-sectional variance in consumption and 55–80 percent of expenditure shocks. But these instruments may weakly correlate with consumption, and more importantly, errors in measuring the instruments may correlate with errors in measuring consumption.

Antman and McKenzie (2005) again use pseudo-panel data to argue that ordinary least squares with a panel substantially overstates mobility. They use 58 quarters of data from 1987 to 2001 in Mexico's National Survey of Urban Employment (ENEU) and construct cohorts according to the birth year and education level of the household head. The OLS slope coefficient of income on its lagged value using panel data is 0.668 or 0.598 including cohort dummies. But their pseudo-panel estimates of this slope coefficient are 0.988 or 0.832 including individual effects. Over five years, their pseudo-panel indicates a coefficient of 0.950. While these results may vary with different cohort definitions, any of these estimates implies a considerable overstatement of mobility.

For our purposes one conclusion should be clear: analysis ignoring these issues is likely to overstate poverty mobility, especially when very few time periods are used in the analysis. Although the fact that any study observing substantial poverty mobility in the data finds significant correlates with different household and community characteristics suggests that a significant part of the observed mobility is genuine, the presence of substantial measurement error cannot be discounted.

How does attrition affect estimates of mobility?

The disappearance of households between baseline and follow-up data—attrition—may bias estimates of mobility and its determinants. Thomas, Frankenberg, and Smith (2001) label this problem the Achilles' heel of panel surveys. Purely random attrition would have no effect other than decreasing precision, since random attrition would merely shrink the survey's sample size. But households disappear due to marriage, migration, violence, business success or failure, or political instability, and these causes that lead households to disappear from the data may also affect households' income mobility. Hence, attrition may cause analyses to underestimate upward or downward mobility.

Respondents' selective refusal to participate in surveys accounts for much attrition in industrial countries but less in developing countries, where the inability to track households plays a more important role (Jasso, Rosenzweig, and Smith 2000; Thomas, Frankenberg, and Smith 2001). One can easily understand why: telephones, the Internet, land titling, and other fixed contact methods work far better in industrial than in developing countries. Furthermore, in more agrarian societies, the gradual movement out of agriculture of large parts of the population is an essential part of development.

Evidence from a few panels shows the varied importance of attrition due to household movement in developing-country datasets. Nearly 60 percent of attrition in Nicaragua's three-year LSMS was due to households leaving their dwellings (Davis and Stampini 2002). In Indonesia's Family Life Survey, which made extensive effort to track households, 82 percent of 1993–97 attrition was due to the inability to find households. IFLS in 1997 asked respondents to list the phone number of a neighbor, friend, family member, employer, or other individual who could contact them, and only 20 percent could provide such information (Thomas, Frankenberg, and Smith 2001). In a small Lesotho survey with a first wave that was not intended as the baseline for a panel, 83 percent of attrition was due to households that could not be tracked (Wason and Hall 2004). Elbers, Gunning, and Kinsey (2002) use a Zimbabwean panel with only 10 percent attrition between 1983 and 1997, but they define a household as the residents of a particular piece of land, so their panel ignores migration and considers only complete disintegration or eviction of a household as causes of attrition. While this approach achieves low attrition, it does not guarantee that a household observed in one wave of a panel is the same household that was observed in a different wave of the panel.

Table 3.6 presents attrition rates, follow-up methods, and analysis of attrition for all datasets from annex table 3.B for which attrition information

TABLE 3.6
Attrition Rates for Different Follow-up Methods
for Selected Panel Data Surveys

Dwellings		Local tracking		Extensive tracking	
Survey	Rate	Survey	Rate	Survey	Rate
Bolivia PIDI	35.0	Egypt EIHS	7.2	Bangladesh BNS	0
Mexico ENEU	35.0	India REDS	17.5	Indonesia IFLS	5.6
Nicaragua LSMS	31.1	Philippines IFPRI	21.4	South Africa KIDS	16.0
Peru LSMS	15.0	Vietnam VLSS	11.0		
Venezuela EHM	50.0	Ethiopia ERHS	7.0		
Mean, median	33.0,	Mean, median	14.0,	Mean, median	7.2,
	35.0		14.0		5.6

Sources: See surveys in annex table 3.B. Attrition rate is the number of households that disappear between baseline and last wave divided by number in baseline. Table includes only surveys for which information could be obtained on both attrition rate and follow-up method. Note that these are household-level attrition rates.

was easily available.[6] Attrition rates range widely, from 0 percent in the Bangladesh Nutrition Survey (BNS) to nearly 50 percent in a survey in Hungary (table 3.7). Selection of survey method is heavily endogenous with investment in the survey, duration of the survey, location of the survey, and other factors, so the numbers in table 3.6 do not accurately measure a causal effect of survey method. Nonetheless, the difference in mean attrition rates is striking: surveys of dwellings achieve a mean attrition rate of 33 percent, while surveys including tracking of households outside their dwellings but only in their local communities achieve a mean rate of 14 percent, and surveys with extensive tracking achieve a median rate of 5.6 percent.

Table 3.7 summarizes the evidence on the nature of attrition in those studies for which more information was available. A review of the tracking rules for each survey shows large variability in the methods used. Similarly, the way in which attrition is discussed and analyzed also varies. From these studies it appears that, generally, households more likely to disappear have younger heads, live in urban areas, and have higher per capita income and more unmarried individuals. These results cohere with intuition—the households most likely to leave their dwellings are the households with characteristics that naturally associate with spatial mobility. Most studies recognize these differences but comment that the magnitude is sufficiently small as to weakly affect estimates of poverty or related income mobility.

TABLE 3.7
Attrition in Selected Panel Surveys

Country and data	Attrition rate (%)	Rules for tracking households	Description and analysis	References
Argentina EPH	1995–2002: 48	Drop a household if any member refuses to answer income questions.	Graph comparing complete and panel sample at baseline: lower income in sample, different poverty rates.	Cruces and Wodon 2003b
Bangladesh BNS	0	For people who moved, village residents who cohabited with departed members were questioned; for people who remained in the village, the original interviewee was also interviewed.	Compare means, analysis of households that would have attrited under different sampling rules.	Rosenzweig 2003
Bangladesh HIES	No information	From village census, baseline sampled 1,245 households in 62 villages, stratified into 8 landowning groups. The follow-up in 32 villages stratified by wealth (rather than land), then followed up original households. So of the 965 households interviewed in follow-up, 695 were interviewed in baseline.	No information	Hossain et al. 2002
Bolivia PIDI	35	Interviewers did not track and follow migrants.	Compare means, probit for attrition. Statistical tests.	Alderman et al. 2001
Chile CASEN	11.8	No information	No information	Contreras et al. 2004
China (rural Sichuan) RHS	No information	No information	They simulate bias if households with different identifying information in the baseline and follow-up had been dropped.	McCulloch and Calandrino 2003

TABLE 3.7
Attrition in Selected Panel Surveys—continued

Country and data	Attrition rate (%)	Rules for tracking households	Description and analysis	References
Côte d'Ivoire CILSS	5–15	No information	Regression showing smaller and younger households attrit.	Kamanou and Morduch 2002
Egypt EIHS	7.2	Interviewed household if it remained in the same primary sampling unit. So loss of households was due to households moving, being absent at time of visit, or refusing interview.	Compare means and determinants of consumption in 1997 for entire sample and panel sample. Rural attritors were poorer, urban attritors were wealthier; neither difference significant.	Haddad and Ahmed 2003
Ethiopia ERHS	1989–94: 7; 1994–97: 2	Identify household head or household that considers itself as the successor household if head has died. Restricted to village.	No specific analysis reported.	Dercon and Krishnan 2002
Ethiopia EUHS	Kedir and McKay: 30.3; Bigsten et al.: 7	Identify household head or household that considers itself as the successor household if head has died. Restricted to particular urban area.	No information	Bigsten et al. 2003; Kedir and McKay 2005
Hungary HHP	Each round: 15; 1992–97: 48	No information	Estimate income equations simultaneously with equation for attrition. Smaller households and households outside Budapest less likely to attrit. They provide estimates corrected and uncorrected for attrition.	Lokshin and Ravallion 2004

India NCAER	No information	Kept if (1) household head in 1970/71 remained alive in 1981/82 and household was still intact; or (2) head remained alive but household members had not stayed together; or (3) household head had died but rest of household stayed intact. They do not use weights, so estimates reflect the sample and not India's rural population.	None	Bhide and Mehta 2004
India REDS	17.5	Lost information on children who moved out of Dadar or who dropped out.	Use *jati* fixed effects in estimation.	Munshi and Rosenzweig 2005
Indonesia IFLS	1993–97: 5.6	Follow households that change dwellings. Median interview time: 6 hours per interview on 17 islands in 20 languages. Main visit: interview households in same dwelling and within generally 30 minutes by public transportation (local move).	Movers were more similar to nonmovers at baseline than at follow-up. Lowest reinterview in capital city.	Thomas, Frankenberg, and Smith 2001
Iran	33.8	No information	Compare means in baseline.	Salehi-Isfahani 2003
Kenya and Madagascar USAID	No information	No information	Probit for attrition; variables jointly insignificant.	Barrett, Bezuneh, and Aboud 2001
Kenya (Nyanza province) KICS	28 women, 33 men	Common reasons for attrition: mortality, migration, not found after three visits, busy, or sick.	Compare means, probit for attrition, BGLW test.	Alderman et al. 2001
Lesotho	34.4	No information	Probit for attrition. Larger households with more pigs more likely to remain.	Wason and Hall 2004
Madagascar 1–2–3	1997–98: 22; 1998–99: 21	No information	Compare means. Attritors younger, better educated, smaller households, less often own their dwellings. But no difference in poverty status.	Herrera and Roubaud 2005

TABLE 3.7
Attrition in Selected Panel Surveys—continued

Country and data	Attrition rate (%)	Rules for tracking households	Description and analysis	References
Mali	7.9	No information	Compare means. No significant difference at baseline.	Christiaensen and Boisvert 2000
Mexico ENEU	35	Follow dwellings only; if household moves it is dropped.	Extensive analysis and compare panels with pseudo-panels.	Antman and McKenzie 2005; Gong, Van Soest, and Villagomez 2004; Wodon 2001
Nicaragua LSMS	31.1	Visit same dwelling; if household has moved, do not follow them.	Compare means, probit for attrition, compare regression coefficients, Heckman regression for regressing consumption and attrition on covariates. Attrition not significant problem.	Davis and Stampini 2002
Peru	1997–98: 12; 1998–99: 3	No information	Compare means. Attritors younger, better educated, smaller households, less often own their dwellings, early 17% more than non-attritors. But no difference in poverty status.	Herrera and Roubaud 2005
Philippines IFPRI	1962 baseline; 1985–94: 21.4	Follow up households in the same village.	No information.	Fuwa 2007
Poland HBS	No information	No information	Wealthier and urban households disappear.	Luttmer 2001
Russia RLMS	No mean information	Follow dwellings only.	No information.	Heeringa 1997
South Africa (Free State)	7.6	No information	No information.	Booysen 2003

South Africa KIDS	15	Interviewers tracked, followed, and re-interviewed migrants and mobile households.	Compare means, probit for attrition.	Alderman et al. 2001; May et al. 2000
Uganda IHS and UNHS	28	No information	Compare means, probit for attrition, compare baseline results with and without attrited households. Insignificant differences between panel and nonpanel, though rural and larger households more likely to remain.	Lawson, McKay, and Okidi 2003; Lawson 2004; Deininger and Okidi 2003
Venezuela EHM	50	Keep only households in same dwelling.	Households that remain have larger size and smaller real income per capita, fewer unmarried individuals, and fewer couples without children.	Freije 2003
Vietnam VLSS	28 individuals, 11 households	Households in the same commune were followed, but households that moved out of the commune were not followed.	Newly formed households underreported; more urban than rural attrition. Also both surveys have same sample frame (Vietnam 1989 census), but rural-to-urban migration since then means the later data represent the country less. They use weights in the first round but not the second round.	Baulch and Masset 2003; Glewwe and Nguyen 2002
Zimbabwe	1982–97: 10	Follow land and define a household as the residents of a piece of land.	10% dropped due to surveying errors, household disintegration, or government eviction.	Elbers, Gunning, and Kinsey 2002

Note: Attrition rate = number of households lost / total baseline households. The attrition rate is unweighted, so it is for the sample, not the population.

For example, Alderman et al. (2001) conducted a careful analysis on this issue for Bolivia's Integrated Child Development Project (PIDI) and Kenya's Ideational Change Survey (KICS), where interviewers did not follow migrants, and for South Africa's KIDS survey, where interviewers did follow migrants. They show that in all three countries, household characteristics in the baseline could not effectively predict attrition, and attrition did not affect baseline regression estimates of the particular relationships of interest to them, for example between family background and education or health outcomes. In other words, relative to baseline characteristics, there are no obvious patterns to the attrition. These results cohere with analysis of attrition in the U.S. Panel Study of Income Dynamics (Fitzgerald, Gottschalk, and Moffit 1998).

This is a difficult issue and this type of analysis cannot entirely settle it. Such studies can only rely on baseline data on the households that have disappeared from the survey to assess whether these households are "different" or not. For example, it could be that the entrepreneurial people left the community, so that inference on moving out of poverty and its determinants may be biased even though there are no observable differences. In a related vein, it could be that negative shocks, such as illness or crop losses experienced after the baseline round, forced some people to leave (or contributed to their deaths). Baseline characteristics would not be able to reveal this, and the underlying causes of mobility would not be identified from the data. In sum, the evidence that attrition may not matter much is potentially seriously flawed.

A number of studies have taken the attrition issue more seriously. By trying to trace more people than would be implied by a typical simple revisit rule, they also provide evidence on the relevance of attrition for analysis in general, and for inference on poverty and mobility. These studies have shown that attrition, particularly in the case of dwelling-based follow-up, will significantly bias results. Indonesia's Family Life Survey achieved only 5.6 percent attrition after four years by a detailed protocol that Thomas, Frankenberg, and Smith (2001) carefully document. Follow-up in the IFLS second round, with interviews in 20 languages on 17 islands requiring an average of six hours each, presented some challenge. One entire enumeration area in Jakarta had been bulldozed and replaced with a shopping and apartment complex, and by extensive tracking the researchers followed 18 of the 20 households originally from that enumeration area. While households that moved locally were generally similar to households that did not move, households that moved far away differed greatly from households that did not move in a variety of characteristics, including simple welfare outcomes.

In mere numbers, these authors report that dwelling-based sampling would have given a follow-up rate of 77–84 percent rather than the 94 percent that they achieved.[7]

Rosenzweig (2003), using an 18-year Bangladeshi panel with a 0 percent attrition rate, argues against the dwelling-based follow-up that the LSMS program suggests (Glewwe and Jacoby 2000) or the intact household (or same head) approach that India's ICRISAT and REDS surveys used. To achieve this zero attrition, previous co-residents of those no longer present in the village were interviewed to collect some basic characteristics of those not present. Rosenzweig reports that using the LSMS criteria would have dropped more than half of males less than age 30 from his data. The impact on assessing mobility over time is shown to be substantial.

The way forward: Long-term panel data with full tracking of individuals

Few if any studies take this issue of attrition a logical step further. When studying mobility, one needs to study welfare outcomes over long periods. But households change over time: children are born, adults leave and set up new households, couples get married, people die. Households split; people move out or move in. To put it simply, there is no such thing as a stable household unit that can be followed over long periods of time. The unit that is followed is based on some judgment that may affect the results. For example, ICRISAT used to follow a household as long as it had the same head, and later, it followed the person who held the land asset of the previous head. In both cases these are choices that are likely to affect the results of the analysis.

While the aforementioned work, linking poverty changes to household and other characteristics and circumstances, makes substantial progress, the results are bound to be problematic unless one thinks carefully about attrition. Poverty mobility is the evolution of the poverty outcomes of individuals and households that try actively to shape their own futures, given what they have, in response to their own circumstances and the general environment they face, including the policy environment. Specifically, households split, move out of communities, and migrate as part of their poverty mobility strategies. Even more regular life-cycle events, such as marriage, birth, and death, are shaped and influenced by the process of trying to move up or failing to do so. In short, attrition is bound to be a crucial and endogenous part of mobility work, even if work that only looks at the impact of attrition using baseline observable characteristics may not find that it is a problem. If panel surveys only look for "original" households in original dwellings or even in the original community, then one crucial part of poverty mobility, spatial mobility—moving elsewhere to try to do better, in response to opportunities or pressures of destitution—is totally ignored. In fact, if development economics theory has anything to say about how poverty reduction takes place, it is that fewer people remain involved in agriculture as jobs are created in other sectors. Thus spatial mobility is likely to be central.

When taking seriously the various split-offs and changes to the household in panel data, one reaches another methodological conclusion as well: following a household does not make sense, since a household changes rapidly over time. Defining what is the "same" household is highly complicated because individuals move in and out. The only feasible solution is to base the sampling and tracking strategy on *individuals*. This is what a number of recent and current studies aim to do. The Bangladesh study reported by Rosenzweig (2003) and discussed above started from a small sample of 50 households initially and tracked all split-off households to result in a sample of 308 households.

In Tanzania, the Kagera Health and Development Study (KHDS) does this systematically on a relatively large scale compared to other current studies (see, for example, Beegle, De Weerdt, and Dercon 2006c). The KHDS began in 1991 and conducted a detailed panel data survey in four rounds between 1991 and 1994. It was implemented in Kagera, a region near Lake Victoria with high HIV/AIDS prevalence. It initially surveyed 900 households. In 2004 a new survey round was launched, aiming to collect data to study the long-term implications of adult mortality and related impacts from HIV/AIDS. It was clear from the start that much had happened to change these initial households, and a decision was made to focus on all *individuals* ever surveyed in the earlier rounds.[8] This led to an effort to trace more than 6,000 people.

At the level of original households, the tracing was successful: 93 percent of original households were reinterviewed, comparable to the best short-term panel data survey and highly successful given the 10-year period since the previous interviews. The result was a survey of 2,774 households, linked to 832 recontacted households. At the individual level, about 87 percent of respondents were reinterviewed as part of the survey, but the implications of spatial mobility are very striking. Only 49 percent of the individuals interviewed in 1991–94 had stayed in the same village. Nineteen percent moved to a nearby village; 20 percent moved further away to another village or town in Kagera region; 10 percent moved outside the region, but still within Tanzania; and 2 percent moved to other countries, including Uganda and Rwanda.[9] In sum, without tracking there would be no way to assess mobility in any spatial sense, and if tracking had been done using "dwelling" or "same village" rules, more than half the individuals would have been lost.

Beegle, De Weerdt, and Dercon (2006c), using some simple descriptive statistics, contend that inferences about poverty and poverty mobility would be very misleading without this tracking. Table 3.8 shows that poverty decreased in the KHDS sample, but to a very different extent across the different locations to which people moved. Those who remained in the village saw the poverty head count fall from 36 to 32 percent, a decline of 4 percentage points. But those who moved to a nearby village had an 11 percentage point decline, those moving elsewhere in Kagera experienced a 13 percentage point decline, and those moving outside Kagera saw poverty decline by 23 percentage points. If sampling had occurred using a "same location" rule, then poverty mobility would have been considered to be substantially lower than what actually took place. Surely, this does not look like "random attrition" according to standard rules. In fact, Beegle and colleagues found that initial observable variables are not at the root of these differences in poverty mobility; if anything, unobservable characteristics drive these differences, as when more able or entrepreneurial individuals move farther away.

Of course, this type of work imposes considerable costs. One alternative is to fill in the "missing" individuals and households by using key-informant interviews. This is effectively what Rosenzweig (2003) did in some survey work. For each individual not present in the village, a simple key-informant interview was conducted, trying to glean a few indicators. But the indicators

TABLE 3.8
Poverty and Spatial Mobility in Kagera, Tanzania: Comparing the Poverty Head Count between 1991 and 2004 by Initial Locality

2004 location	Mean 1991	Mean 2004	Difference means[a]	N
Within village	0.36	0.32	−0.04	2,611
Nearby village	0.33	0.22	−0.11	566
Elsewhere in Kagera	0.37	0.24	−0.13	571
Out of Kagera	0.30	0.07	−0.23	327
Full sample	0.35	0.27	−0.08	4,075

Source: Beegle, De Weerdt, and Dercon 2006c.

a. Significant at 1 percent.

have to remain limited to a few basic assets such as land or education. Such information can help assess the potential bias entailed by attrition—but again on the basis of indirect observable characteristics related to welfare outcomes.

In the "new" ICRISAT surveys, which involve tracking all the individuals ever interviewed in 1975–84, a similar instrument is used, but it is pursued further. Key informants and family are asked not just about assets but also about their perceptions of the welfare situation of the missing individuals, using a seven-step scale from very rich to very poor. But there is still the problem of discrepancies between community or key-informant perceptions of other people's well-being and those people's own self-assessment. In other words, while both perceptions are information about the person, it would be wrong to simply assume both are measures of the *same*, particularly since measurement error may have different properties for self-reported data than for reports on a family member.

Another alternative is to turn the idea of a panel data survey upside down. Rather than starting with a baseline, one could start with interviews for a full sample drawn from a current population and then use recall to establish a baseline for these people. This is effectively what was done by Krishna (2004) and to some extent in the herd histories in Ethiopia. While such studies provide interesting insights and information, as argued earlier, there are caveats in using these methods to assess poverty mobility. For example, in the Ethiopia ERHS, subjective welfare perceptions were elicited in different rounds over a 10-year period. In 2004, the same questions were asked using 10-year recall. The answers were revealing: for example, when asked in 2004, 29 percent said that they had been rich or very rich in 1994. In 1994, only 7 percent of respondents provided this answer.

In short, while recall provides interesting information for assessing welfare outcomes and poverty mobility, one must be careful. Recall is unlikely to give the same information as one would have obtained if the questions had been asked in the past, and this in turn affects inference on poverty mobility. Furthermore, cognitive dissonance may lead individuals to remember events and circumstances that cohere with their life situation but forget or misreport those past events that conflict with their current circumstances. Finally, retrospective studies cause further selectivity bias since only the surviving people that stayed in a particular location are being interviewed. As an indication of the nature of change in terms of poverty in a particular locality, this is particularly fraught. Finding good alternatives to tracing all individuals is clearly a challenge.[10]

Conclusions and Directions for Future Research

In the last few years, many more panel datasets have become available from developing countries. A number have been used for the analysis of poverty mobility and its correlates. Most research has found that household and community endowments, such as assets and infrastructure, matter for allowing people to move out of poverty, while shocks and risk make and keep people poor. Nevertheless, it is difficult to generalize on which factors matter most in different contexts. Furthermore, many studies are not able to provide evidence that goes beyond correlates; rarely if ever has any causality been established convincingly. Better statistical analysis, combined with a careful contextual understanding of the economic and other circumstances constraining poverty mobility, will be essential to move this research forward.

Heavy attrition appears to be present in most panel databases. Following dwellings rather than tracking households worsens attrition. Investing in tracking households substantially lessens at least attrition rates. Good research practice should involve reporting the rate of attrition, comparing means and determinants of attrition, and discussing reasons for attrition.

But just following households is not enough. With longer panel datasets, the future for understanding long-term mobility must lie in methodological innovations. These include an increasing focus on individual mobility and not just household mobility. It is clear that there are no simple shortcuts for this work, whether in quantitative or qualitative studies: some of the people of interest will inevitably move, and this will impose costs in terms of data collection and other logistical requirements. Simple recall and key-informant interviews are unlikely to solve these issues.

Annex. Data Sources for Poverty Mobility Work

The datasets used in recent studies (annex tables 3.A and 3.B) constitute distinguishable categories of surveys. Several LSMS-type household surveys, such as those in Peru and Vietnam, included a multiyear panel designed into the survey. Quarterly or annual rotating panels in Argentina, Mexico, and Venezuela allow study of short-term income dynamics or analysis of attrition and measurement bias. Several data sources designed for evaluation of a specific development intervention—the Bangladesh Household Income and Expenditure Survey (HIES), the Integrated Child Development Project in Bolivia, Progresa/Oportunidades in Mexico, and others—provide insight into mobility as a useful side benefit of impact evaluation.

ANNEX TABLE 3.A
Duration of Panel Surveys Used in Recent Research

Duration	Panel surveys
1 to 5 years	Argentina EPH, Bolivia PIDI, Chile CASEN, China RHS, Côte d'Ivoire CILSS, Côte d'Ivoire FMHS, Egypt EIHS, Hungary, Indonesia UNICEF/BPS, Indonesia IFLS, Indonesia 100 village, Iran, Kenya WMS, Kenya/Madagascar USAID, Kenya KICS, Madagascar 1–2–3, Mali, Mexico ENEU, Mexico Progresa, Nicaragua LSMS, Peru ENAHO, Poland, Rwanda, Russia, South Africa Gauteng, South Africa Free State, Venezuela
5 to 10 years	Bangladesh BNS, Bangladesh Greeley, Bangladesh HIES, Ethiopia ERHS (full), Ethiopia EUHS, India ICRISAT (old), Kenya TAMPA, Uganda, Vietnam
More than 10 years	Ethiopia ERHS (subsample), Ethiopia herd histories, India ICRISAT (new), India NCAER, India REDS, Tanzania KHDS, Lesotho, Philippines, South Africa KIDS, Zimbabwe

Note: Duration is defined according to waves used in articles profiled in this review. The rotating panels in Argentina EPH and Mexico ENEU offer many overlapping one-year panels.

Only five of the 44 are rotating panels, that is, repeated cross-sections where some portion of the respondents remain in the survey for a set period. Mexico's ENEU, for example, surveys a household for five quarters before replacing it. Some panels came from following up a baseline survey that was not originally designed to be part of a panel. Lesotho's 1993 survey, for example, was designed as a rapid assessment of the effects of a drought affecting much of Sub-Saharan Africa, and the original survey did not anticipate a follow-up in 2002 (Wason and Hall 2004). The Ethiopia Rural Household Survey, with six rounds since 1994, has at its core a smaller sample of households interviewed by the International Food Policy Research Institute in 1989 on the effects of the 1984–85 famine. Still other databases, such as the 55-household herd history in Ethiopia, were completed for specific individual papers, largely based on recall data. Only one data source—Kenya's Welfare Monitoring Survey (WMS)—had no panel of households and involved repeated cross-sections used to form a panel of communities.

Most surveys used in research last only a few years, but some panels have longer duration. Of the 44 panel data sources categorized here, nine (20 percent) span six to 10 years and another 10 (23 percent) last more than 10 years. A few long panels cluster: Bangladesh has three panel data sources that span more than five years, while India and Ethiopia each have two (and each has one with a subsample spanning an even longer period). Many of these surveys will have additional waves. At the same time, the panels with longer duration often have samples of fewer than 500 households, and attrition may affect longer panels more severely. Also, despite the increasing presence of long panels, two-thirds of panels still cover a time span of five or fewer years.

ANNEX TABLE 3.B
Datasets Used in Recent Research

Country	Survey name	Type	Waves[a]	n	Coverage	Research using these data
Argentina (Greater Buenos Aires)	Permanent Household Survey (EPH)	Rotating panel	May and October 1990–2002	12 cohorts, average 453 households	All urban Argentina	Fields et al. 2006; Wodon 2001; Garrido and Marina 2002; Cruces and Wodon 2003a; Albornoz and Menéndez 2003
Bangladesh	Greeley survey	Panel	1994, 2001	1,184 households	Comilla and Tangail districts	Kabeer 2004
Bangladesh	Bangladesh Nutrition Survey (BNS)	Panel	1981/82, 2000	50 households initially, 308 households in follow-up	15 villages	Rosenzweig 2003
Bangladesh	Household Income and Expenditure Survey (HIES), also known as BIDS panel	Panel	1987/88, 2000	379 households	21 villages	Sen 2003
Bolivia	Integrated Child Development Project (PIDI) evaluation data	Panel	1995/96, 1998	2,047 households	Poor urban areas	Alderman et al. 2001
Chile	National Socioeconomic Characterization (CASEN)	Panel	1996, 2001	4,700 households	National	Contreras et al. 2004
China	Rural Household Survey (RHS)	Panel	1991, 1995	3,311 households	Rural Sichuan	McCulloch and Calandrino 2003
Côte d'Ivoire	Côte d'Ivoire Living Standards Survey (CILSS)	Rotating panel	1985, 1986, 1987, 1988	800 households	National	Kamanou and Morduch 2002

ANNEX TABLE 3.B
Datasets Used in Recent Research—continued

Country	Survey name	Type	Waves[a]	n	Coverage	Research using these data
Côte d'Ivoire	Farm Management and Household Survey (FMHS)	Panel	1993, 1994, 1995	120 rice-farming households	Three humid to subhumid agro-ecological zones	Barrett, Bezuneh, and Aboud 2001
Egypt	Egypt Integrated Household Survey (EIHS)	Panel	1997, 1999	347 households	National	Haddad and Ahmed 2003
Ethiopia (Borana Plateau)	Herd histories	Panel	1980, 1997	55 households	Selected pastoralists from southern Ethiopia	McPeak and Barrett 2001; Lybbert et al. 2004
Ethiopia	Ethiopia Rural Household Survey (ERHS)	Panel	1994 (2), 1995, 1997, 1999, 2004; also 1989	1,477 households (354 households since 1989)	Rural areas	Dercon and Krishnan 2000, 2002; Bigsten et al. 2003; Dercon 2004a; Dercon et al. 2004
Ethiopia	Ethiopia Urban Household Survey (EUHS)	Panel	1994, 1995, 1997, 1999, 2004	1,500 households (urban)	Urban areas	Bigsten et al. 2003; Kedir and McKay 2005
Hungary	Hungarian Household Panel (HHP)	Panel	6 waves, 1992–97	1,385 households in panel from 2,668 in original	National	Lokshin and Ravallion 2004
India	Rural Economic Development Survey (REDS); National Council of Applied Economic Research (NCAER) panel	Panel	1970/71, 1981/82, 1999	3,319–4,979 households in 2,509 villages	Areas within Mumbai	Bhide and Mehta 2004; Munshi and Rosenzweig 2005

Country	Data source	Type	Years	Sample size	Coverage	References
India	ICRISAT (old) (Maharashtra, Andhra Pradesh, Madhya Pradesh, Gujarat)	Panel	1975–84	400 households; much research on smaller dataset	Rural south India	Gaiha and Imai 2002; 50+ research papers, main papers summarized in Morduch 2004
India	ICRISAT "new" (Maharashtra, Andhra Pradesh)	Panel	2001–6	All households still residing in villages from old ICRISAT survey, plus from 2004 tracking of all split-offs, including migrants	Rural south India	In progress
Indonesia (rural)	100-village survey by UNICEF and Statistics Indonesia (BPS)	Panel	1998, 1999 (4 interviews)	10,640 households	Villages from 8 provinces	Suryahadi, Widyanti, and Sumarto 2003
Indonesia	Indonesia Family Life Survey (IFLS)	Panel	1993, 1997, 2000 (and part of sample, 1999)	2,132 households	Rural areas from 13 provinces	Fields et al. 2003a, 2003b; Strauss et al. 2004; Newhouse 2005; see also IFLS Web site
Iran	Data from Statistical Center of Iran	Panel	1992, 1993, 1994, 1995	3,371 households	National	Salehi-Isfahani 2003
Kenya	Tegemeo Agricultural Monitoring and Policy Analysis Project (TAMPA)	Panel	1997, 2000, 2004	1,500 households	Rural areas	Muyanga, Ayieko, and Gamba 2005

ANNEX TABLE 3.B
Datasets Used in Recent Research—continued

Country	Survey name	Type	Waves[a]	n	Coverage	Research using these data
Kenya	Welfare Monitoring Survey (WMS)	Cross-sections/pseudo-panel	1994, 1997	Panel of 981 clusters, 10 different households in each cluster	Rural areas	Christiaensen and Subbarao 2005
Kenya	Quarterly survey of six sites	Panel	Ongoing		Rural northern Kenya	McPeak and Barrett 2001
Kenya	Kenyan Ideational Change Survey (KICS) for HIV/AIDS knowledge	Panel	1994/95–1996/97	900 women and their husbands	Nyanza province	Alderman et al. 2001
Kenya and Madagascar	U.S. Agency for International Development (USAID) panel	Panel	1993–95	301 households	Rural areas	Barrett, Bezuneh, and Aboud 2001
Lesotho	Lesotho panel survey	Panel	1993, 2002	328 households	Unclear	Wason and Hall 2004
Madagascar	1–2–3 Survey	Rotating panel	1997–98 and 1998–99	1997–98: 1,151 households 1998–99: 2,371 households 1997–99: 1,249 households	Antananarivo (capital city)	Herrera and Roubaud 2005

Country	Survey	Type	Years	Sample size	Coverage	Reference
Mali	Rural survey	Panel	1997–98	274 households	Zone Lacustre	Christiaensen and Boisvert 2000
Mexico	Progresa/Oportunidades evaluation survey	Panel	1997–2000, every 6 months	41,000 households	Rural areas	Skoufias 2001
Mexico	National Survey of Urban Employment (ENEU)	Rotating panel	Quarterly, 1987–2001		Urban areas	Wodon 2001; Gong, Van Soest, and Villagomez 2004; Antman and McKenzie 2005
Nepal	Nepal Living Standards Survey	Panel	1995/96, 2003/4	962 households	National	Bhatta and Sharma 2006
Nicaragua	LSMS	Panel	1998, 2001	3,015 households	Urban and rural areas	Davis and Stampini 2002
Pakistan	Peshawar panel	Panel	1996, 1999	299 households	Villages in Peshawar district	Kurosaki 2006a, 2006b
Peru	National Household Survey (ENAHO)	Panel	1997–99	1997–98: 2,709 households; 1998–99: 1,872 households	Urban areas	Herrera and Roubaud 2005
Peru	LSMS Instituto Cuanto	Panel	1990, 1994, 1996	421 households	Urban areas	Herrera 1999
Philippines	International Food Policy Research Institute (IFPRI) and Research Institute for Mindanao Culture (RIMCU) data	Panel	4 rounds in 1984/85, then 1 round each in 1992 and 2004	352 households	One village in Pangasinan province, Luzon island	Fuwa 2007

ANNEX TABLE 3.B
Datasets Used in Recent Research—*continued*

Country	Survey name	Type	Waves[a]	n	Coverage	Research using these data
Poland	Household Budget Survey (HBS)	Panel	1993–1996	4,919 households	Rural and urban areas	Luttmer 2001
Rwanda	National budget-consumption survey	Panel	Quarterly (4 rounds), 1982–83	270 households	National	Muller 2003
Russia	Russian Longitudinal Monitoring Survey (RLMS)	Panel	1994, 1995, 1996, 1998	3,596 households, 1,970 in panel	National	Luttmer 2001; Lokshin and Ravallion 2004
South Africa (Gauteng province)	Community Agency for Social Enquiry study of urban informal settlements	Panel	1997, 2001	200 households	Urban, Gauteng province	Stevens 2003
South Africa	USAID survey	Panel	May/June 2001, Nov/Dec 2001, July/Aug 2002	355 households in 2 communities	Free State	Booysen 2003
South Africa	KwaZulu-Natal Income Dynamics Study (KIDS)	Panel	1993, 1998, 2004	1,171 households	KwaZulu-Natal	Alderman et al. 2001; Carter and May 2001; Keswell 2001; Fields et al. 2003a, 2003b; Cichello, Fields, and Liebbrandt 2005

Country	Survey	Type	Dates	Households	Coverage	Source
Tanzania	Kagera Health and Development Survey (KHDS)	Panel	1991, 1992, 1993, 1994, 2004,	900 households in 1991–94, all households and split-offs in 2004 (2,774 households)	Kagera	Beegle, De Weerdt, and Dercon 2006a
Uganda	Integrated Household Survey (IHS) and Uganda National Household Survey (UNHS)	Panel	1992, 1999	1992–96: 818 households; 1992–99: 1,005 households	National	Lawson, McKay, and Okidi 2003; Lawson 2004
Venezuela	Household Sample Survey (EHM)	Rotating panel	1997 and 1998	7,744 households	National	Freije 2003; Fields et al. 2003a, 2003b; Fields et al. 2006
Vietnam	Vietnam Living Standards Survey (VLSS)	Panel	1992/93–1997/98	4,272 households	National	Glewwe and Nguyen 2002; Baulch and Masset 2003
Zimbabwe	Bill Kinsey data	Panel	1983/84, 1987, annually 1992–2002	400 households		Elbers, Gunning, and Kinsey 2002

Note: In some cases different papers using the same data use different numbers of households. "National" coverage generally refers to nationally representative surveys, while "rural and urban" refers to surveys that include households in both rural and urban areas but do not necessarily constitute a nationally representative sample.

a. The dates follow the convention that, for example, 1985/86 refers to a round or wave of survey covering 1985 and 1986, while 1985–86 refers to two rounds of the survey, one in 1985 and one in 1986.

Notes

1. On the work of the Chronic Poverty Research Centre, see, for example, *European Journal of Development Research* 17 (1), *International Planning Studies* 10 (1), *Journal of Human Development* 5 (2), and *World Development* 31 (3). Also see the organization's Web site at http://www.chronicpoverty.org. On Pathways From Poverty, see the BASIS Collaborative Research Support Program Web site at http://www.basis.wisc.edu/global_pathways.html.
2. For studies using a panel of geographic areas, see Fofack, Monga, and Tuluy (2001) on Burkina Faso regions and Chomitz et al. (2005) on Brazilian municipalities. Recent theoretical discussions of estimating mobility or comparisons of different measures appear in Gottschalk and Spolaore (2002), Schluter and Trede (2003), and Ligon and Schechter (2004). Discussion of studies in the United States appears in the summer 2002 issue of the *Journal of Economic Perspectives* (see Bowles and Gintis 2002).
3. Related reviews are Hickey (2001) and Lawson, McKay, and Moore (2003).
4. A number of other studies are reviewed in McKay and Lawson (2002), yielding broadly the same conclusions.
5. For the United States and Scandinavian countries, Aaberge et al. (2002) replace survey estimates of income with payroll record estimates, which may measure income with less error. But such data are less available in developing countries and may exclude the more common informal sector income.
6. Often survey documents other than mobility analyses discuss these details. Some such documents appear in the far-right column of table 3.7, while others, such as the local mimeographs mentioned in Barrett, Bezuneh, and Aboud (2001) and Lokshin and Ravallion (2004), are not used here.
7. But note that this is household-level attrition—that is, a household is considered traced if at least one member is traced.
8. The survey instrument used was still largely a household survey instrument, but was applied to the household to which the tracked individual now belonged.
9. One individual, currently residing in Sweden, remains to be interviewed.
10. A "statistical" solution is to drop the analysis of panels altogether and rely on pseudo-panels, or the tracking of a cohort (age, demographic group, other identifiable group) through various cross-sections. For Mexico, Antman and McKenzie (2005) find that disappearing households are younger, less often married, and with smaller households and larger incomes than households that remain in the sample; the effects are significant given the large sample but the effects result from a small number of households.

Bibliography

Aaberge, R., A. Björkland, M. Jäntti, M. Palme, P. Pedersen, N. Smith, and T. Wennemo. 2002. "Income Inequality and Income Mobility in the Scandinavian Countries Compared to the United States." *Review of Income and Wealth* 48 (4): 443–69.

Alesina, A., R. Di Tella, and R. MacCulloch. 2003. "Happiness and Inequality: Are Europeans and Americans Different?" *Journal of Public Economics* 88 (9–10): 2009–42.

Albornoz, F., and M. Menéndez. 2003. "Income Mobility and Equality: The Case of Argentina During the 1990s." National University of La Plata, Argentina.

Alderman, H., J. Behrman, H. P. Kohler, J. A. Maluccio, and S. Watkins. 2001. "Attrition in Longitudinal Household Survey Data: Some Tests for Three Developing-Country Samples." *Demographic Research* 5: 78–124.

Alderman, H., J. Hoddinott, and W. Kinsey. 2006. "Long Term Consequences of Early Childhood Malnutrition." *Oxford Economic Papers* 58: 450–74.

Andersen, L. 2001. "Social Mobility in Latin America: Links with Adolescent Schooling." Research Network Working Paper R-433, Inter-American Development Bank, Washington, DC.

Antman, F., and D. J. McKenzie. 2005. "Earnings Mobility and Measurement Error: A Pseudo-Panel Approach." Policy Research Working Paper 3745, World Bank, Washington, DC.

Barrett, C. B., M. Bezuneh, and A. Aboud. 2001. "Income Diversification, Poverty Traps, and Policy Shocks in Côte d'Ivoire and Kenya." *Food Policy* 26: 367–84.

Barrett, C., P. Phiri Marenya, J. G. McPeak, B. Minten, F. Murithi, W. Oluoch-Kosura, F. Place, J. C. Randrianarisoa, J. Rasambainarivo, and J. Wangila. 2006. "Welfare Dynamics in Rural Kenya and Madagascar." *Journal of Development Studies* 42 (2): 248–77.

Baulch, B., and J. Hoddinott. 2000. *Economic Mobility and Poverty Dynamics in Developing Countries.* Portland, OR: Frank Cass.

Baulch, B., and E. Masset. 2003. "Do Monetary and Nonmonetary Indicators Tell the Same Story about Chronic Poverty? A Study of Vietnam in the 1990s." *World Development* 31 (3): 441–53.

Baulch, B., and N. McCulloch. 2003. "Being Poor and Becoming Poor: Poverty Status and Poverty Transitions in Rural Pakistan." *Journal of Asian and African Studies* 37: 168–85.

Beegle, K. 2000. "Economic Mobility in Indonesia and Vietnam: What Missing Data Can't Tell Us." RAND Corporation, Santa Monica, CA.

Beegle, K., J. De Weerdt, and S. Dercon. 2006a. "Orphanhood and the Long-term Impact on Children." *American Journal of Agricultural Economics* 88 (5): 1266–72.

———. 2006b. "Adult Mortality and Economic Growth in the Age of HIV/AIDS." Policy Research Working Paper 4082, World Bank, Washington, DC.

———. 2006c. "Poverty and Wealth Dynamics in Tanzania: Evidence from a Tracking Survey." World Bank, Washington, DC; EDI, Tanzania; Oxford University, UK.

Behrman, J., A. Gaviria, and M. Székely. 2001. "Intergenerational Mobility in Latin America." Research Department Working Paper 452, Inter-American Development Bank, Washington, DC.

Behrman, J., M. R. Rosenzweig, and P. Taubman. 1994. "Endowments and the Allocation of Schooling in the Family and in the Marriage Market: The Twins Experiment." *Journal of Political Economy* 102 (6): 1131–74.

Bhatta, S., and S. Sharma. 2006. "The Determinants and Consequences of Chronic and Transient Poverty in Nepal." Working Paper 66, Chronic Poverty Research Centre, Manchester, UK.

Bhide, S., and A. K. Mehta. 2004. "Chronic Poverty in Rural India: Issues and Findings from Panel Data." *Journal of Human Development* 5 (2): 195–209.

Bigsten, A., B. Kebede, A. Shimeles, and M. Taddesse. 2003. "Growth and Poverty Reduction in Ethiopia: Evidence from Household Panel Surveys." *World Development* 31 (1): 87–106.

Bird, K., and A. Shepard. 2003. "Livelihoods and Chronic Poverty in Semi-Arid Zimbabwe." *World Development* 31 (3): 591–610.

Block, S., and P. Webb. 2001. "The Dynamics of Livelihood Diversification in Post-famine Ethiopia." *Food Policy* 26: 333–50.

Booysen, F. le R. 2003. "Chronic and Transitory Poverty in the Face of HIV/AIDS-Related Morbidity and Mortality: Evidence from South Africa." Presented at conference, "Staying Poor: Chronic Poverty and Development Policy," University of Manchester, UK, April 7–9.

Bourguignon, F., F. Ferreira, and M. Menéndez. 2003. "Inequality of Outcomes and Inequality of Opportunities in Brazil." Policy Research Working Paper 3174, World Bank, Washington, DC.

Bourguignon, F., C. Goh, and D. I. Kim. 2004. "Estimating Individual Vulnerability to Poverty with Pseudo-panel Data." Policy Research Working Paper 2275, World Bank, Washington, DC.

Bowles, S., and H. Gintis. 2002. "The Inheritance of Inequality." *Journal of Economic Perspectives* 16 (3): 3–30.

Carter, M. R., and J. May. 2001. "One Kind of Freedom: Poverty Dynamics in Post-apartheid South Africa." *World Development* 29 (12): 1987–2006.

Chen, S., R. Mu, and M. Ravallion. 2006. "Are There Lasting Impacts of a Poor-Area Development Program?" Development Research Group, World Bank, Washington, DC.

Chen, S., and M. Ravallion. 1995. "Data in Transition: Assessing Living Standards in Southern China." *China Economic Review* 7 (1): 23–56.

Chesher, A., and C. Schluter. 2002. "Welfare Measurement and Measurement Error." *Review of Economic Studies* 69 (2): 357–78.

Chomitz, K. M., D. da Mata, A. Ywata de Carvalho, and J. C. Magalhães. 2005. "Spatial Dynamics of Labor Markets in Brazil." Policy Research Working Paper 3752, World Bank, Washington, DC.

Christiaensen, L. J., and R. N. Boisvert. 2000. "On Measuring Household Food Vulnerability: Case Evidence from Northern Mali." Working Paper 2000-05, Department of Agricultural, Resource, and Managerial Economics, Cornell University, Ithaca, NY.

Christiaensen, L. J., and K. Subbarao. 2005. "Towards an Understanding of Household Vulnerability in Rural Kenya." *Journal of African Economies* 14 (4): 520–58.

Cichello, P. L., G. S. Fields, and M. Liebbrandt. 2005. "Earnings and Employment Dynamics for Africans in Post-apartheid South Africa: A Panel Study of KwaZulu-Natal." *Journal of African Economies* 14 (2): 143–90.

Contreras, D., R. Cooper, J. Herman, and C. Nielson. 2004. "Dinámica de la Pobreza y Movilidad Social: Chile 1996–2001." Departamento de Economía, University of Chile, Santiago.

Coulombe, H., and A. McKay. 2002. "The Evolution of Poverty and Inequality in Ghana over the 1990s: A Study Based on the Ghana Living Standards Surveys." Department of Economics, University of Nottingham, UK.

Cruces, G., and Q. Wodon. 2003a. "Risk-Adjusted Poverty in Argentina: Measurements and Determinants." Discussion Paper DARP 72, London School of Economics.

———. 2003b. "Transient and Chronic Poverty in Turbulent Times: Argentina 1995–2002." *Economics Bulletin* 9 (3): 1–12.

Dahan, M., and A. Gaviria. 2001. "Sibling Correlations and Intergenerational Mobility in Latin America." *Economic Development and Cultural Change* 49 (3): 537–54.

Davis, B., and M. Stampini. 2002. "Pathways towards Prosperity in Rural Nicaragua: Why Households Drop In and Out of Poverty, and Some Policy Suggestions on How to Keep Them Out." ESA Working Paper 02–12, United Nations Food and Agriculture Organization, Rome.

Deaton, A. 1997. *The Analysis of Household Surveys: A Microeconometric Approach to Development Policy.* Baltimore: Johns Hopkins University Press.

Deaton, A., and C. Paxson. 1994. "Intertemporal Choice and Inequality." *Journal of Political Economy* 102: 437–67.

Deaton, A., and S. Zaidi. 2002. "Guidelines for Constructing Consumption Aggregates for Welfare Analysis." Living Standards Measurement Study Working Paper 135, World Bank, Washington, DC.

Deininger, K., and J. Okidi. 2003. "Growth and Poverty Reduction in Uganda, 1992–2000: Panel Data Evidence." *Development Policy Review* 21 (4): 481–509.

Dercon, S. 2002. *The Impact of Economic Reform on Rural Households in Ethiopia.* Washington, DC: World Bank.

———. 2004a. "Growth and Shocks: Evidence from Rural Ethiopia." *Journal of Development Economics* 74: 309–29.

———. 2004b. *Insurance Against Poverty.* New York: Oxford University Press.

———. 2005. "Vulnerability: A Micro-level Analysis." Paper presented at Annual Bank Conference on Development Economics, Amsterdam, May 23–24.

———. 2006. "Economic Reform, Growth and the Poor: Evidence from Rural Ethiopia." *Journal of Development Economics* 81 (1): 1–24.

Dercon, S., D. Gilligan, J. Hoddinott, and T. Woldehanna. 2006. "The Impact of Roads and Agricultural Extension on Crop Income, Consumption, and Poverty in Fifteen Ethiopian Villages." International Food Policy Research Institute, Washington, DC.

Dercon, S., and J. Hoddinott. 2005. "Livelihoods, Growth, and Links to Market Towns in 15 Ethiopian Villages." Discussion Paper 194, International Food Policy Research Institute, Washington, DC.

Dercon, S., and P. Krishnan. 2000. "Vulnerability, Seasonality, and Poverty." *Journal of Development Studies* 36 (6): 25–53.

———. 2002. "Poverty in Rural Ethiopia 1989–95: Evidence from Household Panel Data in Selected Villages." In *The New Poverty Strategies: What Have They Achieved?*

What Have We Learned? ed. A. Booth and P. Mosley, 172–204. Basingstoke, UK: Palgrave Macmillan.

Dunn, C. 2003. "Assortative Matching and Intergenerational Mobility in Family Earnings: Evidence from Brazil." Department of Economics and Population Studies Centre, University of Michigan, Ann Arbor.

Elbers, C., J. W. Gunning, and B. H. Kinsey 2002, "Convergence, Shocks, and Poverty." Discussion Paper 2002–035/2, Tinbergen Institute, Amsterdam.

Falaris, E. 2003, "The Effect of Survey Attrition in Longitudinal Surveys: Evidence from Peru, Côte d'Ivoire, and Vietnam." *Journal of Development Economics* 70 (1): 133–57.

Ferreira, S. G., and F. A. Veloso. 2004. "Intergenerational Mobility of Wages in Brazil." Banco Nacional de Desenvolvimento Econômico e Social, Rio de Janeiro, Brazil.

Fields, G. S. 2002. *Distribution and Development: A New Look at the Developing World.* New York: Russell Sage Foundation.

Fields, G. S., P. L. Cichello, S. Freije, M. Menéndez, and D. Newhouse. 2003a. "For Richer or for Poorer: Evidence from Indonesia, South Africa, Spain, and Venezuela." *Journal of Economic Inequality* 1 (1): 67–99.

———. 2003b. "Household Income Dynamics: A Four-Country Story." *Journal of Development Studies* 40 (2): 30–54.

Fields, G., M. L. S. Puerta, R. D. Hernández, and S. Freije. 2006. "Earnings Mobility in Argentina, Mexico, and Venezuela: Testing the Divergence of Earnings and Symmetry of Mobility Hypothesis." School of Industrial and Labor Relations, Cornell University, Ithaca, NY.

Fitzgerald, J., P. Gottschalk, and R. Moffitt. 1998. "An Analysis of Sample Attrition in Panel Data." *Journal of Human Resources* 33 (2): 251–99.

Fofack, H., C. Monga, and H. Tuluy. 2001. "Household Welfare and Poverty Dynamics in Burkina Faso." Policy Research Working Paper 2590, World Bank, Washington, DC.

Freije, S. 2003. "Income, Positional, and Poverty Dynamics in Venezuela." School of Industrial and Labor Relations, Cornell University, Ithaca, NY.

Frick, J. R., and M. M. Grabka. 2005. "Item Nonresponse on Income Questions in Panel Surveys: Incidence, Imputation, and the Impact on Inequality and Mobility." *Allgemeines Statistisches Archiv* 89: 49–61.

Fuwa, N. 2007. "Pathways from Poverty toward Middle Class: Determinants of Socioeconomic Class Mobility in the Rural Philippines." *Cambridge Journal of Economics* 31 (1):123–44.

Gaiha, R., and K. Imai. 2002. "Vulnerability, Shocks, and Persistence of Poverty: Estimates for Semi-Arid Rural South India." Economics Series Working Paper 128, Department of Economics, University of Oxford, UK.

Garrido, N., and A. Marina. 2002. "Income Mobility: A Characterization in Argentina Using Archetypes." *Estudios de Economía* 29 (1): 123–38.

Gibson, J. 2001. "Measuring Chronic Poverty Without a Panel." *Journal of Development Economics* 65: 243–66.

Glewwe, P., and G. Hall. 1998. "Are Some Groups More Vulnerable to Macroeconomic Shocks than Others? Hypothesis Tests Based on Panel Data from Peru." *Journal of Development Economics* 56: 181–206.

Glewwe, P., and H. Jacoby. 2000. "Recommendations for Collecting Panel Data." In *Designing Household Survey Questionnaires for Developing Countries: Lessons from 10 Years of LSMS Experience,* ed. M. Grosh and P. Glewwe. Washington, DC: World Bank.

Glewwe, P., and P. Nguyen. 2002. "Economic Mobility in Vietnam in the 1990s." Policy Research Working Paper 2838, World Bank, Washington, DC.

Gong, X., A. Van Soest, and E. Villagomez. 2004. "Mobility in the Urban Labor Market: A Panel Data Analysis for Mexico." *Economic Development and Cultural Change* 53 (1): 1–36.

Gottschalk, P., and E. Spolaore. 2002. "On the Evaluation of Economic Mobility." *Review of Economic Studies* 69 (1): 191–208.

Greeley, M. 1999. "Poverty and Well-Being in Rural Bangladesh: Impact of Economic Growth and Rural Development." Department for International Development, London, UK.

Grootaert, C., R. Kanbur, and G. Oh. 1997. "The Dynamics of Welfare Gains and Losses: An African Case Study." *Journal of Development Studies* 33 (5): 635–57.

Guimarães, S., and F. Veloso. 2003. "Intergenerational Mobility of Earnings in Brazil." Banco Nacional de Desenvolvimento Econômico e Social, Rio de Janeiro, Brazil.

Haddad, L., and A. Ahmed. 2003. "Chronic and Transitory Poverty: Evidence from Egypt, 1997–99." *World Development* 31 (1): 71–85.

Heeringa, S. G. 1997. "Russia Longitudinal Monitoring Survey Sample Attrition, Replenishment, and Weighting in Rounds V–VII." Institute for Social Research, University of Michigan, Ann Arbor.

Herrera, J. 1999. "Ajuste Económico, Desigualdad, y Movilidad." Working Paper DT/99/07, Développement et Insertion Internationale (DIAL), Paris.

Herrera, J., and F. Roubaud. 2005. "Urban Poverty Dynamics in Peru and Madagascar, 1997–1999: A Panel Data Analysis." *International Planning Studies* 10 (1): 21–48.

Hickey, S. 2001. "Chronic Poverty in Sub-Saharan Africa and South Asia: A Select Annotated Bibliography with Special Reference to Remote Rural Areas." Working Paper 1, Chronic Poverty Research Centre, Manchester, UK.

Hossain, M., M. L. Bose, A. Chowdhury, and R. Meinzen-Dick. 2002. "Changes in Agrarian Relations and Livelihoods in Rural Bangladesh." In *Agrarian Studies: Essays on Agrarian Relations in Less-Developed Countries,* ed. V. K. Ramachandran and M. Swaminathan. Proceedings of international conference, "Agrarian Relations and Rural Development in Less-Developed Countries," January 3–6. Kolkata, India: Tulika Books.

Jalan, J., and M. Ravallion. 2002. "Geographic Poverty Traps? A Micro Model of Consumption Growth in Rural China." *Journal of Applied Econometrics* 17: 329–46.

Jasso, G., M. R. Rosenzweig, and J. P. Smith. 2000. "The Effects of Interview Payments and Periodicity on Sample Selection and Attrition and on Respondent Memory: Evidence from the Pilot Study of the New Immigrant Survey." RAND Corporation, Santa Monica, CA.

Kabeer, N. 2004. "Snakes, Ladders, and Traps: Changing Lives and Livelihoods in Rural Bangladesh (1994–2001)." Working Paper 50, Chronic Poverty Research Centre, Manchester, UK.

Kamanou, G., and J. Morduch. 2002. "Measuring Vulnerability to Poverty." NYU Wagner Working Paper WP1012, New York University.

Kedir, A. M., and A. McKay. 2005. "Chronic Poverty in Urban Ethiopia: Panel Data Evidence." *International Planning Studies* 10 (1): 49–67.

Keswell, M. 2001. "Intragenerational Mobility: A Study of Chance and Change in Post-Apartheid South Africa." Department of Commerce, University of Cape Town.

Krishna, A. 2004. "Escaping Poverty and Becoming Poor: Who Gains, Who Loses, and Why?" *World Development* 32 (1): 121–36.

Krishna, A., P. Kristjanson, M. Radeny, and W. Nindo. 2004. "Escaping Poverty and Becoming Poor in 20 Kenyan Villages." *Journal of Human Development* 5 (2): 211–26.

Kristjanson, P., A. Krishna, M. Radeny, and W. Nindo. 2004. "Pathways Out of Poverty in Western Kenya and the Role of Livestock." Pro-Poor Livestock Policy Initiative Working Paper 14, International Livestock Research Institute, United Nations Food and Agricultural Organization, Rome.

Kurosaki, T. 2006a. "Consumption Vulnerability to Risk in Rural Pakistan." *Journal of Development Studies* 42 (1): 70–89.

———. 2006b. "The Measurement of Transient Poverty: Theory and Application to Pakistan." *Journal of Economic Inequality* 4 (3): 325–45.

Lawson, D. 2004. "The Influence of Ill Health on Chronic and Transient Poverty: Evidence from Uganda." Working Paper 41, Chronic Poverty Research Centre, Manchester, UK.

Lawson, D., A. McKay, and K. Moore. 2003. "Panel Datasets in Developing and Transitional Countries, Version 1-07.2003." Chronic Poverty Research Centre, Manchester, UK.

Lawson, D., A. McKay, and J. Okidi. 2003. "Poverty Persistence and Transitions in Uganda: A Combined Qualitative and Quantitative Analysis." Working Paper 38, Chronic Poverty Research Centre, Manchester, UK.

Ligon, E., and L. Schechter. 2004. "Evaluating Different Approaches to Estimating Vulnerability." Department of Agricultural and Resource Economics, University of California, Berkeley.

Lokshin, M., and M. Ravallion. 2004. "Household Income Dynamics in Two Transition Economies." *Studies in Nonlinear Dynamics & Econometrics* 9 (3): 1–31.

Luttmer, E. F. P. 2001. "Measuring Poverty Dynamics and Inequality in Transition Economies: Disentangling Real Events from Noisy Data." Policy Research Working Paper 2549, World Bank, Washington, DC.

Lybbert, T. J., C. B. Barrett, S. Desta, and D. Layne Coppock. 2004. "Stochastic Wealth Dynamics and Risk Management among a Poor Population." *Economic Journal* 114: 750–77.

May, J., M. R. Carter, L. Haddad, and J. A. Maluccio. 2000. "KwaZulu-Natal Income Dynamics Study (KIDS) 1993–98: A Longitudinal Household Database for South African Policy Analysis." *Development Southern Africa* 17 (4): 567–81.

McCulloch, N., and M. Calandrino. 2003. "Vulnerability and Chronic Poverty in Rural Sichuan." *World Development* 31 (3): 611–28.

McKay, A., and B. Baulch. 2004. "How Many Chronically Poor People Are There in the World? Some Preliminary Estimates." Working Paper 45, Chronic Poverty Research Centre, Manchester, UK.

McKay, A., and D. Lawson. 2002. "Assessing the Extent and Nature of Chronic Poverty in Low Income Countries: Issues and Evidence." *World Development* 31 (3): 425–39.

McPeak, J. G., and C. B. Barrett. 2001. "Differential Risk Exposure and Stochastic Poverty Traps among East African Pastoralists." *American Journal of Agricultural Economics* 83 (3): 674–79.

Morduch, J. 2004. "Consumption Smoothing over Space." In *Insurance Against Poverty*, ed. S. Dercon. New York: Oxford University Press.

Muller, C. 2003. "Censored Quantile Regressions of Chronic and Transient Seasonal Poverty in Rwanda." *Journal of African Economies* 11 (4): 503–41.

Munshi, K., and M. R. Rosenzweig. 2005. "Why Is Mobility in India So Low? Social Insurance, Inequality, and Growth." CID Working Paper 121, Center for International Development, Harvard University, Cambridge, MA.

———. 2006. "Traditional Institutions Meet the Modern World: Caste, Gender and Schooling Choice in a Globalizing Economy." *American Economic Review* 96 (4): 1225–52.

Newhouse, D. 2005. "The Persistence of Income Shocks: Evidence from Rural Indonesia." *Review of Development Economics* 9 (3): 415–33.

Perry, G., O. S. Arias, J. H. López, W. F. Maloney, and L. Servén. 2006. *Poverty Reduction and Growth: Virtuous and Vicious Circles.* Washington, DC: World Bank.

Ravallion, M. 1996. "Issues in Measuring and Modeling Poverty." *Economic Journal* 106: 1328–44.

Reyes, C. 2002. "Moving In and Out of Poverty in the Philippines." MIMAP Research Paper 53, International Development Research Centre, Ottawa.

Rosenzweig, M. 2003. "Payoffs from Panels in Low-Income Countries: Economic Development and Economic Mobility." *American Economic Review Papers and Proceedings* 93 (2): 112–17.

Salehi-Isfahani, D. 2003. "Mobility and the Dynamics of Poverty in Iran: What Can We Learn from the 1992–95 Panel Data?" Prepared for the Economic Research Forum for the Arab Countries, Iran, and Turkey.

Schluter, C., and M. Trede. 2003. "Local versus Global Assessment of Mobility." *International Economic Review* 44 (4): 1313–35.

Scott, C. D. 2001. "Mixed Fortunes: A Study of Poverty Mobility among Small Farm Households in Chile, 1968–86." *Journal of Development Studies* 36: (6): 155–81.

Sen, B. 2003. "Drivers of Escape and Descent: Changing Household Fortunes in Bangladesh." *World Development* 31 (3): 513–34.

Skoufias, E. 2001. "PROGESA and Its Impacts on the Welfare and Human Capital of Adults and Children in Rural Mexico: A Synthesis of the Results of an Evaluation by the International Food Policy Research Institute (IFPRI)." International Food Policy Research Institute, Washington, DC.

Skoufias, E., and A. R. Quisumbing. 2005. "Consumption Insurance and Vulnerability to Poverty: A Synthesis of the Evidence from Bangladesh, Ethiopia, Mali, Mexico, and Russia." *European Journal of Development Research* 17 (1): 24–58.

Solon, G. 2002. "Cross-Country Differences in Intergenerational Earnings Mobility." *Journal of Economic Perspectives* 16 (3): 59–66.

Stevens, L. 2003. "Chronic Poverty in Urban Informal Settlements in South Africa: Combining Quantitative and Qualitative Data to Monitor the Impact of Interventions." Intermediate Technology Group, Schumacher Centre for Technology Development, Bourton on Dunsmore, UK.

Strauss, J., K. Beegle, A. Dwiyanto, Y. Herawati, D. Pattinasarany, E. Satriawan, B. Sikoki, Sukamdi, and F. Witoelar. 2004. *Indonesian Living Standards Before and After the Financial Crisis: Evidence from the Indonesia Family Life Survey.* Santa Monica, CA: RAND Corporation.

Suryahadi, A., W. Widyanti, and S. Sumarto. 2003. "Short-term Poverty Dynamics in Rural Indonesia during the Economic Crisis." *Journal of International Development* 15: 133–44.

Thomas, D., E. Frankenberg, and J. P. Smith. 2001. "Lost but Not Forgotten: Attrition and Follow-up in the Indonesia Family Life Survey." *Journal of Human Resources* 36 (3): 556–92.

Wason, D., and D. Hall. 2004. "Poverty in Lesotho 1992 to 2002." Working Paper 40, Chronic Poverty Research Centre, Manchester, UK.

Wodon, Q. 2001. "Income Mobility and Risk during the Business Cycle: Comparing Adjustments in Labor Markets in Two Latin American Countries." *Economics of Transition* 9 (2): 449–61.

Woolard, I., and S. Klasen. 2005. "Determinants of Income Mobility and Household Poverty Dynamics in South Africa." *Journal of Development Studies* 41 (5): 865–97.

4

Intragenerational Income Mobility: Poverty Dynamics in Industrial Societies

Brian Nolan and Robert Erikson

The study of social mobility is one of the central areas of sociology, and studies of income mobility and poverty dynamics have burgeoned in economics in recent years. This chapter draws together leading studies from both disciplines, thus addressing issues about which there is a substantial volume of scientific writing. In addition, we provide new analysis to contribute to the knowledge of mobility processes. The chapter advances the notions that poverty dynamics are best understood when seen within the broader context of income mobility more generally, and that both economics and sociology have something to offer in understanding the key relationships and processes.

Following a nontechnical overview of the field, we examine movements into and out of poverty in relation to mobility in other areas of the income distribution. We discuss long-term stability and change of individual positions in the income distribution and compare income mobility in nations with different welfare regimes. In considering the relation between income stability/change and certain individual or household characteristics, we focus on Sweden as an interesting example. Finally, we ask to what extent outcomes of poverty studies may depend on the definitions of poverty used. Some of these issues have to be dealt with in a more superficial manner than others, with the availability and accessibility of suitable data often being a major obstacle.

The concept of mobility is not clear-cut. What is meant by mobility and how it is measured varies from context to context and from one study to another. Sociologists tend to focus on occupational and social class movements, whereas our focus here is on income changes. We are primarily concerned with income changes that give rise to movements into and out of income poverty over time; however, we also relate these movements to the broader context of income mobility patterns across the overall income distribution. Furthermore, in measuring income poverty dynamics we focus for the most part on income thresholds that move over time in line with average income in the country in question—that is, relative income poverty lines. This is the common approach in European and comparative studies, but it can give very different results than measures that are fixed in purchasing power terms over time, the more usual approach in the United States. While both are informative, we are constrained by the fact that most of the literature on which we draw employs the first approach.

A Nontechnical Overview of the Field

The literature in the area of social and income mobility is very large. Much of this literature focuses on intergenerational rather than intragenerational mobility. Within sociology there is a long tradition of studying intergenerational associations in socioeconomic position using social class or occupational prestige as outcome measures (see, for example, Breen and Jonsson 2005). Economists have been engaged with intergenerational associations since at least the 1980s, mostly focusing on the correlation between the earnings of fathers and sons. These studies show significant variations in intergenerational life chances among countries that are in many respects quite similar.[1]

Norway has the lowest father-son correlation, about 0.13, making it the industrial country where the father's earnings and presumably the son's circumstances during childhood seem to play the smallest role in the son's overall life chances. Estimates for Denmark, Finland, and Sweden are generally on the order of 0.2–0.28, and Canadian studies have produced estimates in a similar range. A German study indicates a slightly higher elasticity. Estimates for the United Kingdom, on the other hand, are like most of those for the United States, at about 0.4.[2]

Research on intragenerational mobility in household incomes (from all sources) is more recent. While intergenerational mobility has been measured from a various types of data collections, longitudinal surveys have dominated the analysis of intragenerational income mobility.[3] These have been available for many years in the United States, notably through the Panel Study of Income Dynamics (PSID), and in Sweden, through the Level of Living Survey. But only since the 1980s and early 1990s have such data been available in other European countries, with national longitudinal surveys in, for example,

Germany, the Netherlands, and the United Kingdom. More recently, panel data for most of the 15 pre-2004 members of the European Union, the so-called EU-15, have been produced from the European Community Household Panel (ECHP). Canada has the Canadian Survey of Labour and Income Dynamics (SLID).

The cross-country comparative analysis of poverty dynamics was pioneered by Duncan et al. (1993, 1995). They compared short-term transitions (over a few years) into and out of poverty in the United States and Canada with those in selected European countries for which panel data were then available. More recently, such data have become available for more countries, notably through the European Community Household Panel survey organized by Eurostat, the Statistical Office of the European Communities.

In broad terms, analysis of short-term poverty dynamics using these sources has revealed what the Organisation for Economic Co-operation and Development (OECD) has described as a seeming paradox: poverty is simultaneously fluid and characterized by long-term traps.[4] Many spells of poverty are short and represent only transitory setbacks, and considerably fewer people are continuously poor for an extended period of time than are observed in poverty at a point in time. On the other hand, the typical year spent in poverty is lived by someone who experiences multiple years of poverty and whose long-term income is below the income poverty threshold on average. Repeated spells help to explain the apparent paradox of fluidity combined with persistence, since many of those who exit poverty in a given year reenter it within a short time. In addition, much of the time spent by such people above the poverty threshold is not very far above it. So the evidence suggests that there is extensive persistence and that this is greater than just looking at spell exits would suggest.

The most popular analytical approach follows Bane and Ellwood's (1986) influential U.S. study in analyzing the duration of single spells and how they start and end. It has become clear, however, that this analysis may be too limited for a host of reasons. First, some people will experience more than one spell in poverty.[5] Second, the availability of information on individual and household characteristics in panel surveys can lead to a neglect of institutional and macroeconomic factors. The chance of being trapped in low pay or poverty over the long term could be much higher in one institutional setting than in another, and it could also be affected by the macroeconomic situation. Third, the extent and nature of mobility in and out of poverty may vary depending on precisely where and how the poverty line is set—for example, a relative versus a fixed poverty line. Fourth, changes in household income may not have an immediate impact on consumption and on levels of deprivation and exclusion, so short-term movements above and below an income threshold may not be as significant for poverty as they appear at first sight (see, for example, Layte et al. 2001). And finally, the time horizon adopted could be critical. Mobility may be much greater over the long term than over a period of just a few years, and a longer perspective might produce rather different patterns within and across countries.

Income Poverty Dynamics and Mobility in Other Areas of the Income Distribution

Household incomes change over time throughout the income distribution. Poverty dynamics measured as movements relative to an income poverty threshold are in that sense simply income changes occurring in a particular part of the distribution. Movements into and out of poverty are special cases of more general income mobility, but stability or change around the poverty threshold might well be greater or less than in other areas of the income distribution; that is, there may be more or less mobility out of the lowest quintile than into and out of the other four quintiles. For example, movements into and out of unemployment or into and out of welfare dependency might be key factors producing change around the poverty threshold but much less important in the middle and upper reaches of the income distribution. It is therefore valuable to look at cross-country patterns of poverty dynamics in this broader context, to see in particular whether cross-country differences in poverty dynamics appear to simply reflect the scale of income mobility more generally or have distinctive features.

We begin with poverty dynamics. A comparative picture of poverty persistence versus mobility in the short term, from one year to the next, can be derived from longitudinal data for most countries of the "old" EU-15 as well as Canada and the United States (from the ECHP, the SLID, and the PSID, respectively).

Figure 4.1 shows some key indicators derived from these sources. These look at poverty dynamics over a three-year period, 1993–95 for most of the countries covered but 1987–89 for the United States.[6] We use a poverty threshold set at 50 percent of median equivalized income in the country in question, though some results using a higher threshold set at 60 percent of the median will also be discussed. The figures refer to the entire sample across all ages and thus cover different cohorts including children, people of working age, and people age 65 or over. The underlying figures, covering 13 European Union (EU) countries, Canada, and the United States, are given

FIGURE 4.1
Poverty Rates, Exit Rates, and Poverty Persistence in the European Union, Canada, and the United States, 1993–95

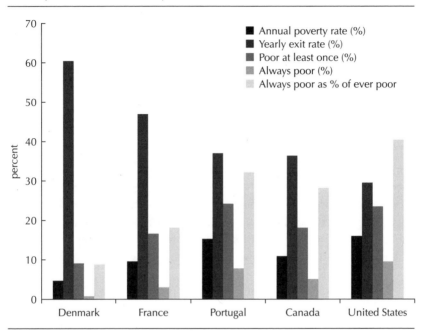

Note: Threshold is 50 percent of median equivalized income. U.S. data are for 1987–89.

in annex 4.1. Figure 4.1 shows three contrasting EU countries for illustrative purposes, together with the two North American ones.

We see from the first bar that the percentage falling below the income threshold ranges from 5 percent in Denmark up to 16 percent in the United States. The second bar shows the percentage of those below the income threshold in one year who have escaped by the next; this ranges from 30 percent in the United States up to 60 percent in Denmark. Countries with high cross-sectional poverty rates also tend to have low escape rates and vice versa, though there are exceptions: Canada's escape rate is lower than its poverty rate would lead us to expect.

The overall numbers experiencing poverty over the period will depend on the cross-sectional scale of poverty in any one year together with the extent of movement into and out of poverty. We see in the third bar that the percentage experiencing poverty at any time within the period ranges from 9 percent in Denmark up to 24 percent in Portugal and the United States. The fourth bar shows the percentage of households that fell below the income threshold in all three years. This is clearly highest in the United States, at almost 10 percent; it is also high in Portugal but is only 3 percent in France and 1 percent in Denmark.

The proportion of those falling below the threshold in any year who were below it in all three years—the "always poor" as a proportion of the "ever poor"—is a useful summary indicator of poverty persistence, shown in the final bar. Once again this is much higher in the United States than anywhere else, with 40 percent of those experiencing poverty in any year remaining below the threshold in all three years. Poverty persistence is lowest in the countries with the lowest cross-sectional poverty rates, though the ranking of countries in terms of persistence is not identical to the ranking by annual poverty rates. One factor that may be at work is that those below the income threshold may be further below it on average in countries where the cross-sectional poverty rate is higher, and they thus have further to go before they escape poverty. (Changing the income threshold can make a significant difference for some countries, as illustrated by results using a 60 percent of median threshold also shown in annex 4.1. However, Denmark and the United States still remain at either extreme.)

Macroeconomic conditions in a country at the time of measurement clearly can affect poverty persistence. As already mentioned, the data in figure 4.1 refer to a different period for the United States (1987–89) than for the other countries shown. Moreover, even for the same period, the business cycle will not always be at the same stage in each country and macroeconomic conditions may differ significantly. However, the broad pattern of variation in cross-sectional poverty rates across countries persists even when cyclical differences are taken into account, and it is likely that the same is true of cross-country variation in poverty persistence. It is certainly the case that the persistence in the United States measured in other periods is still particularly high.

Since the OECD study was completed more data have become available from the ECHP, and a longer horizon can also be adopted for the EU countries it covered. Figure 4.2 shows some indicators of poverty dynamics we have derived using the first five waves of the survey, using the 60 percent of median income threshold (which has become a key point of reference in the EU's social inclusion process). It takes those falling below that income threshold in the first year and looks at the proportion who were still below that threshold one year later, two years later, and four years later. Once again we illustrate the patterns using results for Denmark, France, and Portugal, with the results for these and other EU countries shown in annex 4.1.

FIGURE 4.2
Income Poverty Dynamics in Three European Union Countries, 1993–97

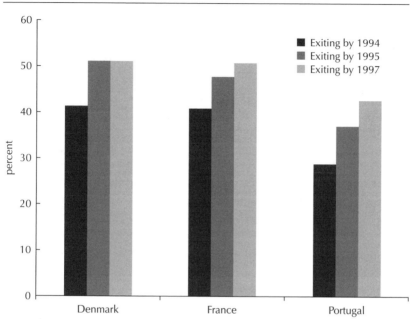

We see that lengthening the observation window naturally increases the percentage exiting from poverty in all countries, but it makes more difference in some countries than in others. The increase in the proportion exiting as we go from one to two to four years is relatively modest in the two countries with high one-year exit rates, Denmark and France. About 40 percent of those below the threshold have escaped after one year, and this has risen to about half after four years. By contrast, countries with low initial exit rates, of which Portugal is a prime example, see a more substantial increase, going from less than 30 percent after one year to 43 percent by the fifth year. Thus when the observation period is lengthened the differences between these EU countries narrow.

How do these patterns in poverty dynamics relate to broader patterns of income mobility throughout the income distribution, again focusing on the short-to-medium-term time horizon? We have seen that the United States appears to be an outlier in terms of poverty dynamics, with a particularly low level of escapes and a correspondingly high level of persistence of income poverty. As already noted, the literature on income mobility has often focused on the issue of American exceptionalism, but it has emphasized that the United States in fact looks similar to other industrial countries when it might be expected to have higher levels of mobility.[7] For example, Fritzell (1990) found that mobility was remarkably similar in Sweden and the United States; Burkhauser and Poupore (1997) found similar mobility patterns in Germany and the United States; Schluter (1998) found little difference between the United States, the United Kingdom, and Germany; and Goodin et al. (1999) found similar levels of mobility in Germany and the United States but more in the Netherlands.[8]

Here we are particularly interested in mobility toward the bottom—poverty dynamics—and overall mobility. Ayala and Sastre (2004) use data from the ECHP and the PSID to compare mobility over a five-year period in the United Kingdom, Germany, France, Italy, Spain, and the United States, and they compare income mobility toward the bottom with movements elsewhere in the distribution. They show that the United States has more mobility than France but less than the other countries they cover, and that both those countries are distinctive in the degree of immobility toward the top rather than the bottom.

We can expand the range of countries covered in analyzing mobility at different points in the distribution, again using the ECHP dataset. We derive measures of mobility based on transition matrices using quintile positions in the equivalized disposable income distribution—that is, whether the person was in the bottom 20 percent, the next 20 percent, and so on—and look at the extent of persistence in quintile ranking from one year to the next and over a five-year period. As far as overall mobility is concerned, the percentage remaining in the same quintile from one year to the next in most countries is around 55 percent. The percentage immobile falls as the observation window is lengthened to five years, with 40–45 percent then remaining in the same quintile. Comparing mobility at different points in the distribution, the consistent pattern—familiar from national studies—is that there is considerably more persistence at the bottom and the top than in the middle three quintiles. Generally persistence is about one-third in the middle quintiles over the five years, but about half for the bottom quintile and often 60 percent or more for the top quintile. As Ayala and Sastre found, countries with high overall immobility appear to have particularly high persistence at the top, Portugal being the outlier with 70 percent remaining in the top quintile.

The relationship between measured poverty dynamics and overall income mobility is a complex one. From a measurement perspective, poverty dynamics are conventionally measured in relation to an income threshold that is set as some proportion of the mean or median income, whereas income mobility is usually measured in terms of changes in ranking, either by income decile/quintile or simply by individual rank in the distribution. We return to such measurement issues below. The second reason why poverty dynamics may give a different picture than overall income mobility is simply that the former involves focusing on a specific part of the income distribution whereas the latter encompasses mobility throughout. The fact that a country has relatively low or high levels of overall income mobility does not necessarily mean that it will display that pattern toward the bottom.

Long-term Stability and Change of Individual Positions in the Income Distribution

Having looked in the previous section at poverty dynamics and income mobility over the short to medium term, we now turn to income mobility over a longer period. We focus first on analysis by the OECD of the Cross-National Equivalent Files (CNEF) of harmonized longitudinal survey data prepared at Cornell University covering Canada, Germany, the United Kingdom, and the United States. We then look at the American Panel Study of Income Dynamics and the Swedish Level of Living Survey, which both started as long ago as 1968 and thus provide a period of observation of more than 30 years.[9]

The OECD (2001) used the CNEF data to look at poverty dynamics over an eight-year period, except for Canada which was restricted to six years. The figures for Canada, Germany, and the United Kingdom are for the 1990s, but those for the United States relate to 1985–92 because of difficulties at the time in obtaining comparable data from the PSID for later years. The results in figure 4.3 show the percentages ever poor and always poor, and the latter as a percentage of the former, all with the 50 percent of median income threshold. The percentage below the income threshold throughout the period was four and a half times higher in the United States than in Germany, with Canada closer to the United States and the United Kingdom closer to Germany. The always poor as a proportion of the ever poor ranged from 13 percent in the United States to less than 6 percent in Germany, but the United Kingdom is now very close to the German level while Canada is little different from the United States.

Yearly exit rates from poverty were also presented and were disaggregated for populations of working and retirement age. These rates are lower in the United States than in the other three countries covered, with the most pronounced difference being for the retirement-age population. For the working-

FIGURE 4.3
Poverty Rates and Poverty Persistence in Germany, the United Kingdom,
Canada, and the United States over Eight Years

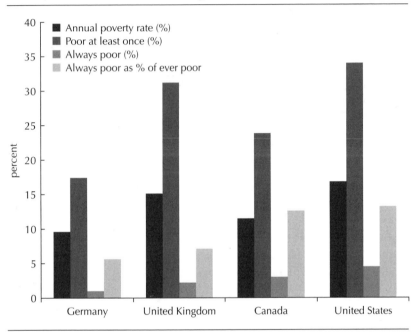

Note: The period for Canada was six years. A threshold of 50 percent of median equivalized income was used for all countries.

age population, the (average) yearly rate of exit from poverty was 30 percent in the United States, compared with 34 percent in Canada and the United Kingdom and 45 percent in Germany. For the retirement-age population the average escape rate was only 18 percent in the United States, compared with 34 percent in the United Kingdom, 39 percent in Canada, and 51 percent in Germany (OECD 2001, 65, table 2.10).

The study by Wu (2003) using the PSID takes a slightly longer time horizon, looking at poverty over the 12 years from 1981 to 1992. The results show that the probability of an individual exiting from poverty falls sharply from the second to the sixth year in poverty and then plateaus for a number of years before falling again. The exit probabilities are considerably lower for older people than for others at each duration, with that gap widening as duration lengthens. After the first three years in poverty, for example, the exit rate for older people was only 7 percent compared with 21 percent for younger people. The majority of older people who spend over three years in poverty can expect to stay there for a long time. About 30 percent of the completed poverty spells of older persons can be expected to last 10 years or more.

We have also derived some relevant results for Sweden, summarized here and set out in more detail in annex 4.2. We look first at income mobility from the early years of the 1990s to the end of that decade among people born in the years 1940 to 1961—potentially in the labor market at both the start and the end of the period. To even out some volatility we focus on average income over three years. Focusing on the bottom, more than three-quarters of those with incomes less than 60 percent of the median in the early 1990s were still in that position in the late 1990s. At the other end of the income distribution, about two-thirds of those with incomes above 160 percent of the median in the early 1990s still had incomes in the same area of the income distribution in the late 1990s. So incomes on the whole were fairly stable in Sweden over that period, with change mostly involving rather small gains or losses.

We also look at income change over a long period for older cohorts born between 1920 and 1939 by comparing their incomes in 1967 and 2000. The results show that Rowntree's (1901) "life cycle of poverty" seems still to be relevant, even in the highly developed Swedish welfare state: moving from employment to retirement still has a considerable impact on income and poverty. In 2000, less than 20 percent of the older cohort had an income above the median among those in the working-age group, and around 40 percent had a disposable income below 60 percent of the median. Only among those who were in the highest income bracket in 1967 was the median income about the same as for all in the working-age cohort. The association between income in 1967 and in 2000 is considerable, and many of those with low incomes in 1967 had fallen into poverty by 2000.

Higher persistence and lower outflows are seen more often at either end of the distribution than in the middle. Does this mean that it is more difficult to leave a state of poverty than other positions in the income distribution, and that those with the highest incomes are more protected than others from sliding down the income distribution? An alternative explanation could be that the lowest and highest income categories are open in the sense that they have no lower or upper limit respectively (except for zero or negative incomes, which are treated as missing values; see Atkinson, Maynard, and Trinder 1983).

We can test this by applying loglinear models to the transition tables. If there are "poverty traps" and "affluence traps"—the latter an ironic term used by Bowles and Gintis (2002)—this should show up in the fitted models.[10]

The results, while not clear-cut, suggest that there were no poverty traps in the 1990s. When we look at income mobility among cohorts born earlier than the mid-1930s and at periods before 1990, we do find some tendency toward "stickiness" at the bottom, as well as at the top. Sweden of is course a rather specific case, with a highly developed welfare state and social protection system, so it is not clear whether similar results would be expected in other countries. The role of welfare regimes in setting the framework within which poverty dynamics play out is the topic to which we now turn.

Income Mobility in Nations with Different Welfare Regimes

It is well established that the size and character of social protection transfers and of broader welfare state institutions influence the degree of income inequality. (This is accepted even though it is difficult to establish the most relevant counterfactual situation—in other words, what would the society in question look like with a different structure or no transfers?) What is less well established is the degree to which income mobility, and particularly movements into and out of poverty, vary with the character of the "welfare regime."

The notion that industrial countries can be usefully categorized into different welfare regimes has a long history, but both the notion and the term have been particularly widely adopted since Esping-Andersen's influential *Three Worlds of Welfare Capitalism* (1990). "Welfare regime" refers to the constellation of socioeconomic institutions, policies, and programs that a country adopts to promote its citizens' welfare, and the key claim is that it is useful to distinguish distinctive combinations of intervention strategies, policy designs, and institutional frameworks. Esping-Andersen distinguishes between "social democratic," "corporatist," and "liberal" welfare regimes. While others as far back as Richard Titmuss (1973) had put forward similar typologies (Goodin et al. 1999), this terminology has now become standard. There has been a good deal of discussion about which countries fit in which categories and whether the set of regimes needs to be expanded or amended. In particular, a strong case has been advanced for adding a fourth, "southern" welfare regime or subprotective welfare state.[11] Despite arguments about the typology and where particular countries fit, the underlying justification advanced for a regime perspective, that it helps focus attention on key processes and outcomes in individual countries, appears to be quite widely accepted at this point.

The key features that have been identified as characteristics of the different regimes may be briefly described. The social democratic regime assigns the welfare state a substantial redistributive role, seeking to guarantee adequate economic resources independently of market or familial reliance. The corporatist regime views welfare primarily as a mediator of group-based mutual aid and risk pooling, with rights to benefits depending on the individual's insertion in the labor market. The liberal welfare regime acknowledges the primacy of the market and confines the state to a residual welfare role, social benefits typically being subject to a means test and targeted to those failing in the market. In the Mediterranean countries of southern Europe family support systems play a distinctive role and the benefit system is uneven and minimalist in nature (Leibfried 1993; Ferrera 1996; Bonoli 1997; Arts and Gelissen 2002).

Sweden, Germany, and the United States are often seen as archetypal examples of the three welfare regimes originally identified by Esping-Andersen (1990), which makes a comparison of these three countries especially interesting. Of the other countries we have been discussing, Denmark can be categorized as social democratic; Canada, the United Kingdom, and Ireland as liberal; Belgium, France, and Luxembourg as corporatist; and Italy, Greece, Spain, and Portugal as exemplifying the southern regime. The Netherlands is often included in the corporatist/conservative regime (see, for example, Ferrera 1996), but Dutch analysts such as Muffels and Dirven (in Goodin et al. 1999) categorize it as social democratic.

If we go back to the results on poverty dynamics and income mobility presented in previous sections and look at them through this welfare regime lens, what do we see? As far as poverty dynamics are concerned, some countries in the liberal regime category can certainly be considered distinctive in the extent of poverty persistence over the short to medium term. Canada and even more so the United States have substantially higher rates of persistence and lower rates of escape from poverty than the EU countries with which they could be compared. However, the other countries with liberal regimes—Ireland and the United Kingdom—display much higher escape rates. If we assess poverty persistence by the summary measure "always poor/ever poor" and use the 50 percent income threshold, Ireland and the United Kingdom are among the countries with the least persistence (together with Denmark and the Netherlands). Even with the 60 percent threshold this remains true of the United Kingdom. When the observation window is lengthened to eight years, the United Kingdom does not look different from Germany, the classic example of the corporatist regime—but Canada and the United States do.

At the other end of the spectrum, Denmark certainly has a distinctively high level of exits from poverty and a low level of persistence, and the Netherlands—if one wants to count it as social democratic—also ranks among the countries with least poverty persistence. Among the southern countries there is considerable variation, with Portugal having a very high level of poverty persistence but Greece, Spain, and Italy being much less distinctive. So as far as poverty dynamics are concerned, the explanatory power of the welfare regime perspective seems to be limited to distinguishing either end of the spectrum: the United States and Canada at one extreme, and the social democratic Scandinavian countries at the other. This still leaves unexplained why other countries with liberal regimes are much closer to other EU countries than to the United States and Canada.

What is very important, though, is that even the limited "fit" with the welfare regime categorization that we do see is the opposite of what might be casually assumed before the evidence is examined. That is, the highest poverty rates go with the least rather than the most mobility out of poverty. It is often casually assumed that Canada and even more so the United States have high cross-sectional poverty rates but that their effect is ameliorated by high levels of mobility, so people are not trapped in poverty or welfare dependency as long as they are in some countries with lower poverty rates. The evidence suggests that the opposite is the case. Those falling below conventional relative income poverty lines in North America are less likely to escape from one year to the next than elsewhere, and more likely to spend a sustained period in poverty. Denmark, by contrast, combines a relatively very low cross-sectional poverty rate and high levels of poverty escape from one year to the next. Layte and Whelan (2003) show that transfers play a particularly pronounced role in poverty transitions in Denmark, in contrast to the very limited role they play in EU countries in the southern regime, where changes in earnings—particularly of the main earner in the household—are dominant.

Clearly countries differ not only in welfare and other institutional structures but also in their population profiles, with differing proportions of older people, single parents, unemployed, and so on. Since such characteristics might be expected to influence poverty persistence, we need to ask whether there remain significant differences across welfare regimes in predicted poverty durations or experiences once such characteristics have been taken into account. Fouarge and Layte's (2005) results using five waves of ECHP data show that countries with social democratic regimes do a better job of preventing both short-term and long-term poverty, those with liberal and southern regimes display much longer durations, and corporatist countries are in an intermediate position. When individual and country variables are used to predict exit rates, welfare regime categories serve as an adequate substitute for individual country effects.

While the extent of poverty persistence is affected by the welfare regime a country has in place, both may also be influenced by the same underlying factors. For example, Alesina and Glaeser (2004) argue that the less generous and more restrictive welfare regime in the United States reflects, among other things, greater social distance between the poor and the nonpoor, with race playing an important role. These factors may be associated with both lower upward mobility and less willingness of the middle class to pay for supportive policies. More broadly, it seems clear that the evolution of the welfare state in different countries is both a product of attitudes toward poverty and an influence on the subsequent development of institutional structures: attitudes and institutions affect each other dynamically. For present purposes, the key message is that welfare institutions do matter to poverty dynamics, although that relationship may not operate in a fashion that is fully captured by conventional welfare regime frameworks.

The Relation between Income Stability/Change and Individual Characteristics

We have seen that poverty dynamics and persistence vary systematically across countries, but how much does the persistence of poverty vary among people with different characteristics within the same country? Below we examine cross-country studies that measure the effects on mobility of key changes or "events" in a household's income or demographic composition. In addition, the importance of various individual and household characteristics themselves can be compared within and across countries.

We have seen that the yearly exit rate using 50 percent of median varies from around 30 percent in the United States to around 60 percent in Denmark, but within each country the chances of being trapped in poverty long-term are likely to depend on the type of individual and household concerned. In trying to understand the factors influencing transitions, econometric modeling of poverty dynamics generally attempts to link observed changes in poverty status over time to changes in the earnings, labor force participation, and composition of the household.[12] The key distinction made is between "income events" such as changes in earnings, benefits, or investment income, and "demographic events" such as the arrival of a new child, partnership formation, death, marital dissolution, or adult offspring leaving home.

For some such events there is a clear a priori expectation that their effects will always be either positive or negative. The arrival of a new child, for example, adds to household needs without adding to income and therefore could produce a poverty entry, but it is hard to see how (arithmetically) it could produce an escape.[13] An increase in the number of people in the household who work, or in the number of hours they work, would usually be expected to produce a poverty escape if anything, while a decrease in household members working or in hours worked would be associated with a poverty entry (though someone could move into work because benefits are exhausted and earn less than the benefit). The effects of some other events are more difficult to predict. Divorce or family splits of other types, for example, would appear at first sight to produce poverty entries; where the entire household was already poor, though, splitting could in fact leave certain members above the income threshold. An adult offspring leaving home could mean that the original household or the newly formed one falls below the income threshold, but in other circumstances it could produce a poverty escape.

The results produced by the OECD (2001) using three-year panels showed a strong association between job-related events and poverty transitions everywhere, but particularly in the United States. About one-third of poverty exits in the United States coincided with an increase in the number of persons at work in the household. Another one-third coincided with an increase in the number of months worked (with an unchanged number of persons at work), and one-third with an increase in earnings (with an unchanged number of workers and months worked). Changes in transfers as well as earnings were seen to be important in the EU and to a lesser extent in Canada, but much less so in the United States. Family and job-related events can be linked: the number of workers in the household often changes because someone joins or leaves the household. For the European countries in the ECHP, 25 percent of entries into poverty and 15 percent of exits coincided with events such as marriages, births, or the establishment of a new family. Such family-related events were observed more frequently in North America, coinciding with 41 percent of entries and 31 percent of exits in Canada and 37 percent of entries and 27 percent of exits in the United States. Separation or divorce was the most common family-related event associated with poverty entry in both the EU and North America, while marriage is associated with an important share of exits in North America but not the EU.[14]

The influence of individual and household characteristics can also be studied in relation to overall experience of poverty over a period. Analysis of three-year panels by the OECD showed that the age, gender, and educational attainment of the household head, the number of workers in the household at the outset, and family composition all have a substantial impact both on poverty exits and on the likelihood of being persistently poor. Exit rates were affected most by the education of the household head, whereas the risk of persistent poverty was affected most by the number of workers in the household.

Analysis of the longer six- or eight-year CNEF panels available for Canada, Germany, the United Kingdom, and the United States brought out the extent to which predicted overall poverty experience over that period varied starkly with individual and household characteristics (see also Valletta 2004). To take an extreme case, a child in a family with a young single head with low education and no workers in the family was predicted to spend 3.5 years in poverty in Canada, 4.7 in Germany, 5.6 in the United Kingdom, and 7.0 in the United States; this compares with a predicted poverty experience of only 0.5, 0.2, 0.7 and 1.1 years respectively in these countries for a couple of prime working age with medium-level education and children.

All these results are based on survey data, where errors in measuring income can have a significant impact on mobility, as we discuss below. It is thus also of interest to analyze income mobility and poverty dynamics using register data available for Sweden, where the income measures are based on administrative information on benefits and taxes. Figure 4.4 shows the

FIGURE 4.4
Persistence of Poverty among Poor, Sweden, 1991–2000

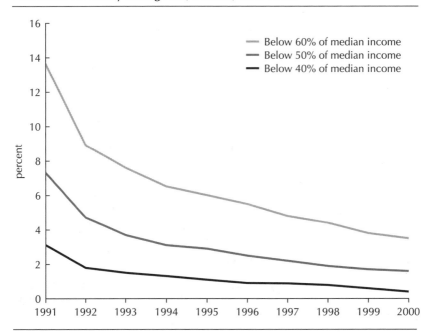

percentage poor in Sweden in 1991 according to the 40 percent, 50 percent, and 60 percent of median income thresholds. It further shows how many of these people remained poor in the succeeding years, so the values for the year 2000 show the proportions who had been poor every year from 1991. All three curves have the same general shape, with a rather sharp fall in the first year and then a slower decrease in the following years. With the 60 percent threshold, 26 percent of those who were poor in 1991 were poor in 2000 and had been so during all the years in between. The corresponding figures for the 50 and 40 percent limits were 22 and 13 percent respectively. This means that 3.5, 1.6, and 0.4 percent of the population (with positive incomes) were poor in all years according to the 60, 50, and 40 percent poverty definitions, respectively.

Concentrating on the 60 percent of median income threshold, we also investigate the degree to which the rate and persistence of poverty differ between men and women in three social classes: the salariat, the intermediate class, and the working class.[15] From figure 4.5 it is clear that the obvious

FIGURE 4.5
Rate and Persistence of Poverty by Sex and Social Class, Sweden, 1991–2000

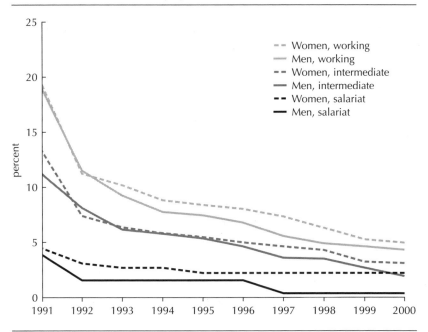

Note: Threshold is 60 percent of median equivalized income.

expectation is borne out: poverty rates are highest in the working class and lowest in the salariat, and generally higher among women than men. It also seems clear that class is more important than sex in determining rate and persistence of poverty since the variation between classes clearly is greater than that between the sexes, at least in terms of family disposable income.[16] The differences in poverty between the classes decrease when we consider more permanent situations, but the relative rates increase so that the relative position of those in the working class actually worsens in terms of persistence.

Obviously poverty rates and poverty persistence differ considerably between social classes. Are there any remaining effects of class origins, that is, of the social class of the parents? Figure 4.6 shows the rates and persistence of poverty, again using the 60 percent of median threshold, for persons from different social origins who belonged to the working class in 1991.[17] We see that the risk of falling into and remaining in poverty is increased among the working class by having one's origin in the working class. The differences according to social origin are quite substantial and the risk of still remaining

FIGURE 4.6
Persistence of Poverty among Working-Class Persons by Social Origin, Sweden, 1991–2000

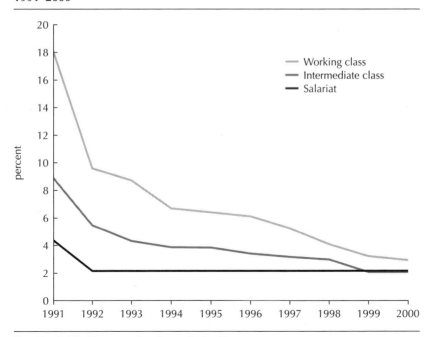

Note: Threshold is 60 percent of median equivalized income.

in poverty in the year 2000 is nearly 50 percent higher for those from working-class origins than for those from intermediate class origins.

Do Poverty Dynamics Depend on the Poverty Measure?

Poverty dynamics are generally measured in relation to relative income thresholds, derived as proportions of mean or median income in the country in question. This is the conventional approach adopted in most comparative studies and the one we have concentrated on up to this point. Poverty thresholds can be established on a different basis and poverty dynamics measured in other ways, however, and we now look at how much difference this could make to cross-country patterns of poverty dynamics.

One option is to focus on mobility out of decile- or quintile-based groups, as is common in income mobility studies. In other words, we could consider the bottom 10 percent or 20 percent of the distribution to be "poor," and measure how many remain in or escape from the bottom of the distribution over time. The picture this conveys can differ in some important respects from that provided by conventional relative income poverty thresholds. This can be demonstrated by reference to some of the results presented by Ayala and Sastre (2004), shown in table 4.1. The right-hand data column shows the percentage remaining in the bottom of the income distribution, defined as the bottom 30 percent. The left-hand data column shows persistence when the bottom group is defined instead as those below 75 percent of mean equivalized disposable income.

TABLE 4.1

Percentage Remaining in Bottom Income Group over Five Years, Alternative Approaches, Selected EU Countries and United States, 1990s

Country	Percentage remaining in "bottom" disposable household income group over 5 years	
	Below 75% of mean income	Below the third decile
France	48.7	31.6
Germany	38.3	32.1
Italy	45.3	29.7
Spain	46.4	26.5
United Kingdom	37.6	26.6
United States	52.3	27.4

Source: Ayala and Sastre 2004, 69, table 5.

The most striking difference is in the position of the United States. As noted earlier, the United States is not distinctive compared with other countries in terms of overall income mobility. In terms of mobility out of the bottom three decile groups it has, if anything, more escaping and a lower percentage remaining than, for example, France or Germany. If we look at the percentage remaining below the 75 percent threshold, on the other hand, the United States is indeed distinctive: it has a considerably higher percentage remaining below that threshold than the other countries covered.

This comes about simply because the United States has a much higher proportion of its population falling below the median-based threshold than the other countries, whereas the proportion in the bottom 30 percent is of course the same in all countries. For the purpose of illustration, suppose that the percentage of the population moving from below to above a particular income threshold (whether median- or decile-based) from one period to the next is actually the same in each country. These "escapers" will represent the same proportion of the bottom 30 percent in each country, but a much smaller share of those below the median-based threshold in the country where the number below that threshold is itself high. So drawing conclusions relating to poverty dynamics from results relating to income mobility from the bottom (as usually measured in income mobility studies) can be misleading, particularly when comparing a country with a particularly high relative income poverty rate such as the United States with others that have much lower poverty rates.

While exits from the bottom decile or quintile group may be hazardous as measures of poverty dynamics, that does not mean that relative income thresholds are unambiguously satisfactory for that purpose. As noted, low income is imperfectly related to deprivation and changes in income may not have an immediate impact on deprivation and exclusion, so it is important to try to capture the dynamics of deprivation as well as income over time (see, for example, Whelan et al. 2001, 2003; Whelan, Layte, and Maitre 2004). More fundamentally, the use of a purely relative threshold may not be universally accepted as the best way to measure poverty over time.

While standards of adequacy change over time as general living standards in the society rise, some may wish to take improving real living standards and falling deprivation levels into account at least to some extent in measuring both the evolution of poverty levels and poverty dynamics. At the extreme, a poverty threshold that is held fixed in purchasing power terms and rises only in line with prices, such as the official poverty threshold in the United States, can be used. Over a period where any significant growth in real incomes toward the bottom is seen, this will convey a very different picture of poverty dynamics than a purely relative threshold.

This can be seen most dramatically in a country experiencing very rapid increases in incomes and living standards, such as Ireland from the mid-1990s onward. Table 4.2 shows cross-sectional poverty rates for Ireland for 1994–2000 on two different bases. With purely relative income poverty lines, set at 50 percent or 60 percent of equivalized disposable income, we see that poverty rose substantially over this period in Ireland. But if the poverty line is set at 50 percent or 60 percent of the 1994 median and subsequently increased only in line with consumer prices—if the poverty line is "anchored"—then we see a substantial decline in poverty.

Low incomes grew at a slower rate than higher incomes, but substantially faster than prices. In particular, social transfers rose substantially in real terms, so pensioners, for example, saw their living standards improve markedly, though they still lagged behind rapidly rising incomes from employment and profits. In such circumstances poverty dynamics as well as poverty rates will look very different depending on the approach adopted: with the anchored approach, most of those in income poverty in 1994 will have exited by 2000. That absolute and relative thresholds can give different pictures of how poverty changes is a point more generally made by Ravallion (2003) in a discussion of change in developing countries. Clearly both the absolute and the conventional relative income approach contain important and relevant information, but neither on its own tells the full story.

In this context, Amartya Sen's (1993) highly influential concept of "capabilities" has served to bring out that the goods required to allow for particular

TABLE 4.2
Alternative Cross-sectional Poverty Measures, Ireland, 1994–2000

	50% of median		60% of median	
Period	Relative poverty line	Anchored poverty line	Relative poverty line	Anchored poverty line
1994	11.9	11.9	20.4	20.4
1995	12.9	11.1	20.8	19.2
1996	12.3	8.5	21.8	16.6
2000	16.5	3.5	22.7	9.0
Percentage change 1994–2000	+38.7	−70.6	+11.3	−55.9

Source: Munzi, Nolan, and Smeeding 2005, box 3.

"functionings" may be very different in a rich than in a poor society. Thus, in industrial countries, as living standards rise, societal standards about what is regarded as adequate will also evolve. That will not necessarily be captured by relative income and purely relative poverty thresholds. Various studies in both Europe and North America have sought to employ nonmonetary indicators of deprivation in order to tap directly into what people with low income can and cannot afford to do—and how that compares with what people regard as "adequate" or as "necessities" (see, for example, Liebfried 1993, Mayer 1993, and Nolan and Whelan 1996). This is beyond the scope of the present chapter, but it needs to be kept in mind in interpreting the evidence about income poverty dynamics.

Of course, income mobility and income poverty dynamics are measured with error, particularly in the household surveys on which most comparative studies rely. The scale of this error may indeed be substantial, and this could lead to a significant exaggeration of mobility and understatement of the persistence of poverty. Several recent studies have sought to model and assess the role of measurement error in poverty dynamics and have concluded that it is substantial.[18] Breen and Moisio (2004) use latent class mover-stayer models to correct for measurement error in estimates of the dynamics of relative income poverty in 10 EU countries measured over four waves of the ECHP. Poverty rates then show less variation across countries and less mobility over time. Rendtel, Langeheine, and Bernstein (1998), using a latent Markov chain model, suggest that almost half the observed income poverty mobility in the German Socio-Economic Panel could be accounted for by measurement error. Whelan and Maitre's (2006) results on poverty persistence in the ECHP, taking measurement error into account, suggest that the broad comparative picture across countries is not affected: there remains a pronounced variation in persistence between Denmark at one extreme and Portugal at the other.

The extent to which household surveys overstate mobility compared with data from administrative registers available for the Scandinavian countries has been directly examined by Basic and Rendtel (2004), who compare five waves of ECHP data for Finland with register data over the same period. The results show that much of the observed movement into and out of poverty in the survey data reflects measurement error, and this has a much greater impact than attrition bias in the longitudinal survey (which tends to receive much more attention from researchers). While these studies suggest that the extent of mobility is overstated, the broad patterns of poverty dynamics across countries may still be reasonably robust.

Conclusions

This chapter has focused on intragenerational income mobility and poverty dynamics in industrial countries, aiming to review and add to what is known about these mobility processes. While a range of studies of income mobility and poverty dynamics have now been carried out, a reliable and comprehensive comparative picture is still emerging.

Income poverty was seen to be both fluid and characterized by long-term persistence. Looking at poverty dynamics over a three-year period, the percentage of those below an income threshold of 50 percent of the median in one year who had escaped by the next year ranged from 30 percent in the United States up to 60 percent in Denmark. Countries with high cross-sectional poverty rates tended to have low escape rates and vice versa, though there were exceptions. Using five waves of data for countries in the EU-15 and a threshold set at 60 percent of median, most countries were clustered around an exit rate of about 50 percent over that length of time. However, while many spells in poverty are short and represent only transitory setbacks, the typical year in poverty is lived by someone who experiences multiple years of poverty and whose long-term income is below the income poverty threshold on average. Many of those who exit poverty in a given year reenter it within a short time. Thus there is more persistence than just looking at the length of individual spells in poverty would suggest.

The relationship between poverty dynamics and overall income mobility is complex. While the United States appears to be an outlier in terms of poverty dynamics,.with a particularly low level of escapes and a correspondingly high level of persistence of income poverty, in terms of overall income mobility the United States appears similar to other industrial countries. This, it should be noted, still contradicts the frequently advanced notion that in the United States the exceptionally high level of cross-sectional income inequality is offset by higher levels of income mobility than in other industrial countries.

Turning to long-term stability and change of individual positions in the income distribution, comparison over a six- to eight-year period showed exit rates from poverty to be lower and persistence higher in the United States than in Canada, Germany, and the United Kingdom, with the most pronounced difference being for the retirement-age population. Data from administrative registers for Sweden allowed income mobility from the early years of the 1990s to the end of that decade to be examined. For the cohort born between 1940 and 1961, few left poverty from 1992 to 1998. In terms of mobility more broadly, their incomes were quite stable and changes mostly small, with those at either extreme of the income distribution particularly likely to be immobile. For older cohorts, there was a high level of persistence in the bottom one-third of the distribution over that period.

The character of the welfare regime—social democratic, corporatist, liberal, and "southern"—does not provide a consistent explanation for differences in poverty transition patterns in the EU. However, the United States' and Canada's less-developed liberal welfare regimes and very high levels of poverty persistence do fit the expected pattern.

The broad comparative picture across countries may not be affected by errors in measuring income, but such errors may cause survey data to overstate the frequency of poverty exits and understate poverty persistence. This makes the examination of income mobility and poverty dynamics using register data, of the sort we have been able to employ for Sweden, valuable.

Changes in the labor market situation of household members and in household structure are critical in "driving" poverty entries and escapes, with the latter more important in the United States than in European countries. The persistence of poverty also varies substantially between persons and households with varying characteristics. Age and gender of the household head, educational attainment, the number of workers in the household at the outset, and family composition have a substantial impact both on poverty exits and on the likelihood of being persistently poor. Analysis of three or five years of panel data for various OECD countries showed that exit rates were affected most by the education of the household head, whereas the risk of persistent poverty was affected most by the number of workers in the household.

The way income poverty is defined and measured can also affect measured poverty dynamics. The conventional approach adopted in most comparative studies is to employ relative income thresholds, but an alternative is to focus on mobility out of the bottom decile or quintile group. The latter reduces measured differences across countries in poverty persistence and escapes, in effect assuming away differences in the underlying level of poverty, and is therefore hazardous as a basis for conclusions about poverty dynamics. Another option is to use a poverty threshold that is fixed in purchasing power terms and rises only in line with prices, such as the official poverty threshold in the United States. Over a period where there has been significant growth in real incomes among those with lower incomes, this will convey a very different picture of poverty dynamics than a purely relative threshold.

Clearly each different approach produces relevant information, and none tells the full story alone. This highlights the complexity of the underlying concept of poverty. Exploring what those on low income can and cannot afford to do—their capacity to participate in their society—complements what is learned by studying income mobility and income poverty dynamics.

Annex 4.1 Background Data

Tables 4.A through 4.D present the background data and sources underlying figures 4.1 and 4.2, including a broader coverage of EU countries, as well as the data and sources for figure 4.3.

ANNEX TABLE 4.A
Poverty Rates, Exit Rates, and Poverty Persistence in the European Union, Canada, and the United States, 1993–95, 50 Percent Threshold

Country	Annual poverty rate (%)	Yearly exit rate (%)	Ever poor (% poor at least once)	Always poor (%)	Always poor as % of ever poor
Belgium	9.8	48.2	16.0	2.8	17.5
Denmark	4.7	60.4	9.1	0.8	8.8
France	9.6	46.9	16.6	3.0	18.1
Germany	12.1	41.1	19.2	4.3	22.4
Greece	14.5	38.8	25.1	6.5	25.9
Ireland	8.2	54.6	15.3	1.3	8.5
Italy	13.5	40.6	21.5	5.6	26.0
Luxembourg	7.8	47.4	12.7	2.2	17.3
Netherlands	7.8	55.7	12.9	1.6	12.4
Portugal	15.3	37.0	24.2	7.8	32.2
Spain	12.0	49.6	21.3	3.7	17.3
United Kingdom	12.1	58.8	19.5	2.4	12.3
ECHP average	*11.7*	*46.1*	*19.2*	*3.8*	*19.8*
Canada	10.9	36.4	18.1	5.1	28.2
United States (1987–89)	16.0	29.5	23.5	9.5	40.4

Source: OECD 2001, 45, 50, tables 2.1 and 2.2. Data are derived from ECHP waves 1–3, except Canada and United States from SLID and PSID respectively.

ANNEX TABLE 4.B
Poverty Persistence in the European Union, Canada, and the United States, 1993–95, 60 Percent Threshold

Country	Ever poor (% poor at least once)	Always poor (%)	Always poor as % of ever poor
Belgium	23.5	5.8	24.7
Denmark	15.9	2.6	16.3
France	25.7	7.3	28.4
Germany	26.1	7.1	27.2
Greece	33.2	10.7	32.2
Ireland	29.8	7.8	26.2
Italy	30.9	10.3	33.3
Luxembourg	22.9	7.2	31.4
Netherlands	20.1	4.3	21.4
Portugal	32.1	12.4	38.6
Spain	31.0	8.3	26.8
United Kingdom	28.2	6.3	22.3
ECHP average	*27.7*	*7.7*	*27.8*
Canada	25.6	9.5	37.1
United States(1987–89)	30.4	14.3	47.0

Source: OECD 2001, 82–83, table 2.B.1, derived from ECHP waves 1–3, except Canada and United States from SLID and PSID respectively.

ANNEX TABLE 4.C
Income Poverty Dynamics in the European Union, 1993–97

Country	% of those below threshold in 1993 exiting by:		
	1994	*1995*	*1997*
Belgium	40.3	47.3	50.6
Denmark	41.4	51.1	51.1
France	40.9	47.8	50.7
Germany	43.0	47.1	55.9
Greece	40.1	44.0	49.9
Ireland	25.6	32.6	45.7
Italy	37.6	45.5	51.6
Netherlands	37.1	45.4	60.9
Portugal	28.8	37.1	42.7
Spain	40.5	48.8	50.1
United Kingdom	32.2	46.3	49.8

Source: Authors' calculations based on ECHP User Data Base micro-data.

Note: Threshold is 60 percent of median equivalized income.

ANNEX TABLE 4.D
Poverty Rates and Poverty Persistence in Germany, the United Kingdom,
Canada, and the United States over Six or Eight Years

Country	Annual poverty rate (%)	Ever poor (% poor at least once)	Always poor (%)	Always poor as % of ever poor
Germany (1990–97)	9.6	17.4	1.0	5.6
United Kingdom (1990–97)	15.1	31.2	2.2	7.1
Canada (1993–98)	11.5	23.8	3.0	12.6
United States (1987–89)	16.8	34.0	4.5	13.2

Source: OECD 2001, table 2.9, derived from CNEF.

Note: Threshold is 50 percent of median equivalized income.

Annex 4.2 Income Mobility in Sweden

This annex gives details of our analysis of income mobility from the early to the late 1990s in Sweden, the results of which were summarized above. Income refers to disposable income adjusted for the size of the family. To even out some of the volatility of income, we use averages over three years (1991–93 and 1997–99), but for convenience we refer to these periods as 1992 and 1998 respectively.

We first divide the sample into 10 groups using income thresholds derived as proportions of the median disposable income in the respective years. Thus the top group had a disposable income above 190 percent of the median, the second group had an income between 190 and 160 percent of the median, and the bottom three groups had incomes between 60 and 50 percent, between 50 and 40 percent, and below 40 percent of the median. Using these median-based income categories we look at changes over time in the location of individuals, cross-tabulating location in the earlier period with location in the later one.

Table 4.E reports outflows from and into each income category from the early to the late 1990s among people born between 1940 and 1961. We see what can be thought of as a mountain ridge along the main diagonal, sloping down evenly on both sides. The numbers are highest in the northwest and southeast corners of the table, that is, at the tails of the income distribution. (If we compare the observed number of cases in the cells of the tables with the numbers expected under independence between incomes in the two years, we find the greatest divergences in the same two corners.)

ANNEX TABLE 4.E

Income Mobility in Sweden 1992–98, for Men and Women Born 1940–61

percent

1992 income as multiple of median	1998 income as multiple of median											
	1.9–	1.6-1.9	1.4-1.6	1.2-1.4	1.0-1.2	0.8-1.0	0.6-0.8	0.5-0.6	0.4-0.5	-0.4	Total	N
1.9–	**64**	19	11	2	2	2	0	0	0	0	100	115
1.6-1.9	15	**35**	27	12	7	2	3	0	0	0	100	103
1.4-1.6	8	18	**26**	27	12	5	4	1	0	0	100	237
1.2-1.4	3	7	13	**34**	31	8	3	2	0	0	100	400
1.0-1.2	1	3	6	15	**39**	28	6	1	1	0	100	599
0.8-1.0	2	1	3	8	19	**35**	25	3	3	1	100	719
0.6-0.8	0	0	1	3	9	27	**41**	15	4	2	100	387
0.5-0.6	1	0	1	2	3	11	34	**28**	15	6	100	179
0.4-0.5	0	0	1	1	0	3	21	25	**26**	22	100	89
– 0.4	3	0	0	0	3	5	9	11	21	**49**	100	80
All	5	5	7	13	20	21	17	6	4	3	100	2,908

Source: Author's analysis.

If we look at the poor or near-poor, that is, the three last rows and the three last columns in the table where incomes are less than 60 percent of the median, we see that few people left poverty in the six-year period from 1992 to 1998. Of those who had a total disposable income below 40 percent of the median in 1992, 80 percent still had incomes below 60 percent of the median in 1998. Also those in the category of less severe poverty (with incomes between 40 and 50 percent of the median) remained as poor or near-poor after six years, as only somewhat more than 25 percent in 1998 had incomes over 60 percent of the median. Those at the other end of the income distribution, say with incomes above 160 percent of the median in 1992, seem on the whole to have been able to remain in the high-income brackets, since around two-thirds still had incomes in the same area of the income distribution in 1998. The basic message is that incomes on the whole were fairly stable in Sweden in the 1990s and that income change mostly concerned rather small increases or losses.

In table 4.F we report the results of a similar analysis for older cohorts, born between 1920 and 1939. A comparison with table 4.7 confirms that fewer older persons remained in the six highest income categories, while many more remained in the three lowest categories. Around 29 percent of those born in the period 1920–39 had incomes below 60 percent of the median in 1998, while the corresponding percentage among those born in the period 1940–61 was 13 percent. The difference between the two age groups in the percentage having low incomes was much smaller in 1992: 15 percent in the older group compared to 12 percent in the younger.

Table 4.G looks at income change over a long period by comparing incomes in 1967 to incomes in 2000. In this table we are comparing the incomes of people who in the earlier year were in the ages 30 to 61, while the income in 2000 was acquired when they were ages 63 to 84. Thus, while the early incomes mostly come from work, the later incomes for the most part consist of pensions and other transfers.

It is clear from this table that the change from employment to retirement still has considerable effects on the income distribution and on the risk of falling into poverty. Thus, Rowntree's (1901) "life cycle of poverty" seems to operate as well in the late welfare state of Sweden. In 2000 less than 20 percent of those born 1916 to 1937 had an income above the median among those of working age, and around 40 percent had a disposable income that placed them in near-poverty or below (below 60 percent of the median). Only among those who were in the highest income bracket in 1967 was the median income about the same as for the working-age population. The

ANNEX TABLE 4.F

Income Mobility in Sweden 1992–98, for Men and Women Born 1920–39

percent

1992 income as multiple of median	1998 income as multiple of median											
	1.9–	1.6–1.9	1.4–1.6	1.2–1.4	1.0–1.2	0.8–1.0	0.6–0.8	0.5–0.6	0.4–0.5	–0.4	Total	N
1.9–	**41**	19	10	19	6	3	1	0	1	0	100	70
1.6–1.9	7	**13**	30	33	13	2	0	0	2	0	100	46
1.4–1.6	4	12	**12**	33	28	7	3	1	0	0	100	94
1.2–1.4	2	3	5	**21**	39	19	8	1	1	0	100	173
1.0–1.2	1	0	1	7	**27**	40	18	4	2	0	100	329
0.8–1.0	0	1	0	2	5	**26**	49	8	6	3	100	507
0.6–0.8	0	0	1	1	1	3	**43**	31	12	9	100	366
0.5–0.6	0	0	1	0	2	5	16	**35**	26	16	100	177
0.4–0.5	0	0	0	0	0	0	10	19	**41**	30	100	70
– 0.4	2	0	0	2	0	2	2	2	29	**59**	100	41
All	2	2	3	7	12	17	28	13	9	6	100	1,873

Source: Author's analysis.

ANNEX TABLE 4.G

Income Mobility in Sweden 1967–2000, for Men and Women Born 1916–37

percent

1967 income as multiple of median	2000 income as multiple of median										Total	N
	1.9–	1.6-1.9	1.4-1.6	1.2-1.4	1.0-1.2	0.8-1.0	0.6-0.8	0.5-0.6	0.4-0.5	-0.4		
1.9–	**10**	11	3	16	10	21	18	4	3	3	100	97
1.6-1.9	7	**1**	3	8	9	22	32	10	3	6	100	120
1.4-1.6	2	2	**2**	4	4	14	37	20	9	5	100	168
1.2-1.4	3	3	2	**6**	6	13	31	20	9	7	100	193
1.0-1.2	2	1	4	3	**9**	12	26	20	12	11	100	293
0.8-1.0	1	0	1	4	10	**16**	26	24	8	10	100	333
0.6-0.8	1	0	2	3	6	15	**26**	23	13	11	100	360
0.5-0.6	1	0	0	0	1	14	24	**22**	20	19	100	111
0.4-0.5	2	0	0	2	2	8	21	27	**17**	23	100	66
– 0.4	0	0	0	0	0	0	10	36	26	**29**	100	42
All	2	2	2	4	7	14	27	21	11	10	100	1,783

Source: Author's analysis.

association between the income in 1967 and that in 2000 is considerable, in spite of the overall decline in income, and it comes as no surprise that many of those with low incomes in 1967 had fallen into poverty by 2000.

For each half of the income distribution, then, the tables show the highest figures in the main diagonal cells—that is, the lowest mobility—for those with the highest and lowest incomes. Does this indicate that it is more difficult to leave a state of poverty than to leave other positions in the income distribution, and that those with the highest incomes are generally protected from sliding down the income distribution? An alternative explanation could be that the lowest and highest income categories are open in the sense that there are no lower or upper limits, respectively, to them (Atkinson, Maynard, and Trinder 1983). We can test which of these two explanations is most compatible with the data by applying loglinear models to several transition tables. By means of such models it is possible to describe the pattern of interaction in a mobility matrix. If there are "poverty traps" and "affluence traps," we should find particularly strong interactions in the immobility cells for the lowest and highest income groups. The actual tests are quite complex and details are available from the authors, but the implications of results are discussed here.

We look in the estimated models at the parameters for interaction in the cells including those who remain in poverty or in affluence, in a table where the income categories are divided by percentages of the median. For the period 1992–98 for those born between 1940 and 1961 these clearly are not significant for any of the relevant cells. Thus, a tentative conclusion is that it does not seem to be more difficult to move from poverty to other income categories than to move between these latter categories in that period. This result is again found when we look at income mobility over the whole of the 1990s, that is from 1991 to 2000. However, when we look at income mobility among cohorts born earlier than the mid-1930s and income mobility in periods before 1990 we do find tendencies toward "stickiness" in the lower part of the income distribution. Thus, for income mobility from 1967 to 1980, immobility parameters for those below 40 percent or 60 percent of the median are significant. For income mobility from 1980 to 1991, the immobility parameter for those below 40 percent of the median again turns out to be significant. Likewise, when income mobility over longer periods, 1967–2000 and 1980–2000, is analyzed, we find significant immobility parameters.

In sum, the results are not completely consistent across cohorts and periods. There may be a weak tendency toward stickiness in the extremes of the Swedish income distribution, or conditions may have changed so that this was the case in the period before but not after 1990. Sweden is of course also a rather specific case, with a highly developed welfare state and social protection system, so it is not clear whether similar results would be expected in other countries.

Notes

1. See Solon (1992); Zimmerman (1992); Solon (2002); Corak (2006); Björklund and Jäntti (1997); Bratberg, Nilsen, and Vaage (2005); Bonke, Hussain, and Munk (2005); and several of the contributions to Corak (2004). Chadwick and Solon (2002) are unusual in studying earnings of parents and daughters.
2. Mazumdar (2005) finds that when misreporting of income and the transitory component in current income are taken into account, the intergenerational correlation is higher in the United States, perhaps close to 0.6.
3. Administrative register data provide an alternative resource but only for a small number of countries.
4. See in particular OECD (2001), Whelan et al. (2001), and Layte and Whelan (2002).
5. Stevens (1999) shows how poverty reentry probabilities as well as exits might be combined to examine the implications for total poverty experienced over a period, but this has not been widely applied.
6. See OECD (2001). The ECHP began in 1994 but the reference period for income was the previous calendar year.
7. Erikson and Goldthorpe (1985) and Ferrie (2005) do not find the United States exceptional in terms of current class mobility compared with other industrialized countries.
8. See also Aaberge et al. (2002) comparing the United States with the Scandinavian countries.
9. Information on the Level of Living Survey can be found in Erikson and Åberg (1987) and Jonsson and Mills (2001).
10. The actual tests are of a rather technical nature, and an annex presenting these results is available from the authors.
11. See, for example, Ferrera (1996), Gallie and Paugam (2000), and Arts and Gelissen (2002).
12. Individual country studies include Jarvis and Jenkins (1997) and Jenkins and Rigg (2001) for the United Kingdom, Cantó (2003) for Spain, Muffels (2000) for the Netherlands, Schluter (1997) for Germany, and van Kerm (1998) for Belgium. Cross-country studies using data from the ECHP include OECD (2001), Whelan et al. (2000), Layte and Whelan (2002), and Fouarge and Layte (2005).
13. The arrival of a child could clearly have a long-term impact on parental behavior and thus on household income, but we are looking here purely at the immediate arithmetic impact of having another mouth to feed.
14. Another study confined to the ECHP but using five waves of data (Layte and Whelan 2003) confirmed that most poverty transitions there were associated

with job- and income-related events rather than with changes in household size and composition.

15. The salariat consists of higher professional and managerial occupations as well as larger employers. The intermediate class consists of lower managerial and white-collar workers, routine nonmanual occupations, small employers, and self-employed persons. The working class includes skilled and unskilled workers. The class position of the household is determined by the "dominant" position in the family (Erikson 1984; Erikson and Goldthorpe 1992).

16. The seemingly high variation at the end of the 1990s between men and women in the salariat should not be given any substantial interpretation since the number of cases is very low.

17. We here restrict the exposition to members of the working class in order to have sufficient numbers.

18. As already noted, in the analysis of intergenerational mobility Mazumdar (2005) seeks to correct for measurement error and finds considerably higher correlation between the earnings of fathers and sons.

References

Aaberge, R, A. Björklund, M. Jäntti, M. Palme, P. Pedersen, N. Smith, and T. Wennemo. 2002. "Income Inequality and Income Mobility in the Scandinavian Countries Compared to the United States." *Review of Income and Wealth* 48 (4): 443–69.

Alesina, A., and E. Glaeser. 2004. *Fighting Poverty in the U.S. and Europe: A World of Difference.* New York: Oxford University Press.

Arts, W., and J. Gelissen. 2002. "Three Worlds of Welfare Capitalism or More?" *Journal of European Social Policy* 12 (2): 137–58

Atkinson, A. B., A. K. Maynard, and C. G. Trinder. 1983. *Parents and Children: Incomes in Two Generations.* London: Heinemann.

Ayala, L., and M. Sastre. 2004. "Europe Versus the United States: Is There a Trade-Off between Mobility and Inequality?" *Journal of Income Distribution* 13 (1–2): 56–75.

Bane, M. J., and D. T. Ellwood. 1986. "Slipping Into and Out of Poverty." *Journal of Human Resources* 21: 1–23.

Basic, E., and R. Rendtel. 2004. "Latent Markov Chain Analysis of Income States with the European Community Household Panel: Empirical Results on Measurement Error and Attrition Bias." Paper presented at the Second International Conference of ECHP Users-EPUNet, Berlin, June 23–26.

Björklund, A., and M. Jäntti. 1997. "Intergenerational Income Mobility in Sweden Compared to the United States." *American Economic Review* 87: 1009–18.

Bonke, J., M. A. Hussain, and M. D. Munk. 2005. "A Comparison of Danish and International Findings on Intergenerational Earnings Mobility." Working Paper 11:2005, Danish National Institute of Social Research (SKI), Copenhagen.

Bonoli, G. 1997. "Classifying Welfare States: A Two-Dimensional Approach." *Journal of Social Policy* 26 (3): 351–72.

Bowles, S., and H. Gintis. 2002. "The Inheritance of Inequality." *Journal of Economic Perspectives* 26: 3–30.

Bratberg E., O. Nilsen, and K. Vaage. 2005. "Intergenerational Earnings Mobility in Norway: Levels and Trends." *Scandinavian Journal of Economics* 107 (3): 419–35.

Breen, R., and J. O. Jonsson. 2005. "Inequality of Opportunity in Comparative Perspective: Recent Research on Educational Attainment and Social Mobility." *Annual Review of Sociology* 31, 223–43.

Breen, R., and P. Moisio. 2004. "Overestimated Poverty Mobility: Poverty Dynamics Corrected for Measurement Error." *Journal of Economic Inequality* 2 (3): 171–91.

Burkhauser, R. V., and J. Poupore. 1997. "A Cross-National Comparison of Permanent Inequality in the United States and Germany." *Review of Economics and Statistics* 79 (1): 10–18.

Cantó, O. 2003. "Finding Out the Routes to Escape Poverty: The Relevance of Demographic vs. Labor Market Events in Spain." *Review of Income and Wealth* 49 (4): 569–88.

Chadwick, L., and G. Solon. 2002. "Intergenerational Income Mobility Among Daughters." *American Economic Review* 92 (1): 335–44.

Corak, M., ed. 2004. *Generational Income Mobility in North America and Europe.* Cambridge: Cambridge University Press.

———. 2006. "Do Poor Children Become Poor Adults? Lessons from a Cross Country Comparison of Generational Earnings Mobility." Discussion Paper 1993, Institute for the Study of Labor (IZA), Bonn.

Duncan, G., B. Gustafsson, R. Hauser, G. Schmaus, S. Jenkins, H. Messinger, R. Muffels, B. Nolan, J-C. Ray, and W. Voges. 1995. "Poverty and Social-Assistance Dynamics in the United States, Canada and Western Europe." In *Poverty, Inequality and the Future of Social Policy: Western States in the New World Order,* ed. K. McFate, R. Lawson, and W. J. Wilson, 67–108. New York: Russell Sage Foundation.

Duncan, G., B. Gustafsson, R. Hauser, G. Schmaus, H. Messinger, R. Muffels, B. Nolan, and J-C. Ray. 1993. "Poverty Dynamics in Eight Countries." *Journal of Population Economics* 6 (3): 215–34.

Erikson, R. 1984. "Social Class of Men, Women and Families." *Sociology* 18: 500–14.

Erikson, R., and R. Åberg, eds. 1987. *Welfare in Transition.* Oxford: Clarendon Press.

Erikson, R., and J. H. Goldthorpe. 1985. "Are American Rates of Social Mobility Exceptionally High? New Evidence on an Old Issue." *European Sociological Review:* 1–22.

———. 1992. *The Constant Flux: A Study of Class Mobility in Industrial Societies.* Oxford: Clarendon Press.

Esping-Andersen, G. 1990. *The Three Worlds of Welfare Capitalism.* Cambridge: Polity Press.

Ferrera, M. 1996. "The Southern Welfare State in Social Europe." *Journal of European Social Policy* 6 (1): 17–37.

Ferrie, Joseph P. 2005. "The End of American Exceptionalism? Mobility in the U.S. Since 1850." *Journal of Economic Perspectives* 19 (3): 199–215.

Fouarge, D., and R. Layte. 2005. "Welfare Regimes and Poverty Dynamics: The Duration and Recurrence of Poverty Spells in Europe." *Journal of Social Policy* 34: 1–20.

Fritzell, J. 1990. "The Dynamics of Income Distribution: Economic Mobility in Sweden in Comparison with the United States." *Social Science Research* 19 (1): 17–46.

Gallie, D., and S. Paugam, eds. 2000. *Welfare Regimes and the Experience of Unemployment in Europe.* Oxford: Oxford University Press.

Goodin, R. E., B. Headey, R. Muffels, and H. J. Dirven. 1999. *The Real Worlds of Welfare Capitalism.* Cambridge: Cambridge University Press.

Jarvis, S., and S. P. Jenkins. 1997. "Low Income Dynamics in 1990s." *Fiscal Studies* 18: 1–20.

Jenkins, S. P., and A. Rigg. 2001. *The Dynamics of Poverty in Britain.* DWP Research Report 157. London: Department for Work and Pensions.

Jonsson, J. O., and C. Mills, eds. 2001. *Cradle to Grave: Life-Course Change in Modern Sweden.* Durham, NC: Sociologypress.

Layte, R., B. Maitre, B. Nolan, and C. T. Whelan. 2001. "Poverty Dynamics: An Analysis of the 1994 and 1995 Waves of the European Community Household Panel Survey." *European Societies* 2 (4): 505–31.

Layte, R., and C. T. Whelan. 2002. "The Dynamics of Income Poverty Risk." In *European Social Statistics: Income, Poverty and Social Exclusion: 2nd Report—Data 1994–1997,* ed. European Data Service, chap. 5. Luxembourg: European Communities.

———. 2003. "Moving In and Out of Poverty: The Impact of Welfare Regimes on Poverty Dynamics in the EU." *European Societies* 5 (2): 167–91.

Liebfried, S. 1993. "Towards a European Welfare State?" In *New Perspectives on the Welfare State in Europe,* ed. C. Jones, 133–56. London: Routledge.

Mayer, S. 1993. "Living Conditions among the Poor in Four Rich Countries." *Journal of Population Economics* 6: 261–86.

Mazumdar, B. 2005. "The Apple Falls Even Closer to the Tree than We Thought: New and Revised Estimates of the Intergenerational Inheritance of Earnings." In *Unequal Chances: Family Background and Economic Success,* ed. S. Bowles, H. Gintis, and M. Osborne Groves, 80–89. Princeton, NJ: Princeton University Press.

Muffels, R. 2000. "Dynamics of Poverty and the Determinants of Poverty Transitions: Results from the Dutch Socio-economic Panel." In *Researching Social and Economic Change,* ed. D. Rose, 165–87. London: Routledge.

Nolan, B., and C. T. Whelan. 1996. *Resources, Deprivation and Poverty.* Oxford: Clarendon Press.

OECD (Organisation for Economic Co-operation and Development). 2001. "When Money Is Tight: Poverty Dynamics in OECD Countries." In *Employment Outlook 2001,* chap. 2. Paris: OECD.

Ravallion, M. 2003. "The Debate on Globalization, Poverty and Inequality: Why Measurement Matters." *International Affairs* 79: 739–53.

Rendtel, U., R. Langeheine, and R. Bernstein. 1998. "The Estimation of Poverty Dynamics Using Different Household Income Measures." *Review of Income and Wealth* 44: 81–98.

Rowntree, S. 1901. *Poverty: A Study of Town Life.* London: Macmillan.

Schluter, C. 1997. "On the Non-stationarity of German Income Mobility (and Some Observations on Poverty Dynamics)." DARP Discussion Paper 30, London School of Economics.

———. 1998. "Income Dynamics in the USA, Germany and the UK." Paper presented at European Meeting of the Econometric Society, Berlin, September.

Sen, A. 1993. "Capability and Well-Being." In *The Quality of Life*, ed. M. Nussbaum and A. Sen, 30–53. Oxford: Clarendon Press.

Solon, G. 1992. "Intergenerational Income Mobility in the United States." *American Economic Review* 82: 393–408.

———. 2002. "Cross-country Differences in Intergenerational Earnings Mobility." *Journal of Economic Perspectives* 16 (3): 59–66.

Stevens, A. H. 1999. "Climbing Out of Poverty, Falling Back In: Measuring the Persistence of Poverty over Multiple Spells." *Journal of Human Resources* 34 (3): 557–88.

Titmuss, R. M. 1973. "What Is Social Policy." In *Social Policy*, ed. B. Abel-Smith and K. Titmuss, 23–32. London: George Allen and Unwin.

Valletta, R. G. 2004. "The Ins and Outs of Poverty in Advanced Economies: Poverty Dynamics in Canada, Germany, Great Britain, and the United States." Working Papers in Applied Economic Theory 2004–18, Federal Reserve Bank of San Francisco.

van Kerm, P. 1998. "Low Income Turnover in Wallonia." Facultés Universitaires Notre-Dame de la Paix, Namur, Belgium.

Whelan, C. T., R. Layte, and B. Maitre. 2004. "Understanding the Mismatch Between Income Poverty and Deprivation: A Dynamic Comparative Analysis." *European Sociological Review* 20 (4): 287–301.

Whelan, C. T., R. Layte, B. Maitre, and B. Nolan. 2000. "Poverty Dynamics: An Analysis of the 1994 and 1995 Waves of the ECHP." *European Societies* 2 (4): 505–31.

———. 2003. "Persistent Income Poverty and Deprivation in the European Union." *Journal of Social Policy* 32 (1): 1–32.

Whelan, C. T., R. Layte, B. Nolan, and B. Maitre. 2001. "Income, Deprivation and Economic Strain." *European Sociological Review* 17 (4): 357–72.

Whelan, C. T., and B. Maitre. 2006. "Comparing Poverty and Deprivation Dynamics: Issues of Reliability and Validity." *Journal of Economic Inequality* 4 (3): 303–23.

Wu, K. B. 2003. *Poverty Experience of Older Persons: A Poverty Study from a Long-Term Perspective*. Washington, DC: AARP Public Policy Institute.

Zimmerman, D. J. 1992. "Regression Toward Mediocrity in Economic Stature." *American Economic Review* 82: 409–36.

5

Escaping Poverty and Becoming Poor in Three States of India, with Additional Evidence from Kenya, Uganda, and Peru

Anirudh Krishna

As some households are coming out of poverty, other households are concurrently falling into poverty. New poverty is being created even as some old poverty is destroyed.

To capture this complex process, the Stages of Progress methodology was developed to examine movements out of and into poverty at the grassroots level. Applied to a sample of rural communities in India, Kenya, Uganda, and Peru, and tracking poverty dynamics for more than 30,000 households, this bottom-up methodology revealed that escape from poverty and descent into poverty have occurred simultaneously in every village. Indeed, even quite well-to-do households have fallen into abiding poverty in some cases. Factors associated with escapes from poverty differ from factors associated with descents into poverty, indicating that two separate sets of poverty policies will be necessary: one to help households escape poverty, and another to head off descents into poverty. Because reasons for escape and descent vary by region, both sets of policies need to be regionally differentiated and locally controlled.

Neglecting the task of preventing descents into poverty is directly responsible for the slow pace of poverty reduction. Up to one-third of those who are presently poor were not born poor; they have fallen into poverty within their lifetimes, and their descents offset the success stories of those that have managed to climb out of poverty. Preventing descents into poverty more effectively should become a key component of the strategy for achieving the Millennium Development Goals.

Gaps in Poverty Knowledge

Policy responses to the problem of poverty are limited by significant gaps in knowledge. Four in particular are especially noteworthy.

First, we are not able to distinguish clearly between two different trends: escaping poverty and falling into poverty. Available statistics tell us about the net change in poverty between two time periods. But looking only at this net figure is inadequate for policy formulation.

A figure for net change can be arrived at under very different circumstances. For example, a 3 percent net reduction in poverty over a five-year period can arise because (a) 3 percent of the population escaped from poverty and no one previously nonpoor fell into poverty during this time; or (b) 8 percent of the population escaped from poverty while 5 percent fell into poverty; or (c) 20 percent escaped from poverty while 17 percent fell into poverty. All of these situations appear equivalent if one looks only at the net figure, but very different conditions underlie these three situations, and very different policy sets are required to deal with them.

Movements upward (out of poverty) respond to one set of reasons, while movements downward (into poverty) respond to another and different set of reasons, as discussed below. Different policies are required to deal with each set of reasons. Depending upon the respective rates of escape and descent, different mixes of the two types of policies will be required in different situations. Differentiating clearly between escape and descent is, therefore, very important: the appropriate policy mix cannot be determined without knowing these separate rates.

Second, it is important also to disaggregate by region and locality. Escapes and descents occur at different rates and for different reasons in different parts of a country, as will be shown. Identifying the particular reasons that operate within each specific region is critical, for only then can we determine what is to be targeted by poverty policies, and only then can we identify regions within which common policies should be applied.

Third, for both these reasons, we will need to study poverty in dynamic context, examining households' movements over time and ascertaining circumstances associated with movements in either direction. Relatively few longitudinal studies are available, however, that track households' movements over a sufficient period.[1] Policies mostly follow the results of cross-sectional studies undertaken at fixed points in time. Some quite erroneous conclusions can result if exclusively cross-sectional studies are relied upon (Krishna 2003).

Fourth, it is also necessary to understand poverty in the terms in which it is defined and lived by those who are poor. Poverty does not exist in a vacuum. It exists in the forms and definitions that we, as analysts, use to understand this term. Let me clarify what I mean by this statement. The definitions that we provide and the measurements that we promote give poverty a particular set of meanings and connotations. Yes, poverty exists even without our seeing it or measuring it. But the *ways* in which we see it and measure it configure the reality that poverty takes on within policy discourse. Statements such as "poverty declined by 5 percent in Country X between 1995 and 2000" have no meaning other than the one we provide. And the meanings that we provide to poverty along with the measures that we adopt lead to the policies that we implement in order to deal with poverty as we know it.

As analysts, we have chosen to measure poverty in particular ways—as a calorific mean, as a dollar-per-day equivalent—and we have elected to treat whole countries as the appropriate units of analysis. These are not the only ways in which to study poverty. Yet we selected these ways because they have allowed us to standardize poverty and to compare progress across different countries. The definition and measures that we have selected are particularly useful for these purposes. But they are not so useful for some other purposes more directly related to assisting households facing poverty.

Households in poverty do not usually sit idle, waiting for growth or program benefits to come their way (Narayan et al. 2000). Instead, they adopt numerous strategies to cope with their difficult situations and tide them over until better times. These household strategies are not guided by any standardized or global definitions of poverty. Rather, locally relevant understandings and definitions give rise to the coping strategies that different households adopt (Chambers 1988).[2]

Household strategies interact with national policies and economic growth to produce results in terms of poverty reduction, but "there is woeful ignorance about [household-level] processes and strategies" (Ellis 2000, 184). To enrich our understanding of poverty, it will be important to learn more about households' coping strategies (Baulch and Hoddinott 2000), and new methods will be required for this purpose. New methods are also required to fill the other knowledge gaps identified above.

The Stages of Progress Method

One such method, an emerging one, which I have termed Stages of Progress, was developed and refined as a result of extensive field investigations carried out in five countries. The first study was undertaken in the summer of 2002 in Rajasthan state, India (Krishna 2003, 2004). Additional studies were carried out in two other states of India, Gujarat and Andhra Pradesh (Krishna, Kapila, et al. 2005; Krishna 2006). With some modifications, this methodology was applied subsequently in similar investigations conducted in Kenya, Uganda, Peru, and the U.S. state of North Carolina.[3] The description of the application below is based primarily on the fieldwork in India.

These Stages of Progress investigations followed seven steps that are recounted briefly below.[4] Three teams of between six and 10 persons each implemented this approach in every community that we studied. Investigations in each country and region were conducted entirely in local languages, so a different team of investigators was selected and trained separately for each community. Typically, each team was composed of two facilitators and four to eight investigators, with equal numbers of women and men. The facilitators are college graduates, while the investigators usually have eight to 10 years of schooling. I trained with each team for about three weeks in each region. After completing training, we implemented the following steps separately in each selected community, regarded here as a unit of habitation, which in rural India is a village.

Villages in each region of India were selected in order to capture the diversity associated with aspects such as distance from markets and major roads, population size, and ethnic/caste composition. A total of 107 villages were studied over the past three years in three states of India: Andhra Pradesh, Gujarat, and Rajasthan. An additional 92 communities were examined in Kenya, Uganda, and Peru, and 13 communities in North Carolina.

Poverty dynamics were tracked for more than 30,000 households in all, and detailed interviews were conducted with a subset of over 7,000 households. These investigations revealed a startling similarity: in every context studied, households are simultaneously escaping from and falling into poverty. Poverty cannot be reduced sustainably until both sets of movements are concurrently addressed through directed policy measures.

The seven steps

Step 1: Assemble a representative community group. In each community studied, an open village meeting was held at the outset. Announcements about this meeting were made in each of the separate caste-denominated neighborhoods. We took particular care to ensure that all segments of the village community, particularly poorer and lower-status ones, were represented at these meetings. Steps were taken to minimize the ever-present danger of elite capture.[5] In some cases, a separate village meeting was convened for women so that women's views would be represented fully—and cross-checked against those provided by men.

Step 2: Present the study's objectives. We introduced ourselves as researchers, and we made it clear that we did not represent any government agency or nongovernmental organization (NGO), so there would be no benefits or losses from speaking freely and frankly to us. We mentioned these facts in order to remove any incentives people might have had for misrepresenting the poverty status of any household in their village.

Step 3: Describe "poverty" collectively. Community groups in each village were asked to delineate the stages of progress that poor households in their locality typically follow on their pathways out of poverty. "What does a household in your community typically do," we asked the assembled community members, "when it climbs out gradually from a state of acute poverty?" "Which expenditures are the very first ones to be made?" "Food," was the invariable answer in every single village. Which expenditures follow immediately after? As more money flows in incrementally, what does this household do in the third stage, in the fourth stage, and so on? Lively discussions ensued among villagers in these community groups, but the answers that they provided, particularly about the first few stages of progress, were relatively invariant across all villages of each state.

After drawing up the progression of stages in each village, we asked the assembled villagers which stage a household must cross to be considered no longer poor. The placement of this poverty cutoff and the nature of the initial stages (that is, those below the poverty cutoff) differed somewhat across villages in the three different Indian states.

Among villages located within the same state of India, however, there was virtually no difference in these local understandings of poverty. It was villagers and not researchers who defined these stages of progress; the similarity in stages is more remarkable for this reason. Villagers within each state identified the same initial stages of progress and the same poverty cutoff (table 5.1).

Notice the progression in stages as households gradually make their way out of poverty. In villages of Rajasthan, for example, the first four stages are food, primary education, clothing, and debt repayment. The poverty cutoff is drawn immediately after the fourth stage. In Andhra Pradesh villages, similarly, the poverty cutoff is drawn immediately after the fourth stage. Three of these first four stages are similar in the Rajasthan and Andhra Pradesh

TABLE 5.1
Stages of Progress and the Poverty Cutoff in Three States of India

Andhra Pradesh	Gujarat	Rajasthan
1. Food	1. Food	1. Food
2. Minor house repair, particularly patching leaky roofs	2. Some clothing to wear outside the house	2. Sending children to school, at least to the primary level
3. Retiring accumulated debt in regular installments	3. Sending children to school, at least to the primary level	3. Some clothing to wear outside the house
4. Some clothing to wear outside the house	4. Retiring accumulated debt in regular installments	4. Retiring accumulated debt in regular installments
----------------	5. Minor house repair, particularly patching leaky roofs	----------------------
	6. Renting a small tract of land to farm as a sharecropper	

Note: Heavy dashed line indicates the poverty cutoff in each state.

villages, but instead of primary education, reported as the second stage in Rajasthan villages, making minor house repairs was reported as the second stage in villages of Andhra Pradesh.

Later stages of progress beyond the first few are not reported in table 5.1. They included digging an irrigation well on one's own land; purchasing cattle to start a dairy business; starting a small retail business; constructing a new house; purchasing jewelry; acquiring radios, fans, and tape recorders; and, finally, purchasing a motorcycle, tractor, or small car. These are, however, discretionary expenses, and depending upon the taste of a household's members, purchasing a radio can precede or come after acquiring jewelry, for example. There was, consequently, more variation in the ordering of these later stages in different villages.

The first few stages of progress are not so discretionary: they are both physically and socially essential. Unmet physical needs—for food, for clothing, for protection from the elements—combine with low social recognition to constitute the definition of poverty that is prevalent within these communities.[6] It is a commonly known and widely agreed-upon understanding of poverty, and this everyday notion of poverty is much more real for these villagers than any definition that is proposed from the outside.

These locally constructed understandings of poverty constitute the criteria within these communities for identifying who is poor. They also constitute a threshold or an objective that defines the goals and the strategies of poor people: what people do in order to deal with poverty depends on what they understand to be the defining features of this state. Villagers participating in community groups developed these criteria among themselves, and they used these well understood and commonly accepted criteria to classify which households are poor at the present time and which households were poor 25 years ago.

A period of 25 years was selected for this exercise because it corresponds roughly to one generation, which is appropriate, according to Walker and Ryan (1990, 99), for examining household mobility. Nine years, the period of time that they considered, is too short, they conclude, for analyzing "issues that pertain to income mobility, which ultimately can only be addressed with intergenerational data." Households devise their strategies in terms of generational time horizons. Parents send children to school, for example, so they can improve their life chances many years later. It helps, therefore, to trace the process backward for as long as is feasible in a given context. In these long-established rural communities it was feasible and worthwhile to ask about events 25 years ago, though we also inquired about an interim period of eight to 10 years ago. In some communities that were studied later, for instance, in North Carolina or in Nairobi or Mombasa, Kenya, it was not feasible to go back any longer than 10 years, and we selected a 10-year period for these studies.

Step 4: Inquire about households' poverty status today and 25 years ago. In this step a complete list of all households in each village was prepared. Referring to the shared understanding of poverty developed in the previous step, the assembled community groups identified each household's status at the present time, 25 years ago, and also for an intervening period, eight to 10 years ago.[7]

Households of today formed the unit of analysis for this exercise.[8] Household composition has been relatively stable in these villages; relatively few households, less than 2 percent in all, have either migrated in or migrated out permanently from any village. Individual members of households, particularly younger males, have left these villages in search of work, but very few members have left permanently, and fewer still have left permanently with their families.[9]

By studying households that exist at the present time, we could elicit, particularly in the case of younger households, the difference between an individual's inherited and acquired status. Did a person who was born into poverty remain poor at the end of the period, or did he or she manage to escape poverty in the past several years? Is another person who was part of a nonpoor household 10 years ago still nonpoor, or has she, regrettably, fallen into poverty during this time? Compiling these trajectories of stability and of change helped us to assess the overall evolution of poverty over time. More important, learning about the reasons for change in each individual case helped to identify chains of events associated with escaping or falling into poverty.

Step 5: Assign households to particular categories. After ascertaining their poverty status at the present time and 25 years ago, each household was assigned to one of four separate categories:

Category A: Poor then and poor now (*remained poor*)
Category B: Poor then but not poor now (*escaped poverty*)
Category C: Not poor then but poor now (*fell into poverty*)
Category D: Not poor then and not poor now (*remained not poor*)[10]

Step 6: Inquire about reasons for escape and reasons for descent in a random sample of households. We took a random sample of about 30 percent of the households within each category and inquired in detail about causes and contributory factors associated with each household's trajectory over the past 25 years. This inquiry was conducted initially in the community meeting. The event history for each selected household was ascertained independently from the community group convened in each village.

Step 7: Interview household members again. Reasons indicated by the community groups for each selected household were cross-checked separately through individual interviews with members of the household concerned.[11] At least two members of each household were interviewed separately in their homes. Male members of our team spoke with the men of these households, while female members interviewed the women. Multiple sources of information were thus used to ascertain reasons associated with the trajectory of each selected household.

It took a team of six to 10 researchers about three days on average to complete these inquiries in one rural community, which has on average about 150 households. These were not standard eight-hour days, but it was an enjoyable learning experience for my colleagues and me.

The Stages of Progress method provided us with a useful methodological device, a benchmark or yardstick, for assessing how high or low on the ladder of material prosperity a particular household had moved over time. It should be noted that the Stages of Progress methodology deals exclusively with a *material* understanding of poverty; it does not take up a more expansive notion of poverty concerned with social and political empowerment. It is an emerging methodology that can certainly be improved, as discussed later, but even in its present shape it helped to fill the four important knowledge gaps identified above.

We were able to elicit separately the rates of escape and descent, identify reasons associated with escape and descent in each separate region, and examine households' situations in dynamic context. Most importantly, we adopted for these investigations an understanding of poverty that is understood and shared by local residents.

Reliability

How reliable are the results derived from applying this methodology? Recall can be quite imperfect, as every researcher knows. However, nearly all exercises measuring poverty at the individual or household level rely upon recall data of some kind. While studies using a monetary or calorific definition of poverty ask respondents to recall all items consumed over the past 15 or 30 days (and in some cases, over the past year), the Stages of Progress method asks them to recall locations along a sequence of stages for some period in the past. Both kinds of recall are subject to lapses of memory and sometimes even willful errors, so it is important to build in some safeguards and cross-checks.

The Stages methodology has several safeguards built in. First, it relies on retracing *large* steps that are better remembered, rather than fine distinctions that are more easily forgotten. Each movement upward along the Stages of Progress represents a significant improvement in material and social status. People remember, for instance, whether their household possessed a motorcycle or a radio at the time the National Emergency was in force, whether they lived in a mud or a brick house, whether they could afford to send their children to school, and so on. By seeking recall data in terms of these clear, conspicuous, and sizeable referents, the Stages of Progress method adds reliability to recall. Members of particular households remember quite well where they were located along this clearly understood hierarchy of stages, and these recollections are verified by others who have lived with them for long periods.[12]

Still, some individuals might forget or actively misrepresent their material status. This risk is alleviated to a considerable extent by asking about each household's status in an open community meeting. Groups locating each household's position on a common yardstick do not so easily engage in willful misrepresentation. Triangulation of all data collected helps to further verify recall. Information about each household is obtained separately at both the community and the household levels. Discrepancies are rare, but when found they bring forth repeat interviews, with community groups and the household verifying each other's account.

Another risk associated with subjective inquiries is that people will think back to some mythical golden age in their lives when "everything was better." This overly rosy view of the past is effectively limited when communities are asked to think in terms of distinct stages, and not in terms of better or worse. These stages are visible to all in the community, so community members are able to say which households are positioned at each stage, both now and in the previous periods chosen.

Finally, asset data are also collected separately for each household that forms part of the sample interviewed. Subjective as well as objective data are collected for these inquiries, and these data have been found to be quite closely matched.

Households' stages recorded for the present time are closely correlated with the assets that these households currently possess. Households that were identified as poor according to the Stages of Progress assessment were also found to be living more often in mud or thatch (rather than brick or stone) houses. They possess fewer heads of livestock and other assets than other households, and most are almost or entirely landless. In fact, there is a monotonically increasing relationship between current stage and assets currently possessed (Krishna, Lumonya, et al. 2006; Krishna, Kristjanson, et al. 2006).

But what about stage as recorded for a previous period? Does it also accord well with the actual material status at that time? In order to convert this hypothetical question into one that could be answered using the available evidence, I conducted a study in 2004 in the same group of 61 villages in Rajasthan, India, where I had undertaken a study seven years earlier, in 1997. In the community meetings in 2004, villagers were asked to recall their own households' stage of progress in 1997. I found that their recollections of their stage at that time closely correlated with the number of assets they had actually possessed seven years earlier, as recorded in the survey conducted in 1997. Table 5.2 presents these data.

TABLE 5.2
Stage of Progress Recalled Versus Assets Actually Possessed Seven Years Earlier in 61 Communities of Rajasthan, India

| Stage in 1997, as recalled in 2004 | Assets actually possessed in 1997 | | | |
	Land (bighas)	Large animals (no.)	Small animals (no.)	Kaccha (mud) house (%)
Very poor (stages 1–3)	3.6	1.8	2.8	86
Poor (stages 4–5)	5.5	2.5	3.7	77
Middle (stages 6–8)	8.1	3.1	5.1	51
Better off (stages 9+)	10.6	4.3	3.1	22

Objective data from a more distant past are not readily or abundantly available; if they were, we would not have needed to develop any such methodology. However, land ownership records are available continuously from the early part of the 20th century in Rajasthan, and by checking these records for an earlier period it is theoretically possible to compare households' landholdings at present with their landholdings of 25 years ago. In practice, however, it is an arduous task. Backtracking land ownership records requires manually locating, collating, and compiling diverse handwritten registers, which are most often not available at a single location. It is especially difficult to do for a period as long as 25 years. With generous assistance provided by the administration of Udaipur district, we were able to track the historical record for a small sample of households.[13] A total of 25 households were selected at random from among all those who have fallen into poverty in five selected villages, and their extent of landownership was traced backward over 25 years.

These inquiries revealed that among these 25 households, all of which have suffered descents into poverty, 22 (88 percent) simultaneously lost all or some part of their previous landholding; that is, they were forced by their circumstances to sell off their lands. About half of these households lost *all* of the lands that they previously owned, and they have become entirely landless. The rest had to part with significant portions of their landholdings.

The land records data closely matched the recall data that we had collected, justifying faith in the 25-year recall period used within these specific communities of Rajasthan. As mentioned above, however, such a long period of recall might not work equally well in other communities, and some shorter period for comparison, such as seven to 10 years, might instead have to be employed. We used a 10-year period for our study in 13 North Carolina communities.

Results: Diverse Trends in Different Localities

In every village we studied, a significant number of households have escaped from poverty over the past 25 years. At the same time, however, a significant number of households have also fallen into poverty. Table 5.3 provides the aggregate results for communities in the three Indian states.[14]

Notice the large proportion of households that have fallen into poverty in the villages of each state, and consider what might have happened, instead, if descent into poverty had been better controlled. Instead of a paltry 1.9 percent net reduction in poverty that was observed in the 36 Andhra Pradesh

TABLE 5.3
Poverty Trends in Villages of Three States of India

State	Districts	Escaped poverty (%)	Fell into poverty (%(	Net reduction in poverty (%)
Andhra Pradesh (36 villages)	Nalgonda, Khammam, East Godavari	14.1	12.2	1.9
Gujarat (35 villages)	Dahod, Panchmahals, Sabarkantha, Vadodara	9.5	6.3	3.2
Rajasthan (35 villages)	Ajmer, Bhilwara, Dungarpur, Rajsamand, Udaipur	11.1	7.9	3.2

villages, a much healthier rate, as high as 14.1 percent, could possibly have been achieved if no one had been allowed to fall into poverty in these villages. Because 12.2 percent of households actually fell into poverty, a much lower pace of progress resulted. Similarly, instead of the small 3.2 percent net reduction witnessed in the Rajasthan and Gujarat villages, much higher rates, as high as 11.1 percent and 9.5 percent respectively, could have been attained if descent into poverty had been more effectively controlled.[15]

Results from investigations in Kenya, Uganda, and Peru convey a similar picture of two opposite movements operating in tandem everywhere. National statistics tend to hide these simultaneous up-and-down movements. In Uganda, for example, poverty nationwide fell from 56 percent in 1992 to 35 percent in 2000. In 36 Ugandan communities where I studied households' movements over the past 10 years, a total of 14 percent of households made an escape out of poverty, but another 13 percent of households fell into poverty simultaneously. Newly impoverished households live side-by-side in these communities with others that have recently overcome poverty. In 20 communities in western Kenya, 18 percent of households came out of poverty over the past two decades, but another 19 percent fell into poverty during the same period. Net change in poverty was minus 1 percent, but a total of 37 percent of households suffered a change in their poverty status.

Introducing a separate focus on falling into poverty is an important contribution of the Stages of Progress method. Very large numbers of households are falling into poverty everywhere. Yet very few policies are directed specifically toward reducing these frequent and often needless descents.

Considering separately the numbers for escape and descent also helps to answer another question, noted at the start of this chapter: What percent-

TABLE 5.4
Divergent Poverty Trends at the Local Level in Six Indian Villages

Village	Number of households	Escaped poverty (%)	Fell into poverty (%)	Poor today (%)	Change in poverty over 25 years (%)
Nalgonda district, Andhra Pradesh					
Sultanpurthanda	89	49.4	3.4	29.4	+46.1
Guroamboduthanda	114	4.4	51.8	84.2	−47.4
Panchmahals district, Gujarat					
Balaiya	215	23.7	4.2	64.7	+19.5
Chikhali	214	9.3	20.6	70.1	−11.2
Udaipur district, Rajasthan					
Barda	146	12.3	14.8	47.3	−2.5
Gowla	111	13.5	3.6	9.9	+10.0

age of poor people were not born poor but have become poor within their lifetimes? In the 35 Rajasthan villages, for example, almost *one-third of those who are presently poor were not born poor:* they have become poor for various reasons.

Differentiating between escape and descent is a prerequisite for gaining such knowledge. Disaggregating geographically is equally important. Different trends and causes operate in different regions and localities, and targeted rather than blanket solutions need to be devised and implemented.

Different trends can operate even in villages in the same district, as illustrated by table 5.4. Just over 29 percent of households are poor at the present time in Sultanpurthanda village of Nalgonda district in Andhra Pradesh; in Guroamboduthanda village in the same district, as many as 84 percent of households are presently poor. Thus the level of poverty differs substantially between these two villages that are located no more than 20 kilometers apart. Similarly divergent trends are also visible when we look at villages in districts of the other two states.

While almost half of all households have escaped poverty in Sultanpurthanda over the last quarter century, only 3.4 percent of households have fallen into poverty in this village. In Guroamboduthanda, the opposite trend has occurred: more than half of all households in this village have fallen into poverty and a mere 4.4 percent of all households have escaped from it. This vast divergence in poverty trends between two villages in the same state, district, and subdistrict is not easy to understand without undertaking a disaggregated and localized inquiry.[16]

Substantial geographic divergence is also apparent when we look at data for any of the 199 communities studied in the five different countries. This diversity in both level and trends will need to be acknowledged and accommodated much better in plans that are made in the future to combat poverty more effectively.

Differences in the reasons for escape and descent will also require that two different sets of poverty policies be put in place in each region. Disaggregated inquiries will be important for uncovering these reasons. Without knowing what reasons are most prominent for escape and for descent in any particular locality, appropriate interventions cannot be identified. Programs formulated without knowing such locality-specific trends can have relatively little impact upon poverty in a region.

Asymmetric Reasons for Escape and Descent

Escape and descent are not symmetric in terms of reasons. In each region that we studied, one set of reasons is associated with the experiences of households falling into poverty, while another and different set of reasons is associated with escaping poverty.

Two separate sets of poverty policies are necessary, therefore: one set to help promote escapes from poverty, and a different set to control against descents into poverty. To the extent that the reasons for descent or escape are similar across an entire state or region, policies can be devised that have a larger geographic scope. To the extent, however, that reasons vary locally, more decentralized policies will be required.[17]

In either event, whether the ultimate policy response is centralized or not, the initial investigation into causes and reasons is better carried out locally. One needs to know first what the causes of poverty are in any particular region; one cannot assume that the same causes operate and the same policy is required everywhere.

Reasons for descent

No single set of circumstances is usually associated with falling into poverty. Most often, a combination of reasons has operated to plunge a household into abiding destitution. An elderly respondent in one Rajasthan village put it succinctly as follows: "A single blow can be endured, but when several blows fall upon us one after the other, it becomes hard to cope . . . and the result [quite often] is poverty endured by generations to come."[18]

The ability of any household to suffer successive blows is related clearly to its income category, and households that live closer to the margin of poverty can withstand fewer blows, especially when the extended family is also relatively poor. However, richer and poorer households alike have fallen into poverty on account of similar combinations of factors. Another village respondent in India narrated the following account:

> We were quite well-to-do at that time [25 years ago]. My father had a reasonable amount of land, and we three brothers helped with the farming tasks. But then my father fell ill. No one knows quite what it was [that afflicted him]. But the local remedies did not help. He became more and more sickly. Finally, we took him to the district hospital. We borrowed 20,000 rupees [about $2,000 at that time, equivalent to about two years' minimum wage] to spend on doctors and medicines, but it did no good. My father died.
>
> Then our kinsmen told us that we had to perform a death feast, inviting the extended clan from the adjoining eight villages. So we borrowed and spent another 15,000 rupees. . . . The rate of interest was going up all this while. . . . And then my brother fell ill, . . . the same story was repeated, . . . and we came under [accumulated] debt of more than 50,000 rupees. . . . Soon after that, I had my two daughters married. We must have spent about 10,000 rupees on each wedding [resulting in] more debt. . . . We were paying a rate of 3 percent a month as interest, and our land was pledged as security. . . . The debt only kept growing. We had to sell our land. We are poor now, my brothers' families and mine. We work hard, wherever and whenever we can find work, . . . just to repay our debt.[19]

This account, like all others considered here, was verified independently by at least one other member of this household and also by the village community. It corresponds closely in its details to the life histories that many other newly impoverished households narrated in other communities, not just in India but also in Kenya, Uganda, and Peru. Table 5.5 brings together the reasons for descent compiled for the three Indian states.

Ill health and high health care expenses lead the list of common reasons for falling into poverty. They were mentioned as important reasons in nearly 60 percent of all descents into poverty recorded in Rajasthan, 74 percent of those in Andhra Pradesh, and as many as 88 percent of those in Gujarat. Despite being located within a relatively rich and fast-growing state, villagers in Gujarat faced a significantly greater threat of falling into poverty for health-related reasons.

TABLE 5.5
Reasons for Falling into Poverty in Three States of India

Reason	Percentage of households that fell into poverty			Remarks
	Andhra Pradesh (36 villages)	Gujarat (36 villages)	Rajasthan (35 villages)	
Ill health and health-related expenses	74	88	60	Commonly the most prominent reason for descent
Social expense: marriage/dowry	69	68	31	The lower incidence in Rajasthan districts reflects the positive impact of dowry-rejection campaigns among particular social groups
Social expense: death feast	28	49	64	Associated with almost every caste group in Rajasthan but only with specific caste groups in Andhra Pradesh
High-interest private debt	61	52	72	Also associated with debt bondage in Gujarat, particularly in some villages
Irrigation failure	44	22	18	Particularly important in one part of Andhra Pradesh

Note: The numbers in each column add up to more than 100 because multiple causes are usually associated with each case.

Ill health was also the most important reason for descent in the other four countries studied. Moreover, there is evidence to show that health has risen in importance as a reason for descent. A comparison in India of households' expenses over time shows that average expenditure on all classes of medical treatment increased manifold between 1986 and 1995. Average expenditure on outpatient care rose from Rs 76 to Rs 176, while average expenditure on inpatient care increased even further, from Rs 597 to Rs 3,202 (Sen, Iyer, and George 2002).

Many more households in Rajasthan have succumbed for health reasons during the last 10 years than fell into poverty on this account in the 10 previous years. An elderly villager in Rajasthan summarized philosophically:

> In the old days, the aged people would fall sick and they would die. Their survivors would grieve and be unhappy, but they would pick up their lives

eventually and carry on much as before. Now, the old people fall sick, and their children run up huge debts caring for them. The old people die, nevertheless, and they leave behind ruined families.[20]

After ill health and health expenses, the second most important reason for descent into poverty relates to customary expenses on marriages and death feasts. While marriages and death feasts are involved in roughly the same percentage of descents in villages of the three states, the ratio between the two ceremonies varies. Expenses on marriages are a more important reason for descent in villages of Gujarat and Andhra Pradesh, while death feasts matter more in Rajasthan villages. Further disaggregation of these numbers shows that each type of expense is variously high or low among different social groups resident in different villages. Addressing this particular reason for descent, through social reform movements or community actions, will require attention to such variations.

Social and customary expenses on marriages and death feasts are also associated with large numbers of descents in some other countries. Expensive funerals and funeral feasts are associated with large numbers of descents in parts of Kenya and Madagascar, while expensive wedding ceremonies and dowries were found associated with descents in Uganda and Peru. Some social practices tend to place the burden of new poverty disproportionately upon women; for example, land inheritance by surviving male relatives tends to leaves female survivors impoverished.

The third most significant reason for descent has to do with high-interest private debt. Villagers most often deal with high health care expenses and expenses on marriages and death feasts by taking out high-interest loans from private moneylenders. No institutional sources are usually tapped for such loans. Even in villages of Andhra Pradesh, where self-help groups and rotating savings and credit associations have spread rapidly in the last decade, hardly any villager has been able to avert descent by taking loans from such institutions. Private sources are most often drawn upon for such purposes, and private rates of interest—as high as 10 percent *per month*—are paid. The high burden of debt that results helps push households downward into poverty.

A very large part of the debt incurred by poor families in India and elsewhere arises on account of large health care expenses (Dilip and Duggal 2002). In rural Vietnam, 60 percent of poor households were found to be in debt, and more than one-third of these households cited medical expenses as the main reason for indebtedness (Ensor and San 1996).

Indebtedness takes a particularly vicious form in Gujarat, where we found debt bondage to be a frequent practice in many villages. As many as

79 percent of poor scheduled tribe households, 35 percent of poor scheduled-caste households, and 45 percent of poor backward-caste households in the villages of Vadodara district that we studied were involved in relationships involving bondage to creditors.[21] A scheduled-tribe member of a village in this district recalls the impact of *chakari*—the local word for debt bondage—on his family during his childhood:

> I remember my mother working as a bonded laborer in the fields of [a rich person in this village]. My parents worked for their entire life, as far as I can remember, doing *chakari* for these people. I remember quite well that after working the entire day in their fields, my mother would bring some grain to our house and fill our stomachs. I still shudder to think of those times. We had no alternative. When education came to this village, then my parents and another two or three Adivasis [scheduled-tribe members] of the adjoining houses sent their children to study, and we have all progressed to some extent . . . but even today, many Adivasis serve as *chakar* in the fields and homes of [these rich people]. Whenever there is any urgent need for money, for instance, to treat somebody's illness or for some wedding or funeral expenses, this amount has to be taken as [a] loan from these [rich people], and the individual who borrows this money is required to do *chakari* as part of the agreement.[22]

Debt bondage is not quite so pronounced in villages of Sabarkantha district, Gujarat, and it was not mentioned in any village that we examined in Rajasthan or Andhra Pradesh. But it is apparent in villages of Panchmahals district and most prominent in villages of Vadodara district, the most industrialized of the four Gujarat districts that we studied.

Irrigation failure constitutes the last important factor associated with large numbers of descents in each region. However, the effect of this factor varies considerably across a state. In Andhra Pradesh, villagers of Nalgonda district cited irrigation failure much more often than villagers of the other two districts, Khammam and East Godavari, indicating that the same factor could have significantly different effects even within the same state.

It is worth mentioning that drunkenness and laziness are not significantly associated with households falling into poverty. We asked explicitly about these two factors (and also about other factors, such as health and jobs). Villagers were not shy in speaking about any of these aspects, even in community meetings. Yet laziness was mentioned as a contributing factor in less than 4 percent of all cases of descent into poverty in villages of all three states, and drunkenness was also mentioned in less than 4 percent. Nor are these factors any more important in any of the other countries where we studied these trends.

Even among households that have remained persistently poor (as opposed to having fallen recently into poverty), laziness and drunkenness are associated with only a tiny minority of cases. Other precipitators of poverty, such as ill health, health care expenses, social and customary expenses, and high-interest private debt, are implicated much more often in keeping these households poor.

The conclusion that emerges is that poor people do not become poor or remain poor on account of bad habits or lack of ambition. Rather, they are plunged into poverty most often because of factors beyond their control.

Reasons for escape

Escaping poverty is also responsive to different factors in different regions. Table 5.6 provides some aggregate figures for the three Indian states.

Diversification of income sources has been the most important reason associated with escaping poverty in these villages. It has involved villagers

TABLE 5.6
Reasons for Escaping Poverty in Three States of India

	Percentage of households that escaped from poverty			
Reason	Andhra Pradesh (36 villages)	Gujarat (36 villages)	Rajasthan (35 villages)	Remarks
Diversification of income sources	51	35	70	Different kinds of diversification have helped more in different states
Government job	11	39	11	A one-time increase in schoolteacher jobs was important in the case of Gujarat villages
Private sector job	7	32	7	
Irrigation	25	29	27	
Help from some government or NGO scheme	14	6	8	

Note: The numbers in each column add up to more than 100 because multiple causes are usually associated with each case.

taking up a range of specific high-return activities.[23] Although diversification of income sources is a leading reason for escaping poverty in all three states, different sets of activities have been more important in different regions.

In villages of Rajasthan, for example, activities taken up by villagers include rearing goats; making charcoal; and hiring out for labor in mining, transportation, and agricultural activities. But many more villagers have sought new sources of livelihood in cities, and they have gone as far as Mumbai, Bangalore, Chennai, and Pune, several hundred kilometers away, to work as carpenters, cooks, ice cream vendors, laborers, masons, plumbers, sign painters, tea stall assistants, truck drivers, and waiters. Younger males make up most of those who move to the city for this purpose, and in nearly all cases they travel by themselves, leaving their families in the village. The positions that they occupy in the city are hardly very secure, and it is both more reliable and cheaper to have one's family remain behind. Consequently, permanent migration of entire households from villages to cities has occurred in relatively few cases.

Diversification of income sources has involved a different set of activities in villages of Andhra Pradesh. Broadly, two types of activities have been taken up in different parts of the state. First, some households have set up tiny businesses of their own or they have sent one of their members to a city, where he or she has found some work in the informal sector. These types of activities have been more frequent in villages of Nalgonda and Khammam districts. Second, some households have diversified into nontraditional crops while still holding on to a mainly agricultural lifestyle. This diversification within agriculture has been more important in villages of East Godavari district. In Gujarat villages, similarly, diversification has involved a proportionately larger component of income from dairy activities.

Because different kinds of diversification are more important in each particular state and subregion, different policy supports will be required to promote escape through diversification within different regions of any state. More precise location-specific poverty knowledge is also useful for this reason.

Employment in the formal sector is the second reason associated with escapes, but it is much less important in terms of overall numbers. In Andhra Pradesh and Rajasthan villages this factor was associated with just 7 percent of all recorded escapes out of poverty. In Gujarat, the proportion was higher, 32 percent—as could have been expected, given that industry has grown at a much higher rate in this state.

Even in Gujarat, however, where the state domestic product grew by more than 5 percent per year in the 1980s and more than 9 percent per year in the 1990s (Ahluwalia 2000), only 9.5 percent of households in the villages studied managed to escape poverty. More than half of all village households continue to remain poor despite high growth. And of the 9.5 percent of households that did, in fact, escape poverty, *less than one-third* found their escape routes through jobs provided by the private sector. Along with rising capital intensity (Kundu 2000), two other factors have a bearing on the relatively slow transformation of industrial growth into job creation for village residents. First, a considerable number of the jobs created by industry have been assigned to casual laborers who have come in (or who were brought in) from other states of India.[24] Second, the jobs that local residents are assigned are quite often of low quality and liable to vanish at short notice.[25]

In Nalgonda district of Andhra Pradesh, all 12 villages that we studied are located alongside a cluster of privately owned cement plants.[26] However, less than 10 percent of all households that escaped poverty in these villages were assisted in this transition by private sector employment. Relatively few jobs were created by industry in the first place. Furthermore, the conditions of employment are such that obtaining a job does not always represent a pathway out of poverty. Local residents who work in the cement industry do so in most cases as casual labor. They are hired by intermediaries and contractors and not directly by the cement factories, and they are paid, often for years on end, on a day-to-day basis, with no benefits and little security.[27]

Studies undertaken by other analysts and in other countries also show that industrial growth has not always generated jobs in numbers large enough to make a significant dent in poverty.[28] The conditions in which industrial growth can make a bigger impact need to be better understood. Jobs in the formal private sector accounted for no more than 13 percent of all escapes observed in the 36 Ugandan communities, 9 percent in the 20 Kenyan communities, and even fewer households in the 40 Peruvian communities.

It is also important to note that jobs were not available in any state for all the educated, talented, and hard-working villagers who were looking for jobs. Contacts who provided *information* were critical for most cases of successful job search. In more than 85 percent of all successful searches, the availability of a friend, or more often a relative, who was already established in the city was critical. Households that have such contacts have been able to tap into economic growth and make use of the opportunities for self-advancement that growth undoubtedly provides. Other households, equally well qualified in most respects but lacking well-placed contacts, have been less able to use formal sector employment or even diversification as a pathway out of poverty in these three states.

The story is not dissimilar in other parts of India. Based on close observation in villages of Uttar Pradesh, one team of researchers (Jeffrey, Jeffery, and Jeffery 2004, 978) concludes that "to obtain a government job one must build relations of trust with a 'source' [who] supplies information about employment opportunities." For people who do not have access to such information networks, "development initiatives focused on formal education are likely to be only partially successful" (963).

It is a sorry fact that even as the government of India has pledged to support market-led economic growth, a path followed by other developing countries as well, it has not at the same time made market-based information easier to access by ordinary citizens. Instead, people rely mostly on kinship-based channels: those who are lucky enough to have relations in cities are the ones who are most able to diversify and break out of poverty. It is also noteworthy that an increase in full-time employment is *not* the main channel through which economic growth has translated into poverty reduction in these contexts. Both these facts are important to recall as we consider policy responses in the following section.

Irrigation represents the last significant pathway out of poverty. While irrigation has been associated with roughly one-quarter of all escapes from poverty in these villages, the remedy of irrigation is not equally available in all villages. It is also not a sure bet: failed wells and dried-up irrigation schemes have served to deepen existing poverty in quite a significant number of households in these regions.

Finally, as the figures in table 5.6 show, government or even NGO assistance schemes have not been associated so far with large numbers of households escaping poverty. In other countries as well, this factor has been relatively unimportant. Less than 4 percent of escapes observed in the 20 Kenyan communities and the 36 Ugandan communities were associated with any program-based assistance to the households concerned.

This finding should not be interpreted to mean that such interventions are inherently not useful or needed. Government schemes and NGO programs can help in very significant ways to reduce poverty—provided they address important reasons associated with escape and with descent. It is when development programs follow a centralized logic based on some preconceived notions, rather than on any close examination of local conditions, that they are least likely to be successful. Better-targeted NGO and government schemes based on understanding local reasons for escape and descent are more likely to succeed in alleviating and reducing poverty.

Conclusion: Toward Disaggregated Knowledge and Targeted Public Action

People are falling into poverty in the developing world even as other people escape poverty. There is a hole in the bucket, and this hole needs to be fixed relatively quickly so that people do not continue falling through. It will not be enough merely to support faster growth; even when it is pro-poor, growth will not suffice to prevent the problem of poverty creation.[29]

Controlling descents more effectively will require specific public actions. Different reasons for escape and descent operate within different regions (and within different communities in the same region), and obtaining localized information on these reasons should be the first step in combating poverty more effectively. Formulating and implementing pinpointed schemes based on a close knowledge of local conditions is the second critical step.

Health and health care expenses constitute the single most important factor associated with descent into poverty in the three Indian states we studied, and they have been found to be critical for deepening poverty in other countries as well (Deolalikar 2002; Krishna et al. 2004; Krishna, Gibson-Davis, et al. 2005; Krishna, Lumonya, et al. 2006; Pryer, Rogers, and Rahman 2003; Sen 2003; Whitehead, Dahlgren, and Evans 2001; Xu et al. 2003). Analyzing data from 15 major states of India for the period 1973–2000, Gupta and Mitra (2004, 203) conclude that "further reduction in poverty is probably not possible without significant improvements in the health condition of the population."

Policy in this regard has often been misinformed by the belief that economic growth will itself constitute an appropriate response to health-related problems. However, Mahadevia (2000) found otherwise in the state of Gujarat. "In spite of rapid economic growth observed in the state since its formation in 1960, the diseases of poverty remain widespread," she writes. "Budgetary allocation to the health sector has declined continuously for over a decade from the mid-1980s. . . . Despite its relatively richer status, the state of Gujarat spends less on health care than the average for other Indian states [and it ranks] fourth from the bottom out of 25 states and union territories." Richer as well as poorer households in the Gujarat villages that we studied have fallen into abiding poverty on account of health shocks and health care expenses.

Growth will not suffice for making health care better, more accessible, and more affordable; carefully directed public policies and well-targeted nongovernmental actions are necessary. The experience of Panelav village in Panchmahals district of Gujarat shows what can and should be done to provide better health care. Only seven out of a total of 106 households in Panelav have fallen into poverty—a significantly lower number than in other villages of this region—and in only one of these seven cases was health a significant reason for the descent. A locally based NGO runs a health clinic in this village. Doctors and attendant staff are regularly available, and the fees charged are within the reach of even quite ordinary villagers. Interviews with villagers in Panelav revealed the very significant impact that this service has had on the status of health in Panelav and surrounding villages.

Such public actions are important to undertake in a wider area if a critical reason for decline is to be addressed more effectively—and it does not seem likely that NGOs alone can do this work. The state can neither abdicate nor be absolved of its responsibilities. Government health agencies will also need to play a more effective role. More important than the nature of the agency concerned, however, is the nature of its working partnership with local residents. In principle, government departments, nongovernmental agencies, and private businesses can run effective health care facilities; the critical element lies in being accountable to area residents and responsive to their concerns.

Governments cannot, however, deal as effectively with the second major reason for falling into poverty in these regions, social and customary expenses; societal forces can deal better with these. The story from some Rajasthan villages is illustrative in this regard. All caste groups in Rajasthan are equally vulnerable to descent on account of such social expenses. The only exception is the scheduled tribes (STs) of Dungarpur district, among whom we did not find a single case of death feasts or marriage expenses resulting in descent. There is no other caste group in these villages of Rajasthan for whom social expenses are not an important reason for descent, including, surprisingly, STs of the adjoining Udaipur district. STs of Dungarpur are alone in this respect, in that they abjure death feasts and spend relatively small amounts on marriage parties. They have been assisted in this respect by a powerful social reform movement that became widespread in this district about 20 years ago.[30]

The third important factor associated with falling into poverty in the regions studied—high-interest private debt—is critically associated with the first two factors. When health care becomes available more accountably and at lower cost, and when people are persuaded to spend less on marriages and death feasts, their need to borrow from moneylenders will be commensurately reduced. Until these long-term policy goals are accomplished, however, people will continue to make these expenditures, so steps should be taken to enhance their access to reliable and cheaper credit.

Last—but very far from least—it will take large amounts of information to root out poverty. Information about job opportunities and career planning is crucially lacking in most rural areas and small towns of India (Krishna and Brihmadesam 2006). Providing more regular and more reliable information, not only about jobs and careers but also about several other factors, will be critically important in the fight against poverty. Information about where to dig a well, for instance, and where not to; about what diseases are most prevalent in an area and how to avoid them; about how and where to complain about teachers who do not teach and health workers who do not heal—these are the kinds of knowledge that diverse agencies can helpfully provide.

New methods need to be pioneered for generating and communicating appropriate knowledge about poverty and its causes. Why people fall into poverty needs to be more closely examined, with special attention to why only some people and not others are able to benefit from opportunities generated by growth.

The Stages of Progress methodology described here is being adapted and implemented by various agencies in different parts of the developing world.[31] Building on a rich history of participatory approaches (e.g., Chambers 1997; Salmen 1987), the Stages methodology is rigorous but relatively simple to apply. After some initial training, community groups can use these methods on their own to track poverty in their midst, to isolate reasons for escape and descent, and to develop strategies to deal with these reasons.[32]

Some limitations will need to be addressed as this methodology is extended. First, the methodology will need to look more closely at intrahousehold differences, particularly those based on gender.[33] Second, it is being adapted to deal better with newly formed communities, particularly those in large cities.[34]

It needs to be mentioned that the reasons for escape and descent identified in these studies are all micro-level and proximate, as experienced by households and individuals. More distant and macro-level reasons related to national policies and international economic conditions are not directly identified using the Stages of Progress methodology, so combining these micro-level analyses with a macro-level examination of policies and structures will help provide a more complete picture. It would be useful to undertake such a synthetic micro–macro study. It would also be interesting to undertake a study that combines monetary measures of poverty with community-based ones. Other methods also need to be used to look at dimensions of poverty other than the material one.

No single method can suffice to study all the important aspects of poverty. Depending upon the questions that a study is intended to address, different methods may be more appropriate and different definitions of poverty more useful. The Stages methodology is particularly strong in identifying reasons and pathways that take households into or out of poverty. These reasons and pathways can be compared across regions and countries. However, because somewhat different poverty lines are identified in different countries, cross-country comparisons of trends and numbers are not precise using this method.[35]

Combinations of methods, rather than any single method, are necessary for gaining a comprehensive view of poverty and for filling important gaps in poverty knowledge. It is my hope that more synthetic methods will be developed and utilized. Critical for this process of synthesis will be "a willingness to break down the hierarchical relationship between social scientific ways of knowing and other forms of expertise—to recognize, that is, the legitimacy and importance of knowledge that is grounded in practice . . . that takes the production of knowledge out of or at least beyond traditional or expert venues and into a variety of communities" (O'Connor 2001, 293–94). Progress in poverty reduction will be better as a result.

Notes

Research for this project was funded in part by the Ford Foundation and by the Cross-Sectoral Public Policy Program at Duke University. Earlier versions of this paper were presented at the Institute of Rural Management, Anand, India on December 6, 2004; at a workshop on "Understanding Rural Poverty" organized at the India International Center, New Delhi, on February 10, 2005; to members of the Triangle South Asia Consortium in Durham, North Carolina, on March 29, 2005; at a workshop on the "Post-Liberalization State in India: Inter-disciplinary Perspectives," Stanford University, June 5–6, 2005; and at the School for Advanced International Studies, Johns Hopkins University, on October 31, 2005.

Comments from participants at these events helped to improve this paper, and valuable input was also received from Chris Barrett, Robert Chambers, David Hulme, Mary Katzenstein, Sunil Khilnani, Ruth Meinzen-Dick, Philip Oldenburg, Elinor Ostrom, Ed Oyer, Neelakantha Rath, H. S. Shylendra, Ole Therkildsen, Norman Uphoff, and two anonymous reviewers. I acknowledge with gratitude the assistance provided by Chitra, a research support agency based in Jaipur, India, and by two NGOs, SARATHI in Gujarat and DISHA in Andhra Pradesh. This research project is a shared effort that has the stamp, most importantly, of hundreds of villagers who gave freely of their time and helped us to understand the nature and causes of poverty in their regions. The usual disclaimers apply.

1. See, for example, Baulch and Hoddinott (2000), Bhide and Mehta (2004), Carter and May (2001), CPRC (2004), Deininger and Okidi (2003), Grootaert and Kanbur (1995), Jodha (1988), Van Schendel (1981), and Walker and Ryan (1990).

2. As Jodha's (1988) seminal study points out, quite different conclusions can emerge when poverty in a region or community is viewed from the alternative viewpoints of professionals and of local residents. Jayaraman and Lanjouw (1999) bring together results from different community-based studies in India.

3. These investigations are described in, respectively, Krishna et al. (2004), Krishna, Lumonya, et al. (2006), Krishna, Kristjanson, et al. (2006), and Krishna, Gibson-Davis, et al.(2005). Results from these studies are also available at http://www. pubpol.duke.edu/krishna.

4. A detailed manual on applying the methodology in practice is available free of charge at http://www.pubpol.duke.edu/krishna.

5. For instance, we did not begin formal discussion until lower and upper castes were both present. We also learned techniques for rotating community respondents and isolating domineering speakers by taking them aside for separate interviewing. One other part of the Stages of Progress process helped reduce the impact of elite domination: all facts ascertained in the community meeting were separately verified in household interviews held privately. To the extent that the fear of elites does not also extend into private spaces, imbalances arising in the community group were ironed out at this point in the study process.

6. It is important to note that social recognition matters as much as economic conditions in defining the shared understandings of poverty within these (and other) communities. For instance, in Gujarat, the fifth stage, fixing leaky roofs, usually entails an expenditure that does not in most cases exceed Rs 400–500 (about $10), and it is a one-time expense, not often incurred year after year. Even though it is a relatively modest outlay, it is significant in terms of status and recognition: people who are not poor in this region do not have leaky roofs. The sixth stage in Gujarat villages, renting small tracts of agricultural land, also has a distinct social significance that is peculiar to this region of India. Advance payment to rent a small parcel of land is not very large (roughly Rs 1,500–2,000, or $40, on average). It is recouped at the end of the year when the harvest comes in. Renting a small tract of land does not necessarily imply any considerable increase in net income. However, the act of renting even a tiny parcel of land elevates the household concerned to a perceptibly higher status. Most significantly, it raises this household above the status of households that are or that might at any time become bonded debtors in the village. The continued presence of debt bondage in these Gujarat villages, discussed later, motivates this desire to differentiate one's status from that of debtors.

7. In order to denote the earlier periods clearly, we made reference to some significant event that is commonly known. For instance, in India we referred to the national emergency of 1975–77, which is remembered clearly, particularly by older villagers. In Kenya, similarly, we referred to the year of President Jomo Kenyatta's demise.

8. A potential weakness, common to all longitudinal studies, has to do with the changing composition of communities and households. Households 20 or even 10 years hence will not be the same as the households of today. Some of today's households will not be in the same place when a later study is conducted, while new households will have been set up by young adults and new immigrants.

Because households do not remain the same over time, some simplifying assumptions have to be made in longitudinal studies. Panel data studies consider households in the starting year of the study. They compare these households over time, neglecting all newly formed households. This neglect does not, however, detract from the purpose of these studies, which is to understand and trace households' trajectories over time. The Stages of Progress method involves an equal though opposite neglect. By considering households at the end of the period, this method ignores all households that have faded away during this time. We have found in a few locations where we inquired that roughly equal numbers of very rich and very poor households disappeared, with members of both groups typically leaving to try their luck in some city. Permanent migration out of these villages has been relatively small, as discussed below.

9. Breman (1996, 37) reports from his experience in southern Gujarat that "surprisingly few . . . households leave the village for any prolonged time or even permanently . . . I have seldom come across cases of households who left in their entirety to seek a new life elsewhere."

10. A residual category, E, was also defined, and households that could not be classified otherwise because of lack of information were assigned to this category. Very few households, less than half of 1 percent in all, were placed within this category.

11. The purpose of correlating facts emerging from household interviews with those ascertained from the community groups was to form a complete and accurate picture of the reasons related to a particular household's trajectory. In some instances, the reasons narrated by the household supplemented those related by the community group. It was only when these accounts of reasons contradicted one another—for example, if the community ascribed a household's descent to drunkenness and laziness whereas members of the household concerned mentioned an accident or illness—that reconciliation was necessary in order to arrive at the truth.

12. I remember, as I suppose each of us can, my situation 25 years ago in terms of some clear and easily recalled referents: Did we have enough food (yes) and clothing (yes)? Could we send children to school (yes)? Did we own a color TV (yes)? Did we own the house we lived in (no)? I find it harder to remember what I ate 15 days ago. See also Krishna (2003).

13. I thank Shikhir Agrawal, collector and district magistrate, Udaipur district, for encouraging his staff members to work with us to uncover this information.

14. It should be noted that the Stages of Progress and the poverty cutoff reported in the three separate regions are roughly similar without being exactly alike. Percentages of poor people reported in table 5.3 are thus approximately but not precisely comparable across regions. Similar questions about cross-regional comparability have also been raised in relation to more conventional poverty measures. See in this regard Johnson (2002), Reddy and Pogge (2002), Schelzig (2001), Sen and Himanshu (2005), and Wade (2004).

15. Analysts distinguish between chronic poverty (situations where people remain poor over long periods of time) and transitory poverty (where there are frequent

oscillations into and out of poverty). See, for instance, Gaiha (1989) and Hulme and Shepherd (2003). An important distinction has also been made between stochastic (fluctuating and reversible) and structural (better-rooted and more abiding) poverty transitions (Carter and Barrett 2004). Here, we were concerned primarily with chronic poverty and structural transitions, identifying households that have made an abiding changeover in either direction.

16. The introduction of a lift irrigation project together with electricity to power the lifts enabled almost 50 percent of all households to escape poverty in Sultanpurthanda village. On the other hand, the failure of irrigation, in this case canal irrigation, was largely responsible for the downturn observed in Guroamboduthanda. Quantitative methods employing small-area estimation techniques have also begun to explore such differences across localities (Bigman and Srinivasan 2002).

17. One would expect that such local-level policy formulation (or adaptation of national policies) would be undertaken by decentralized authorities with local participation, thus eliciting the kinds of local knowledge unearthed by a Stages of Progress inquiry. I thank an anonymous reviewer for this suggestion.

18. Interview with Prabhu Khoral, Badla village, Ajmer district, June 15, 2002.

19. Interview with Kishan Gadari, Muraliya village, Bhilwara district, May 20, 2002.

20. Interview with Chaturbhuj Gujar, Balesariya village, Bhilwara district, June 11, 2004.

21. "Scheduled caste" (SC) refers to the former untouchables and "scheduled tribe" (ST) to what are, loosely speaking, India's aborigines. These categories are recognized by India's constitution, which provides schedules listing specific castes and tribes as SC and ST. "Backward caste" is a more recent administrative listing that includes some other caste groups that have historically suffered from discrimination.

22. Interviewed on May 26, 2003. Respondent's name and village have been omitted at his request.

23. It needs to be clarified that "diversification" as used here does not usually refer to one individual doing many different things at the same time; rather, it refers to engagement in specific high-return activities that are different from and pursued in addition to a household's previous occupation. I thank an anonymous reviewer for helping make this distinction.

24. Based on his study of south Gujarat, Bremen (1996, 19) claims that "employers show a definite preference for these alien workers" from other states, "with the result that men and women who belong to the region are denied access to branches of industry that have shown rapid growth." M. Chatterjee of SARATHI, a Gujarat NGO, explained that "companies like to give employment to people from outside, because these outsiders do not get involved in labor unions" (personal communication).

25. We came across several instances in which people had given over their land to factories in exchange for the promise of jobs, but these jobs had vanished when the factories became or were declared "sick" (i.e., nonperforming) units. The land was no longer theirs to cultivate, and monetary compensation awarded by

the state land acquisition authority was relatively meager and could not last very long. Hirway (2000) explicates these issues further.

26. The first cement plant of this area started production in 1981, 14 more plants started production subsequently, and all are currently in operation at full or near-full capacity. Interview with N. Bhaskar Reddy, general manager, Sagar Cements, Mattapalle, Nalgonda district, January 15, 2004.

27. Interview with K. Suryanarayana Reddy, labor contractor for Nagarjuna Cement Limited, Mattapalle, Nalgonda district, January 20, 2004.

28. Ravallion and Datt (1996) show that 84.5 percent of the recent significant poverty reduction in India was due to growth in the agricultural sector. Using data from 27 countries for the period 1962 to 1992, Timmer (1997) also finds that agricultural growth is a central force in lowering poverty and unemployment. His findings show that growth in the manufacturing sector reduces poverty very slightly, but there is far greater impact from growth in the agricultural sector. Mellor (1999) also concludes that growth in the agricultural sector is pivotal in reducing poverty and unemployment. His findings indicate that "in fast-growth, low-income countries, upwards of three-quarters of all employment growth comes from the sum of agriculture and agriculturally stimulated growth."

29. Achieving higher economic growth "is only one element of an effective strategy for poverty reduction in India" (Datt and Ravallion 2002, 106).

30. Despite the lower significance of these social expenditures, poverty remains larger by far in Dungarpur than in the other four districts. More than 85 percent of all village households in Dungarpur belong to scheduled tribes, a historically marginalized and impoverished group, and their health care status gives considerable cause for concern.

31. Entities using the methodology include, among others, the government of Kenya, the World Bank, Humboldt University, India's Self Employed Women's Association, and researchers associated with the Consultative Group on International Agricultural Research.

32. None of this implies, of course, that communities will be self-sufficient in the resources required to address these reasons and problems.

33. Asking about the status of entire households does not help uncover gender differences where they exist. Females within households, like female-headed households, are more likely to be poor. In our 36 Gujarat villages, for instance, we interviewed members of a random sample of 133 female-headed households. Of these households, 99 (74 percent) have remained poor over 25 years and another 15 percent have become poor during this time, for a total of almost 90 percent who presently live in poverty.

34. See the discussion of these adaptations in Krishna, Gibson-Davis, et al. 2005. Further improvements have been made as the Stages of Progress method has been used within big-city neighborhoods in Nairobi and Mombasa.

35. However, according to Reddy and Pogge (2002) and Wade (2004), comparability problems are also severe when a standardized monetary metric is used.

References

Ahluwalia, M. S. 2000. "Economic Performance of States in Post-Reforms Period." *Economic and Political Weekly* (Mumbai), May 6, 1637.

Baulch, B., and J. Hoddinott. 2000. "Economic Mobility and Poverty Dynamics in Developing Countries." *Journal of Development Studies* 36 (6): 1–24.

Bhide, S., and A. Mehta. 2004. "Correlates of Incidence and Exit from Chronic Poverty in Rural India: Evidence from Panel Data." Working Paper 15, Indian Institute of Public Administration and Chronic Poverty Research Centre, New Delhi.

Bigman, D., and P. Srinivasan. 2002. "Geographical Targeting of Poverty Alleviation Programs: Methodology and Applications in Rural India." *Journal of Policy Modeling* 24: 237–55.

Breman, J. 1996. *Footloose Labour: Working in India's Informal Economy.* Cambridge: Cambridge University Press.

Carter, M., and C. Barrett. 2004. "The Economics of Poverty Traps and Persistent Poverty: An Asset-Based Approach." *Journal of Development Studies* 42 (2): 178–99.

Carter, M., and J. May. 2001. "One Kind of Freedom: Poverty Dynamics in Post-Apartheid South Africa." *World Development* 29 (12): 1987–2006.

Chambers, R. 1988. "Poverty in India: Concepts, Research, and Reality." Discussion Paper 241, Institute of Development Studies, University of Sussex, Brighton, UK.

———. 1997. *Whose Reality Counts? Putting the First Last.* London: Intermediate Technology Publications.

CPRC (Chronic Poverty Research Centre). 2004. *The Chronic Poverty Report 2004–05.* Manchester, UK: Chronic Poverty Research Centre.

Datt, G., and M. Ravallion. 2002. "Is India's Economic Growth Leaving the Poor Behind?" *Journal of Economic Perspectives* 16 (3): 89–108.

Deininger, K., and J. Okidi. 2003. "Growth and Poverty Reduction in Uganda, 1992–2000: Panel Data Evidence." *Development Policy Review* 21 (4): 481–509.

Deolalikar, A. B. 2002. "Access to Health Services by the Poor and the Non-Poor: The Case of Vietnam." *Journal of Asian and African Studies* 37 (2): 244–61.

Dilip, T. R., and R. Duggal. 2002. "Incidence of Non-Fatal Health Outcomes and Debt in Urban India." Working Paper, Center for Enquiry into Health and Allied Themes, Mumbai, India.

Ellis, F. 2000. *Rural Livelihoods and Diversity in Developing Countries.* New York: Oxford University Press.

Ensor, T., and P. B. San. 1996. "Access and Payment for Health Care: The Poor of Northern Vietnam." *International Journal of Health Planning and Management* 11 (1): 69–83.

Gaiha, R. 1989. "On Estimates of Rural Poverty in India: An Assessment." *Asian Survey* 29 (7): 687–97.

Grootaert, C., and R. Kanbur. 1995. "The Lucky Few amidst Economic Decline: Distributional Change in Côte d'Ivoire as Seen through Panel Data Sets, 1985–88." *Journal of Development Studies* 31 (4): 603–19.

Gupta, I., and A. Mitra. 2004. "Economic Growth, Health, and Poverty: An Exploratory Study for India." *Development Policy Review* 22 (2): 193–206.

Hirway, I. 2000. "Dynamics of Development in Gujarat: Some Issues." *Economic and Political Weekly* (Mumbai), August 26, 3106.

Hulme, D., and A. Shepherd. 2003. "Conceptualizing Chronic Poverty." *World Development* 31 (3): 403–24.

Jayaraman, R., and P. Lanjouw. 1999. "The Evolution of Poverty and Inequality in Indian Villages." *World Bank Research Observer* 14 (1): 1–30.

Jeffrey, C., R. Jeffery, and P. Jeffery. 2004. "Degrees without Freedom: The Impact of Formal Education on Dalit Young Men in North India." *Development and Change* 35 (5): 963–86.

Jodha, N. 1988. "Poverty Debate in India: A Minority View." *Economic and Political Weekly* (Mumbai), November, 2421.

Johnson, D. 2002. "Insights on Poverty." *Development in Practice* 12 (2): 127–37.

Krishna, A. 2003. "Falling into Poverty: The Other Side of Poverty Reduction." *Economic and Political Weekly* (Mumbai), February 8, 533.

———. 2004. "Escaping Poverty and Becoming Poor: Who Gains, Who Loses, and Why?" *World Development* 32 (1): 121–36.

———. 2006. "Pathways Out of and Into Poverty in 36 Villages of Andhra Pradesh, India." *World Development* 34 (2): 271–88.

Krishna, A., and V. Brihmadesam. 2006. "What Does It Take to Become a Software Engineer? Educated Parents, Information Networks, and Upward Mobility in India." *Economic and Political Weekly* (Mumbai), July 29, 3307.

Krishna, A., C. Gibson-Davis, L. Clasen, M. Markiewicz, and N. Perez. 2005. "Escaping Poverty and Becoming Poor in Thirteen Communities of Rural North Carolina." Working Paper, Sanford Institute of Public Policy, Duke University, Durham, NC. Available at http://www.pubpol.duke.edu/krishna.

Krishna, A., M. Kapila, M. Porwal, and V. Singh. 2005. "Why Growth Is Not Enough: Household Poverty Dynamics in Northeast Gujarat, India." *Journal of Development Studies* 41 (7): 1163–92.

Krishna, A., P. Kristjanson, J. Kuan, G. Quilca, M. Radeny, and A. Sanchez-Urrelo. 2006. "Fixing the Hole at the Bottom of the Bucket: Household Poverty Dynamics in Forty Communities of the Peruvian Andes." *Development and Change* 37 (5): 997–1021.

Krishna, A., P. Kristjanson, M. Radeny, and W. Nindo. 2004. "Escaping Poverty and Becoming Poor in 20 Kenyan Villages." *Journal of Human Development* 5 (2): 211–26.

Krishna, A., D. Lumonya, M. Markiewicz, F. Mugumya, A. Kafuko, and J. Wegoye. 2006. "Escaping Poverty and Becoming Poor in 36 Villages of Central and Western Uganda." *Journal of Development Studies* 42 (2): 346–70.

Kundu, A. 2000. "Globalizing Gujarat: Urbanization, Employment, and Poverty." *Economic and Political Weekly* (Mumbai), August 26, 3172.

Mahadevia, D. 2000. "Health for All in Gujarat: Is It Achievable?" *Economic and Political Weekly* (Mumbai), August 26, 3200.

Mellor, J. W. 1999. "Pro-Poor Growth: The Relation Between Growth in Agriculture and Poverty Reduction." Report prepared for U.S. Agency for International Development, Washington, DC.

Narayan, D., R. Patel, K. Schafft, A. Rademacher, and S. Koch-Schulte. 2000. *Voices of the Poor: Can Anyone Hear Us?* New York: Oxford University Press.

O'Connor, A. 2001. *Poverty Knowledge: Social Science, Social Policy, and the Poor in 20th Century U.S. History.* Princeton, NJ: Princeton University Press.

Pryer, J., S. Rogers, and A. Rahman. 2003. "Work, Disabling Illness, and Coping Strategies in Dhaka Slums, Bangladesh." Paper presented at the international conference on "Staying Poor: Chronic Poverty and Development Policy," Manchester, UK, April 7–9. Available at http://idpm.man.ac.uk/cprc/Conference/conference papers/Pryer%20Jane%20Workdisab28.02.03.pdf.

Ravallion, M., and G. Datt. 1996. "How Important to India's Poor Is the Sectoral Composition of Economic Growth?" *World Bank Economic Review* 10 (1): 1–25.

Reddy, S., and T. W. Pogge. 2002. "How *Not* to Count the Poor." Department of Economics, Columbia University. Available at http://www.columbia.edu/~sr793/count.pdf.

Salmen, L. 1987. *Listen to the People: Participant-Observer Evaluation of Development Projects.* New York: Oxford University Press.

Schelzig, K. 2001. "Escaping Poverty: Behind the Numbers." *Public Administration and Development* 21: 259–69.

Sen, A., and Himanshu. 2005. "Poverty and Inequality in India." *Economic and Political Weekly* (Mumbai), September 18, 4247, and September 25, 4361.

Sen, B. 2003. "Drivers of Escape and Descent: Changing Household Fortunes in Rural Bangladesh." *World Development* 31 (3): 513–34.

Sen, G., A. Iyer, and A. George. 2002. "Structural Reforms and Health Equity: A Comparison of NSS Surveys, 1986–87 and 1995–96." *Economic and Political Weekly* (Mumbai), April 6, 1342.

Timmer, P. C. 1997. "How Well Do the Poor Connect to the Growth Process?" CAER Discussion Paper 178, Harvard Institute for International Development, Cambridge, MA.

Van Schendel, W. 1981. *Peasant Mobility: The Odds of Life in Rural Bangladesh.* Assen, Netherlands: Van Gorcum.

Wade, R. H. 2004. "Is Globalization Reducing Poverty and Inequality?" *World Development* 32 (4): 567–89.

Walker, T. S., and J. G. Ryan. 1990. *Village and Household Economies in India's Semi-Arid Tropics.* Baltimore: Johns Hopkins University Press.

Whitehead, M., G. Dahlgren, and T. Evans. 2001. "Equity and Health Sector Reforms: Can Low-Income Countries Escape the Medical Poverty Trap?" *The Lancet* 358 (September 8): 833–36.

Xu, K., D. Evans, K. Kawabata, R. Zeramdini, J. Klavus, and C. Murray. 2003. "Household Catastrophic Health Expenditure: A Multi-country Analysis." *The Lancet* 362 (July 12): 111–17.

6

Poverty, Caste, and Migration in South India

T. Scarlett Epstein

Policies intended to reduce poverty often fail to do so because they reflect the perspectives of policy makers and not the realities of the poor. I illustrate this by looking first at India's food distribution program, the largest in the world, and at misplaced attempts to improve efficiency by moving from a universal to a targeted program. This experience points to the need to understand the complex social hierarchies and status distinctions that operate within communities that analysts broadly characterize as "poor."

This is followed by highlights of my work over the past half century in two South Indian villages that experienced rising inequality and extreme poverty during a period of transition to modern agriculture and a commercialized rural economy. Caste differences are central to this story. The chapter then examines processes driving large flows of rural workers into cities and the very unequal opportunities available to migrants of different castes in the urban environment. The chapter closes with a call for development strategies that give higher priority to rural areas and to approaches that foster more inclusive and diversified rural markets through a paradigm of rural–urban partnerships.

Poverty as Perceived from Above and Below

Experts who deal with poverty reduction at the macro level often seem to make assumptions about the poor that are far removed from realities on the ground. For instance, they tend to assume that the poor constitute a homogeneous entity. In real life, of course, poor people are a heterogeneous lot composed of individuals and groups whose struggle for survival often forces them to compete with each other for access to limited opportunities and resources. They come from different cultural backgrounds and have different needs and aspirations. Administrators seldom attempt to discover how poor people themselves perceive their poverty, how they cope with it, what their aspirations are, and what they would consider as an improvement in their standard of living. Unless these views from below are taken into account, poverty reduction policies have little chance of succeeding.

A case in point is the recent change in India's system of food distribution to the poor. The first U.N. Millennium Development Goal calls for halving the proportion of very poor people in the world by the year 2025. There is a general consensus among aid agencies and governments that to achieve this, scarce resources must be targeted toward the poor, and these agencies and government have in many cases switched from universal entitlement to targeted programs (World Bank 2000). In line with this trend, the Indian government decided in 1997 to change its nondiscriminatory Public Distribution System (PDS) of food into a Targeted Public Distribution System (TPDS).

The TPDS substantially increased the value of benefits to poor households, from approximately Rs 7 per household per month in 1993 to as much as Rs 48 in 1999. Policy makers expected that these higher benefits would significantly improve poor people's nutritional levels. But the data reveal that the effect on caloric intake was marginal. The primary reason, it turned out, was that a very small proportion of the poor availed themselves of the TPDS, so that the quantities of subsidized food grains actually purchased fell far short of the entitlements. Indeed, the discrepancy between intended and actual benefits under the TPDS exceeded that under the PDS.

Within a few years of the change, various analysts concluded that the poor had been better served by the universal program (Swaminathan 2000, 2001; Dreze 2001; Bunsha 2002). In 2002 even the government's own high-level committee on grain policy recommended an end to targeting and a return to the universal PDS, with uniform prices for rice and wheat for all households.[1]

A study conducted a few years earlier may indirectly shed some light on the failure of the TPDS. Dr. P. Pushpamma, who monitored the health of some of the poorest children in rural Andhra Pradesh, was puzzled when she found that these children's nutritional levels had declined during a period when incomes of the rural poor had been rising at least slightly. Her inquiry into the reasons for this pointed to the central importance of prestige. These villagers resented the fact that their sorghum-based diet marked them as the poorest, while the better-off villagers ate rice. When these poorest households got a bit more income, the first thing they did was aim for a higher social status by changing to rice as their staple food. But rice is more costly than sorghum, so they could afford to buy less. Moreover, rice is also less nutritious than sorghum. Smaller quantities of a lower-quality food eventually led to declining health levels among the children of households aspiring to climb the social ladder (Pushpamma 1994).

Dr. Pushpamma next conducted a social marketing campaign that succeeded in raising awareness among upper-strata households of the advantages of sorghum, particularly as a breakfast food. Once sorghum gained favor among wealthier households, this helped remove the social stigma attached to eating sorghum and encouraged the poor to return to a sorghum diet. Her action-research clearly illustrates the important role that prestige concerns play in the lives of even the poorest, a fact that does not seem to be appreciated by those who operate at the macro level.

The image the poor have of themselves differs from the image policy makers have of the poor. I would therefore hypothesize that the change from the PDS to the TPDS made the poor resent the targeted subsidies that now marked them as occupying the bottom of the social hierarchy and in special need of help.

An understanding of how the poor themselves perceive poverty and how they cope with it cannot be derived from brief visits and questionnaire surveys. It can be gained only by carrying out extended participatory observations among groups of the poor and by listening carefully to what they say. The argument presented here results from precisely such studies.

1954–56: In-Depth Studies of Two South Indian Villages

The investigation I began in 1954 focused on the impact that access to irrigation had had on the socioeconomic system of villages in what was then Mysore and is now Karnataka state, in South India. The village of Wangala, my first study site, had access to canal water. After staying one year in that village I spent another year in Dalena, a dry land village in the same area.[2] During my two years in the villages I shared most aspects of village life and came to be known as Kempamma. I have even been assured that I shall be reborn as a Wangala or Dalena villager, which I find very comforting to know.

Over the past 50 years, I have tried to keep track of the changes that have occurred in these two villages. I returned in 1970 and 1996 for updates. In 2004 I returned to the area once again, this time with the intention to find and interview individuals who had migrated from Wangala and Dalena to the nearest big city, Bangalore.[3]

Wangala, a wet land village

The large Krishnarajasagar canal irrigation scheme that was started in Mysore state in the mid-1920s triggered a period of rural development in villages that obtained access to canal water. Before irrigation, Wangala, like many other Indian villages that depended on rain-fed agriculture, basically had a subsistence economy. Irrigated agriculture facilitated the growing of sugarcane and paddy cash crops and thereby monetized the village economy. Some years later, Wangala farmers also began to use new high-yield paddy seeds that require especially large amounts of water.

Wangala's population, like the populations of all other Indian villages, was and still is composed of different endogamous castes organized in a hierarchical structure. In Mysore state, the Vokkaliga caste consisted of landowning peasants who had hereditary patron-client relationships with a number of resident functionary caste households. These included the Veerachari, a blacksmith caste, and the local Adikarnataka, scheduled caste (SC), most of whom were landless laboring households. Each peasant patron household offered its clients a modicum of social security by providing them with an annual reward in kind at harvest time; in return, the clients were committed to perform different types of services such as craft or farm labor, for which they usually also received a daily wage. Clients were also expected to provide political support and ritual services for their patron households; for example, the SC client would have to carry the torch ahead of his patron's funeral procession.

In 1954 the poorest section of Wangala's poorest stratum was made up of Vodda immigrants and SC households. Both these castes were considered to be below the caste barrier and were not allowed to draw water from the village caste wells. Yet the Voddas belong to a stonecutting caste that originates in Tamil Nadu, where they are considered to be above the caste barrier. Lack of income in their native villages had forced them to become migrant laborers. They settled in Wangala, where landowners were pleased to employ them on a contract basis to help with the cultivation of paddy and sugarcane, their new cash crops. The Voddas's lack of a permanent home gave resident SCs the chance to treat them as inferior, a judgment they displayed by refusing the newcomers access to the SC source of water.

Peasants constituted the dominant caste in Mysore villages, not only in terms of land ownership but also in numbers and in economic and political power. Of the 192 Wangala households, 66 percent belonged to the peasant caste, which owned 89 percent of the village lands. SCs made up 15 percent of the village households and owned no more than 6 percent of Wangala lands. Voddas constituted 3 percent of the households and owned no land at all.

Housing styles clearly displayed the economic differentiation within the village. Almost all peasant houses were reasonably sized and had tiled roofs. SCs lived in small thatch-roofed mud huts, and Voddas in improvised tiny mud huts. Residential patterns also reflected the boundaries between castes. The major village settlement was occupied by many peasant families and a few functionary caste households; it was separated by open space from the SC colony on one side and from the Vodda huts on the other side. SCs and Voddas were not allowed to enter peasant homes or the village temples and coffee shops. Peasants would enter the SC or Vodda quarters but only rarely their homes. Children grew up inculcated with the notion of caste differences. Whenever I walked around the peasant part of Wangala, I was always followed by a flock of peasant children. But they left me as soon as I crossed the invisible line to the SC or Vodda area, where I was taken over by the children of that caste.

The introduction of sugarcane and paddy cash crops raised the total economy of Wangala and made everyone better off, though not to the same extent, of course. It also reinforced the traditional social system. Those peasants who had the largest holdings of irrigated lands benefited most, but their SC clients also benefited because they earned additional daily wages for the additional work that the new crops required. Cash cropping thus strengthened the traditional hereditary patron-client relationship between peasant and SC households, which in turn reaffirmed the traditional social and ritual differentiation between the two castes. All this happened at a time when the constitution of newly independent India made caste discrimination a criminal offense and offered the SCs a number of privileges.

Wangala SCs at the time were not aware of the privileges the Indian constitution had awarded them. It took an SC Congress Party politician from nearby Mandya town to encourage the Wangala SC to rebel against peasant domination in a symbolic incident (see Epstein 1962, 183). A drama performance was to be held in the town. The politician insisted that the SC actor playing the king should sit on a throne and thus be higher than the peasant audience sitting on the ground. The Wangala peasants strongly resented this and let it be known that they and their fellow caste members from neighboring villages would boycott the performance.

The SCs, advised by their politician sponsor, went to great expense to stage the drama in their own residential area. He promised them a large audience, including the district commissioner and other high-ranking administrators from the nearby district headquarters. Unfortunately for the SCs, on the day of the performance a light rain began to fall just as these officials started out for Wangala, which gave them an excuse to turn back. In the end the audience was made up of only a few entrance-paying SCs from neighboring villages, and me. Though well performed, the drama was a financial disaster for the SCs. Furthermore, the village panchayat, of which only peasants were members, decided to punish the SCs for their rebellion by introducing a lockout of SC labor. To get this lockout lifted, each SC had to pay a fine for disobedience. This taught the SCs a lesson they have not forgotten to this day, though many things have changed since then.

The drama episode amounted to a political action by economic dependents against their masters and employers. The masters, however, formed a united front against their rebellious subordinates and used economic sanctions to reassert their traditional sociopolitical dominance.

Dalena, a dry land village

Dalena belonged to the same cultural area and had the same caste structure as Wangala. The two villages are part of the same ward and the same regional economy. In 1955 Dalena had 153 households, of which 80 percent were peasant households owning 97 percent of the village lands. SC households made up 10 percent and owned no more than 2 percent of the lands.

Dalena's lands lie above irrigation level and thus have remained dry, yet residents also consider the advent of canal irrigation in the region as the turning point in the recent history of their community. Across the canal they could see land getting greener and villagers getting wealthier, whereas their own village lands remained dependent on scarce rainfall. This encouraged peasants to try to participate in the growing regional economy by diversifying their economic activities and reaching outside their own village. They began providing the services needed by farmers in neighboring irrigated villages, for instance by carting the sugarcane grown in these villages to the Mandya sugar factory and by acting as cattle traders. Each of these activities reinforced their links with the wider economy.

A number of Dalena peasants secured employment at the Mandya sugar factory and commuted daily to work. Village peasants used intra-caste loyalties to get these jobs, as the factory management at the time consisted only of peasant caste members. This meant that none of Dalena's poor SCs could secure employment at this or any other Mandya factory, though these were all unskilled jobs for which they should have qualified.

Dalena peasants soon realized that education and a knowledge of English were necessary preconditions of success in the wider economy. Already in 1955 Dalena included a few university graduates, who took up professional positions outside their native village. With the money they earned many of them helped their kin in Dalena buy irrigated lands when these came on the market in neighboring villages.

As long as Dalena had a subsistence economy, peasants had the same type of hereditary patron-client ties with SC households as existed in Wangala. But when Dalena peasants acquired irrigated lands outside their own village, it became more economic for them to hire contract farm labor on a daily basis. This led to the gradual disappearance in Dalena of the traditional labor relationships. Yet peasant patrons still expected their SC clients to perform the traditional ritual functions, which the SCs understandably were not prepared to do. This caused a great deal of friction in the village.

Dalena SCs also faced great difficulties in finding work as farm laborers in surrounding irrigated villages. The different impacts of irrigated agriculture on the lives of Dalena's peasants and SCs led to growing economic polarization. The SCs lost their minimal social security, while peasant wealth increased considerably.

Most of the poor SC households in Dalena were deeply in debt to moneylenders. To pay the interest on their debts, some of them arranged to have their children work as bonded domestic labor in their creditors' homes. Other SC children had to work as daily laborers so as to contribute to the family income. This meant that hardly any of the SC children managed to take advantage of the educational opportunities the state offered them.

1970: Update Study

The first restudy took place in 1970, with six weeks of fieldwork. I was delighted to have the opportunity to catch up with my old village friends and see how their lives had changed, even though I could stay only a short time.

Wangala update

The most striking change since I had left Wangala 15 years earlier was the high rate of population growth. Since 1955 the population had increased from 958 to 1,603 at an average annual compound rate of 3.15 percent. More government land in Wangala had come under irrigation and was being planted with high-yield seeds. This resulted in higher agricultural productivity and a booming market for *jaggery* (unrefined sugar), ensuring that Wangala's land could sustain the increasing numbers of people. There was thus a continuing process of village introversion: the village remained inward-looking and economically self-contained, even though the gap between the rich and the poor had widened.

Much of the new irrigated acreage had been purchased by local peasants. This happened in spite of land rules that specified that at least 50 percent of government land available for disposal in any village should be sold to persons belonging to scheduled castes or scheduled tribes (STs) at a price well below market. However, most SC clients were heavily indebted to their peasant patrons, and the latter shrewdly utilized these circumstances to acquire lands the government had intended for SCs and STs.

The increased wealth among peasants who owned large areas of irrigated lands showed itself in their more and more elaborate living conditions. At the other end of the economic scale, the SCs' standard of living had deteriorated, and thus the gap between wealthy peasants and poor SCs had widened. Daily wage rates paid to SCs had fallen considerably in real terms. Taking 1955 as the base year, the wage index for a male labor day in 1970 was 160, while the consumer price index had risen to 280. This meant that the SCs, most of whom had to buy a large part of their food, had become worse nourished and clothed and their huts were more dilapidated.

When I asked some of my SC friends how they were keeping, my Western cultural background made me expect them to say, "Can you not see our health has deteriorated and we wear torn clothes because we now earn less money to buy food and clothes." To my surprise this was not what they told me. Instead, I heard them say, "We are worse off now because we cannot celebrate the weddings of our children and our other rituals in our accustomed style." Their own perceptions of their poverty thus differed considerably from what most Westerners would expect.

SCs were still not allowed to enter the village coffee shops, but had to send the money in and receive the coffee in crockery kept specially for SCs. One day Nanjeya, a young SC, saw a coffee shop empty and ventured inside with his cup of coffee.[4] Unfortunately for him, his household's patron, Boregowda, walked past and saw him sitting in forbidden territory. The patron immediately ordered Nanjeya to leave and threatened that he would beat him if he refused to do so. When Nanjeya refused to obey a fight ensued, which left him with a bleeding head injury. The commotion caused a crowd to gather, and Nanjeya then threatened that he would take Boregowda to court for having unfairly discriminated against him and injured him. Boregowda in turn threatened that if Nanjeya took him to court, he would not only discontinue his hereditary relationship with Nanjeya's household but would also claim repayment of all the money the family owed him.

The SC headman who had been observing the incident began to worry that the dispute had gone too far and could have repercussions for other SC households. He tried to quiet Nanjeya and made him go home while the crowd dispersed. However, Boregowda was so enraged by what he considered as Nanjeya's impertinence that he carried out his threat and cancelled his hereditary relationship with Nanjeya's family. At first the family thought that the patron would need their labor and would therefore relent, but another Wangala SC household quickly offered its services. Boregowda switched his relationship, leaving Nanjeya's family to struggle for survival.

This case clearly indicates that village patrons can ignore the state's legislation that exists to protect SCs against discrimination and get away with it. It also shows the competition that exists among some of the poorest SC households. Another SC had no compunction about depriving his fellow SCs of their security as long as his own family benefited from it. This throws into relief how extreme poverty promotes competition for scarce sources of income, rather than encouraging united actions among the poor. Poverty made the SCs accept social subordination as the price they had to pay for securing a livelihood.

The increased wealth among Wangala peasants that resulted from cash cropping enabled them to boost their prestige by withdrawing their wives from participation in farm work. This meant that peasant women ceased to be economic assets, which in turn led to a change from bride-wealth to inflationary dowry payments. Lavish wedding feasts became a matter of conspicuous consumption.

Among the poor SCs, women's labor continued to be an important part of their household income, yet they were keen to emulate the change that had occurred among the peasants. Prestige considerations motivated them also to change to a dowry system. This made many SC households incur high debts just to pay for their daughters' wedding expenses.

Dalena update

The village of Dalena, too, had grown in numbers over the years. But its agriculture still depended on scarce rainfall and there were hardly any alternative opportunities in the village to earn income. As a result, Dalena villagers continued to look outside for their income, continuing the pattern of village extroversion. Increasing numbers of Dalena peasants had either left the village for work in the wider economy or had secured jobs in Mandya's factories and commuted daily. The only employment SCs could find outside Dalena was as daily farm laborers.

Among the peasants there evolved the formation of "share families" whereby one or two brothers would do factory work in the nearby town while one brother remained in the village and cultivated the lands owned by his employed brothers. This was an effective reciprocal arrangement: the farming brother passed a part of the farm produce to his urban-based kin and they in turn met his cash expenses out of their wage earnings.

The peasants realized that education in general and knowledge of English in particular were necessary preconditions for success. Peasant fathers put more and more emphasis on having their sons go through the educational system, and increasing numbers of young boys from Dalena became university graduates. This was a luxury hardly any SCs could afford; they still needed their children to earn money.

Since the poor SCs had little chance of securing factory employment in nearby towns and their increasing numbers made it difficult for them to find work as farm laborers within Dalena, they too increasingly sought farm work in neighboring villages that had irrigated lands.

Predictions for the year 2000

Having studied the same micro-societies at an interval of 15 years and analyzed the changes that had occurred between 1954–56 and 1970, I decided to try to predict how these villages and others like them would change over the next 30 years—by the year 2000 (see Epstein 1973).

First of all, I expected that the rate of population growth would continue to increase in both Wangala and Dalena.

Second, I judged that Wangala's process of village introversion and Dalena's village extroversion would continue with greater intensity. Wangala villagers would continue to focus most of their work and attention on activities in the village, which would ensure the continued functioning of their social system. By contrast, Dalena's increasing ties to the wider economy would lead to a breakdown of intra-village social relations.

Third, I reasoned that the differential economic progress of different categories of villagers might lead to the development of an intra-caste class structure.

1996: Restudy and Evaluation of Predictions

In 1996 it was time to do a restudy to find out to what extent my predictions had been right and where and why I might have gone wrong.

Wangala restudy

The picture in Wangala after a quarter century was one of intra-village economic diversification.[5] Growing farm incomes resulting from new agricultural technologies and rising *jaggery* prices had led to a widening demand pattern and new economic activities among villagers. Building contractors were busy putting up new and larger two-story houses, motor-scooter drivers provided transport to Mandya, and fertilizer shops met farmers' needs. Several new coffee shops and retail stores had flourishing businesses selling goods not only to Wangala villagers but also to people from neighboring villages who came to Wangala to visit the bank or the group *panchayat* headquarters. Children from the surrounding area who attended the Wangala school complex bought goods from the retail stores. This busy and thriving village economy and the considerable increase in real daily wage rates for farm laborers also ensured at least a minimum livelihood for the local landless poor. Only a few male peasants had moved out of the village in search of a better life elsewhere.

Also apparent was the important role one man can play. T. Thimmegowda was eight years old when I first moved to Wangala in 1954. He obtained a master's degree in economics and became a highly respected officer of the Indian Administrative Service. Yet he continued to identify with his native village and attempted to boost its development, making sure that the village benefited from services the central and state governments provided for the rural sector. With his help, Wangala became the headquarters of the group *panchayat* and received a piped water system, a primary health center, a veterinary center, a bank, a large school complex, an SC student residence, and several other facilities that are not usually available in villages. Thimmegowda also succeeded in reducing factional fighting among Wangala's peasants by encouraging the establishment of a "core group" composed of highly respected local peasants. Moreover, he acted as patron for a few young Wangala peasants by helping them secure jobs and homes in Bangalore.

He had little success, however, in bridging the socioeconomic gap that still existed in Wangala between peasant farmers and the poverty-stricken SCs. Wangala's social system continued to function in 1996, but there were signs that it would not last much longer. Population increase and the introduction of agricultural technologies, coupled with the arrival of migrant laborers willing to accept lower wage rates, made it increasingly difficult for Wangala's indigenous SCs to secure farm labor jobs. The migration of some younger male peasants to Bangalore also disrupted traditional patron-client ties. These combined factors led to the beginning of the breakdown of the hereditary labor relationships between peasant patrons and their SC clients and deprived increasing numbers of SC households of their minimum social security. Most SCs remained among the poorest, yet only few of them were prepared to take the risk of leaving their native village in hope of a better life in a city.

Also persisting was the gender gap. Liberal state legislation had reduced the degree of women's subordination on paper, but in practice the relationship between male and female villagers remained far from equal. Indeed, drinking and gambling among men had resulted in declining living conditions for many women and in a growing problem of domestic violence. There was as yet no strong women's lobby in the villages to claim women's human and constitutional rights. By 1996, seats were reserved for women in the *panchayats*, but female councilors still tended to act as the mouthpiece of their male sponsors rather than representing the demands of village women. This was especially true in the case of SC female councilors.

Education held out hope for improving the status of both women and scheduled castes. Yet in 1996 the proportions of female and SC students were still well below their proportions in the village population, especially at higher levels of schooling.

Dalena restudy

By 1996, the growing population and the lack of income-earning opportunities within Dalena had forced increasing numbers of villagers to seek an income outside their native place. This process contributed to the development of a regionally integrated economy. A division of labor developed whereby villagers with dry lands provided services, such as flour mills and cane crushers, that farmers of irrigated lands needed. This proved to be an economic solution that had disadvantageous social effects. Indeed, as the increasing village extroversion dismantled the structure of Dalena village society, concern for the less fortunate members of the community disappeared almost completely.

The expanding regional economy provided increased urban employment opportunities. In particular, the establishment of an industrial center within easy reach of Dalena created more jobs. However, most of the business managers were peasants and they preferred to employ fellow caste members. Not only Dalena peasants but also peasants from more distant places found employment on this industrial estate. A number of the peasants from other villages who took these jobs found it convenient to live in rented accommodation in Dalena, where peasants quickly responded to these new opportunities and began building houses for renting out.

The poorest Dalena SCs, on the other hand, could scarcely earn enough to sustain their families. While peasants monopolized urban job openings in southern Karnataka, the mechanization of agriculture had reduced the need for farm labor. As a result, a number of Dalena SCs were forced to consider urban migration as a survival strategy. But only one, who had achieved the necessary educational level, had managed to get a position in Bangalore's public service. He built a nice house in Dalena for his wife and children and visited them regularly. All the other poor Dalena SCs who had migrated to Bangalore had ended up in one of the city's slums. They found it extremely difficult to eke out a living for themselves, let alone send money to the families they had left behind in Dalena.

Evaluation of earlier predictions

Only one of the predictions I made in 1970 for the year 2000 turned out to have been wrong, while the others proved correct. This seems to augur well for the possibility of using longitudinal micro-society studies to provide the basis for sound predictions of societal changes.

The erroneous prediction concerned the rate of population growth: my estimate turned out to have been too high. I realized that I had ignored the importance of education, largely because the 15 years between my first two studies had been too short a period for the impact of education to become apparent. Yet in the years after 1970, education made its mark on fertility behavior and thus on population growth. The village doctor in Wangala assured me that almost all couples of reproductive age were now using one or another means of contraception. As a result, the average annual rate of population increase had declined in both Wangala and Dalena.

My prediction of Wangala's continued village introversion with maintenance of its traditional social system and Dalena's continued village extroversion with breakdown of its traditional social system turned out to have been correct. One positive development in Dalena was that in line with government regulations, Dalena peasants no longer objected to SCs entering the village coffee shops.

In both villages there were obvious signs of the development of class within caste, more so among the peasants than among the SCs. The equal-inheritance rule among sons when applied to Wangala farmlands meant that a man's economic status was largely determined by the number of brothers he had and by the size of his father's landholding. Many young Wangala men inherited unsustainably small holdings, leaving them no option but to sell their land and join the landless village households. A few lucky young men were the only sons of fathers with large landholdings. They further increased their holdings by purchasing the lands that came onto the market. Among villagers in general, the expectation of land constraints for their sons made parents realize the importance of education, which was considered the passport to a public service job (Dore 1997).

The increasing size of Wangala's population encouraged the government to release more land located south of the SC quarter to house the additional numbers of landless villagers, without regard to their individual caste membership. The old SC colony was now sandwiched in between the peasant residential area and the new housing area. In the new multi-caste settlement, homes of peasant and functionary caste members from landless families were interspersed with SC homes. Yet there had not yet developed any shared class identity among them.

In both villages, a few of the SC households had succeeded in rising to a higher economic stratum by identifying themselves as SCs and taking advantage of the preferential treatment the government offered them. Similarly, landless peasants perceived that their only chance of improving their lot was to stress their peasant identity. This enabled them to take advantage of the privileges offered to "backward castes," which include the peasants. Thus in 1996 caste remained the overriding principle of social organization in these two South Indian villages, but within each caste an incipient class structure was emerging.

2004: Study of Rural–Urban Migrants from the Villages

When I returned in 2004, I found that the lack of rainfall in Karnataka state between 2000 and 2003 had caused canals to run dry and crops to fail. The entire "irrigated region" where Wangala and Dalena are located, which had depended on agriculture and animal husbandry, had suffered greatly. There was great distress among farmers of land that had previously had access to irrigation, as they now could not pay debts they had incurred when purchasing farm inputs. Their desperate situation was reflected in a rising number of suicides. The worst-affected by the drought were the village poor—the landless laborers. The doctor at Wangala's Primary Health Centre told me that about two-thirds of the villagers who come to consult him suffer from symptoms of stress.

Migration had become a primary survival strategy. The combination of drought and limited land availability constrained income-earning opportunities in the villages, yet their populations continued to grow, with continuing high fertility rates among the poorest families. This forced many villagers to seek a livelihood elsewhere, mostly in nearby cities. The continued urban bias among developers led to urban industrial development that stood in stark contrast to the poverty of the rural areas. To poor rural migrants, the big cities offered an array of employment, housing, and education opportunities that seemed to promise a solution to all their problems. A few "made it," but for most, these dreams would remain unfulfilled. They ended up living in appalling conditions among strangers in urban slum settlements without any income or access to the basic requirements of life—and no one to turn to for help.

I began my studies of migrants by asking my village friends in Wangala and Dalena for the names of people who had left the villages since my previous stay in 1996. In most cases they did not know the urban addresses of these rural–urban migrants and could only tell me the city to which they had migrated; most of them had gone to Bangalore. It took a difficult piece of detective work to find these migrants in the capital city, whose population of 6 million is swelling with an influx of 1,000 new migrants a day. But I did manage to locate most of the names on my list.

Using a set of interview guidelines I prepared, I undertook to discover how different categories of rural migrants from Wangala and Dalena had fared in the urban environment.[6] I was interested in why these men from different backgrounds had migrated to Bangalore, what they did there, how they perceived the differences between life in the village and the city, and how and where they would like to spend the rest of their lives. Boxes 6.1 through 6.4 present profiles of two peasant migrants and two SC migrants from Wangala and Dalena. Their stories give a glimpse of the range of experiences of village migrants in Bangalore.

Analysis of case studies

The 33 case studies I collected in Bangalore in 2004 point to a number of factors as key determinants of how a rural–urban migrant fares in the city. Leading the list is caste status and the network of connections associated with caste. These strongly influence not only the migrant's chances of securing a job, but also what kind of a job he will get and where he will live. Crucial to success in the city is having a sponsor, a powerful individual who can use

CASE STUDY
Shivagowda, a Wangala Peasant

Shivagowda is about 50 years old and speaks English reasonably well. After completing his master's degree in sociology, he worked as a part-time lecturer in a small-town college for two years. In 1987, T. Thimmegowda, Wangala's chief patron, recommended him for the post of social worker in Bangalore's cancer hospital. Since then, Shivagowda has been promoted to permanent employment as assistant social welfare officer at the hospital.

During his first few years in Bangalore, Shivagowda stayed in rental housing. Then Thimmegowda again came to his aid, this time to help him acquire a building site in a nice residential area. He also helped Shivagowda get a bank loan to pay for the site and the building of his house, which has become a lovely, well-furnished urban home.

Shivagowda married a woman from Bangalore who also has an MA degree and works in the same hospital. Their 11-year-old son attends a school where English is the language of instruction. They hope he will become a medical doctor, though they expect to find it difficult to pay the high fees for his studies.

Shivagowda's only brother is married and still lives in Wangala, where he cultivates the 2.5 acres of dry land that their father passed onto his two sons. Though the brothers own the property jointly, Shivagowda has no intention of claiming his share. He has maintained close contacts with Wangala and with his own kin in particular, although his visits are not as frequent as before because of the pressures of his job. He is always prepared to offer financial help to his brother whenever he may need it.

Shivagowda and his family insist that "We owe our existence in Bangalore to T. Thimmegowda." Indeed, their attitude borders on hero worship. They are happy to have settled in the city and look forward to staying there for the rest of their lives. Although his personal ties to a generous patron were instrumental in helping Shivagowda move up, he seems convinced that those who fail to succeed in the city do so because they have adopted bad habits, such as drinking alcohol or using drugs. He considers that urban migration offers every villager a chance of a better life.

his or her contacts and resources to help the migrant find work and a place to live in the new environment. Every one of the migrants who had settled reasonably well into urban life stressed that he owed his success to a sponsor. Not surprisingly, migrants of the peasant caste are far more likely than SC migrants to have acquaintances in powerful positions.

Rural caste norms continue to operate among rural people who have moved to the city. When I heard that a meeting was being organized in Bangalore for all migrants from Wangala and Dalena, I encouraged all the migrants I had met in Bangalore, without respect to their caste or economic situation, to attend this meeting. Most of them promised to do so, yet only 14 showed up, and all were peasants from Wangala. No scheduled caste migrants from Wangala or Dalena attended the meeting. Moreover, each of those who attended owed his successful stay in Bangalore to an urban patron. T. Thimmegowda was the sponsor of 12 of the 14 peasants, and the gathering was held in the home of one of his clients. After the event, the SCs and lower-caste migrants who did not attend told me that they did not come because they were not formally invited and they did not think that a peasant would want to have them in his home.

At the meeting, Thimmegowda, who now occupies an important position in Bangalore, announced the formation of a Wangala Migrant Trust. He urged each man present to put into this trust as much money as he could spare, thereby offering help to the people who still live in Wangala. Since the participants were all Wangala peasants, the trust is obviously a totally peasant-dominated, peasant-focused affair. There is no evident intention to help any of Wangala's poorest SCs, although Thimmegowda did stress that the trust would also aim to relieve poverty in Wangala.

Beyond caste and connections, other influential factors in how a rural–urban migrant fares in the city include age, gender, health, education, skills, and character. Being a healthy male is essential to employability. Unless a female migrant is extremely well qualified or has a special skill, her only chance to find a job in the city is as an unskilled laborer, and even this is often difficult. This is true even if a female migrant belongs to the peasant caste.

A university degree is a great help in securing a better life in the city. So is knowledge of English. Most urban migrants who have their families with them try to send their children to schools where English is the language of instruction.

Those migrants who have acquired a specific skill that is in demand in the city, for instance as a bus driver, find it easier to get employment than the many unskilled laborers who migrate. It is interesting to note that hardly any of the Wangala and Dalena migrants had become self-employed business people.

Given the obstacles that confront migrants, patience and perseverance become essential character traits. A large proportion of rural–urban migrants return to their native villages after having tried for no more than a few months to settle into city life. Every one of the Wangala and Dalena migrants

I interviewed complained about the lack of community spirit in the urban setting, where nobody cares for anyone but himself and his near kin. They miss the company of their family and village friends and would gladly stay in the village if it provided the necessary income-earning opportunities.

In sum, rural–urban migrants who have the best chance to raise their economic status in the city are healthy young males of the regional dominant caste who have some education and skills and who have a patron in a position of power. This sets the bar rather high. For most of the rural poor, migration to urban centers means scrounging for low-paid work, living in a slum, and suffering an extremely low quality of life.

Policy Implications

Rural economies in most areas of the developing world used to depend almost exclusively on agriculture. In response to concerns about population growth and low agricultural productivity, international crop research institutes worked to develop new varieties that would optimize the productivity per unit of land. This research began with the assumption that land is *the* scarce factor of production; little consideration was given to the availability of water. The high-yield varieties of seeds that were created require a larger amount of water than traditional varieties. This in turn spurred international donors to invest in irrigated agricultural development. Many such projects have been success stories; the Krishnarajasagar irrigation scheme in South India is considered to be one of them.

However, during the last decade conditions in South India have begun to change. The large South Indian canal system had to be closed down for three years because of drought. The state governments seemed not to fully appreciate the havoc this water shortage created in the rural areas. Villagers in drought-prone areas like Rajasthan complained that "government does not know the situation on the ground. . . . If there is no rain this year, we will leave the village. Last year we survived, but this year it is a big burden" (*Financial Times*, May 23, 2000, 12). The international crop research institutes have yet to develop crops that maximize the productivity per unit of water rather than per unit of land.

Even if agricultural productivity can be increased, this is not a solution to the problems of rural economies. As village populations are still increasing (though rates of growth are declining), even a reasonably sized holding is soon divided into unsustainably small units if there are more than two sons to claim the inheritance. The prospects are bleaker still for poor landless villagers.

CASE STUDY
Shivaram, a Dalena Peasant

Shivaram is one of three brothers who shared the inheritance of two acres of dry lands in Dalena and three acres of wet lands in a neighboring village. Their father encouraged his sons to get an education because he realized that the family's landholdings would not suffice for all three. Shivaram took his father's advice and is now a lawyer at Bangalore's High Courts.

When asked how someone of his modest background managed to become a high-powered lawyer, he says it is all due to Dr. Sudha Rao. He was her research assistant when she conducted her field studies on education and rural aspirations during the early 1980s in Dalena.[9] She encouraged him to study for a law degree, and she took him to Bangalore and introduced him to people in important positions who were able to assist him. She also helped him get a job as an accounting clerk while he was taking evening law classes in Bangalore, and often gave him money to supplement his meager income during that time. "But for Sudha Rao, I would not be in the position I hold today," he says.

As a law graduate he was in great demand as a bridegroom. A marriage was arranged with the daughter of a wealthy family from a village near Mandya. His in-laws not only paid for an elaborate wedding but also provided a handsome dowry. Recently they presented him with a valuable housing site in one of Bangalore's elite residential districts. His first son is studying electronics at a city engineering college. He wants his second son to become a medical doctor, but he is not sure whether he will be able to afford the fees.

Presently, the family occupies on mortgage the upper floor of a large house in one of Bangalore's comfortable districts. They look forward to building a nice house on the site his in-laws have given them. Although Shivaram appreciates the better housing, educational facilities, and amenities in the city, he criticizes the lack of community spirit, and he considers urban life to be a continuous rat race. Shivaram maintains contact with his parents and brothers and with Dalena villagers in general, visiting frequently and returning for marriages and important rituals. He hopes eventually to build a large house in Dalena for the couple's retirement, if his wife and son agree.

Although productivity may increase, the demand for farm labor continues to decline in tandem with increasing mechanization. Globalization, with its possibilities of access to world markets for India's agricultural products, offers no hope for the landless poor. They have nothing to sell but their labor.

Nor does rural–urban migration help most poor people escape poverty, as my case studies clearly show. Urban job creation cannot keep pace with the increasing numbers of unskilled migrants arriving in the cities. Moreover, such migration has an adverse impact on both urban and rural sectors. Urban crime and violence is on the increase, while village societies are being denuded of their productive labor force.

CASE STUDY
Putta, a Scheduled Caste Person from Wangala

Putta, the son of landless SCs, is about 25 years old. He has had only primary education and does not speak English. About three years ago, after searching unsuccessfully for farm employment, he decided to try his luck in Bangalore.

When Putta first arrived in Bangalore, he had nowhere to go. He soon met two other young SCs who were in the same predicament; they told him about places where labor contractors come every morning to recruit day laborers for construction sites. Putta went to the site early in the morning and after a few days he and his newfound friends were lucky enough to be selected.

With the money they earned, they rented a tiny room in a slum area where there was already an SC colony. The room was just large enough for the three of them to lie down side by side. They shared a filthy wash place and toilet with 25 other slum dwellers.

Putta returned home to Wangala once a month at first, but then he realized his travel money would be better spent if he sent it to his parents. Since then he comes home only when rituals require him to return. He tries hard to save money from his meager earnings to support his parents but does not often succeed in doing so. Three more young Wangala SCs have followed Putta to Bangalore, and he has helped them find casual employment and housing in the slum area where he lives. This makes Putta feel that at least he has a few of his village friends with him now, and he does not feel so cut off any more.

Putta is glad to earn an income in Bangalore, but he misses his family and friends. In the village he always felt a strong bond with the people whose lives he shared, but in the city he misses this sense of belonging and identity. His housing conditions are appalling. Unless he can find a way to get a better-paid job, Putta fears, he will have no option but to accept his fate.

What, then, can make a positive difference? Every one of the villagers I interviewed in Bangalore, as well as those that still live in their villages, stressed the need to introduce income-generating activities in India's rural areas. The creation of off-farm income-earning opportunities for the rural poor in their native places offers them the best, and possibly the only, chance to escape poverty. However, special care will be needed to ensure that the SC poor have the first chance to participate in new income-generating activities. Creating new employment opportunities in the villages will not reduce poverty if the dominant landowning households are allowed to monopolize them.

Diversification of rural economies is key to creating off-farm income-earning opportunities. This implies a decision to strive for balanced rural–urban development policies, rather than policies that channel the bulk of development funding and efforts to urban industrialization. Urban and rural development need to be considered as complementary processes rather than as competing for limited resources. The benefits of such an integrated approach will by far outweigh its costs.

It is likely to prove more cost-effective to improve rural rather than urban infrastructure. Most work associated with infrastructure improvements is highly labor-intensive, and wages are lower in rural than in urban areas. Villagers often can be motivated to offer some of their assets and/or labor free as long as they are assured that the venture will benefit their own community. Moreover, a wealthier rural sector will create increased demand for industrial products and thus will help boost the country's gross national product. Though growing urbanization increases the demand for farm produce in the cities, in many developing countries food prices are kept artificially low to keep labor costs at a minimum for infant industries, thereby obliging the rural sector to subsidize industrialization.

A rural–urban partnership development paradigm

Diversification of village economies, I would suggest, might be achieved by the implementation of a three-tier rural–urban partnership that links rural growth areas and rural growth centers with the urban centers (figure 6.1).[7] The aim is to stimulate economic expansion in rural areas, enabling more people to make their livelihoods in their home villages. Such rural–urban partnerships can reduce rural–urban migration, improve both rural and urban standards of living, and provide a sustainable development option as part of the ongoing process of globalization.

FIGURE 6.1
Rural–Urban Partnership Linkages

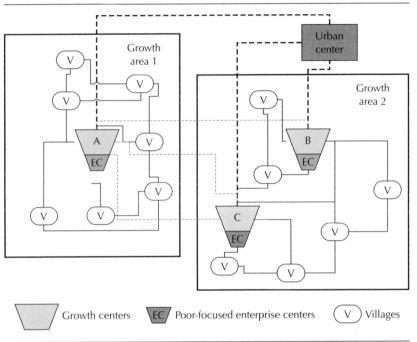

Drawing on resource and market surveys, development planners should be able to calculate the most effective size of individual rural growth areas. There should be easy access and communication not only between the different settlements that constitute one rural growth area, but also between different growth areas and the urban centers. Each such area could also represent a democratically elected political entity.

A rural growth center will form the nucleus of each growth area. It will have two-way socioeconomic relationships with neighboring villages and linkages with urban and rural suppliers and markets. These rural growth centers will provide formal services for the population residing in the growth area. Comparative advantages enjoyed by the different settlements within one growth area will determine the role each such center will play in the development of its area.

Urban centers should have an increasing volume of network linkages with rural partners, suppliers, and buyers. Linking urban-based businesses with rural small-scale producers has been done successfully in Taiwan and the Republic of Korea, among other places. In these countries, urban manufacturers of small consumer goods maintain only small workshops in the city, with consequently low overhead. They rely on rural households for the bulk of their production. Trainees, most of whom are women, are accommodated near the firm's workplace while they learn the production process. They then return to their rural villages, taking one or more machines on a hire–purchase basis. The manufacturer continues to supply them with raw materials (such as cut pieces of garments), collects the finished articles, enforces strict quality control, pays piece rates, and markets the products using the firm's in-country and export marketing links.

This rural–urban partnership has proven to be an extremely cost-effective productive process, and it has helped Taiwanese urban manufacturers capture export markets. Villagers earn reasonable incomes without having to worry about how to market what they produce. The partnership development paradigm proposed for India represents an adaptation of this decentralized production model. The urban–rural linkage can create a mutually beneficial network of relations involving farmers, agro-based processing enterprises, and domestic industrial units in rural growth areas. The telecommunications revolution that is underway in many parts of rural India will help make this possible.

In addition, small-enterprise promotion centers should be established in the rural growth areas. These centers should offer existing and potential rural small entrepreneurs access to expert advice on starting new business ventures.[8] To encourage groups of villagers to establish small enterprises, appropriate shareholding arrangements with legally binding obligations need to be made available to villagers. Such arrangements should be formalized under a local statute or regulation.

A number of preconditions have to be met before such a paradigm can be expected to succeed. First of all, a political commitment to balance rural–urban development is of foremost importance. So is local participation and interest in a revised development strategy. Villagers have to be convinced that the authorities are now really committed to promoting not only urban but also rural development.

Education and training is a second precondition. Facilities should be decentralized to ensure that students from villages acquire appropriate skills. Their studies should not alienate them from their rural background. Open-university type courses in business management and simplified accountancy should be offered. Such courses should explain the advantages and disadvantages of different types of business structures so that villagers can make

CASE STUDY
Ramana, a Scheduled Caste Person from Dalena

Ramana, about 39 years old, is a married SC whose family owns a small plot of dry land in Dalena. He studied up to SSLC standard but could not pass, having had to leave school to assist his parents in cattle and sheep rearing. After a series of temporary day-laborer jobs as a construction worker, gardener, and electricity contractor's assistant, he found himself unemployed. Ramana did not want to work for wages in the fields of his fellow villagers, doing heavy physical labor in the hot sun for very low pay. Moreover, he said, the village landowners treated him with disrespect, as he belongs to a scheduled caste that they considered a former untouchable caste.

His mother advised him to go to Bangalore to seek help from the husband of her sister's daughter, who worked as a marble polisher in Bangalore. Ramana left Dalena and cycled all the way to the city, leaving his wife and two sons in the village with his mother. In the city, his relative introduced him to a work contractor and he became a helper in marble polishing. During his training he earned Rs 45 to Rs 50 per day, less than $1. It took him about six months to learn the trade.

Initially, he stayed with his cousin's husband, but the house was small and he soon moved in with one of his friends. They slept in a bar after the business closed, usually after midnight. Because the bar owner often had to open again around 5 a.m., Ramana frequently had only a few hours' sleep. Eventually, he wound up sleeping in doorways, cycling home once a fortnight to wash his clothes and bathe.

As a marble polisher in Bangalore, he faced many problems. If the polishing equipment needed repair, the contractor would declare a holiday and the workers would earn no pay until it was repaired. The building owner or the contractor might also stop work due to financial difficulties. Ramana often had no money for food. The first contractor for whom he worked treated him well, but others demanded more and more work from him with fewer benefits.

At present, he shares a room in a slum area with two other young men. The peasant landlord does not let rooms to SCs, but Ramana claimed to be a peasant. The room is so tiny that it is impossible to open the door when three people are sleeping inside. It has no furniture, only hooks on the wall for clothing. Bathing and toilet facilities are outside and are shared with about 50 neighbors.

As a skilled marble polisher, Ramana earns Rs 175 per day. When he gets work at least six days in a week, this pays for his subsistence but leaves little to support his family. On days when he has no job, he faces a serious problem of survival. The cost of living is high in the city, Ramana points out, although living conditions are far below those in the villages. His work as a marble polisher takes him to the most luxurious homes in Bangalore, from which he returns to the squalor of his tiny room.

Nonetheless, he believes city life offers several advantages. First, there is in practice no caste discrimination, as it is usually impossible to identify a person's caste. Ramana has successfully concealed his true identity as an SC, and his neighbors now show him the respect due a peasant; he gets invited to their festivals, rituals, and marriages. Second, wages in the city are higher than in the rural areas, and working conditions are better. Whatever the trials of marble polishing, it is less arduous than farm labor. Third, urban work, unlike farm labor, is not seasonal. If one is lucky in the city, one can continue working year round.

Despite his own difficulties, Ramana is optimistic about his children's future. He hopes they will manage to get public service jobs. However, securing a government job requires payment of a very high bribe, he notes, that is beyond the means of poor SCs. If he cannot get his sons government jobs, he is confident that he can find them employment in private enterprise by using the connections he has made in Bangalore.

Ramana emphasizes that city life gives SCs the opportunity to shed their caste identity and frees them from the demeaning social subordination they endure in the villages. He also feels that Dalena peasants treat him with less disrespect since he has established himself in Bangalore and helps support his wife and children. At the same time, he misses the company of his family and village friends and says he would return to live in Dalena if he were assured a livelihood there.

---

informed choices to become self-employed or engage in private partnerships, cooperative ventures, or other forms of business.

With respect to agriculture, international crop research institutes should be encouraged to focus on developing high-yield seed varieties that require little water. The Green Revolution ceases to be green if there is insufficient water available to grow the crops, and research objectives at these institutes must change in line with changing conditions. In promotion of agro-based industries, vertical integration toward the market will offer employment opportunities and will retain more income within the rural sector, leading to overall increases in demand for goods and services.

An effective road network linking rural growth centers to nearby towns is an essential precondition for success. In addition, over time, rural infrastructures have to be improved to ensure ready access to education, sanitary water, primary health centers, hospitals, banking, and reliable power supplies. Public works ventures to improve infrastructure will have the added benefit of offering decentralized income-earning opportunities.

The single most important factor needed to redress the imbalance between living standards in the city and countryside is the political will to bring about balanced rural–urban development. Only with such a commitment can a rural–urban partnership succeed in keeping people productively employed in the villages, reducing the rate of urban growth and easing severe poverty in both the rural and urban sectors.

Notes

1. The committee's report is available on the Web site of the Ministry of Consumer Affairs, Food, and Public Distribution, http://fcamin.nic.in/dfpd_html/index.asp. For one explanation of the low participation in the TPDS, see Kochar (2005).
2. The late professor M. N. Srinivas, a leading social anthropologist, advised my choice of doctoral research and helped me identify my first study site. These village studies constituted the fieldwork for my PhD at the University of Manchester, UK. The revised version of my thesis was published in 1962. In my publications I have changed the names of the two villages slightly so as to conceal the identities of my informants.
3. My thanks are due to the Nuffield Foundation for providing one of their small research grants, which made this study possible.
4. Wherever possible I have given my informants pseudonyms to ensure their anonymity.
5. I conducted the Wangala restudy jointly with A. P. Suryanarayana, my research assistant, and T. Thimmegowda, the "one-man major patron" of Wangala. Together we published *Village Voices: Forty Years of Rural Transformation in South India* (1998). We also acted as consultants for a film team from the German Institute of Scientific Film, which made a documentary with the same title as the book.
6. I gratefully acknowledge the devoted help I received from Dr. V. Ramaswamy, a staff member of the Institute for Social and Economic Change in Bangalore. A selection from my case studies formed the basis for a documentary film titled *Back to the Village*. It was filmed jointly by Nagathihalli Chandrashekhar, from Bangalore, and Richard Wasserman, with T. Thimmegowda and I serving as consultants. The film was financed by the Swedish development agency Sida and the Asian Development Bank.
7. This section draws on Epstein and Jezeph (2001). I am indebted to T. Thimmegowda for discussing with me his conviction of the importance of establishing rural growth areas and centers.
8. Such small enterprise promotion centers already exist in the United Kingdom and other developed countries and are considered to have helped successful

establishment of small enterprises. The need for such centers is greater in India's rural sector than in the industrial countries, yet in India few such centers exist.

9. Sudha Rao was my PhD student and I supervised her research in Dalena. See Rao (1986).

References

Bunsha, D. 2002. "The Human Face of Adjustment." *Frontline* (India) 19 (1): 5–18.

Dore, R. 1997. *The Diploma Disease*. London: University of London, Institute of Education.

Dreze, J. 2001. "The Right to Food and Public Accountability." *The Hindu* (India), December 5.

Epstein, T. S. 1962. *Economic Development and Social Change in South India*. Manchester, UK: Manchester University Press.

———. 1973. *South India: Yesterday, Today, and Tomorrow*. London: Macmillan.

Epstein, T. S., and D. Jezeph. 2001. "Development—There Is Another Way: A Rural–Urban Partnership Development Paradigm." *World Development* 29 (8): 1443–54.

Epstein, T. S., A. P. Suryanarayana, and T. Thimmegowda. 1998. *Village Voices: Forty Years of Rural Transformation in South India*. New Delhi: Sage.

Kochar, A. 2005. "Can Targeted Food Programs Improve Nutrition? An Empirical Analysis of India's Public Distribution System." *Economic Development and Cultural Change* 54 (1): 203–35.

Pushpamma, P. 1994. "Sorghum and the Nutrition of the Poorest in Andhra Pradesh, India: A Case Study." Development Market Research (DMR) and Social Marketing (SM), BBC World Service, London, and SESAC, Sussex.

Rao, S. V. 1986. *Education and Rural Development*. New Delhi: Sage.

Swaminathan, M. 2000. *Weakening Welfare: The Public Distribution of Food in India*. New Delhi: Leftword.

———. 2001. "A Further Attack on the PDS." *Frontline* (India) 18 (2).

World Bank. 2000. *India: Reducing Poverty, Accelerating Development*. New Delhi: Oxford University Press.

7

Elusive Pathways Out of Poverty: Intra- and Intergenerational Mobility in the Favelas of Rio de Janeiro

Janice E. Perlman

This chapter is based on findings from a longitudinal multigenerational study in the favelas, or shantytowns, of Rio de Janeiro from 1969 to 2003.[1] Large political transformations took place in Brazil during this period, from dictatorship to "opening" to democracy. At the same time, the economy progressed from a boom to hyperinflation and crisis to relative stability, and policy toward the favelas shifted from removal to upgrading and integration with the city at large. However, these positive political and economic changes have not significantly reduced urban poverty in Rio de Janeiro. In fact, both the absolute number of poor people and the percentage of Rio's population living in favelas have increased steadily over these three decades.

The study began in 1968–69 in three favela communities where I lived for 18 months, collecting survey data and conducting interviews with residents. Thirty years later I returned to these same communities in search of the original study participants and their descendants. Over the course of two years, I found 41 percent of the original participants, quite a high percentage given the large time gap.

Interviews were conducted in 2001 with these original interviewees and with a random sample of their children and grandchildren. With basic information on the parents of the original sample, I was able to trace the dynamics of poverty and social-spatial mobility across four generations. This follow-up on individuals was supplemented with a restudy of the communities themselves.

Some things had clearly changed for the better. The physical conditions of the study communities and the overall education levels of their residents showed significant improvement over the three decades and with each succeeding generation. On other important dimensions, however, the results were more mixed. Unemployment nearly doubled, income gains did not fully reflect educational advances, and few people had found professional jobs. Even fewer had been able to move into the more desirable areas of the city. There was also a continuing lack of voice and political participation despite the return to democracy in 1985.

Barriers to upward mobility in the favelas include economic obstacles, especially labor market conditions, extreme inequality, and the stigma of favela residence, which creates an impediment to being hired. Political obstacles include lack of legal documents and scant protection of the state under the rule of law, as well as post-dictatorship forms of corruption and clientelism. An additional factor is the spike in lethal violence related to trafficking in drugs and arms.

Some people were able to overcome these obstacles thanks to high aspirations and a sense of agency, optimism, and perseverance. These individual characteristics significantly correlated with several measures of success, including higher socioeconomic status, higher income, exit from the favelas, political participation, and self-reported satisfaction. Males, young people, people with smaller families, and those raised in communities close to the upscale neighborhoods of the city had a distinct advantage in socioeconomic and spatial mobility. Despite the daunting challenges of everyday existence, about half the sample in each generation reported that their lifetime achievements had exceeded their expectations.

The chapter draws upon life history narratives, open-ended in-depth interviews, and participant observation, as well as our survey data and secondary data from existing sources. It addresses four main questions:

- What changes occurred in the lives of the original interviewees over three decades and how did their children's and grandchildren's lives differ from theirs?
- Is poverty sticky? How strong is intra- and intergenerational transmission of poverty?
- What are the subjective perceptions of satisfaction and future prospects?
- Why are some people successful and not others? What patterns were found that relate to upward mobility and success?

The concluding section summarizes the findings and offers some reflections on inequality in Brazilian society as a constraint to moving out of poverty.

The Original Study and the "Myth of Marginality"

Favela is the Brazilian term for an informal settlement or shantytown in an urban area. Migrants from the countryside, lacking the means to rent or buy housing in the city, "invade" unused parcels of land and build their homes there. These lands are most often in undesirable locations such as steep hillsides, marshlands prone to flooding, landfills, or narrow parcels alongside roads, water basins, or riverbeds. Communities form over time as the migrants are joined by members of their extended families or others from their home towns who come to join them in the city.

For the original research in 1968–69, I selected three communities at varying distances from the center of Rio de Janeiro, representing the three areas of the city where poor people could then live. They were

- Catacumba, a favela on a steep hillside abutting a rock cliff in the wealthy South Zone, between Copacabana and Ipanema on the Lagoa Rodrigo de Freitas. By 1970 the Catacumba community had been eradicated and the residents forcibly relocated to public housing complexes, as discussed further below.
- Nova Brasília, a more spacious favela extending up a hill just off the Avenida Itaóca in the industrial North Zone.
- Duque de Caxias, a municipality in the Baixada Fluminense, located in Rio state but outside the city of Rio which was then the Federal District. Caxias was the least desirable of the options at that time, being the farthest from the opportunities and services afforded by the central city.

Within Caxias there were better-off neighborhoods closer to the municipal seat and poorer ones farther away. The latter had already been laid out in legal lots (*loteamentos*), but these had a quasi-rural aspect as they were not included in the urban network of paved roads, electricity grids, water and sanitation systems, or garbage collection that the better neighborhoods enjoyed. The lots were rented or sold at very low prices, providing an alternative to favela squatting for some of the migrants.

I lived for six months in each of the three sample areas. With a team of Brazilian students, I interviewed 750 people, 250 in each site. Of these 250, 200 were selected at random from the population of men and women ages 16–65. The remaining 50 in each site were community leaders who were selected based on their position and reputation. Eighty-two percent of those interviewed were migrants who had arrived in Rio from the countryside, and 18 percent were first-generation Rio-born (Perlman 1976, 82).

The resulting book, *The Myth of Marginality: Urban Poverty and Politics in Rio de Janeiro* (1976), was part of a paradigm shift, from depicting favelas as a problem to seeing them as a practical solution to the lack of affordable housing for rural migrants in the city. The book contested the stereotypes equating *favelados*, or favela dwellers, with criminals, vagabonds, prostitutes, parasites on the economy, political radicals, and social misfits. The research revealed that most migrants to Rio were not pushed out from the countryside because they were the least capable, but rather were pulled toward the city by its opportunities, aspiring to give their children better lives. Favela residents were not economically marginal but exploited, not socially marginal but excluded, not politically marginal but manipulated to preserve the status quo. The negative stereotypes were used not simply to stigmatize and dehumanize the favela population but also to justify policies of massive favela eradication.

Although an array of poverty alleviation policies and programs were put in place, they proved disappointing and left local, national, and international policy makers wondering what to do. Even as some slums were upgraded, new ones formed and grew. There was a sense of futility at being behind the curve. A better understanding of the dynamics of urban poverty was clearly needed, not a snapshot of a single moment or set of moments in time, but a grasp of the ongoing processes perpetuating poverty or overcoming it across time and generations.

The Restudy: Rationale and Design

Few longitudinal studies exist on urban shantytowns. Those that have been attempted tend to study the same communities but not the same individuals.[2] We are still ignorant of what happens to people over their lifetimes, what happens to their descendants, and why. A few studies have tried to answer these questions by using secondary data rather than primary fieldwork to explore social mobility, creating similar cohorts of people as proxies for a panel of the same individuals, and working with household survey data over time to explore social mobility (see, for example, Gacitúa Marió and Woolcock 2005).

A restudy of the same individuals and their descendents, I hoped, would fill this void in the literature about the dynamics of urban poverty over time and across generations. Only through a panel study of the same people, their children, and their children's children can we see how patterns of context, attitudes, behavior, and luck play out in the struggle to overcome the exclusion and dehumanization of poverty.

Although I had stayed in touch with the families from the original study, the restudy proved to be a formidable challenge. The danger of violence in the favelas was much greater. It was difficult to recontact families because of the general lack of street addresses and because many in the sample had moved. In order to protect anonymity during the height of political repression, I had not used the last names of the study participants.[3]

Eventually, with the help of local community residents that were hired and trained in research techniques, I succeeded in finding 308 of the 750 people in the original study, or 41 percent. Half of them were located in the same communities where they had been living; the other half were found in various locations around Rio and in six other states, where I went to interview them. The teams continued to follow up on leads for locating other original interviewees until the end of the fieldwork in 2001. In cases where the original study participant had died, the life history matrix for that person was filled in with the help of family members, but the full survey instrument was not used.

The restudy was carried out in three phases:

- Phase I (1999–2000) was a feasibility study to determine the viability of tracing original interviewees (OIs) and to begin contextual research on the communities themselves.
- Phase II (2001–2002) focused first on reinterviewing the 308 original interviewees who could be located. The research team used questionnaires and life history matrices with those who were still living and able to respond (165) and filled in the life histories with the closest living relative for those who were deceased or were physically or mentally incapable of being interviewed (143).[4] We also interviewed a random sample of the children of OIs (367) and of those children's children (208). We wanted to see whether the dreams of the original study participants had had been realized in their children's or grandchildren's generation.
- Phase III (2003–2005) was a restudy of the same three favela communities that were researched in 1968–69. The purpose was to compare the profiles of the communities in 1969 to their profiles in 2003 to see changes in their demographic composition, quality of life, and position within the city of Rio. This also enabled us to better assess attrition bias

in the longitudinal study. New random samples of 400 people and leadership samples of 25 were drawn from each community (with an additional 24 people from the housing complexes where most of those evicted from Catacumba had been sent). An updated version of the original survey instrument and life history matrix were used along with open-ended interviews and participant observation.

The total sample size for the restudy was therefore 2,182, of which 883 were from Phase II and 1,299 from Phase III. Finally, as follow-up, we conducted in-depth interviews with the most and least successful people from the random and leadership samples.

The problem of bias due to attrition

Given that 59 percent of the original sample was not located, attrition was a serious concern. The people not found could have included the most upwardly mobile, who had moved to better neighborhoods, or the most downwardly mobile, who had gone to live on the streets or under bridges or returned to the countryside. One method we used to test bias was to compare the characteristics of the entire random sample in 1969 with the 1969 characteristics of the subset we were able to find 30 years later. When we compared these two groups we found no statistically significant differences in socio-demographic variables such as gender, race, number of children, access to domestic goods, status of education, income, occupation, political participation, home ownership, number of people in the household, or number of rooms in the home as of 1969.[5]

The second way we checked for bias was to compare the sample we located with the new random sample, holding age constant, by using the children of the OIs (since the OIs had an average age older than 65, which was the age limit of the new random sample). We found that children of the original interviewees were slightly better off than their same-age counterparts from the new random sample in the same communities.

Neither approach revealed systematic bias in any direction. The 1969 socioeconomic profiles of those who were found and those who were not found were quite similar. This means there were no apparent socioeconomic traits in 1969 that correlated with the probability of our locating the person later (although this does not rule out the possibility that these two groups may have had different life outcomes in the intervening decades). The findings did reveal what I call the "urban advantage": Rio-born children had an edge over those born elsewhere, and those with Rio-born parents tended to do even better. For migrants, in general, the longer a person has been in the city, the better off he or she will be.

Our analysis here focuses on how the people we did find had changed over three decades and how their lives compared with those of their children and grandchildren. Our findings are not based on the assumption that the 30-year "survivors" of the original panel are representative of all original interviewees or of the favela population at large in 1969 or in 2001. One of the reasons we drew new random samples in the same communities was to look at how our group of survivors compared with the current residents of those communities, and we found them to be quite similar.

The Setting: Brazil, Rio, and the Favelas

Brazil is not a poor country. Its per capita gross domestic product (GDP) places it in the middle-income category, between the highly industrial countries of the North and the underdeveloped countries of the South. It is among the richest countries in Latin America, along with Chile, Argentina, and Mexico, and is considerably better off than most Asian and African countries.

Brazil's rapid growth and public policy changes have reduced poverty in recent decades, from about 40 percent in 1977 to 36 percent in 2000. But the poverty rate is still high in comparison with other countries with similar income per capita (Paes de Barros, Henriques, and Mendonça 2001). Moreover, any gains have been offset by the persistence of extreme inequality. Brazil ranks among the most unequal countries in the world, with a Gini coefficient of 0.56–0.60 that has remained relatively constant over time (Ferreira, Leite, and Litchfield 2006). The top 10 percent of Brazilians account for 50 percent of the national income, and the poorest 20 percent account for only 2.5 percent of the national income. The wealthiest 1 percent earn more than the poorest 50 percent (Paes de Barros, Henriques, and Mendonça 2001). This inequality in income distribution not only puts a damper on mobility but limits economic growth as well.[6]

The mobility patterns of Rio's *favelados* from 1969 to the present—and the mobility of their children and grandchildren—can best be understood in light of certain macro-level political and economic transformations in Brazil and in the city of Rio de Janeiro over this period.

The original study was conducted at the height of the Brazilian dictatorship, which began with a military coup on April 1, 1964. A gradual political opening (*abertura*) started in 1974. It was followed by a series of incremental steps toward redemocratization until the end of the dictatorship in 1985 and the return of direct vote for mayor, governor, and president. After a long period of repression of civil liberties, the "right to have rights" movement prevailed. The new constitution of 1988 expanded the space for community groups, federations of community groups, and nonprofits, creating the expectation that life for the urban poor would improve.[7]

There were equally dramatic transitions in Brazil's economy during this period. The country went from the economic "miracle" of the 1960s, when it enjoyed one of the fastest-growing economies in the world, to triple-digit inflation in the 1970s. The so-called lost decade of the 1980s was followed by relative stabilization achieved through Fernando Henrique Cardoso's 1994 "Plano Real," which pegged the value of the Brazilian currency to the U.S. dollar. Inflation was brought under control but growth rates have been disappointing, averaging about 2.5 percent per year (Gacitúa Marió and Woolcock 2005). Contagion from other countries' economic crises, exorbitant interest and tax rates (which inflate the informal economy, now at almost 40 percent of GDP), and stark levels of inequality have kept Brazil from reaching its full potential.

Rio de Janeiro in perspective

The economic position of the municipality of Rio de Janeiro in relation to other metropolitan areas in Brazil declined over the three decades between the two studies.[8] Contributing factors included the loss of national capital status to Brasília; the shift of the country's financial, service, intellectual, and cultural headquarters to São Paulo; deindustrialization; and a decline in tourism due to violence. Rio's GDP per capita is relatively high, but its growth is not keeping pace with the rest of the country. During the period of the restudy, in 1999 and 2002, the city of Rio had a lower growth rate of GDP per capita than the city of São Paulo, the state of Rio, all the major regions of the country, and Brazil as a whole.

The proportion of Rio residents under the poverty line decreased by 3 percent between 1991 and 2000, from about 16 percent to 13 percent. But the number of indigent poor increased slightly to about 6 percent (Bourguignon, Ferreira, and Menéndez 2003).

The relatively high per capita GDP of Rio as compared with other cities and regions masks stark disparity between rich and poor. Rio's level of inequality (the municipal Gini index is 0.616) is worse than that of Brazil as a whole (0.593). Moreover, the gap between poverty and prosperity in the "marvelous city" widened during the 1990s (IPP 2005).

This has resulted in strikingly different rankings for different parts of the city on the United Nations Development Programme's Human Development Index (HDI). The neighborhood of Gávea in the city's South Zone enjoys a quality of life comparable to that of Belgium, which ranks 9th on the HDI. Meanwhile, the Complexo de Alemão in the North Zone of Rio has a quality of life close to that of Vietnam, which ranks 108th. Complexo de Alemão is a large favela that sprawls over several hillsides; Nova Brasília, one of our study favelas, is part of this complex. The average per capita income of Gávea, at 2,140 *reais* per month, is more than 12 times that of Complexo de Alemão, at 177 *reais*. Residents of Gávea have a life expectancy of 80; those in Complexo de Alemão, just 65.

There is also a striking income gap between favelados and non-favelados within the same residential zone. According to the 2000 census, non-favelados in the wealthy South Zone had 5.5 times more income than favelados in the same zone. In the poorest area of the city, the West Zone, non-favelados had only 1.5 times more income than favelados in that zone.

Favela growth over five decades

Rio had 752 favelas in 2000, according to the Instituto Pereira Passos, the city's urban planning agency. With 1.1 million favelados as of that year, Rio has the largest favela population of any Brazilian city. In 2000, 19 percent of Rio's total population of 5.8 million inhabitants lived in favelas. If the population in favelas is added to low-income Rio residents in other forms of informal housing, a total of 38 percent of the city's population can be considered at risk (IPP 2005).

Despite political and economic advances, poverty programs, and community improvements, both the absolute number of poor people and the percentage of Rio's population living in favelas have increased steadily over the past six decades. Growth of the favela population has outpaced population growth in the city as a whole in every decade including the 1970s, when over 100,000 favela dwellers were removed and relocated by the dictatorship. In the 1980s, the population of Rio grew by less than 8 percent while the favelas swelled by 22 percent. In the 1990s, Rio grew by about 7 percent and the favelas by 24 percent (IPP 2005).

Our three study favelas had somewhat different experiences during the 30-year research period. By 1970 the Catacumba community had been eradicated and the residents forcibly relocated to public housing complexes in various parts of the city. Families were divided up according to income level: some were taken to the *Cidade de Deus,* made infamous by the widely distributed film *City of God,* but most were sent to the adjacent housing complexes of Quitungo and Guaporé. Nova Brasília never benefited from any government upgrading project. It became one of the most violent communities in the city as it grew up and over the mountain, joining with seven other favelas into what is now called the Complexo de Alemão. The Caxias favelas, while considerably improved with respect to physical conditions, are also in an uphill battle against stigma and violence. The closer-in Caxias loteamentos, however, have been gradually upgraded and incorporated into the urban fabric of the municipality as legitimate low-income neighborhoods.

How People's Lives Changed over Time and Generations

To get a picture of individual trajectories for those in our study samples, we looked first at place of residence: who had managed to move out of the favela to a better neighborhood and who remained. We then examined changes, both positive and negative, in the lives of individual participants and attempted to identify key obstacles to upward mobility.

Where are they now?

If the favelas are a trap, as suggested by Wacquant (1996, 1999) in his provocative work on the new marginality, nearly all surviving members of the original sample and nearly all of their descendants would still be there 30 years later. In fact we found that only 37 percent of the random sample had remained in favelas. Another 25 percent, almost all of them former residents of Catacumba who had been forced out, were living in housing complexes (*conjuntos habitacionais*). These massive, deteriorated structures consist of small apartments in five-story walk-up buildings. While they are legal, the conjuntos are still stigmatized spaces, with levels of drugs and gang violence similar to the favelas. These housing projects are technically within neighborhoods of Rio, but the word "neighborhood" (*bairro*) is reserved for communities characterized by market-based houses and apartments, often mixed with some commercial use. Thirty-four percent of the original random sample had succeeded in moving into these better neighborhoods, albeit at some distance from the center city (table 7.1).

This finding that the majority of the original sample and their descendants no longer live in favelas raises the question of whether they have moved

TABLE 7.1

Location of Original Interviewees and Their Descendants in 2001

percent

Category	Favela	Public housing complex (conjunto)	Neighborhood with market-rate housing (bairro)
Original interviewees	37	25	34
Children	36	16	44
Grandchildren	32	13	51

Note: Percentages do not add up to 100 as the remainder are in loteamentos. The shrinking percentage of people in housing projects is largely explained by the projects' inability to physically expand. As families grew over generations, descendants moved either to favelas or to neighborhoods.

out of poverty. Does geographic mobility out of the stigmatized space of the favela translate into socioeconomic mobility and integration into the city as a whole?

Our research results show clearly that those who remained in favelas have significantly lower scores on measures of socioeconomic status (SES). They have lower incomes, a lower percentage of nonmanual jobs, and lower educational levels than those who moved to neighborhoods. The indicators for those in public housing projects fall somewhere between favelas and neighborhoods on each of these measures. This does not tell us whether those in neighborhoods were better off *before they left* the favelas or housing complexes, and for that reason had financial freedom to exit, or whether they began doing better *after they started living in the neighborhood* because of greater access to jobs, quality schooling, and diverse network connections. We found a two-way relationship: those with greater assets and resources had a greater chance of moving into a neighborhood, and once they were there, freed from the stigma attached to favela residents, they were able to increase their relative advantage still more.

One way we approached this question was by comparing SES differences among children in favelas, conjuntos, loteamentos, and neighborhoods; all of their parents were still living in the favelas. As seen in figure 7.1, the children still in favelas have negative SES scores, while those in neighborhoods have the highest scores, with loteamentos and conjuntos in between but closer to the neighborhood scores. Holding constant the favela location of the OIs reveals a distinct disadvantage for children who stayed in the favela and a distinct advantage for those who moved into a neighborhood.

What affects the likelihood of escaping the favelas? The results of a probit model on factors affecting the likelihood of moving from a favela into a neighborhood are as follows:

Positive correlations
Father's education
Own education
Political knowledge

Negative correlations
Home ownership (or perceived ownership)
Formal labor contract (with official signed document)
Membership in a neighborhood organization or association

The literature would lead us to expect the first two positive correlations, that is, that education of oneself and one's parent would be significant pre-

FIGURE 7.1
SES of Children Whose Parents Stayed in a Favela

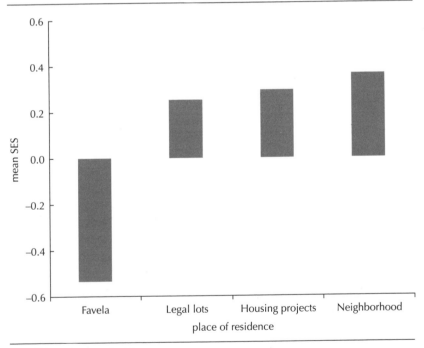

Note: SES = socioeconomic status.

dictors of mobility (Gacitúa Marió and Woolcock 2005). Political knowledge (as measured by correct answers to a set of political questions) would be a likely correlate of more years of schooling and better-educated parents.

The more perplexing and even paradoxical findings emerged from the significant negative correlations. Why would the apparent elite of the favelas—those who boasted the resources to own their homes, who enjoyed formal employment with a labor contract guaranteeing them full worker benefits, and who had the energy and initiative to join a local organization—be more likely to stay than to leave? Only when one lives in the communities and gets to know the people firsthand does this finding begin to make sense. Of the original interviewees still residing in the favelas, over 11 percent had the economic means to move out (equal or higher SES scores than those who did move out), yet chose to stay. The answer is that they were the ones with the strongest ties to their favela community, as reflected in home ownership (although very few had legal documents), nearby employment, and active participation in neighborhood-based organizations of one type or another.

Home ownership in favelas (or perceived home ownership, when actual title is in doubt) implies several things. First, many of those who said they owned their homes had invested much of their disposable income over decades into expanding and improving their dwellings. Not only was the house their greatest asset, but in all likelihood their extended family lived there as well and it had grown upward and outward into a family compound. While it might have been financially feasible for a single person or a couple to move into an apartment in a bairro, or to buy a small plot of land on the urban fringe, it would imply leaving the rest of the family behind, as a large living space elsewhere would be unaffordable.

The second significant factor in remaining in the favela is the possession of what Brazilians call a *carteira assinada*, or signed work permit. This is a valuable document indicating a formal work contract with all of its attendant benefits, such as a guaranteed minimum wage (which varies by place according to living costs), the right to an extra month's salary bonus at the end of the year, overtime wages, paid vacation, and retirement benefits. Those who have it are the elite of the labor force. Favela residence offers a close-in, affordable place to live that is close to work opportunities; other affordable housing would likely be at a great distance from the central city.

The last factor is the most obvious. Levels of community participation are generally low. People who are members of any organization or association presumably have particularly close ties to that community and to the people living there, and they would thus be less likely to want to move away.

What improved over 35 years?

Across the study sample, the lives of the original study participants and their offspring became better in some ways and worse in others. While it would make for a more concise chapter if the findings were consistently positive or negative, the reality did not turn out that way. To better understand this mixed picture, I found it useful to compare the original study participants in 1969 with their children in 2001, as these two samples reflect comparable stages in the life cycle. The mean age of the original random sample in 1969 was 35.7 years and the mean age of their children in 2001 was 39.6. This puts both in the range of their highest earning power, often defined as 20 years after their first jobs.

In 1969, electricity in the favelas was provided by illegally tapping into power lines. Water was available only at collective spigots slowly dripping at the bottom of the favela hillsides, and sewerage ran down the slopes in open channels, often overflowing into pathways and homes during heavy rains. As shown in table 7.2, there was dramatic improvement over time and generations in home building materials, plumbing, and electricity. The near univer-

TABLE 7.2
Improvements over Time and Generations
percent

Indicator	1969 OIs	2001 OIs	Children	Grandchildren
Brick home	43	94	97	97
Indoor plumbing	54	76	98	99
Electricity	73	98	97	96
Refrigerator	36	98	97	96
Television	27	93	98	96
Washing machine	0	50	67	63
Air conditioner	0	39	69	68
Telephone line	0	68	88	89
Car	0	14	29	34
Computer	0	10	22	25
Illiterate	72	45	6	0
Some/all high school	0	1	29	45
Mean years of education	2.37	2.49	7.36	8.88
Had nonmanual job for most of working life	6	20	37	61

Note: OI = original interviewees.

sality of urban services in 2001, even in communities that were not included in formal upgrading programs, is notable.

Striking gains were also made in ownership of household goods and in education and occupation. While 75 percent of the parents of the OIs and 45 percent of the OIs were illiterate, only 6 percent of their children were, and none of the grandchildren. At the other end of the spectrum, none of the OIs or their parents had attended high school, but 45 percent of their grandchildren had, and 11 percent of the grandchildren had gone on to university. With respect to occupation, we looked at the category of job the individual had held for the majority of years since starting work. We found this to be more reliable for comparison than either "current job," "first job," or "job 20 years after first job," and we had answers to this exact question about the fathers and mothers of the original interviewees. Clearly, nonmanual work became more common with each generation.

What was disappointing?

Migrants, favela dwellers, social scientists, and policy makers see education as the key to moving out of poverty. If that were so, the impressive educational gains recorded in the favelas would go a long way toward mitigating poverty and ensuring a successful life. Due to the perversity of prejudice, however, those who make the greatest sacrifices for their education and need it the most do not see the same returns on schooling as those who have the luxury of taking education for granted.

Valéria Pero (2003) found that educational gains for favelados are not fully reflected in income. For every additional year of schooling after the first four, the gap in expected income between favelados and non-favelados grows wider (figure 7.2). This holds up even when one controls for age, race, and gender. This gap likely reflects differing levels of quality in education, differing social and cultural environments in favelas than in neighborhoods, and discrimination against people from favelas in the job market.

In light of this, it is no wonder that many favelados became disillusioned with education. This showed up in their responses when they were asked to name "the most important factor for a successful life." Whereas in 1969 the vast majority responded that education was most important, by 2001 a large majority of both the OIs (79 percent) and their children (96 percent) named either a "good job" or "a career" (figure 7.3). They further explained that they would be happy with either employment in the formal sector (*emprego*) or independent work (*trabalho*), as long as they had a chance to do "decent work with decent pay."

FIGURE 7.2
Income Returns to Education for Favela Dwellers and Others

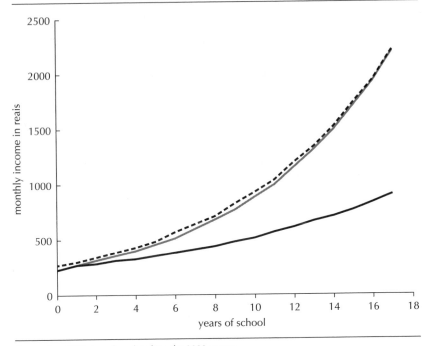

Source: Pero 2003, based on data from the 2000 census.

FIGURE 7.3
OI Children's Views on Most Important Factor for a Successful Life

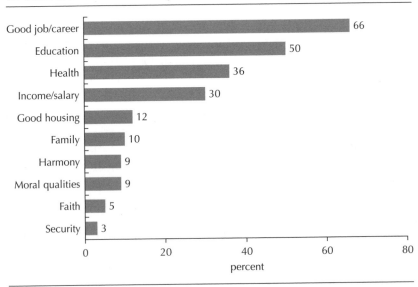

OI = Original interviewees

Following individual families enabled us to do a case-by-case analysis comparing each person with his or her own parents. While 85 percent of the children had more education than their parents, only slightly more than half (56 percent) had better jobs. In part this reflects the fact that educational requirements for the same jobs has also been rising. A higher educational bar to employment also contributes to the higher unemployment rates for each succeeding generation despite greater educational attainment. Between the first study and the restudy, the proportion of our sample that reported being unemployed (or *parado*, inactive, if they worked in the informal sector) for more than six consecutive months at any point in their working lives rose from 32 percent to 51 percent. This rate was higher in the favelas than in the housing projects or neighborhoods.[9] The average unemployment rate in the city of Rio was 10 percent at the time of the restudy.

We also found indications of absolute poverty: 35 percent of the OIs, 18 percent of their children, and 13 percent of their grandchildren had gone hungry in the not-too-distant past. Twenty-three percent claimed to have no income, compared to 17 percent in 1969.

One former leader from Nova Brasília, who had earned good pay as a truck driver for the nearby Coca Cola factory until it closed, was living in a shack in the backyard of what was once his own home. When I asked him what should be done for the poor, by which I meant families like his own, he replied by referring to others less fortunate: "I always try to help someone in need and do whatever I can for them." When I asked him what his biggest problem was, he said "the choice between buying diabetes medicine for my wife or milk for my grandson." His pension was supporting at least seven family members. He supplemented it with a monthly *cesta básica* (minimum food basket) distributed by the church and by sending the children to collect leftovers from the local produce markets.[10]

What are the obstacles to mobility?

Barriers to upward mobility include *community-level obstacles* (increased violence related to drug and arms traffic and decreased social capital, sense of trust, and community unity); *political obstacles* (lack of voice, absence of the protection afforded by the rule of law, and postdictatorship forms of corruption and clientelism); and *economic obstacles* (the stigma that favela residents face in getting a job, labor market conditions, and extreme inequality).

The biggest single change I saw in the lives of the favelados was the constant, all-consuming fear caused by drug-related violence. This is a population with great ingenuity and unfailing humor and vitality. Even in the face of severe deprivation they had always found ways to make their homes and communities warm and welcoming. Today, however, violent battles between competing drug factions and between drug traffickers and the police cast a shadow over daily life. At the start of the restudy in 2000, about half the favelas in Rio still had independent residents' associations with popularly elected presidents. One by one the local leaders were driven out or killed, and by 2005 almost all the residents' associations were controlled by drug traffickers. The one exception, Rio das Pedras, is drug-free but is controlled by *matadores*, death squads made up of retired or active police who use lethal force to keep drug dealers out. Poor people feel trapped between the warring sides. Drug-related violence creates a climate of fear not only in the favelas but also in the conjuntos and increasingly in the low-income neighborhoods where the poor have gone to escape the violence.

In the 2001 multigenerational interviews we asked each person: "Have you, or a family member, ever been a victim of violent crime?" The percentages responding affirmatively ranged from a low of 1 percent for rape and sexual abuse to a high of 56 percent for robbery (figure 7.4). One of every five people interviewed had lost a family member to homicide.[11] Contrary to what the news media, particularly the Brazilian newspaper *O Globo*, would lead one to believe, levels of lethal violence are not higher in favelas than in other types

FIGURE 7.4
Reported Experiences of Violent Crime

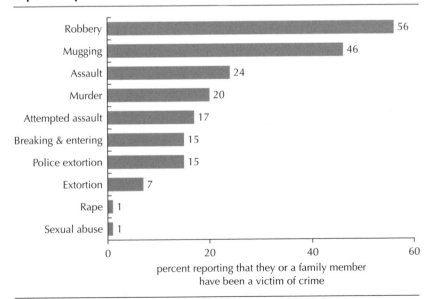

percent reporting that they or a family member
have been a victim of crime

of low-income communities, whether conjuntos or bairros. Reported levels of violence were the same regardless of age, generation, or gender.

The pervasive violence has had a dampening effect on social capital as measured by the sense of community unity. In 1969, 85 percent of the OIs said their communities were "united or very united." By 2001 this had dropped to 51 percent of the OIs, 45 percent of children, and 42 percent of grandchildren. The frequency of socializing with friends and neighbors and the degree of trust in neighbors had plunged. In 1969, 51 percent reported that they could count on "most or all" of their neighbors, but by 2001 only 31–35 percent said they could—among all three generations.

Rising violence has also contributed to declines in community participation by weakening the community associations and by making it dangerous to leave home after dark to attend meetings (figure 7.5).

During the first study, the residents' associations played a critical role in the life of the favela communities. By 2001 the study favelas had full infrastructure, if not land tenure, and the vitality of the residents' associations had diminished. Most of them had lost their independence to takeovers by one of the several competing drug factions. If the elected president did not agree to this changeover, he and his family were often found murdered or were given 24 hours to leave the community. In such cases, the police provided "protection" to the evicted

FIGURE 7.5
Participation in Community Organizations, 1969 and 2001

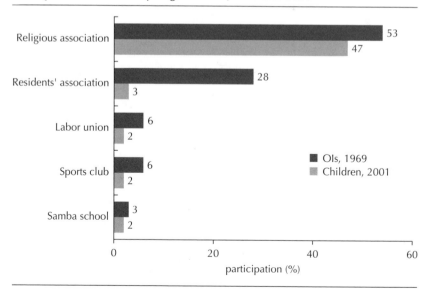

family rather then confronting the dealers. At the same time, the conjuntos had difficulty organizing any associations at all due to distrust and disinterest, and the neighborhoods had their own associations but also with low memberships.

Over the same period of time, labor unions, sports clubs, and samba schools in the study communities also went from low participation to almost no participation. Religious groups were the only organizations to maintain active membership, predominantly the evangelical churches and primarily with female members.

Along with declining membership in local organizations we found a lower level of socializing among friends and neighbors. What I call the "sphere of fear" (or *mundo de medo*) discouraged people from going out, visiting or receiving visitors, and congregating in public areas as they used to do. This reduced level of socializing in turn reduced the casual exchange of tips about work opportunities, odd jobs needing to be done, or school scholarships being distributed. The violence also depressed the sale or rental value of homes, forced many local shops and restaurants to close, discouraged new investments in the area, and scared away service providers (teachers, health care workers, nonprofit organizations, and commercial deliveries).

In terms of marginality, the degree of violence reported in the press and on television serves to reinforce the stigma associated with favelas. Job interviews typically end when the applicant's address is requested and identified as a favela. For all generations, the stigma of favela residence trumps the stigma of race and all other forms of discrimination, including being born outside Rio (those from the northeast of Brazil or the interior of Minas Gerais are particular targets of derision) (figure 7.6).[12]

The OIs' children hold similar perceptions of discrimination as the OIs, but the grandchildren report somewhat less awareness of stigma. This may be a sign that they are in fact less excluded. Still, 78 percent of the grandchildren say there is stigma against favelados, 45 percent against dark skin color, 57 percent against people who do not look like they are from the South Zone, and 57 percent against those from outside Rio. The trend is in a positive direction, but these young people still endure stigmatization on multiple levels, helping explain their high levels of unemployment.

In terms of citizenship, those who lived through the dictatorship report feeling more excluded now and having less bargaining power than they did before the return of democracy 20 years ago. People have won back the right to vote. But without any accountability or rule of law, new forms of corruption and clientelism are disenfranchising the poor, preventing them from exercising their voice and leaving them without recourse for seeking justice.

FIGURE 7.6
Sources of Stigma: Perceptions of Three Generations

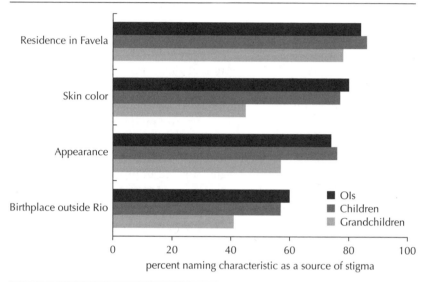

Note: "Appearance" is a loose translation of the slang expression *pinta,* which has to do with the way the person presents himself or herself, including type of clothing, shoes, hairstyle, accessories, speech, posture, behavior, politeness, cleanliness, and eye contact.

The above-mentioned obstacles are exacerbated by the decline in Rio's economy and the tight labor market. Deindustrialization (which occurred earlier than in other cities) and the decline of the shipping industry created massive job losses for blue-collar workers. Work in construction, which had earlier absorbed a large proportion of male newcomers and favela dwellers, fell off as the city's South and North zones became completely developed and mechanization replaced manual labor in many arenas. Domestic service, the major source of income for women in earlier times, also contracted, a result of higher costs (after household work became covered by labor laws), the economic squeeze on the middle class, wider availability of labor-saving household appliances, and new food take-out services.

Service jobs spun off by the federal government were lost when the capital moved to Brasília. Technological advances meanwhile eliminated many labor-intensive jobs and raised educational requirements for entry-level jobs, so that getting work has become extremely difficult for those without an advanced degree.[13]

Finally, as many studies have shown, the extreme inequality in Brazil and in Rio presents an obstacle to social mobility (Bourguignon, Ferreira, and Menéndez 2003; Gacitúa Marió and Woolcock 2005).

Why Some, and Not Others?

"Por que uns e não outros?" The question of why some people succeed while others from similar circumstances do not has been raised in regard to which favela youth succeed in getting into a university (Souza e Silva 2003). The same question could be asked regarding upward mobility in general.

Despite the myriad of obstacles they encountered along the way, many of the original study participants and their first- and second-generation descendants have made considerable progress toward improving their lives. It is true that only a handful made it into the upscale South Zone of the city or obtained professional jobs (5 OIs, 13 children, and 3 grandchildren). Yet some did much better than others over their lifetimes. Was it sheer luck and happenstance, or are there patterns in attributes, attitudes, beliefs, and behaviors that increase the probabilities of success?

As successful outcomes go far beyond the standard per capita family income, we look at four dimensions in the move away from poverty, exclusion, disenfranchisement, and despair:

- *Economic mobility* as measured by socioeconomic status and individual income
- *Geographic mobility* as measured by exit from favelas into legal neighborhoods
- *Political mobility* as measured by citizenship participation, both political and civic
- *Psychological mobility* as measured by aspirations, satisfaction, and perceived mobility relative to various reference groups[14]

The analytical framework shown in figure 7.7 allows us to systematically explore the relationship between "givens" (such as age, gender, race, origin, and household composition), mindset (fatalism, optimism, agency), social capital (both "bonding" based on internal networks and "bridging" based on external networks), and the successful outcomes described above.

Across all of the generations and time periods, we found significant bivariate correlations among all five measures of success, with the single exception that citizenship participation was correlated only with SES and not with any of the other measures. This may be due to the low level of political participation in general (Perlman 2007).

FIGURE 7.7
Analytical Framework for Successful Outcomes

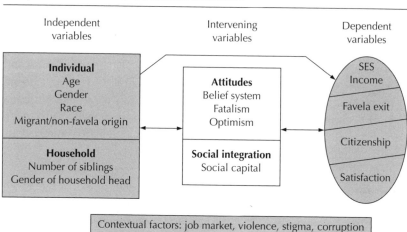

In looking for patterns based on the ascribed characteristics of a person's profile, we found that stage in the life cycle influenced attitudes and outcomes. Outcomes were better for the young or those in mid-career, as would be expected; being male or in a male-headed household conferred distinct advantages as well. Being young and male also correlated positively with intervening variables such as agency and optimism, which in turn increased the likeliness of upward mobility, thereby compounding the age/gender advantage and creating a virtuous cycle.

Race, on the other hand, made surprisingly little difference within this low-income population. In the grandchildren's generation, we did find a correlation between lighter skin color and higher SES, but there was no significant relationship between race and any of the other outcome variables. Underclass status seems to have trumped skin color, confirming what the interviewees had reported about the stigma of poverty (signified by favela residence) weighing more heavily than the stigma of race.

The other strong findings were that being Rio-born rather than a migrant was positively correlated with higher SES in all three time periods (1969, 2001, and 2003). I call this "the urban advantage," and it is cumulative. There is also a "small family advantage." Average family size is dropping in the favelas, but it is still higher than in the city as a whole, and within our sample those with smaller families scored significantly higher on every measure of SES, income, and satisfaction.

In terms of intervening variables, fatalism was negatively correlated with successful outcomes across all generations. People who believed that whatever happened was destined to occur (rather than the result of individual effort), or who said that Brazil's future depended on God or luck (rather than work of the people or good government), were less likely to be proactive in seeking out opportunities, less likely to have a strategy for getting ahead, and thus less likely to succeed. This in turn reinforced their passivity and fatalism. Conversely, optimism about the future was positively correlated with SES and political participation in the children's generation and with satisfaction across all generations, which reinforced agency and a proactive mindset.

The relationship between social capital and successful outcomes was determined by the *type* of networks, memberships, and socializing behavior. Those with greater "bridging networks" (significant ties external to one's own community) had significantly better-than-average outcomes in SES, income, and political participation. Those with greater "bonding networks" (internal ties within the community) had worse outcomes.[15]

On the issue of satisfaction, there were clear differences among the generations. For the OIs, community unity was highly important for satisfaction, but it made little difference for their descendants. Only for the children's generation was SES a strong factor in satisfaction. For the grandchildren, one important factor was holding title to their house (not land title, which was a separate variable). The other was indebtedness. Perhaps surprisingly, the more debt a person in this generation held, the more satisfied he or she professed to be.

From living with the families and knowing the grandchildren well, I can explain the apparent paradox of more debt leading to greater satisfaction. The debt is consumer credit, and consumption is a badge of prestige for the young. They buy everything—from cell phones to sound systems to shoes and shirts—on time in multiple installments, often paying interest that amounts to several times the price of the item. The more they owe, the more they have to show off, impress their friends, and approximate the images they see on TV.

Perceptions and relative mobility

Given that perceptions affect identity, motivation and action, the way individuals look at their own situation influences their chances of breaking out of the poverty trap. Mobility is a relational concept implying a reference group for comparison. People's measurable achievements in absolute terms are often not as important to their sense of well-being as their achievements relative to their past, their aspirations, and the aspirations their parents had for them, or relative to significant reference groups. Even television advertisements create a kind of reference group against which a person can feel relative deprivation.

I therefore asked several questions about relative mobility and perceived satisfaction. I used the 10-step "ladder" technique employed by Latinobarómetro to assess respondents' perceptions of their success relative to the past and to other generations (Birdsall and Graham 2000). The first question in this sequence ascertains each person's view of what would constitute a "successful life" (*vida bem-sucedida*). Using their own definition, respondents are then asked to place their current lives on the rungs of a ladder with step 1 at the bottom (the worst life) and step 10 at the top (the best life). Six comparative questions follow, each answer being registered as a position on the same ladder relative to where the respondent had placed his or her own life at the current moment. Table 7.3 shows the percentages who responded "better" or "much better" to each of the six comparisons.

For most of these questions, the percentage registering positive assessment in the comparisons (by indicating a higher position on the ladder) is surprisingly similar across all three generations. Despite all of the disappointments and obstacles discussed above, an average of 61 percent in all generations rated their current lives as better than they had been in the past (Q1). But they did not see this upward trend continuing for their children. (Q3), with only about 44 percent saying their children's lives were (or would be) better than their own. Similarly, the answers to how their lives had evolved relative to

TABLE 7.3
Perceptions of Progress toward a Good Life

Question	% responding "better" or "much better"		
	Ols	Children	Grandchildren
Q1: My life now versus 30 (or 10) years ago[a]	59	60	65
Q2: My life versus my parents' lives	53	35	27
Q3: My children's lives versus my life	43	44	47
Q4: My life versus my expectations	48	52	52
Q5: My life versus my parents' expectations	58	49	50
Q6: My family versus other families in this community	41	27	19

a. We asked about 30 years ago for Ols and 10 years ago for children and grandchildren.

their own and their parents' expectations (Q4 and Q5) yielded similar results for all generations, split about half and half, with slightly more of the OIs saying their lives had exceeded their parents' expectations (perhaps because their parents, being migrants, had minimal expectations).

Perceptions about the lagging outcomes for younger generations can also be seen in the discrepancy in generational responses to Q2: 53 percent of OIs but only 35 percent of children and 27 percent of grandchildren placed their lives higher than their parents' lives on the ladder. Here, the question of social mobility and moving out of poverty is shown to concern more than just the attainment of greater goods and services. The feeling of losing ground, a pervasive theme in the open-ended interviews, comes through clearly.

The feeling of being worse off than others in the community shows up in Q6, again most dramatically among the grandchildren, who are the highest in all measures of well-being. Only 19 percent in this generation ranked their families as better off than the other families around them, compared to 27 percent of the children and 41 percent of the OIs. All three generations feel they are not doing as well as others, but the ranking on this measure is the inverse of the poverty ranking. This may be because a greater share of each succeeding generation has moved into neighborhoods where the average standard of living is higher than in the favelas, and where they feel they are less well off than their neighbors. But the sense of being one step down is true for every generation.

This suggests that even as progress is being made at the material and educational levels, the goal of breaking out of poverty—of becoming *gente*, respectable people—is a moving target. The closer one gets to this desired social category, the more excluded one feels. Thus the grandchildren, who are the closest to the working or middle class by many indicators, are the ones who feel they have the farthest to go. One person said he had assumed that if he made many sacrifices, married well, and worked hard all his life he could become *gente*, but after all these years, he still feels "light years away."

Somehow, economic achievements are not erasing the sense of lingering marginalization, disrespect, and exclusion that poor Brazilians feel. Equality and full inclusion is a receding target, always elusive and out of reach.

What about the future?

Finally, respondents were asked about their expectations for the future. Did they expect a better life in the next five years for themselves, for their community, for Rio, for Brazil as a whole? They were most pessimistic about

FIGURE 7.8
Optimism about the Future

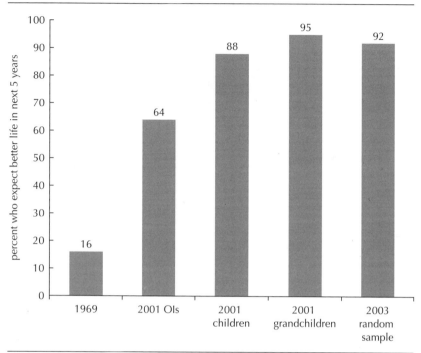

prospects for Brazil in the next five years and most optimistic about prospects for their own lives—and this held true for all generations. As this was one of the questions I asked back in 1969 and we also asked it of the new random sample in 2003, we have five points of comparison (figure 7.8).

There is a secular trend of increasing optimism. In the 2003 random sample of people ages 16–65, 92 percent said their lives will be better in five years. This optimism peaks among the grandchildren, 95 percent of whom expect better times to come. These responses are particularly striking given that only 16 percent of the OIs in 1969 who were in the same age range and the same communities expressed such optimism. As Brazil was in the midst of an economic boom at that time, and the interviewees were on a marked path of upward mobility, I would have expected a higher degree of optimism about the future. I would also have expected a lower degree of optimism on the part of these same individuals in 2001, by which time most were living on

FIGURE 7.9
Virtuous Cycle: Two-Way Positive Correlations

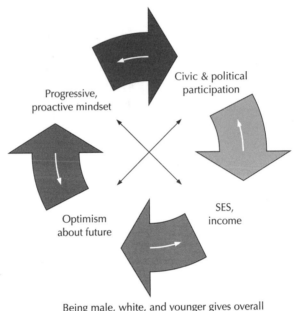

Being male, white, and younger gives overall
advantage, but relationships shown still hold
when analysis controls for race, gender, and age.

fixed pensions or retirement benefits, Rio's economy was relatively stagnant, and the drug wars were worsening.

Overall, we have seen a virtuous cycle for those who are moving away from—if not out of—poverty. Figure 7.9 shows these multiple relationships.

Successful outcomes versus greatest mobility: Comparing profiles

We use two distinct but complementary ways of analyzing what it means to move away from poverty: one depending on *successful outcome* and the other on the *degree of upward movement*. Looking at the characteristics of both types of "winners," we found many overlaps but some clear differences. We created a typology of mobility patterns, each with a set origin and destination point, to explore the correlates of upward mobility (as we explored the correlates of success earlier in the chapter). We then looked at the individual profiles of everyone in each generation who had moved up three quintiles or more.

Among the OIs, the most upwardly mobile between 1969 and 2001 were the younger ones, the most highly educated, those with smaller families, those with strong external networks and weak internal networks, those who voted in the last election, and those who were most optimistic about their lives. They were also the people who managed to find stable jobs and who had moved out of favelas and into neighborhoods.

Among the children, those with the greatest upward mobility in comparison to their parents were 31 to 45 years old, had moved into neighborhoods, and expressed greatest satisfaction with their lives. These findings are consistent with the findings on the five outcome measures used above in the analytical framework.

The differences are more illuminating. Whereas white males were the most successful by outcome measures, mulatto females were most upwardly mobile. In terms of original location, the most successful were from the subdivisions in Caxias (who started out slightly better off than those in favelas), but those from the favela of Catacumba in the upscale South Zone had the highest mobility. While education was a determining factor in successful outcomes for the OIs, those who went from the lowest to the highest quintiles were not the most educated of their peers; some were illiterate and many had low or no schooling. It was in the mobility of their children and grandchildren where education, especially university education, made a notable difference.

These findings are as far as survey data analysis can take us. To understand the more nuanced qualities that distinguish the "poverty escapers" from the "poverty prisoners" or "poverty plungers," we turn to the life histories and personal narratives that came out of multiple in-depth interviews I conducted over the years.

Is Poverty Sticky? Is It Inherited?

A basic premise of this volume is that poverty is not necessarily chronic over a person's lifetime (born poor, stay poor).[16] Nor does being born to a poor parent necessarily condemn a child to poverty (parents poor, children poor). Different social systems at different times and in different places offer greater or lesser prospects for mobility. If we understand the endogenous and exogenous factors that facilitate upward mobility, we may be able to support or accelerate the process. For intragenerational mobility we want to know, "Is poverty sticky?" And for intergenerational mobility we ask, "Is poverty inherited?"

TABLE 7.4
Intra- and Intergenerational Transmission of SES
percent

OIs 1969—OIs 2001	0.275
OIs 1969—children 2001	0.358
OIs 2001—children 2001	0.314
Children 2001—grandchildren 2001	0.498
OIs 1969—grandchildren 2001	0.239
OIs 2001—grandchildren 2001	0.09 (not significant)

To address these questions, we ran correlations of the SES means for OIs at two points in time (1969 and 2001) and across three generations. Table 7.4 shows that all but one of the correlations are positive and statistically significant, but none of them are strong correlations.

In short, an OI's socioeconomic status in 1969 is not a good predictor of his or her SES in 2001. Nor is the parent's SES in 1969 a good predictor of the children's SES in 2001, while they are at the same general stage in the life cycle. An OI's 2001 SES is an even weaker predictor of the children's position. The strongest correlation (0.498) is between the children and their children (that is, the children and grandchildren in 2001). But this is artificially high because 22 percent of the grandchildren are living with their parents, so the household consumption and density components of the SES index are identical, leaving only education as a differentiator.

Life Narratives: Pathways Away from Poverty

Once all of the survey and life history data had been analyzed, I selected the 10 most and 10 least successful members of the random and leadership samples for follow-up interviews. Several individual traits and contextual circumstances emerged as themes from these narratives, but they can be seen only as patterns fostering mobility (table 7.5). Not all of them were necessary conditions, and none of them alone was sufficient to bring about a move out of poverty.

I had expected that macroeconomic and political shifts and major public policy initiatives might turn up in narratives regarding the life trajectories. The change of currency to the *real* as part of the 1994 Plano Real, an anti-inflation measure pegging the value of the Brazilian currency to the U.S. dollar, raised purchasing power and seemed a likely positive benchmark in the lives of the poor. So did the end of the dictatorship, with restoration of the vote. Public

TABLE 7.5
Emergent Themes from Life Narratives

	Individual	Contextual
Givens	Drive	Proximity to upscale areas
	Persistence	Social networks
	Abilities	Family support (for education, skills training, job, etc.)
	Talent	
		Family culture and values
Choices	Spouse	Tradeoff between living in a favela closer to city center, or in a neighborhood farther away
	Limit number of children	
	Strategic planning (money, education, etc.)	
	Learn a trade, start a business, get a job	

policy initiatives such as Favela-Bairro, the massive favela upgrading project, might be expected to affect living conditions, along with community-level improvements such as the installation of piped water or electricity or the opening of a daycare center.

But none of these themes emerged as part of the uncensored stories about people's movements into or out of poverty. The themes and patterns that did emerge repeatedly, and that would not likely show up on any standardized survey, are summarized in table 7.5. They are divided into individual and contextual factors and into givens (personality traits or abilities evident at an early age) and choices. In a finding that would surely dismay many social scientists and policy makers, random elements of luck and timing also made a difference in many lives. Some of the most important events were thus entirely out of individual or policy control.

Many of these traits have appeared in the literature. In his review, Yaqub (1999, 19) identified eight "mobility filters" that distinguish "poverty escapers" from "poverty prisoners." They are parental income, education, gender, race, caste, community, class, and culture. For our interviewees all of these (except caste) played a role, but family culture turned out to be the best distinguisher between those who moved up and out of poverty and those who did not.

Family support and the "privileged connections" it can confer on children arose as extremely important in Krishna's (2004) work in Kenya. He concludes that "education, intelligence and hard work are not enough per se to escape from poverty," and he notes that access points and the advantageous opportunities family can provide are essential. Likewise, Platt's (2005) research on pathways out of poverty for ethnic minorities in Great Britain concluded that educational opportunities opened through parental support and particularly through the culture of the mother in the family are more important than class by itself in securing professional or managerial jobs for the next generation. Roemer (2003) specifies the channels through which family culture operates as provision of social connections, formation of beliefs and skills through family culture and investment, generic transmission of poverty, and formation of preferences and aspirations.

These themes are reflected below in the narratives of seven people who found pathways out of poverty—or did not.

The ant and the grasshopper: Edson and Adão

Edson is one of the poorest individuals in the random sample. When I arranged to meet him in Nova Brasília, he said it would be safer to meet at the house of his elder brother Adão, whose life and home were more orderly (*arumado*) than Edson's own further up the hillside. They were both waiting for me when I arrived. Once Adão's son had been sent to buy Coca Cola for the three of us (this being the ultimate sign of hospitality for a distinguished guest), we sat down to talk. It became obvious that both brothers would be participating in the interview.

They had come to Rio from a small town in the interior of the state of Minas Gerais, and both had started working at the age of eight. But their lives took divergent paths early on.

Edson lives in a precarious two-room shack without a plaster finish or proper roof (*laje*). He lives with eight dependents. None of his children are in school and none are working. He is an odd-jobber (*biscateiro*), picking up construction work here and there, but he has no steady income. He was formerly a construction worker and had a small bar where he sold local liquor called *cachaça*. At that time he had a car and a savings account and was a big spender, but he got into trouble and had to flee. He has had several wives and several children with each of them.

He is living on the edge. He says that is partly because he never thought about the future and lived from day to day, only caring about women and fun, and he spent whatever he earned without ever saving. His current wife was working but stopped when they married. He has no pension because he got angry one day when the social security system was on strike and he needed medical care, so he stopped making his monthly payments and was cut off. That, he says, is when he lost his way (*descaminho*) and his life began to spin out of control (*descontrolou*).

When asked how he manages, he explained that "now things are really rough . . . everyone is suffering. I used to get by borrowing from my neighbors here and there, but they can no longer help even themselves." He is ashamed to go to the produce markets to pick up leftover produce at the end of the day:

> It's like this. You arrive and there are other people who got there first and I don't have the courage to stay there picking through the spoiled leftovers— would you? How can you, when you see little children, shameless, who are there playing with the tomatoes or oranges and throwing them back and forth. For me this is no game.

He was getting the *cesta básica*, a basic basket of food staples that the government distributes to the poor once they prove their need. But it is distributed through the local Pentecostal church and when he does not attend services, they deny him the food. He is eligible for the Bolsa Escola program, which pays a stipend to the families of poor schoolchildren, but only if his child never misses a day of school. Moreover, the check of 100 *reais* per month barely lasts a week and then the family is hungry again. He tried moving back to the countryside at one point, but things were even worse there.

He said his brother is doing better because "he believed in work and planned his life for tomorrow." But their sister, who still lives in Minas, and who also saved and planned ahead, had a stroke, is blind, and had both legs amputated due to diabetes. Thus chance and vulnerability enter the picture.

When I asked what made work so hard to find these days, his brother Adão answered, saying "the poor don't have a chance anymore"(*o pobre não tem vez*). He went on:

> Before, there wasn't so much mechanization. Now there are even robots to do the work we used to do and the boss doesn't have to think about anyone. In the Campo Grande garbage dump, which employed lots of people, there is now only one worker, a robot, and a computer. Formerly there were garbage men who threw the trash into the truck. Now there is a machine that scoops it up and dumps it into the truck, so only the driver has a job.

Materially, Adão's life is much better than Edson's. Recently widowed, he lives in a three-bedroom, very well appointed house with his son and daughter in a loteamento adjacent to Nova Brasília. He was able to move there because he had worked for the owner of the land for nine years as caretaker. Out of his loyalty and vigilant work and due to good luck at being in at the beginning, he was able to buy a lot when the owner decided to subdivide. He lives quite well on his retirement pay for a lifetime of service as a janitor for Kibon, the ice cream company. He has a *carteira assinada* (a signed work card, serving as a record of employment) and all the documents of full citizenship.

He and his wife had only two children, an older girl who is now studying to be a nurse and a younger boy who is not working or studying and who spends his days flying his kite from the rooftop and watching television. Adão is in debt due to the high cost of his wife's funeral three months before the interview, but he has a plan to pay back the money. His biggest worry is his son, who threatens to join the drug traffic if any demands are made upon him. Life is not easy for Adão, but he is able to hold things together, pay for his daughter's nursing school, and help his brother by employing him to tile his kitchen and bathroom.

When I asked him what he thought accounted for the differences in their lives, Adão said,

> There is always one in every family who likes to work harder and wants to get ahead more. All my life I have liked to save money and I never spent all I earned. If I got 30 *contos* [an older currency], I would spend 15 and put the other 15 away. I was never interested in women or drink, and my wife and two children were the center of my life.

Soccer and smarts: Hélio Grande

Hélio is one of the most memorable people from the early days in Catacumba. He was 45 years old at the time of the first interview, a tall, charismatic community leader who was friendly with everyone. He was active in the residents' association, the youth athletic club, the samba school, and community events such as dances and picnics. Later in life he joined a labor union and became active in political parties as well.

Even as a youth, he had contacts outside the favela. Catacumba was located between Ipanema and Copacabana, two wealthy neighborhoods, and the poor kids from the favela played soccer with the rich kids. Once when Hélio was about 15, he was walking home from a party in the predawn hours and the police picked him up for vagrancy and held him in jail overnight. In the morning the police chief arrived and said, "Helinho, what are you doing here?" Hélio played soccer with the chief's son and had been to his house. He was immediately released, with apologies.

Of all the people I reencountered, Hélio had done the best in life. Although he only had a junior high school education, he was one of the very few to be living in the South Zone, and he had integrated into life in the middle-class neighborhood of Glória. In short, he had become *gente*.

I interviewed him in his two-bedroom apartment on a tree-lined street, a far cry from his shack in the favela. Hélio recalled that he and his family had been relocated to the housing project in Guaporé in 1970 when Catacumba was torn down. Through a combination of intelligence, contacts, and luck, he had landed a job as security guard at a bank. Within a few years he was transferred to Brasília, where he worked as a functionary in the Ministry of Justice. By working hard and living practically rent-free, he had saved enough money to return to Rio and buy his Glória apartment in cash.

> I always managed; I did whatever it took. We never had money. . . . My family was really poor, there was not enough to eat and we often went hungry . . . but I was never destitute. I always found a way to survive. Whatever sort of work came my way, I always grabbed it (*correu atrás*) and did it, and the hardest times passed that way. . . . Success is having luck provide an opportunity and then acting on it. . . . I had health, friendship, and soccer, and I made the rest happen.

He never felt any type of work was beneath him, he said, and thus he was never unemployed for long. He set goals for himself and met them. He believed that people should go after things they believe are right and not depend on others for their well-being. He also discussed his strategy of staying in Catacumba, rent-free, even after he started to earn a better living, and investing his money in property elsewhere when land values were cheap.

He has a son who is a professional soccer player and a grandson who married a Norwegian woman and lives in Oslo. But Hélio is most proud of his daughter, who attended private school, passed the entrance exam to the Federal University of Rio de Janeiro, graduated with flying colors, and completed two advanced degrees.

> I was able to do for her what I was never able to do for myself; this was my dream. I wanted to be an accountant. Then I wanted to be a lawyer, but I never had a chance to study seriously. And this girl [his daughter] is both: she's an accountant and a law graduate. Can you imagine?

Strategy and sacrifice: Maria Giselda

In 2001 Maria had the highest SES score among all of the random-sample original interviewees we found. In 1969, when we first met, she was living in Centenário, one of the unserviced loteamentos in Caxias, and now she lives in a small, spotless apartment in Copacabana. Each of her four children started working at age 14, and they helped buy her this apartment after her husband died. Her children prefer not to live in the South Zone; they've remained in or close to Caxias, and Maria visits them there on weekends.

Her family was from the Northeast and valued education and hard work as the road to success. In her words, they "fought for their lives and ran after any opportunity they could to survive and improve." Maria says that studying, personal drive, and parental support were the critical factors in her life success.

> I fulfilled my responsibility to raise my kids. I didn't want to leave them with anyone else so I stayed home with them and didn't work. It was a financial struggle for [my husband and me] to support our kids, but we did it, thank God. I think I raised them well. They haven't disappointed me at all—they make me so happy. The sacrifice I made to send them all to private school was worth it, and they have all worked hard.

Three of Maria's four children have good jobs. Her sons are both lawyers with good political connections that they made during high school, and together they bought and managed a local pharmacy where they had worked when they were in law school. Her younger daughter is a bank clerk in Copacabana. Her older daughter had to stop working because of heart problems.

Maria moved to Copacabana in 1989 after her sons sold their pharmacy in Caxias. But it was apparently her daughter who bought the South Zone apartment for her. Maria and her husband had also owned their home in Caxias, which she now rents out for additional income.

Today Maria is retired and cares for her ailing daughter. She also travels when she can. She says that she's able to live on retirement pay because she was a good financial planner and tucked away money each month during her working life. She made the most money when she started trading in gold jewelry, buying it cheaply in São Paulo and selling it for a profit in Rio. This was lucrative until the dollar rose, along with gold prices. In addition to her current retirement she receives her deceased husband's pension and rent payments from the house in Caxias.

Father knows best: Alaerte Correia

Alaerte had the second-highest SES of the random-sample individuals who were reinterviewed in 2001. He makes his living as a barber. His wife also contributes to family income, but the revenue from his barbershop was always the major source. He attributes his success to his father's pushing him to learn a trade:

> My father was 100 percent responsible for [my success]. When I was 13 years old, he said, "Son, you're going to go far in life." One of his buddies from back in the countryside had a barbershop near his house. My father asked him to teach me how to be a barber. I said "Oh, Dad, I don't

have the slightest desire to learn this. I don't want to learn to cut hair, no way." He said "No, my son, you're going to learn and learn well because a profession is never a waste." I remember as if it were yesterday. When I was 13, I learned to cut hair and at 15 I started working in the barbershop. My father's friend didn't like working; he liked soccer and drinking, so I ran the shop alone. At 18 I worked as a barber in the military for a year and eventually opened my own barbershop. If I hadn't learned this trade, I don't know what I would have been. I learned because [my dad] wanted me to learn it, he made me learn it, and I can now say that my life is better because of him. He gave me a profession.

Over time Alaerte has managed to acquire a significant amount of real estate, including an apartment in the conjunto Fazenda Botafogo, two studio apartments, a house in Campo Grande, a store in the city center, and a piece of land in Fazenda Modelo on the road to Teresópolis. For Alaerte, having a successful life depends on a solid family structure and a steady salary. And it was finding his trade that made all the difference.

No fruit on the table: Djanira

Djanira was one of the charismatic leaders in Vila Operária, the most organized of the three favelas in Duque de Caxias. She fought for the land, organizing street demonstrations and fighting in the courts for legalization of land title. She was once arrested and held in jail when she was nine months pregnant. She is brilliant, articulate, and beautiful. She went back to finish high school at the age of 40, after having 11 children, and then got a job in the health department of the Caxias municipality, working in DETRAN, the malaria prevention division. Barbosa, her partner for several decades and the father of her six youngest children, was a community benefactor who arranged to get the land for the residents. He owned land, stocks, and bonds and had a good job with a large pension plan. Their house was always full of people and activity, and there was always plenty to eat for anyone who dropped in around mealtime.

Today Djanira is practically destitute. She became ill from overexposure to the spray used to control mosquitoes (probably a toxic form of DDT). Each worker carries a canister of it on his or her back, with a hose and nozzle, and spends six days a week going door to door and shop to shop, spraying and breathing in the fumes. Now Djanira is short of breath and cannot work or get workers' compensation. She has been waiting for 12 years to get the pension that her partner signed over to her. But since she was not his legal wife, the required process of testing the DNA of her children has dragged on and on.

She still lives in the same house, but the street has become crime-ridden and bullet holes dent her front gate. The residents' association has been taken over by one of the drug factions and no one dares go out at night. Several of her grown children and their families live there as well, but all of them are struggling. One daughter cooks lunches for the school next door and another takes care of young children for her neighbors to earn some spending money. Djanira's son was in a bus accident and has never recovered his mental or physical abilities. He sells candies on the street where they live. One of her daughters lives in a nonurbanized loteamento further away in Caxias on a small plot she bought. It is much like Vila Operária in the old days, with its dusty dirt roads and lack of water, sanitation, garbage collection, and other urban amenities, but it is legal.

Money is so scarce that Djanira often has to choose between buying food or her blood pressure medication. Last time I visited she was making crocheted baskets and trying to sell these from home. She apologized to me for not having her usual bowl of fruit on the table.

Light years away: Nilton sums up

Nilton is a success story by other people's standards but a failure by his own. When I met him in Catacumba in 1969, he was 26 years old—bright, handsome, and full of promise.

His parents had managed to send him to a private Jesuit secondary school. After the removal to Guaporé he got a job with the military police, and after retirement he became a security guard and then a traveling salesman. His wife was a seamstress in a textile factory and after her retirement she continued working from home.

Both their daughters went to private schools and were the first in their community to get a desktop computer when they turned 15. One gave up her studies to marry. Her husband doesn't want her to work, but he is a traveling salesman and she stays with her parents many nights because it is too dangerous to stay in her apartment alone when he is working late or traveling. The other daughter dropped out of university when she broke her leg in a fall on campus. She became a telemarketer, paid below minimum wage and off the books, with long hours, but had to leave that job because it was making her deaf. She never returned to school.

Nilton lives in a family compound he built between the conjunto of Guaporé and the polluted river that runs alongside it. He sold his apartment and invaded this land to build a house for himself and his family, and relatives joined him one by one. They now have a little gated community with a two-car garage. It is protected by the fact that two family members were in the military police and have made it known that no drug dealers or gangs are welcome on "their" property.

Although Nilton is by no means poor, he is still relegated to a second-class existence as a squatter in a public housing complex in a zone controlled by warring drug gangs. He fears for his wife and daughters every time they go out. He cannot afford to retire, so he is now a salesman. By this point in life he had expected to be living like *gente*—a real person with dignity, who is not invisible as the poor are—in a legal house built on his own property, perhaps in the South Zone. He feels like a failure because he never managed to move his family out of this stigmatized setting and into a decent neighborhood, which would have enabled his daughters to study in better schools, choose from a wider array of job options, and meet different kinds of men. As he said to me when we met again after many years, he was beginning to get cynical and feel defeated:

> Janice, when I first met you I thought if I worked hard all my life, married well, had a small family and kept on saving, that I would be close to becoming *gente* . . . but now I feel light years away.

These stories are revealing and fascinating in their own right, but it needs to be emphasized that the beliefs and behavior patterns we identified among the most successful favelados by no means guarantee success for all. Some of the narratives show downward mobility among individuals who shared many of the traits and talents in table 7.5, being well educated, hard-working, persistent, and highly motivated.

There are dozens of people whose stories merit telling and whose lives are full of courage and creativity in the most daunting of circumstances. Space here does not permit further discussion of their struggles, setbacks, and successes.[17] Perhaps what stands out most is the persistence of hope, even when discouragement or despair seems more warranted. Hope itself becomes a critical resource for mobility upon which Rio's poor can and do draw.

Summary and Reflections

One of our principal findings is that the expression and the feeling of poverty and exclusion change over time and with each generation. Moving out of poverty is by no means simply a function of gaining access to better goods and services, although this is an important step. For the original migrants, the move to the city and the exchange of rural poverty for urban poverty was a leap forward. Access to jobs, education, health care, and unexpected opportunities opened up new prospects for their lives. Their struggles were to bring electricity, water, sewerage, and paved streets into their favela communities and avoid eviction. Those were collective struggles and created a sense of solidarity that their descendents rarely experienced.

The most powerful state intervention mentioned by our respondents was not pro-poor but universal: the pension system. It is regressive and expensive, yet the little that does come to the poor is literally a life saver. That is why when asked "Who was the politician who most helped people like you?" most of the older generation named Getúlio Vargas, who put the pension system into place.

For the children, born in the city, the quest was to obtain higher education, enough resources to get out of the favelas, and a measure of recognition and respect. In the grandchildren's generation, educational attainment is high, over half are living in legal neighborhoods, and the consumption of household goods is nearly the municipal average. Their challenge is to find work—over half are unemployed—and to avoid being killed in the pervasive drug-related violence. While an economist looking at census data may see many of the grandchildren as having moved out of poverty, within the current context of Rio de Janeiro they are still expendable, disenfranchised, and dismissed.

The youth are the best educated and most knowledgeable, but also the most cynical and most vulnerable. The years between the ages of 14 (when they can leave school) and 18 (when they can join the military) are the years of greatest risk. Child labor laws prevent those under 18 from being hired except as interns, and this makes it all the more tempting to go for the easy money and status of drug trafficking. Many youths still live with their parents, with the entire household surviving on the pension of the grandfather, as illustrated by the life stories above.

A recent ethnographic study commissioned by the Instituto de Economia, Trabalho e Sociedade (IETS) showed that youth who are no longer in school and not working spend most of their time sleeping, grooming, and watching TV.[18] They do not feel included in the life of Rio. In my interviews, I found that even favela youth with better jobs in the formal sector feel subservient and behave in a deferential manner when dealing with upper-class people or South Zone residents. The feeling of marginality persists even among those who have completed school, hold a job, and own a car and/or a computer.

What comes into focus when looking at all of these findings and narratives is a juxtaposition of positive changes at the community level—notably expanded urban services and infrastructure—and a mixed, less positive picture at the individual level. The lives of our interviewees continue to be marked by high unemployment, low political participation, and disappointing income returns to educational investment. Contextual barriers to individual mobility persist at the macro level, both in the economic environment (labor market conditions, high levels of inequality) and the political environment (lack of voice, low participation). These are compounded by community-level constraints, including drugs, violence, and decreased social capital, and by personal constraints such as passivity, fatalism, and low self-esteem.

There is no level playing field in the pathway out of (or away from) poverty and exclusion. Personal attributes matter, especially being male, light-skinned, and young, coming from a small family, and living close to an upscale neighborhood. Likewise, personality plays an important and often overlooked role. Without drive (*pique*) and persistence (*persistencia*), no one would succeed in moving out of the favelas or out of humiliating work conditions.

Our aim was not to generate policy prescriptions, but a few obvious ones suggest themselves. If jobs are the most important factor in success, as our interviewees asserted, emphasis should be placed on income generation at every level. Given that income returns to education are substantially lower for favelados than for non-favelados in Rio, the quality of education must be addressed. But better education alone will not improve the job prospects of favela youth as long as the stigma of favela residence, tied to high levels of violence, continues. It is essential to control the sale of arms and drugs and reduce the corruption that permits impunity.

For favela dwellers, legal documents such as identity cards, work cards, birth certificates, marriage licenses, and voter registration cards are badges of citizenship, allowing access to a range of services. Programs run by legal volunteers to help favelados secure these documents should be supported, along with an existing government program to give favela dwellers legal rights to their homes.

If poor people living close to upscale neighborhoods do better over their lifetimes due to contact with the nonpoor, as our research suggests, it may be useful to foster such contact by developing mixed-income land uses through urban planning and zoning regulations. For newly arrived migrants, who traditionally have found housing in the urban periphery, smaller areas closer to the center could be set aside.

Because attitude plays a significant role in getting ahead, emphasis should be placed on programs that motivate youth and provide legitimate role models as an alternative to drug dealers. Recreational and job-readiness programs run by communities, nongovernmental organizations, and government agencies should be scaled up.

But enlightened policies will go only so far as long as the entrenched culture of inequality continues. Our research over 30 years suggests that inequality is the fundamental impediment to upward mobility, economic growth, poverty alleviation, and reduction of violence. To address the persistence of poverty and to create conditions for upward mobility based on merit and effort, the entire social contract condoning radical inequality will have to be confronted. There must be a direct challenge to the comfortable culture of privilege that makes Brazil the second most unequal country in the world.

Notes

Acknowledgments. I would like to thank Sarah Anthony for her excellent help as a research assistant during the critical period of interpreting the analytic findings coming from our Rio project office. Her help was sorely missed during the last year of completion of this manuscript. I am also grateful to the Rio research team for their diligent work under difficult conditions. The team was directed by Professor Ignacio Cano of the Sociology Department at the Universidade do Estado do Rio de Janeiro, who supervised the methodology of Phase II, the entire research process of Phase III, and the data analysis. This work would not have been possible without the careful and insightful work of Graziella de Moraes, our first full-time Rio research assistant, and those who followed her: Lia Mattos da Rocha, Emanuelle Araujo, and Gisele Rocha. All of my friends in the communities are the real heroes and heroines of this work, and their willingness to take the risk of honesty made all the difference in what we found. Many others contributed and to all I am very grateful.

1. The full study will be published as *Marginality from Myth to Reality: The Favelas of Rio de Janeiro, 1968–2005*. Further information is available from the Mega-Cities Project, http://www.megacitiesproject.org/.
2. There are of course many panel studies, but very few in urban shantytowns, in part because conditions are nearly prohibitive. No street addresses, registries, or official records of slum populations exist, and people tend to use nicknames because so many have the same names. It was always a risk to conduct research in what the city considers a "no-man's-land," but that risk has increased exponentially with the rise of drug traffic and violence among gangs and police. It is no surprise that our restudy took five years to complete in these conditions.
3. In order to find the people, we started by locating their original household within the favela. If they had moved, we asked for help from the current occupants of the residence as well as neighbors, local organizations, stores, bars, etc. Often a family member, relative, or friend was able to tell us where the original interviewee was living or where other family members could be found. As many people have the same names, we asked a battery of questions (such as parents' place of birth, their own place of origin, occupation, schooling, and the names of their children) in order to verify that the person identified was indeed the person we had interviewed in the original study.

4. The 165 living OIs whom we reinterviewed included 126 from the random sample and 39 leaders. The 143 who had died or become incapacitated included 90 random and 53 leaders. For details on sample selection in Phase II, see Perlman (2003).

5. For a description of the way we tested bias from attrition, see Perlman (2003). There were built-in biases due to our method of relocation that led to overrepresentation of those with greater social networks and larger families. For example, Catacumba residents, who we assumed would be the most difficult to find as they had been forcibly relocated years earlier, turned out to be the easiest to find because their collective struggles had created lasting bonds. Those in the Caxias loteamentos, on the other hand, were underrepresented, as they were not squatters but renters or owners and had fewest ties to the community; once they moved, they were harder to track down. Among those found still living, females and younger people were overrepresented, as would be expected from longevity statistics. A full discussion of how the study handled questions of bias and attrition is included in Professor Ignacio Cano's "Phase III Report for Rio Re-Study," available from the Mega-Cities Project.

6. See Perry et al. (2006). According to the United Nations Development Programme, Brazil ranks 63rd of 177 countries on the Human Development Index, below its Latin American counterparts such as Chile (37th), Argentina (34th), and Mexico (53rd).

7. It seemed at first that this movement would be led by the independent "residents' associations" and federations of associations that had developed during the dictatorship as a voice for the favelas. These associations bargained for community improvements, especially infrastructure and urban services. They were courted by political parties and made alliances with them in the first few postdictatorship years. By the 1990s, however, drug dealers began taking over the residents' associations, and by 2000 only half were still independent. By 2005 the only residents' association *not* controlled by the drug factions was in Rio das Pedras, where death squads ran the association and kept the community free of drugs.

8. Rio de Janeiro is a municipality (6 million inhabitants), a metropolitan region (12 million), and a state (14.4 million). Unless specified otherwise, we refer to the municipality in this chapter.

9. The relative disadvantage of those in favelas is also reflected in the prevalence of the desirable nonmanual jobs. In 2001, among those in our study living in neighborhoods, 40 percent of those working held nonmanual jobs. In housing projects the figure dropped to 34 percent, and in favelas it was only 27 percent.

10. At the time of the study, Bolsa Familia, the conditional cash transfer program, had not yet reached urban areas. Since eligibility is based on a standard poverty measure, regardless of location, the program's benefits will continue to go mostly to the rural areas of poor states in the Northeast before reaching anyone in the large cities.

11. This rate is comparable to a country in civil war. The homicide rate for young males is higher in Rio than in Colombia (Rio: 268/100,000; Colombia: 213/100,000) (Cano 2004).

12. According to Moore (2005), social exclusion and adverse incorporation interact so that people experiencing discrimination and stigma are forced to engage in economic activities and social relations that keep them poor. Yaqub (1999) calls this "the poverty of the working poor."
13. The federal university system is free, but there remain major impediments to earning a university degree. These include the low quality of public schools in poor areas, the high cost of private schools, and the even higher cost of the *cursinho*, a preparatory course for the university entrance exam.
14. Our SES index was composed of education, consumption (of domestic goods), and density (people per room). The political participation index was based on four questions: have you ever signed a petition, attended a political meeting, participated in a political rally, or worked for a candidate or political party? We removed voting from the earlier index as it is now mandatory. Aspirations are based on what Appadurai (2004) calls "capacity to aspire." To create the satisfaction index, we gave one point for each positive answer to the following comparisons: your life today compared to your life in the past; your life today compared to your parents' lives; your family's life compared with the other families in the community; your life compared with your expectations/aspirations; your life compared with your parents' expectations/aspirations; and your life now compared to five years ago.
15. Networks were measured by the geographic proximity of the four closest family members or friends of the interviewee. Internal networks were considered high if three or four friends or family members lived inside the interviewee's community. Low internal networks consisted of one or two members, and no internal network meant that all one's closest family and friends lived outside the community. The same applies for external networks (high external = three to four friends/family members living outside the community, and so on). These two variables have a perfect negative correlation (see Granovetter 1973).
16. We owe a debt of gratitude to Shahin Yaqub for the terminology used throughout this chapter. His "Born Poor, Stay Poor?" (1999) is an excellent review of the literature on mobility.
17. I go into this in detail in my forthcoming book, *Marginality from Myth to Reality.*
18. Andre Urani, former city secretary of labor and president of IETS, personal communication, September 2005.

References

Appadurai, A. 2004. "The Capacity to Aspire: Culture and the Terms of Recognition." In *Culture and Public Action,* ed. V. Rao and M. Walton, 59–84. Stanford, CA: Stanford University Press.
Birdsall, N., and C. Graham, eds. 2000. *New Markets, New Opportunities? Economic and Social Mobility in a Changing World.* Washington, DC: Brookings Institution and Carnegie Endowment for International Peace.
Bourguignon, F., F. Ferreira, and M. Menéndez. 2003. "Inequality of Outcomes and Inequality of Opportunities in Brazil." Policy Research Working Paper 3174, World Bank, Washington, DC.

Cano, Ignacio. 2004. "O Impacto da Violencia em Rio de Janeiro." Working Paper, Universidade do Estado do Rio de Janeiro.

Ferreira, F., P. G. Leite, and J. A. Litchfield. 2006. "The Rise and Fall of Brazilian Inequality, 1981–2004." Policy Research Working Paper 3867, World Bank, Washington, DC.

Gacitúa Marió, E., and M. Woolcock, eds. 2005. *Mobilidade Social no Brasil.* Brasilia: Instituto de Pesquisa Econômica Aplicada; Washington, DC: World Bank.

Granovetter, M. 1973. "The Strength of Weak Ties." *American Journal of Sociology* 78 (6): 1360–80.

IPP (Instituto Pereira Passos). 2005. "Favelas in Rio: Data and Changes." PowerPoint presentation by Sergio Besserman, IPP president, Rio de Janeiro.

Krishna, A. 2004. "Escaping Poverty and Becoming Poor in 20 Kenyan Villages." *Journal of Human Development* 5: 211–26.

Moore, K. 2005. "Thinking about Youth Poverty through the Lenses of Chronic Poverty, Life-Course Poverty and Intergenerational Poverty." Working Paper 57, Chronic Poverty Research Centre, University of Manchester, UK.

Paes de Barros, R., R. Henriques, and R. Mendonça. 2001. "A estabilidade inaceitável: Desigualdade e pobresa no Brasil." Texto Para Discussão 800, Instituto de Pesquisa Econômica Aplicada (IPEA), Rio de Janeiro.

Perlman, J. E. 1976. *The Myth of Marginality: Urban Poverty and Politics in Rio de Janeiro.* Berkeley: University of California Press.

———. 2003. "Longitudinal Research Methodologies in Rio de Janeiro's Favelas." In "Urban Longitudinal Research Methodology," ed. C. Moser. DPU Working Paper 124, Development Planning Unit, University College, London.

———. 2007. "Redemocratization in Brazil, a View from Below: The Case of Rio de Janeiro's Favelas, 1969–2003." Mega-Cities Project, New York.

Pero, V. 2003. "Mobilidade Social no Rio de Janeiro." Instituto de Economia, Universidade Federal do Rio de Janeiro.

Perry, G., J. H. Lopez, W. F. Maloney, O. Arias, and L. Servén. 2006. *Poverty Reduction and Growth: Virtuous and Vicious Circles.* Washington, DC: World Bank.

Platt, L. 2005. *Migration and Social Mobility: The Life Chances of Britain's Minority Ethnic Communities.* Bristol, UK: Policy Press. http://www.jrf.org.uk/knowledge/findings/socialpolicy/0545.asp

Roemer, J. E. 2003. "Equal Opportunity and Intergenerational Mobility: Going Beyond Intergenerational Income Transition Matrices." Paper presented at conference, "Frontiers in Social and Economic Mobility," Cornell University, Ithaca, NY, March 28–29. http://inequality.cornell.edu/events/papers/EOp-IITM.Roemer.pdf.

Souza e Silva, J. 2003. *"Por que uns e não outros?" Caminhada de jovens pobres para a universidade.* Rio de Janeiro: Sette Letras.

Wacquant, L. 1996. "The Rise of Advanced Marginality: Notes on Its Nature and Implications." *Acta Sociológica* 39 (2): 121–39.

———. 1999. "Urban Marginality in the Coming Millennium." *Urban Studies* 36 (10): 1639–47.

Yaqub, S. 1999. "Born Poor, Stay Poor? A Literature Review." Technical report, Institute of Development Studies, University of Sussex, Brighton, UK.

8

Resisting Extreme Poverty: Learning from Families in Burkina Faso and Peru

Xavier Godinot, Claude Heyberger, Patricia Heyberger, Marco Ugarte, and Rosario Ugarte

After 50 years of development efforts, many areas of the developing world have experienced little or no prosperity. How is it that after several decades of unprecedented increases in global wealth combined with continued international development financing, Sub-Saharan Africa has seen a rise in extreme poverty and stunningly high child and maternal mortality rates? How is it that progress on poverty in Latin American and the Caribbean has been slight, while large inequalities persist?

Many development agencies and nongovernmental organizations have addressed these issues in recent years. They have come up with an array of intertwined political, economic, and geographic explanations.[1] These include the lack of voice for poorer countries in global governance, which results in rules that are unfair and costly for them; the deterioration of terms of trade for many developing countries; market failures and imperfections; deliberate distortions of competition; the burden of debt; a lack of public investment in basic infrastructure and services; scant amount and poor quality of overseas development aid; persistent differences in power and status between groups that perpetuate inequalities within countries; poor domestic policies that magnify rather than attenuate inequalities at birth; bad governance and corruption; adverse agro-climatic conditions—and the list goes on.

We contend that a fundamental factor in the increase or persistence of extreme poverty in Africa and Latin America is all too often overlooked. The development interventions promoted by rich countries can harm the capacity of people in developing countries to resist extreme poverty by the specific means they have developed and implemented for centuries. People in traditional societies have a great many effective strategies for countering extreme poverty and degradation. These strategies are based on creating and maintaining strong links of interdependence, reciprocity, and sharing between members of the same community, providing a modicum of security for each person within a general context of frugality. Community ties provide access to fundamental rights such as employment and education. Yet these ties have been devalued, states Nobel Peace Prize winner Wangari Maathai of Kenya (2004):

> Historically, our people have been persuaded to believe that because they are poor, they lack not only capital but also knowledge and skills to address their challenges. Instead they are conditioned to believe that solutions to their problems must come from outside. . . . Solutions to most of our problems must come from us. . . . Culture may be the missing link in the development of Africa. Africans, especially, should rediscover positive aspects of their culture. In accepting them, they would give themselves a sense of belonging, identity, and confidence.

Despite the abundance of means at their disposal, rich countries have failed to eradicate chronic poverty within their own borders. Even the most developed countries have vast numbers of people living in poverty. These countries cannot claim to have all the answers, and they have much to learn. Indeed, says former United Nations official Majid Rahnema, the societies of the developing world "still have a great deal to teach us. They have just as much to teach us as those countries that produced the Industrial Revolution. It is vital for us to extract from the knowledge of this common heritage everything which could enrich our present" (2003, 18, 171). It is not a question of wishing to return to a golden age that never existed. Nor is it a question of refusing modernity. Rather, we need to ensure that in their efforts to promote human rights and development for all, societies of the global north and south learn from each other. Societies must share the best of what each has achieved while respecting the identity and culture of all.

People in Poverty as Experts on Poverty

ATD Fourth World has long maintained that the foremost experts on poverty are those living in extreme poverty themselves. Like any experts, they have valuable knowledge and opinions that need to be heard. In much of the current research and writing on poverty, the people living in poverty are completely excluded from the process. The result, although clearly not the intention, is that such scholarship may keep those living in poverty powerless and voiceless. The alternative is to bring them into the process as co-producers of knowledge. A recent World Bank report argues that "engaging poor clients in an active role as co-producers can tremendously improve performance . . . [and] is a welcome tonic to the top-down technocratic orientation that has characterized much development thinking until now" (2003, 64–65).

The research carried out by ATD Fourth World seeks to gain insight into the lives of people enduring chronic poverty and to understand the dynamics in their local communities (box 8.1). The two monographs presented in this

BOX 8.1
ATD Fourth World

ATD Fourth World is an international nongovernmental organization that challenges individuals and institutions to acknowledge and support the daily efforts of people living in extreme poverty. With no religious or political affiliation, it works to advance a society where the equal dignity of each human being is recognized and where extreme poverty and social exclusion are eradicated.

Founded in 1957 by Joseph Wresinski (1917–88), who himself came from a very poor family, ATD Fourth World now has teams in 30 countries, both industrial and developing, on five continents. It is in contact with a broader network of individuals and organizations who work with people living in poverty in over 100 countries around the world.

ATD Fourth World's primary objective is to reach the poorest members of society, breaking down their isolation and exclusion and working with them to recover their basic rights and responsibilities. Through relationships of mutual trust built over time, projects are initiated in partnership with those living in poverty according to their particular needs, hopes, and aspirations. These projects include street libraries, creative workshops, computer workshops, discussion forums, health promotion projects, and housing and employment programs.

While firmly grounded in grassroots initiatives, ATD Fourth World also carries out research, representation, and public awareness projects at the local, national, and international levels. This work includes engaging in advocacy; understanding and documenting the lives and knowledge of the poorest; and collaborating with public authorities, organizations, and institutions to allow people living in extreme poverty to have a voice in the decisions that affect their lives.

To raise awareness of extreme poverty, ATD Fourth World inspired the launch of the International Day for the Eradication of Poverty. Recognized by the United Nations and observed every year on October 17, the day invites the public at large to hear the voices of people living in poverty and encourages all to look for ways to combat poverty and defend human rights.

Source: http://www.atd-fourthworld.org.

chapter were written by full-time volunteers who lived and worked alongside the subject families, for over eight years in Burkina Faso and 12 years in Peru. The stories were completed with the full agreement and participation of the subjects; as such, they are the result of knowledge and trust gained through long-term commitment to and action with very deprived families. An important aspect of this approach is that all of the central actors in each life story are expected not only to describe the events and situations they lived through but also to give their opinions on them.

This approach—building knowledge together with families living in poverty over a long period of time—differs sharply from the usual academic approaches that concentrate on short-term interviews, discussion groups, or participatory appraisals. The reality for most research teams is that establishing trust with people who have many reasons to be distrustful can be extremely difficult, making a truthful relationship virtually impossible to achieve. "The bottom poor are a blind spot in development . . . They are often difficult to reach and help" state the authors of *Voices of the Poor* (Narayan et al. 2000, 264–65). Clearly, these types of monographs cannot replace other means of knowledge building like forums and surveys, but they provide an important and necessary complement.

The monographs are designed to reflect the daily struggles and concerns not only of the individual or family in question, but of a broader population as well. Certain criteria were followed to ensure the representative nature of the work. The individual or family had to live in poverty or in extreme poverty, and their life story had to be generally consistent with the lives of other individuals or families known to ATD Fourth World.

While individuals and families in chronic poverty are at the center of the monograph-writing process (see Brun 2001), they are not the only ones who can be considered experts on poverty. Just as outside researchers cannot claim pure objectivity, neither can people living in poverty or the volunteers who work with them. Each of these groups has its own particular perspective and understanding. When their knowledge, experience, and expertise is brought together, this allows different ideas to be compared, contrasted, and verified against one another. Where common ground or a common understanding emerges, we are more likely to come close to a truth that can strengthen the fight against poverty by informing projects and development.

The monographs, in this sense, might better be called plurigraphs, since they are attempts to merge these three distinct types of input: the knowledge gained from direct, first-hand experience of living in extreme poverty; the knowledge born of action conceived with and executed alongside people in poverty; and academic knowledge.[2]

Monograph: Paul of Burkina Faso— Balancing Village and City Life

This monograph is the result of 10 years of work and action carried out with children and youths living on the streets of Ouagadougou, the capital of Burkina Faso.[3] It charts the life of Paul from his initial sojourn as a teenager in the city through two returns to his natal village, where members of his extended family and community provided key support, enabling him to develop and mature. As the story ends, Paul returns once more to the city to work but continues to nurture and draw on the strength of his family and community ties.

Paul's story is one of a search for balance—between the relationships that bind a young man to his family and community, on the one hand, and his personal aspirations for socioeconomic progress and independence, on the other. His life provides insight into the lives not only of children and youths living on the streets in West Africa, but also of many young people in rural areas across the developing world.

On the streets of Ouagadougou

Paul first came into contact with the Burkina Faso team of ATD Fourth World in September 1996, when he became a regular presence at the street library. He was approximately 15 years old at the time. The street library was usually held in the evening, around 8:30 p.m. Two ATD volunteers would take books to places where children living on the streets would gather, as a first step in meeting the children. Presenting the books under the street lamps, they would encourage the children to ask questions and express themselves. One of the books told the story of Yacouba, a boy sent by his family to hunt a lion whose life he ends up saving. It was Paul who said out loud, "If someone has no mercy in their life, that is not good."

Paul was quiet and pleasant, and he had appeared at a number of street libraries before. But his life on the streets was marked by deep insecurity— odd jobs in the informal sector, petty theft, drugs.

He had arrived several years earlier from his village in the countryside. As soon as he stepped off the bus that brought him to Ouagadougou, Paul began to look for work.

> When I arrived at Goughin market, I found a woman who was walking with a bag. I asked her for work. She was going to the market to buy flour to make cakes. She asked me to go to her house, which was on the edge of Goughin market. In the morning, I took the cakes and walked around selling them in the city. She gave me 75 francs [CFAF 75, about 15 cents] in the morning and 75 francs in the afternoon to pay for food. In the evening, I ate at her house.

Paul sold cakes for only three weeks before he found another job. In walking around the city he met the younger brother of a kiosk owner who was looking for someone to work for him, selling coffee and snacks by the roadside. Paul worked at the kiosk for eight months before leaving in the wake of an argument over whether he should pay for glasses that broke while he was washing them. A third job was with a woman who cooked and sold dishes of rice, but Paul left when the woman continually failed to pay him on time. Yet another job was sweeping and cleaning the courtyard of a large house, but he was soon forced to leave after an argument with the owner's daughter.

These informal jobs made for a precarious existence. To his employers, Paul had no identity, no ties to a family or community that could provide stability and protection. Without a protective network of social relationships, it was not surprising that Paul ended up sleeping on the streets.

During the periods when he was without work, the darker elements of life on the streets took over.

When I left the kiosk, I went back to the city and looked for work near the Great Market but I didn't find any. When night came, I slept outside a multi-storied building. I slept there for 12 days. There were other children even younger than me who came to sleep there as well. When there wasn't anything to eat, we would hang around outside restaurants and eat the leftovers.

At the Great Market we stole pieces of fabric, shoes, boxes of Nescafé, chains, watches. . . . Sometimes, we would go and hide in ditches because someone had stolen women's handbags. Moussa and Salif did that. I did not do that because it wasn't easy. If you weren't fast enough, they could catch you. I only did it once and it worked. We also went out at night. We entered people's courtyards in the various districts. We went in two at a time, so as not to be scared. We took whatever we saw: radios, money, shoes. We went to sell them at the Great Market.

I was inhaling rubber solution. If you inhale it, you can do things. You can steal what you want. If you don't inhale it, you can't do those things because you get scared. We made money but, as there were four of us, we spent it all. This is why I lasted so long with them. We paid for our food, we paid for the drugs we smoked and the rubber solution. . . .

In the city, Paul's social setting was turned upside down. Unlike in the village, nothing was familiar and he had nobody close to him. Like all children living on the streets, he could be greatly humiliated by the suspicion and disgust that people often showed him. He no longer had the social relationships that required him to use the behaviors and values he had learned with his family. The border between good and bad faded into a blur.

First return to the village: Learning to live together again

From the beginning of 1997, Paul was invited on a number of occasions to come to the Courtyard of a Hundred Trades to participate in a workshop.[4] He took his time deciding to do so, only agreeing in September of that year. So that children can participate fully in the week of activities and make the most of the experience, they are often paid a wage during the workshop. When asked what he was going to do with this money, Paul said he had decided to use it to go back to his village. "I saw that what I was doing on the streets was no good. You should not leave your family like that. You should help your parents when they no longer have the strength to work."

At the end of the workshop, Paul set a date with the Courtyard team on which he would come back and plan his return to the village. But he failed to turn up. After a few weeks the team went to look for Paul and found him under the influence of drugs in the area near the Great Mosque in the center of town. It was mid-December.

As agreed, Paul arrived at the Courtyard a couple of days later. He repeated his determination to return home before the Christmas holidays, and to encourage him, a member of the team offered to accompany him. Paul set off for his village on December 20, 1997. It had been nearly four years since he had left home.

After reuniting with his family in the village, Paul followed the wishes of his parents and went to work for an uncle in another village about 20 kilometers away. Paul and the uncle sold bottles of gasoline at the market. Later they were able to add a table selling coffee, tea, and buttered bread.

Regular visits by members of the team at Courtyard of a Hundred Trades revealed more about the life to which Paul had returned. There were clear signs of material poverty. Every structure in his family's compound was traditionally constructed of clay and natural materials. Most families in the village had at least one small building with a metal roof to better weather the rainy season, but Paul's family did not. The family did not own a plow. They had no donkey or cow, only a couple of goats, a pig, and some chickens. Paul's parents were living as a nuclear family, without any other children or relatives except for Paul's paternal grandmother, a situation relatively rare among rural families and indicative of this family's constrained situation.

Paul's family also had a history of migration. Paul's father had left the family when Paul was young and worked for several years on plantations in Côte d'Ivoire. When he returned to Burkina Faso, he moved with his young family to a more fertile area for seven years, only returning to the village upon the death of his own father. Paul was the only child of the family who completed his primary school education; the other children either were refused entry on account of their age or abandoned their studies very quickly. These two indicators—the history of migration in Paul's family and the fact he had completed primary school—appear to have played a role in Paul's decisions both to leave for the city and to return home.

In the culture of the ethnic group to which Paul and his family belong, the Mossi, such departures of young people from their homes can be understood as a modern form of the traditional initiation into adulthood (Badini 1994). In leaving the natal village, young people set out to prove to their community that they are adults and mature enough to face up to the difficulties and responsibilities of adult life. According to Amadé Badini (2004), a professor at the University of Ouagadougou,

> Emigration itself is a component of traditional education. . . . The child
> will therefore travel, to destinations near or far, and will return with new
> practices, new ideas, and new knowledge to be invested in the group. In
> real terms, [people] have gone to learn something other than what there is
> to be learned in the village and they return with this knowledge which is
> new to the village and which will be called upon to be used for its benefit.

Traditionally, the expectation is that the young adult, having grown richer as a result of this experience, will return to the family and the village. The successful integration of those who have left and later returned has always enriched the social and cultural fabric of the community. Today, however, the aim of earning money is so deeply entrenched that children often leave the village at too young an age and without the necessary protection and support for their departure. Those who have been to school are often especially eager to go to the city to seek work because their aim in attending school was to become anything other than a farmer.

Paul was affected by his schooling experience, which raised his aspirations and drew him to the opportunities offered by city life. But having grown up in the village, Paul was shaped by its culture as well. In rural Africa it is understood that every child will be educated and raised by the extended family and larger community, not by the parents alone. The daily lives of different families, especially kin, are bound to one another, and understanding how these links work is much harder than simply measuring a community's material situation. Paul's early socialization in the village partly explains why he was willing to go live and work with an uncle on his return.

Nonetheless, his spell with the uncle selling gasoline lasted only four months before he made his way back to Ouagadougou. Paul's aspirations for his life went beyond the opportunities that seemed to be available in the village at this time. He later recalled, "I left for the city. I never returned to [my] village because I didn't have enough money [to do business]. Other young people were buying chickens and sheep to sell to merchants who had come from the city, but I couldn't do the same."

On his return to the city, Paul spent eight months in a privately run center for street children, neither visiting his family in the village nor contacting the team from the Courtyard of a Hundred Trades. Once he left the center, Paul again began to visit the Courtyard, but the visits were intermittent. He had recurring thoughts about returning to the village again. Eighteen months after his first return, Paul made a second attempt. This second return would see Paul remain in the village for four years and would reveal the many ways in which the community can be a true partner in a young person's self-development.

Second return to the village: Education and earning

Back in the village, Paul became involved in a number of income-generating activities with the help of family and friends. These allowed him to begin contributing to the welfare of his family while also laying the foundations for his own future.

After working with his parents during the rainy season, Paul left to do seasonal work in the garden of an uncle.

> I went to help my uncle Philippe water his garden. If we produced something from the garden that we could sell, he would share the money with me and his children, Xavier, René, and Emilienne. One day, he told me to find something I could plant for myself for my own benefit and to begin planting it in the garden. He gave me tomato plants. He showed me how to plant them and when to water them. I learned lots of things, like how to treat diseases in the garden. To grow things, there are also days when you need to plant or add fertilizer. He showed me everything. I watched, but he also explained.

A second uncle also employed Paul to work on his farm with a tractor, paying Paul for his labor. A third uncle took Paul on to work at his second-hand clothing stall in the market. Once he had learned the vagaries of the trade and the price of the clothes, Paul was able to sell some of them at a higher price and share in the profit. Another uncle introduced Paul to buying and selling chickens to merchants from the city who came to the market to buy poultry. Paul also worked with friends and relatives to make clay bricks for building houses. Finally, Paul was also involved in breeding animals, including chickens, goats, and pigs.

It was during Paul's second return to the village that the team at the Courtyard of a Hundred Trades began to provide, at various times, financial support to Paul and his family for their activities. The sums involved were small, but always significant in the sense that each donation or gift—as opposed to a loan—either involved Paul and his family in a joint project or demonstrated the Courtyard team's support of projects important to the family. Such support took the form of money to buy chickens and a pig, both for breeding, or products such as seeds and trees for the garden project.

However, each donation was also evaluated for the effect it could have on the family and on Paul's reintegration into village life. In making each gift, the Courtyard team took pains to ensure that it did not preempt the role of someone in the community who could have provided assistance. It was important not to lessen the community's input to the projects of Paul and his family. The team was also careful to avoid giving too much money, which might be poorly used. This could have led to tension within the family, provoked the family into lying to or hiding things from the team, or even precipitated the departure of Paul. Large donations would also have singled out the family by placing excessive means at their disposal, which would have endangered existing networks of solidarity in the community. Last, the team sought to avoid creating any unspoken expectation that could have influenced the relationship between the family and the team.

The Courtyard team was well aware that accompanying Paul and his family as they developed their activities would be a step-by-step process. Because struggling families often find it difficult to evaluate the potential of their projects beforehand, they often move forward on a trial-and-error basis. The donations allowed the family to go ahead at its own pace. Furthermore, by supporting the family's activities as well as Paul's own projects, the donations contributed to strengthening the human and economic resources of the family and the whole community. They were seen as investments in Paul's effort to establish himself in the village with the close involvement of his parents and extended family.

The challenge of interdependence

After Paul had been home for two years, his father began sending him to represent the family at certain village ceremonies. This helped nurture Paul's interest in customary practices rooted in the family, the village, and the community. Paul expressed his own understanding of the importance of this development: "We will be taking over from the older generation, so we are obliged to learn." His time in the village also allowed Paul to visit friends, relatives, and village elders on a regular basis and profit from the experiences of others and the relationships he built. He later said of this period, "I have good friends in the village. . . . We never did anything stupid because we talked to the old people. Three or four of us would go and sit with men older than my father. They would give us advice about things we didn't know."

Paul's participation in these activities show that he was able to live in his rural community despite his years on the streets of the city. How was this the case?

All the income-generating activities that Paul undertook after returning to the village involved a member of his family or of the community. Paul agreed to work in his uncle's garden without knowing whether he would be paid for this work; implicitly, he also accepted that his uncle would watch over him on behalf of the family. That he accepted such conditions testifies to the strong influence that Paul's upbringing had on him. From a young age, Paul was taught to work cooperatively with members of his extended family and community. Once Paul showed that he could still function within the family framework, his uncle offered him the chance to plant a garden for his own benefit. The uncle shared his expertise with Paul so that the garden would be a success. "The fact that I worked with members of the family changed their opinion of me. They told me I had changed."

Paul thus found a way to live and work with others and accepted his dependence upon them. This in turn allowed the community to reciprocate by providing him the support he needed to succeed with his projects. This acceptance was the fruit of his early education—not formal schooling, but learning how to live in the environment in which he grew up.

These village relationships contrasted sharply with those in the city. In Ouagadougou, Paul managed to find a number of jobs for himself and worked largely for money, shelter, and food. But at no point during his time in the city was Paul ever afforded training or real protection. Not one of his employers tried to trace his parents, and in several cases a single argument terminated the employment. Working in the village, by contrast, Paul received little money, but he did benefit from the protection of his family and community and he received training, such as gardening expertise.

Paul's experience in the village demonstrates that the stability and coherence of the family and community setting provides a level of access to fundamental rights such as education, work, and training. Interdependence within the community is not always a burden or a hindrance to personal aims. Rather, it can effectively advance the individual's development as well as the development of the community.

Even so, village life can be a difficult adjustment after life in the city. Personal ideas, projects, and desires can come into conflict with those of the community. After one year back in the village, Paul sold his pig in order to finance a departure to Côte d'Ivoire for work. Paul was attracted by the lure of something new and foreign, but the money raised by the sale of the pig wasn't enough to pay for a ticket. Looking back, Paul says, "I thought about going to Côte d'Ivoire to work. I had an uncle who wanted to send me there so I could watch over his cacao and coffee fields. . . . The old woman [his grandmother] told me not to go. . . . Friends also told me to stay. . . . Today I no longer want to go. I think it was better to stay."

A new life in the city: Maturity and stability

In early 2003, after four years in the village, Paul once again left home and headed for the capital to find work. Even as he did this, he had his own project in mind and ideas about what the future could bring.

> It is difficult just to farm without trading. I came to Ouagadougou in search of money to start trading. . . . I want to sell new clothes in the village: hats, caps, Nike sportswear, shorts, belts. . . . I am looking to be able to work in Kobodogho because it is my village and I want to help my parents and my brothers.

Within a month of his arrival in the city, Paul found a job working in a restaurant and housing in the same area. As he had done the first time he lived in the city, Paul found the job by walking around and asking for work. However, there were also great differences from his first sojourn in the city. When he arrived this time, Paul did not go back to sleeping and living on the streets. Rather, he went and stayed with a relative while he searched for his own place to live. A second difference was in the attitude of the restaurant owner, who consistently raised Paul's salary until it reached CFAF 25,000 per month (about US$51) and also made a contribution toward the cost of Paul's accommodation after less than six months of employment. Paul works during the afternoons and evenings to sell roast chicken and look after the cash register, a sign of the proprietor's trust in him.

The responsibility and stability of this job means that Paul's most recent departure for the city bears little resemblance to the escapism of an adolescent looking for adventure. Instead, this is the kind of adult migration that has become the reality of contemporary rural life in Burkina Faso. Paul returns to the village every third Sunday, on market day, to visit his parents and grandmother, leave them some money, and deposit his own savings with an uncle. Such acts make it clear that Paul, although living in the city because it offers more income-generating opportunities, still continues to define himself and his projects in the context of his family, the community, and the village. Life in the village remains permanently connected to life in the city.

In July 2004, Paul's father was able to look back and see the difference:

> Paul has changed. He doesn't have the same character as before. He has more money now than when he was in the village: he is able to look after himself and make ends meet. He manages to hold down a job and wants to earn a living, little by little. Whatever he is today is thanks to what he must have learned in school. Paul was not the first to apply for his current job; there were others wanting to work there. It was perhaps due to their lack of schooling that the owner decided not to take them on.

Two types of education

The father's comment reflects the importance of an academic education to rural African families. Paul's father tried to send all his children to school, expending both money and effort to do so, but none of his other children attended long enough to improve their situation. The father attributes Paul's current employment in some measure to the fact that he managed to complete his primary education; he learned to read, write, count, and speak some French. For the father, these qualities played a part in persuading the restaurant owner to give Paul certain responsibilities. Formal education thus helped Paul gain employment, even though he did not learn a trade at school.

At the same time, Paul's improved status is also due to the social education he received from his community. Without this, he would never have been able to manage his farming activities and other projects and his relationships in the village. This training helped him build the solid foundation from which he was able to leave once more for the city, this time with more success.

In sum, Paul's development is the result of two types of education: academic education in school and social education in the community. Reconciling the two and drawing on both is essential in resisting extreme poverty. Toward this end, school education should be considered as a complement to that provided by the family and the community, and not as the only way to become educated. Instruction in both contexts should not be limited to the transmission of knowledge, but must also focus on how to behave, how to share, and how to work alongside others. Dialogue should be encouraged between teachers and the community so that the content and rhythms of teaching can promote the reconciliation of social and academic education.

Who can define who is poor?

After having raised six children, Paul's parents have only one child left at home to help them cultivate their land. The older children have all left to find work elsewhere, including Paul in Ouagadougou and another sibling in Côte d'Ivoire. No other child has been entrusted to the family's care. The household has neither the labor power nor the technical means to significantly improve its agricultural productivity or invest in better land farther away. There are other signs of persistent financial insecurity. The home in their compound is still built from traditional materials and has hardly been improved in the past decade. The family herd continues to consist of only a few animals. And, tellingly, the family did not send Paul's younger brothers to school when they reached school age.

However, these signs of financial insecurity are not the only ones to be considered in asking whether the family has made progress in moving out of poverty. In and of themselves, they do not necessarily define Paul's family as poor within its own community. Many families in the rural environment share similar circumstances.

It is difficult for outsiders to define an individual, a family, or a community as poor. It is much more interesting to consider the definition of poverty that they themselves use. In Burkina Faso, according to Badini (2004),

> Poverty is not determined in relation to material or monetary ownership; it is the sense of belonging to a group that is important. Mossi culture teaches that in order to be rich, it is necessary to have people with whom this wealth can be shared. This means that a person is rich because of the opportunity they have of helping, participating and working with others. . . . Life, even material life, is not just about money. References in our countries are mainly social and relational: a person is poor if he or she has no relations.

This is something that is all too easily overlooked. Development projects often address problems related to water supply, health, or participation in the economic life of a country, but very few seem to emphasize the value of living together in a community. Families and communities need to form their own understanding of themselves, their knowledge, and their resources so that they can define for themselves what it means to "succeed in life."

Paul's own definition of his success is simple. In June 2004, he reflected on his current situation:

> What is good is that I have work. If you don't have work, you don't know what you are going to do to earn money. What is also good is that I am nearby [the village]. I go to see my family and I come back. I am lucky that if I go back to live in the village, I will always find work and the people will always show me what to do.

Monograph: The Rojas-Paucar Family of Peru—Struggling to Work and Stay Together

This monograph is the result of dialogue and interaction with the Rojas-Paucar family over more than 12 years. The parents, Benigno Rojas and Alicia Paucar, both originate from the region of Cusco, in a mountainous area of southern Peru. The family has four children: Margarita, Laura, Miguel, and Fernando. Margarita, the eldest, was born in 1982; Fernando, the youngest, was born in 1996.

The family lives together in the El Mirador neighborhood on the outskirts of the city of Cusco. When asked to participate in the writing of the monograph, they replied that they would be happy to be involved, on one condition: that the work and the monograph itself would serve others—not by contributing to alleviating poverty, but by helping to bring an end to poverty.

Benigno's path

Benigno Rojas was born into a farming family in 1951, in the province of La Convención in the department of Cusco. He was the eldest of eight children of Pedro Rojas and Ana Huaman. As the 1950s progressed, tensions grew between large landowners and peasant trade unions in the area. It was against this backdrop that Benigno's father was accused of theft and spent the next six years in jail in the city of Cusco.

These events were disastrous for the family. Benigno's mother followed her husband to Cusco so that she could be present at the legal proceedings. To do so, she left her son in the care of a sister-in-law, but returned to collect Benigno and take him to Cusco when the aunt and nephew did not get along. Benigno remembers this period:

> In Cusco, we lived in La Almudena. My mom rented a room in front of the jail. We would go to the potato fields in Huancabamba together. My mom,

like the men there, would carry sacks of potatoes. I did too, as much as I could. We would take the sacks down to Cusco to sell potatoes, beans, and root vegetables. Mom would sell some of them, and we would keep some for ourselves to eat. Sometimes she prepared food to sell in the central market.

But my dad wasn't idle. He worked in the jail. He made wooden combs, spoons . . . lots of things. There was his workmanship as well. Mom used to go to the jail on visiting days. He would give her what he had made and she would sell it. That's how we used to live sometimes.

The second consequence of Benigno's father's imprisonment was that the family sold the land and all it had owned in P'ispitayoq. The crops and the buildings that the family sold had been the fruit of many years' hard work. Although Benigno believes the land sold for less than it was worth, the money did allow Benigno's father on his release from jail to find work buying cattle in a province outside of Cusco and taking them to be slaughtered in the city.

In the early 1960s, the family was given the opportunity to return to farming. One of Benigno's uncles was a foreman on a ranch in Paltaibamba, a little farther north than the family's original holding in P'ispitayoq, and he offered Benigno's father land to cultivate. The province of La Convención was still experiencing tension between landowners and peasants. Following a number of confrontations between the two groups, in 1969 an agrarian reform law was passed that forced the landowners off their land in order to create agricultural cooperatives. The lands that the peasants had worked passed into their own hands. Benigno's parents thus became landowners again, and they still live today on this plot in Paltaibamba.

Benigno finished primary school in Paltaibamba, but as his home was far from the secondary school, he could not continue studying there. So at the age of 16 Benigno left for Cusco, where he found a job doing auto body repair. With the help of an uncle, he reached the third level of secondary school before his father asked Benigno to return to Paltaibamba and work on the land. But the relationship between father and son was difficult and Benigno, with his father's blessing, soon left to join the army.

Two years later Benigno left the army and returned to Cusco, where he worked as a builder. He met his first partner and they moved to Urubamba, where they had a child and spent eight years selling small hardware goods on the streets. His partner then left him and took their son with her. Benigno wandered between farming work in Paltaibamba and construction jobs in Urubamba and Cusco, where he met Alicia, his current partner.

Alicia's path

Alicia Paucar was born in 1961 to Juan Paucar Flores and Maria Rios Pérez in the province of Anta in the department of Cusco. She was the third of three daughters. Not long after she was born, Alicia's parents separated. Her mother moved to Lima to be with her new partner, taking Alicia with her. Alicia looked back on her relations with her family in June 2004:

> We were three sisters but we grew up separately. When my mom left my dad, my dad gave the younger of my two older sisters to my aunt Francisca. My other sister was brought up by my aunt Dionicia and I was brought up by my mom.
>
> When I was eight years old, my grandma came to pick me up and then she picked up my sister Rosa. Rosa and I have become closer. We have gone through everything. When I had a problem, she was the one who supported me.
>
> My other sister, Carmen, grew up at Aunt Dionicia's side. They had a business. She met her husband when she was there and now she lives in Quillabamba. We never grew close. We have always been apart.

Alicia's childhood was marked by constant movement. After living with her mother for four years, Alicia was sent to live with an aunt who made her work as a servant. At eight, Alicia began living with her grandmother, for whom she also had to work, preparing candies and ice cream to sell in the markets on Sundays. When she was 12, Alicia ran away from her grandmother's house and worked for a year caring for an elderly woman. Alicia eventually returned to her grandmother, only to run away a second time. This time she headed for Quillabamba in order to be with her elder sister, Rosa, who had previously run away from their grandmother and gotten married.

In Quillabamba, the two sisters worked together selling fruit in the market. A year later, when Alicia was just 14, the sisters moved to Cusco to work. Rosa made a great effort to enroll Alicia in school, and although Rosa was jailed for nearly two years for her part in a fight, Alicia managed to finish primary school while continuing to sell goods on the streets and in the markets. One of her jobs was to sell coffee in the early morning near San Pedro train station, and it was there that Alicia met Ruben Pastor. She was only 15 years old. The couple stayed together for seven years and had three daughters. When her partner left, he took their two eldest daughters with him while the youngest, Margarita, stayed with Alicia. Alicia returned to selling fruit, vegetables, and cheese to earn money. This was how she met Benigno.

The challenge of building a family

For the first five years of their life together, Alicia and Benigno lived in the same area of Cusco, near their relatives and friends. They found work and appeared settled where they were. However, difficulties with the local housing association eventually forced the family to move. In 1989 the family, which now included younger children Laura and Miguel, found a place in the El Mirador neighborhood with the help of one of Benigno's friends.

El Mirador sits atop a steep hill. When the neighborhood was originally developed, the land was divided into 90 lots, and the trees on the hill were cut down to make way for the development. Eucalyptus trees were planted, but it was not enough to keep the ground stable. A landslide in 1984 spread fear among the landowners; many of them were reluctant to continue living in their damaged homes, and so the houses and rooms left standing were offered for rent at low prices. It was just such a room that was offered to the Rojas-Paucar family in 1989.

The room measured four meters by five meters. It had a slanting roof of tiles and corrugated iron, a small door, and no windows. In exchange for the room, Benigno agreed to participate in community work organized by the neighborhood association every Sunday.

The family's life quickly became more difficult in El Mirador. Benigno could not find a permanent job. Alicia brought money into the house by selling vegetables in San Pedro central market, work she had done before the family moved. It was also at this time that Margarita, Alicia's daughter, began to work in La Almudena cemetery.

> Every Saturday and Sunday, all day long, I went to sell water. From Monday to Friday I worked in the afternoon. In the morning, I studied and at two o'clock, after lunch, I took my bucket down to the cemetery. I got changed out of my school uniform and went to sell water in my old clothes. I went to sell water so as to bring something back for breakfast, maybe, to help my mom and my little brother and sister.

Tensions mounted within the family. Throughout these years, particularly when material problems weighed most heavily, there were a number of occasions when either Benigno or Alicia left the family home. Such separations could last a few days or much longer, but every time the one who had left would return to the family. After one particular separation, the reconciliation was more difficult than usual, but still Benigno and Alicia worked to bring their family back together again. According to Benigno,

I said to Alicia, "For how long are we not going to talk to each other? How are the children going to react?" She looked at me but didn't say anything. In the afternoon, she came back very calm. Leaving the house, she said to me, "So people won't gossip, we're going to walk in the street hand in hand. I know that they're going to tell tales but are you going to believe them?" I said, "No. I'm not bothered about gossip." She said to me, "Listen, why don't we go and eat some chicken?" As I had some money from my work, we went out to eat and since then we've always been together.

This was the reality of the family's life when it first encountered ATD Fourth World through the participation of Margarita and Laura in various activities and workshops that were organized for children, young people, and adults in the area. Margarita greatly enjoyed these activities:

People from ATD came to teach us how to draw, read and "be sociable." That's what I loved most. I liked it when they came and said, "We're going to do some acting and dancing," because that's what I liked . . . They taught me. They saw how we lived and helped us feel better.

The hardships the family faced did not turn them inward. In fact, they made even more active efforts to establish links between themselves and the community around them. In 1989, Benigno and Alicia had Laura baptized at the age of two years and eight months. The man who agreed to be her godfather was a shopkeeper in San Pedro who had befriended Alicia when she was working in the market there. In keeping with this important role in Peruvian society, the godfather helped support Laura by sending her clothes on her birthday and at Christmas. Another important relationship was with Margarita's godparents, named at the time of her first communion in 1993. Four years later, it was one of these godparents who fought to enroll Margarita in night school after she had been forced to drop out of school for financial reasons.

The family also took care to build friendships in El Mirador. Like neighborhoods the world over, El Mirador is a web of complex and overlapping relationships. By cultivating these relationships, neighbors attempt to come together and create a single community. But this very closeness can also make any sense of rejection extremely painful for those who live there.

The Peruvian government's Glass of Milk program supports families by providing quantities of milk, beans, and corn or quinoa flour to be distributed each morning to mothers who are breastfeeding or have children under the age of six.[5] To be eligible for the program, all those who benefit from it pay a certain amount each month to cover the costs of transporting the food.

Those who cannot pay are usually offered an alternative, such as preparing the breakfasts over a number of days. This poses problems for those who work as vendors because the early morning is when they need to go to market to buy the fruits and vegetables that they will later sell in the streets. The humiliation for Alicia was that her name was not put forward to help prepare the breakfasts so that her family could benefit from the program and also repay the community.

The family's struggle to build relationships in El Mirador suffered again in 1995 when Benigno fell out with the friend who had helped the family secure the house in the neighborhood. The owner subsequently asked the family to leave. The family found another house in the neighborhood, but paying rent on a set day every month proved too demanding and the family once again found itself looking for a home. They moved to the nearby neighborhood of San Juan, taking a simple room with a slanting roof and no electricity, water, or toilet. Benigno participated in the Sunday communal work with the housing association of this neighborhood and it was during the family's two years in San Juan that their youngest child, Fernando, was born. In early 1998, hoping to maintain and build on friendships they had had in El Mirador, the family returned to that neighborhood, where they continue to live today.

Working to survive

Benigno and Alicia's story highlights the importance of the relationships that a family is able to build with those around them, and particularly with inhabitants of their neighborhood. But the well-being of the family also depends upon its relationship with work. Without work, the family cannot survive. This is not only a question of income; even if it does not bring much money into the home, work is still identified with success.

Since 1989, Benigno has found it harder and harder to find regular work. This is in part the result of a more difficult economic context,[6] but it also reflects the wearing down of his health and his ability to do manual labor. He has therefore focused on finding work that can bring concrete gains to the family, such as housing. Benigno has succeeded several times in getting a position as watchman in the neighborhood of El Mirador or nearby. In this role, Benigno participates in collective neighborhood work on Sundays and represents the owner in community meetings. In exchange, the family is allowed to live in the room that they occupy and Benigno can claim that his efforts guarantee a roof over their heads.

Benigno also worked hard to contribute to the family's food supply by growing potatoes in the village of Huancabamba, a three-hour walk from El Mirador. Benigno was able to work in the rural environment of Huancabamba by maintaining and building on the relations that his mother had established with that community. The peasant on whose land Benigno works and with whom he shares the crop was invited to become Fernando's godfather, further strengthening the family's village connection.

Margarita's experience also underscores the crucial role of work. She began selling water and flowers in the cemetery at a young age. While this may raise questions about child labor, Margarita took pride in making a contribution toward the survival of the family. Later she began working at the local bus stop that had been built near El Mirador. At first she sold wares at the bus stop, building friendships with the bus drivers. Relying on these friendships, Margarita then asked for work riding the buses, recruiting customers and selling tickets for the route. A boss from one of the bus companies gave her the opportunity and she spent five years doing this work.

> I was paid a set wage of ten *soles*, which I gave to my mom. My wages went to her to pay the rent and the electricity or so that she could cook something and buy the daily food. The rest I kept for my clothes so that I could wear something. There were a lot of expenses but we tried to get on by supporting each other, my mom, my dad, and me.

As Margarita grew older, the role of work in her life changed subtly. While she still provided support to her parents and family, she was now also able to see the work as helping lay the groundwork for the rest of her life. Eventually she moved on from working on the buses to selling pens, key rings, card games, and acrylic boards with her partner.

Education: Hope and struggle

The relationship of the Rojas-Paucar family with the education system was, and remains, far from easy, even though the whole family made great sacrifices for the sake of the children's future.

There are two types of education: formal and informal. Informal education that the family provides, often by setting an example for children, helps prepare a person to take on various responsibilities. In this way both Margarita and Laura learned how to contribute to their family's support, Margarita by earning money and Laura by doing chores such as fetching water, looking after her younger brothers, cleaning, and helping prepare food.

Ideally, formal education complements the education within the family. Schooling allows people to acquire knowledge and skills that will bring recognition, further integration into society, and wider opportunities in the world of work. Toward this end, the Rojas-Paucar family invested as much as they could in making it possible for their children to succeed in school. And yet such success was far from automatic. The difficulties that Laura faced in school demonstrate the obstacles the family had to overcome.

In Peru, education is nominally free of charge. However, budgetary limitations mean that the state's spending on education tends to cover little more than the salaries of teachers, leaving parents' associations to decide the level of financial contribution that parents will have to make to cover school equipment and maintenance. Indeed, it is estimated that families contribute one-third of overall public spending on education in Peru (Pasquier-Doumer 2003, 25).

Benigno insisted that Laura should enroll in school. But he also had to find a way to explain the family's situation and persuade the school to allow them to pay the enrollment fee over several months. Benigno missed the first meeting because of a broken rib sustained in a fall; without money to get medical attention, he was home-bound as he recovered. On the last possible day for enrollment, Benigno walked seven kilometers to the school with Alicia, since neither of them had money for transport. "Each step I took, I felt a sharp pain in my side and the pain was unbearable."

Laura enrolled and was able to start school. This was a source of pride to the family but the financial burden was heavy. The compulsory school uniform included a sweater that the family had to purchase. "For Laura to start school, I bought a sweater on credit which I paid off over two years," Alicia noted. "Thankfully, that sweater lasted the five years she was at school."

Laura herself also had to endure difficult moments throughout her years in school as a result of her family's situation:

> For computer class, they always asked us for diskettes. My mom put money aside especially on Saturday to buy the diskettes. But, during the week, they also wanted money for photocopies. As I went to school without any money, I asked them, "Sir, can I have one? I'll pay you tomorrow." Some teachers would accept this and give it to you, but they would only give you one chance. If you didn't pay them the next time, they wouldn't give you any. There were days when mom didn't have the money or couldn't pay for photocopies so the teacher wouldn't give them to me at the next class.
>
> I felt sad because I saw that my classmates could pay for the photocopies, that they had money and could buy things. They had more than me. But I had to put up with it as I knew that mom couldn't give me any money.

Laura was sometimes humiliated by her family's circumstances. She had to walk from home to the center of town to arrive at school. Since the streets of her neighborhood are unpaved, her shoes were dirty by the time she made it to school. One day a teacher stood her up in front of her classmates and drew attention to her shoes by literally stepping on Laura's toes, saying loudly, "These shoes are so dirty that it doesn't matter if we dirty them some more. This will teach you to come to school in clean shoes."

In September 2002 Alicia was involved in a traffic accident and had to be treated in a hospital. When she came home, there were days when she could not get out of bed unaided and so both Laura and Miguel began to miss days of school as they cared for their mother at home. As a result of her many unexplained absences, the school threatened Laura with expulsion. After a meeting to explain her absences, the school gave Laura a conditional enrollment, meaning that any further absence would result in her definitive expulsion.

Laura successfully completed school in December 2003. Each step forward in the struggle to have the family's children complete their schooling has been hard won, but each child has helped to define the path, making it easier for the next to follow. Margarita reached the second year of high school; although she did not finish, she laid down a path for her sister to follow. In the same way, Laura may have opened the way for Miguel and Fernando to follow her and finish their schooling. This is the family's hope.

Health crises threaten security

Like many families living in very difficult circumstances in El Mirador, the Rojas-Paucar household looks to traditional medicine to deal with their health problems. It is only when an illness gets worse despite the traditional treatments that the family will go to a local health center or hospital. Even then, they do so with a certain level of suspicion and distrust.

Health problems have emerged time and again in the lives of the Rojas-Paucar family as genuine dangers to the family unit, threatening to take away the little security they have. The birth of Margarita's first child in 1999 is one example.

> I didn't have a normal birth. I had a Caesarean and had to spend 15 days in the hospital. I didn't have any money to get out of hospital or for the medicine. My mom had to go begging everywhere. The nurses wanted to keep the baby because we owed 500 *soles* for the medicine and the bed. My mom went to the social worker to get a discount. She said that we had to pay 250 *soles* but we didn't even have that.

Then the nurse arrived and said, "If you don't pay, we'll take the baby off you. Why are you going to take the child if you can't raise him? If you haven't even got enough to get him out of the hospital, you're not going to be able to feed him, breastfeed him, or bring him up." Then she said to me, "Let him stay. We'll give the baby away in adoption to people who can offer him a better life."

We were very sad and started to cry. I said to mom, "Go and borrow money from anyone. Pawn my TV first of all." But she didn't have enough: the TV only came to 70 *soles*.

With the support of ATD Fourth World and other people around the family, Margarita was able to pay for her treatment and leave the hospital with her son. But it is exactly this kind of experience that is so humiliating for those living in extreme poverty.

A similar crisis erupted at the birth of Margarita's second child, in February 2004, when Alicia had to use money that had been saved for school enrollment fees to pay the hospital costs. The family thus had to make a difficult tradeoff between health and education. The situation was further complicated by the fact that Laura, who was then working as a saleswoman, was fired by the shop owner because she missed work on the day that Margarita's baby was born. Alicia eventually found the money to enroll Miguel in school, but she had less than half the money needed to enroll Fernando and had to take out a loan to register her second son.

On another occasion, Miguel developed a toothache and the tooth became infected. This local infection became generalized, at which point he went to a hospital but was not examined. Miguel then went to a health center run by a local association and received treatment over a period of three months. When his health continued to deteriorate, he was taken to a state hospital. There, difficulties continued for Miguel and the family. On a number of occasions, the treatment given to Miguel was made conditional on payment, even as his condition became so serious that his kidneys began to fail. As a result, he now needs to undergo dialysis three times a week.

Friends rallied around the family and informed Alicia of a national program, the Comprehensive Health System (SIS), which is set up to support disadvantaged families. There is only one hospital in Cusco capable of performing dialysis, but administrative problems meant that Miguel could not be treated there. However, the director of the SIS in Cusco provided valuable support to the family. Understanding their situation, he used agreements signed by different hospital and care centers with the SIS to have Miguel sent to Lima, where he can, free of charge, have access to the treatment he so desperately needs. Once Miguel becomes an adult, the situation will change again and new means will have to be found to continue his treatment so a new health scare does not once again threaten the fragile foundations of this family.

Family lifeline: Community reciprocity and support

In building a family and meeting challenges of work and health, community relations and community recognition have been vital for the Rojas-Paucar family. They are interdependent with other families living in poverty in El Mirador in a network of mutual help and support.

Speaking of her relationship with one particular family, Alicia said,

I'm the godmother of one of Irma's daughters and my late sister too. That's why we treat each other like family. . . .

In the past, there were good times. She sometimes said to me, "Let's get together to cook something, Alicia." . . . The children grew up together. We've got photos of the times we went to the cemetery, when her children were small and so were mine. It was on All Saints Day one time. We took photos, food, and drink.

We've knitted together as well. She used to say to me, "Alicia, knit me a shirt for Meche. She's expecting another baby." She helped me prepare the wool. We got on well. But recently the relationship started to dry up. It's partly down to our children seeing each other and I don't really agree with that.

Such relationships led to Margarita being invited by other young people to go to the cemetery to begin selling water and flowers. And the same kind of relationship allowed Benigno to continue working the land in Huancabamba by maintaining community ties that were first established by his mother.

The importance of community support was reflected in the godparents that Benigno and Alicia chose for their children. Each time, their choice reflected a desire to create or reinforce links with people that the family could rely on and who would support the family in their daily life.

The concept of *ayni* is the basis of Andean society and culture. *Ayni* is reciprocity, the act of giving so as to receive. It is an ancient value for Andean people on which everything else is based. It permeates relationships between people of the same social level and shapes every aspect of daily life, particularly in a neighborhood such as El Mirador. "Everything in life is *ayni*," according to the Andean people.

Hope for the future

The Rojas-Paucar family continues today to face many difficulties, but in two of the areas it values most—education and family cohesion—clear differences exist between the family's situation today and in the past.

In terms of education, Margarita studied until the second year of high school. Laura finished high school, and Miguel, his illness permitting, is on course to finish as well. Both younger children have far surpassed their parents in formal schooling and have built upon the progress that their older sister made.

Concerning the ability to keep the home together, both parents and the children are aware that their family has lived through moments of profound tension. Yet somehow they have managed to avoid splitting up, a fate that sadly befalls many families trapped in difficult circumstances. Even though Margarita now has her own partner and children and lives far from her parents and siblings, she still sends support to her family and cherishes her relationship with them. This is in contrast to what Benigno and Alicia had to live through, not only with their parents but also with their own first relationships.

It is this success and sense of progress that allows Benigno and Alicia to look forward to a better future for their children. For Benigno,

> What really hurts is poverty, which affects us a lot as a family. We're shaken by it and I'm really looking for ways to get out of it and get my children out of it as well. That's my struggle. It's a very difficult thing and although I'm trying to get out of it, I can't. I'm faced with too many problems. That's what I am really sad about. I want my children to continue on a better path. But I'm always trying to get out of this poverty.

Alicia, for her part, is clear on what it means for her to get out of poverty.

> I want my children to have a stable job and be someone in life. I want to carry on helping them as much as I can. I'm happy when my son Miguel says to me, "I'm going to be a doctor." Laura always says to me, "Mom, I'm going to study to be a tourist guide." We're always supporting my daughter, thinking that she'll carry on studying and perhaps go to university. . . . If only they can finish school and be someone. I've always wanted to see my children do well in life, even if it's just one of them.

Discussion: What Does It Mean to Escape Poverty?

The life stories of Paul and the Rojas-Paucar family provide a glimpse of the forces that allow individuals and families to escape extreme poverty and also those forces that keep them trapped in extreme poverty. But what does moving out of poverty or extreme poverty actually mean in the case of Burkina Faso and Peru, countries characterized by widespread material deprivation that affects the majority of the population?

Poverty, extreme poverty, and social exclusion are multidimensional

To begin with, the two stories illustrate the need to distinguish between poverty and extreme poverty, as well as between extreme poverty and social exclusion. Commonly used definitions of poverty and extreme poverty consider the amount of money a household has to live on each day. A slightly different definition was proposed by Joseph Wresinski, founder of ATD Fourth World, and adopted by the French Economic and Social Council in 1987 and the United Nations Commission on Human Rights in 1996.

> Lack of basic security is the absence of one or more factors that enable individuals and families to assume basic responsibilities and to enjoy fundamental rights. Such a situation may become more extended and lead to more serious and permanent consequences. Extreme poverty results when the lack of basic security simultaneously affects several aspects of people's lives, when it is prolonged, and when it severely compromises people's chances of regaining their rights and of reassuming their responsibilities in the foreseeable future (Wresinski 1994a, 25).

Wresinski underlines the continuity between poverty and extreme poverty. He also highlights their multidimensional nature by noting that extreme poverty brings long-term insecurities in many aspects of life. It becomes ever harder for those living in extreme poverty to protect their rights on their own, without the support of the community and the society at large. Thus they can lose their capacity for autonomy.

Because the extreme poor lose their access to fundamental rights, Wresinski (1994b) emphasizes that extreme poverty—not poverty—must be considered a violation of human rights. Many agencies of the United Nations have now adopted this concept. This approach has similarities with the one put forward by Amartya Sen, the 1998 Nobel Prize winner in economics. Sen (1999) contends that "poverty must be seen as the deprivation of basic capabilities," and he defines development as "a process of expanding the real freedoms that people enjoy."

Although extreme poverty is a condition, social exclusion is a process that implies a dynamic: one is excluding others, or one is being excluded by others. The concept of social exclusion, which seems to have been used for the first time by French researchers 40 years ago, describes a breakdown in the relationship that links an individual to society (Klanfer 1965). All the links between people and the society around them—family ties, social and economic integration, citizenship—are at risk of being severed or damaged.

When he was living on the streets of Ouagadougou, Paul found himself in a state of extreme poverty and social exclusion. His economic integration was precarious, social and citizenship links were lacking, and his family ties were in danger of being permanently broken. The prospect of a definitive break with the family is a threat that looms over all young people living on the streets. After several years of support from the ATD Fourth World team, Paul revived his relationship with his family, took advantage of the economic opportunities that these family links make possible, and escaped from extreme poverty by accepting the more ordinary poverty experienced by his parents. He eventually found a job that offered him more financial rewards than those available in the village. However, he continued to fulfill his responsibilities to his family.

Despite their many efforts to build relationships in El Mirador, the Rojas-Paucar family also endured extreme poverty and a degree of social exclusion. For instance, Alicia Paucar was deeply humiliated when her name was not put forward to help prepare breakfasts so that her family could benefit from the Glass of Milk program and also repay the community. Laura was equally humiliated when her teacher stepped on her toes in front of her classmates because her shoes were dirty. Social exclusion results when a person is despised or discredited and deemed no longer capable of contributing to society as a direct result of extreme poverty. It is a vicious cycle: extreme poverty leads to social exclusion from the community, and the resulting isolation in turn increases the insecurity and vulnerability that leads to extreme poverty.

The importance of belonging

The individual and nuclear family profiled in the two monographs have strong feelings of belonging to their extended family and community. Their experiences of interdependence and reciprocity are deeply rooted in the Mossi tradition in Burkina Faso and the Andean tradition of *ayni* in Peru. These traditions allow the community and the family to play strong roles in the formation and education of each individual and to share in the responsibility for his or her welfare.

People living in extreme poverty gain dignity and identity from sharing in this group dynamic and being recognized as members of the community. As such, they share in the riches of the culture and the community, giving them strength to continue to fight against poverty in their lives. The links they build with their community become a means of resisting exclusion and achieving a certain security. The overwhelming reality is that when systems of social protection do not work, do not exist, or simply do not reach those trapped in chronic poverty, family and community solidarity is the best defense against privation.

These links obviously are not an unconditional guarantee of well-being. Families and communities, some of them very frail, vary in their capacity and means to fulfill their protective role. Nonetheless, the director of the United Nations Division for Social Policy and Development believes that "families all over the world remain the most vital force in the battle to eradicate poverty. . . . The irony is that, often, the central role played by the family has escaped the attention of policymakers. . . . [They] are only beginning to realize that programs to eradicate poverty and to provide basic services must recognize and support the ongoing efforts that families already make" (Schölvinck 2004).

The dominant materialist concept of development tends to view economically poor communities in the least developed countries as poor in all respects. This devalues those communities by failing to take into account their cultural wealth and the strength of their social fabric, making it more difficult for such communities to believe in the educational and economic resources they have to offer (Rahnema 2003; Traoré 2002).

The critical importance of work

The informal economy and child labor are omnipresent in the two monographs as strategies for basic survival. These inherently precarious strategies are made somewhat more secure through the process of sharing. Each time Paul or the Rojas-Paucar children earn some money, they provide aid to their families. Inculcated with values of sharing from a young age, Paul and the Rojas-Paucar children would not think of earning money without using it to help the people around them. Small sums of money achieve greater impact when they are invested in a community that is able to redistribute them.

A more individualist and materialist vision of well-being considers this practice as preventing the individual from becoming rich, or at least from avoiding poverty. According to this view, group obligations trap individuals by preventing them from escaping poverty on their own; to prosper, a person has to move beyond the traditional community ties that hinder individual freedom. This vision, which permeates many development projects, alienates people from their surroundings and leads them to define themselves only in terms of material wealth or poverty. Their dignity and identity would be better respected if they could define themselves in terms of the cultural and community riches they share, which help them resist poverty. An excessively individualist form of development, which rewards the strongest to the detriment of others, contributes to large disparities that destabilize society and erode fundamental rights to peace and security.

In Sub-Saharan Africa and in Latin America, the informal economy has grown at a faster rate than the formal economy over the past decade. People living in extreme poverty who work in the informal sector are particularly vulnerable: they have no fixed employment, no social protection, no benefits linked to their work such as days off, no collective representation, and very little power of negotiation with their employers. Employment in the informal sector may well allow those living in extreme poverty to survive, but it rarely allows them to move out of poverty.

Promoting decent work should be at the core of anti-poverty strategies. Yet it seems to be almost completely absent from the objectives of most Poverty Reduction Strategy Papers, development guidelines prepared by developing-country governments under the supervision of the international financial institutions. For the International Labour Organization (ILO), promotion of decent work has four basic aspects: *ensuring the right to employment,* which implies supporting policies that favor microfunding and microloans for workers and businesses in the informal economy; *providing social protection,* by supporting initiatives for the creation of health cooperatives and for protection against the dangers of informal labor; *application of basic work standards,* such as those appearing in international labor agreements (freedom for unions and protection of the right to organize and negotiate collectively, banning forced labor and the worst forms of child labor, etc.); and finally, *promotion of social dialogue* and the participation of unions and associations in the definition of strategies to reduce poverty (ILO 2002).

Reconciling community education and school education

Education, of course, is an opportunity for children. But the financial burden of school fees can regularly put other necessities, such as rent, food, and health care, at risk. Academic education is also poorly matched to the rhythm of daily life in communities where children must work for part of the day in order for the family to eat. Parents may fear that schooling will turn their children away from traditional activities and culture.

Academic education needs to be reconciled with the education that comes from parents, families, and communities. This family- and community-based education is fundamental to fighting poverty but still comes into confrontation with academic education, whose values and priorities are different. According to Badini (2004), the values of academic education "are based on competition, the emergence of the individual rather than the group, and they concentrate on personal success rather than the individual's contribution to the success of the group. It is precisely this latter point that, for me, is the special characteristic of [community] education." The solution, then, consists of social and educational policies that are both adapted to and respectful of community priorities and values. This can be seen in two main issues: primary schooling and lifelong learning.

To enable all children to complete their primary education, it is not enough simply to eliminate school fees. It is just as important to imbue "education for all" with content adapted to each country, most notably by prolonging the education given by the community and having it endorsed by the school system. Toward this end, dialogue between schools, teachers, and those populations living in extreme poverty is an absolute necessity.

In a similar vein, lifelong learning is not simply a question of finding places and teachers so that adults can learn to read and write. It is important for adults to develop their own skills and trades and have them brought into the sphere of education where they can be reinvested in the community. Teaching "knowledge of how to live together" should be at the heart of every intervention concerned with education and development.

Toward a more participatory and community-based development process

An approach to development genuinely rooted in the principle of "living together" must necessarily question the dominant ideas of poverty and the way in which development is implemented. The development field remains dominated by economics-based approaches in which the notion of well-being is completely subordinated to the notion of economic growth. Yet nongovernmental organizations have played an influential role in motivating governments and international institutions to adopt an integrated approach to human rights and development issues, an approach that most U.N. agencies have now endorsed (Nyamu-Musembi and Cornwall 2004). In a globalization process where criteria of modernity are largely dictated by the West, people and countries must try to find their own path toward modernization without sacrificing their identity or culture.

The stories of Paul and the Rojas-Paucar family highlight the conflicts that can arise between cultural identity and modernity, especially for people who go through the formal education system. Development programs promoted by international institutions and governments could ease this conflict by encouraging the merging of knowledge and cultures, as well as the affirmation and promotion of specific cultures. In developing countries, most communities are eager to combine their traditional knowledge with modern technology in order to improve their living conditions, provided that their identity and culture are respected. "Indigenous and global knowledge working together in a democratic, self-determined way is the best combination to foster sustainable development," according to a former president of Tanzania (Mkapa 2004, 3). It is the responsibility of politicians and decision makers to provide the space for this to happen.

Living together in the community produces a level of security for people in extreme poverty. Those who would fight poverty need to look for ways to support these practices and integrate them into development programs. These programs can bring in resources from outside, but they must also work to reinforce and draw on the economic, cultural, and educational resources of the community itself. Placing people in extreme poverty at the center of these efforts and learning from their knowledge can help foster sustainable development for all.

Notes

This chapter summarizes research carried out by the Research and Training Institute of ATD Fourth World (http://www.atd-fourthworld.org) and coordinated by Xavier Godinot. The authors thank Jean-Marie Anglade, Amadé Badini, Bruno Bambara, Caroline Blanchard, Anne-Claire Brand, Guillaume Charvon, Cristina Diez, and Paul S. for their collaboration. This summary version of the report was prepared by Andrew Hayes under the supervision of the study authors.

1. See, for instance, U.N. Millennium Project (2005) and World Bank (2005).
2. Godinot and Wodon (2006) explore the epistemological basis of this approach.
3. This work fed into the study published as *How Poverty Separates Parents and Children: A Challenge to Human Rights* (ATD Fourth World 2004). This study was based on interviews with children and parents living in extreme poverty and also included contributions from social workers, partners in state agencies and international institutions, researchers, and members of ATD Fourth World.
4. The Courtyard of a Hundred Trades was created in 1983. Michel Aussedat, a full-time volunteer with ATD Fourth World, initiated the project with others. He emphasizes that the Courtyard was not established to provide children with food, clothes, or medication, or to compensate for their lack of housing or jobs. "Not only did we lack the resources, but taking on such a responsibility would risk undermining [the children's] own efforts and marginalizing them even further, making them dependent, something deep down they really didn't want."

Rather, the Courtyard is a meeting place where the poorest children are always welcome. It is "a place where the children find the means to understand their own lives, take back control, and direct their efforts towards projects that respect their family and their culture" (Aussedat 1996, 92).

Among other activities, the Courtyard conducts week-long workshops with children living on the streets. Activities are offered with the help of local craftsmen, who are sensitive to the fate of the children and want to share their know-how with them. Beyond enhancing the youths' skills, the workshops provide a peaceful space for dialogue that often ends up encouraging the youngsters to return to their families (ATD Fourth World–Burkina Faso 2002).

5. The Glass of Milk program began in the 1980s in Lima under Mayor Alfonso Barrantes. In 1985, a national law extended the program to all provincial towns in the country.

6. A neoliberal economic model that was set up in 1990 to control inflation brought about cuts in many subsidies and increased the rate of unemployment (Ugarteche 2003). In 2000, the job market could employ less than half the labor force, leaving a large section of the population to fend for themselves in the informal sector (UNDP 2002, 26).

References

ATD Fourth World. 2002. *Rapport Moral 2002*. Ouagadougou, Burkina Faso: ATD Fourth World–Burkina Faso.

———. 2004. *How Poverty Separates Parents and Children: A Challenge to Human Rights*. Méry-sur-Oise, France: ATD Fourth World.

Aussedat, M. 1996. *La Cour aux Cent Métiers*. Pierrelaye, France: Editions Quart Monde.

Badini, A. 1994. *Naître et grandir chez les Moosé traditionnels*. Paris and Ouagadougou: Sépia-ADDB.

———. 2004. Paper presented at international seminar on "Writing Monographs of Families Living in Poverty," Pierrelaye, France, October.

Brun, P. 2001. *Emancipation et connaissance: Les histoires de vie en collectivité*. Paris: L'Harmattan.

Cabrera Sotomayor, G. *El financiamiento de la educación en el Perú: Alternativas de solución*. Lima: Peruvian Education Ministry, Office for Educational Planning.

Godinot, X., and Q. Wodon, eds. 2006. "Participatory Approaches to Attacking Extreme Poverty: Case Studies Led by the International Movement ATD Fourth World." World Bank Working Paper 77. Washington, DC: World Bank.

ILO (International Labour Organization). 2002. *Decent Work and the Informal Economy*. Geneva: ILO.

Klanfer, J. 1965. *L'exclusion sociale: Etude de la marginalité dans les sociétés occidentales*. Paris: Science et Service/ATD Bureau de Recherches Sociales.

Maathai, W. 2004. Nobel Lecture, Oslo, December 10.

Mkapa, B. 2004. "Indigenous Knowledge: A Local Pathway to Global Development." In *Indigenous Knowledge: Local Pathways to Global Development*. Washington, DC: World Bank.

Narayan, D., R. Chambers, M. K. Shah, and P. Petesch. 2000. *Voices of the Poor: Crying Out for Change*. New York: Oxford University Press for the World Bank.

Nyamu-Musembi, C., and A. Cornwall. 2004. "What Is the 'Rights-Based Approach' All About? Perspectives from International Development Agencies." Working Paper 234, Institute of Development Studies, University of Sussex, Brighton, UK.

Pasquier-Doumer, L. 2003. "L'évolution de la mobilité scolaire intergénérationelle au Pérou depuis un siècle." Document de travail DIAL/Unité de Recherche CIPRÉ. Institut Français d'Etudes Andines, Lima; Institut d'Etudes Politiques, Paris.

Rahnema, M. 2003. *Quand la misère chasse la pauvreté*. Paris: Fayard/Actes Sud.

Schölvinck, J. 2004. Foreword to *How Poverty Separates Parents and Children: A Challenge to Human Rights*, by ATD Fourth World. Méry-sur-Oise, France: Fourth World Publications.

Sen, A. 1999. *Development as Freedom*. New York: Knopf.

Traoré, A. 2002. *Le viol de l'imaginaire*. Paris: Fayard/Actes Sud.

U.N. Millennium Project. 2005. *Investing in Development: A Practical Plan to Achieve the Millennium Development Goals*. New York: U.N. Millennium Project.

Ugarteche, O. 2003. "Después del ajuste estructural: Donde estamos y adónde vamos." *Revista Actualidad Económica* (Lima), December.

UNDP (United Nations Development Programme). 2002. *Human Development Report 2002: Deepening Democracy in a Fragmented World*. New York: Oxford University Press.

World Bank. 2003. *World Development Report 2004: Making Services Work for Poor People*. New York: Oxford University Press.

———. 2005. *World Development Report 2006: Equity and Development*. New York: Oxford University Press.

Wresinski, J. 1994a. *Chronic Poverty and Lack of Basic Security: The Wresinski Report of the Economic and Social Council of France*. Landover, MD: Fourth World Publications. Orig. pub. 1987 as *Grand Pauvreté et Précarité Economique et Social* (Paris: Journal Officiel).

———. 1994b. *The Very Poor: Living Proof of the Indivisibility of Human Rights*. Paris: Editions Quart Monde.

9

Moving Away from Poverty: Migrant Remittances, Livelihoods, and Development

Anthony L. Hall

Since time immemorial, people have sought new life chances in other countries when opportunities at home are scarce. Today, entrenched poverty, inequality, and political strife in many parts of the developing world have persuaded growing numbers that their only chance of improving their lot is to seek employment overseas, either temporarily or on a permanent basis. A convergence of interests between rich and poor countries has fueled this trend: while the poor desperately need jobs, wealthy nations need workers to plug gaps in the labor market that their own ageing populations cannot fill. The labor market has never been as globalized as it is today, and migrant flows are higher today than ever. Moving out of poverty, it seems, is increasingly a matter of moving *away* from poverty.

International migration has doubled in volume since 1980, according to United Nations data. There are up to 200 million international migrants living and working outside their countries of origin, about two-thirds of whom have settled in the industrial countries (GCIM 2005). Some 20–25 million migrants are nationals of Latin America and the Caribbean (LAC), and over 80 percent of them live in the developed economies of North America, Europe (especially Spain, Portugal, and Italy), Australia, and Japan (IOM 2005).

Emigration was expensive even before the events of 9/11; since then, the tightening of security has driven costs still higher. Costs are also increased by the restrictions that are introduced periodically as immigrants become pawns in domestic electoral battles in the United States and in Europe.[1] Sustained by murky interests, people trafficking is big business. In Ecuador, for example, an investigation by the newspaper *El Comercio* estimated this trade to be worth over US$60 million a year (Hall 2005). There, traffickers (known as *coyotes* in Latin America) charge up to US$15,000 per head, three times the average annual salary, for passage to the United States through Central America and Mexico. Emigrants are frequently obliged to mortgage their houses to raise the capital to migrate, while their families back home may face threats of violence if repayments to moneylenders are delayed. If migrants are caught and deported, their investment is lost.

Emigration is also often life-endangering. The press regularly carries harrowing tales of abandonment by coyotes on the high seas or in the desert, as well as the sexual abuse of migrant women and children on their journeys (Hall 2005). In 2005, 465 people trying to cross into the United States from Mexico died of cold, heat, thirst, or hunger, or were shot (Baldwin 2006).

The phenomenon of "illegal" migration reflects widespread desperation. The population of undocumented immigrants in the United States was estimated at 11–12 million in 2006 (Passell 2006). One study of first-time migrants to the United States from Mexico found that no fewer than 91 percent were undocumented (McKenzie 2005).

Not all emigrants are fleeing poverty and civil turmoil. Wealthier and better-qualified international migrants, such as the majority of Ecuadorians and many Mexicans, also seek new avenues of opportunity abroad.[2] The growing importance of migration to Latin Americans of every social and income level has led to ever-larger portions of LAC populations moving north. About 4.5 percent of Latin Americans overall live and work outside the region, but this proportion is much higher in some countries such as Mexico (20 percent), Ecuador (15 percent), and Guatemala (9 percent) (IOM 2005).

These flows of people have had an array of social, political, and economic consequences, but none more important than the tidal wave of funds that migrants who have found work abroad send back to their home countries. Sent in small amounts, often outside of the formal financial system, migrant remittances are notoriously difficult to count and track. They have long been omitted from official statistics on international financial flows, or appended as an afterthought. Indeed, one analyst calls it "the case of the missing billions" (Terry 2005, 1). But as the magnitude of these transfers is increasingly recognized, their uses and impact are the subject of growing attention.

Officially recorded remittances worldwide leapt from US$173 billion in 1999 to US$232 billion in 2005 (Maimbo and Ratha 2005; IDS 2006). Of this, US$167 billion went to developing countries—an amount double the level of foreign aid. India and China lead the field with over US$21 billion each in remittances, followed by Mexico with US$20 billion. In Latin Amer-

FIGURE 9.1
Worker Remittance Flows to Latin America and the Caribbean, 2004

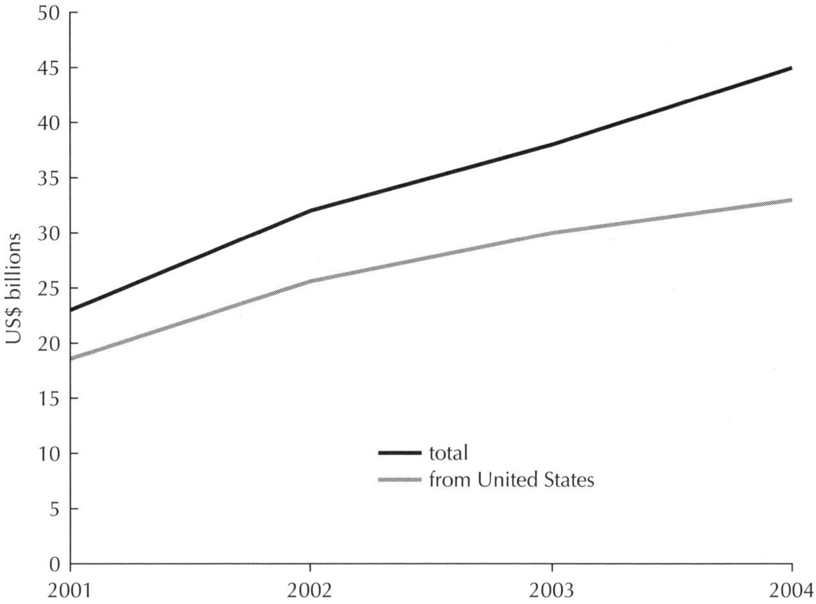

Source: IDB 2004.

ica, the world's largest remittance-receiving region, such transfers constituted 2 percent of gross domestic product (GDP) in 2004 (Orozco and Wilson 2005).[3] In 2005 Latin America received US$56 billion, including US$35 billion per year from the United States alone, more than the combined total of foreign direct investment and foreign aid to the region (figure 9.1).

Mexico, with US$20 billion, is by far the largest recipient of worker remittances in Latin America (figure 9.2). It is followed by Brazil, a distant second (US$6.4 billion), Colombia (US$4.1 billion), Guatemala (US$3.0 billion), El Salvador (US$2.8 billion), the Dominican Republic (US$2.6 billion), Peru (US$2.5 billion), and Ecuador (US$2.0 billion). According to the Inter-American Development Bank (IDB), cumulative remittances to LAC from 2001 to 2010 are expected to approach US$500 billion.

Migrant remittances tend to be discussed as if they constituted a unitary pool of resources, but in practice they perform several very different roles and

FIGURE 9.2
Remittances to Selected Latin American and Caribbean Countries, 2005

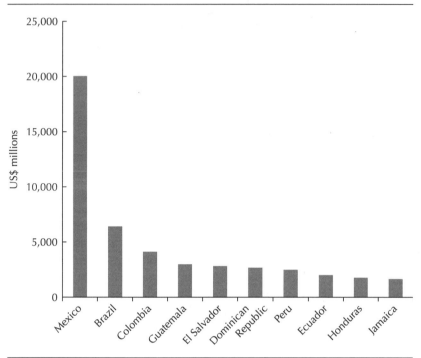

Source: IDB 2005.

address distinct needs in the receiving communities. Consistent with Gold-ring (2004), this chapter distinguishes between (a) family transfers sent by individuals to meet the basic household needs of their kin back home, such as food, clothing, consumer durables, health, and education; (b) collective remittances sent by groups of migrants for community social infrastructure projects such as the construction or refurbishment of churches, schools, and recreational facilities; and (c) entrepreneurial remittances from successful expatriates seeking profitable investment opportunities that also contribute to local economic development.

Although the vast bulk of remittances have traditionally supported migrants' families and to a lesser extent community needs, the pool of migrant financing is becoming very appealing to policy makers seeking additional funding for local economic development. This involves private sector development through small and medium enterprises that can both create jobs and stimulate local economic activities. The present chapter draws out the distinctive nature and role of the three main categories of remittances and raises questions about the potential for shifting transfers away from personal and community support into more directly "productive" business activities.

Remittances and Development: Two Views

The literature on international migration has devoted increasing attention to contrasting views on the development potential of migrant remittances. The more optimistic analysts regard migrant remittances as a vast, unitary pool of wealth that is still relatively untapped. Application of the right policies and incentives, they contend, could unleash the potential of these funds to promote local economic development. Donald Terry of the IDB's Multilateral Investment Fund contends that "the huge scale of LAC remittances can be a powerful lever to open up financial systems, mobilize savings, generate small-business loans, and multiply the economic impact for millions of individual families, as well as the communities where they live" (2005, 11).

A more pessimistic school of thought sees strict limits to this development potential. These analysts argue that almost all cash transfers are used to satisfy basic family consumption needs, leaving little surplus for investment in wider economic activities. There is some validity in both of these perspectives, and the true potential of harnessing remittances for development purposes probably lies somewhere along this "optimistic-pessimistic" continuum.

A starting point is to recognize that there are diverse categories of remittances that, on the whole, serve distinctive development needs. Goldring (2004, 800) argues that "migradollars" do not constitute a monolithic or uniform category, but may be broadly disaggregated into three major types. *Family remittances* to relatives in the home country are used to cover basic household needs such as food, clothing, and consumer goods, as well as family members' health and education costs. *Collective remittances* are sent by organized groups of migrants to finance social or community activities, including health and education infrastructure, public works, or festivities, most often in their home towns. Finally, *entrepreneurial remittances* may be sent by economically successful expatriates in the form of investment capital to finance productive ventures such as small businesses.

Remittances, then, can be conceived as serving diverse but complementary livelihood needs. The concept of livelihood has been defined as comprising "the capabilities, assets (including both material and social resources) and activities required for a means of living" (Scoones 1998). In Latin America and many other parts of the developing world, international migration is an increasingly critical component of people's livelihood strategies, not only for the migrants but also for the family members they leave behind. In a rational sense, "Migration is the result of individuals and households weighing the utility that is attainable under different migration regimes with the utility from not migrating" (Mora and Taylor 2005, 25). For growing numbers, overseas migration is a carefully calculated move to boost job prospects, income-earning opportunities, and the general welfare of entire extended families. The process is facilitated, supported, and driven to a large extent by family members living and working abroad and sending money home.

Pessimists generally take the view that the vast bulk of remitted funds are absorbed by household support and to a lesser extent by community-based social investments, leaving hardly any surplus to boost investment in local development through private enterprise initiatives. Early studies carried out during the 1970s seemed to reinforce that view (for example, Böhning 1975). Even today, research suggests that only about 5–10 percent of total remittances overall are invested in microenterprises, real estate, or other assets in the home country. Yet recent surveys have revealed the diverse and complex economic motivations underlying the sending of remittances home, ranging from altruism, loan repayments, and insurance to inheritance, service exchange, and investment (Docquier and Rapoport 2006).

Concern for mobilizing a larger proportion of migrant remittances to fund local economic development has been growing on the international policy agenda. As noted above, the optimistic school of thought believes that significant personal wealth has been accumulated by migrants and that this could be harnessed to fund private enterprise and encourage local development, beyond that already stimulated indirectly through individual family support and collective social infrastructure. The different categories of remittances would require different interventions in order to redirect a portion of them to local development. Based on the assumption that remittances are fungible, albeit to an undetermined degree, many policy makers believe that this investment potential can be boosted using one or a combination of the following strategies:

- Divert a proportion of family remittances into more "productive" activities. This is based on the perception that while remittances are conventionally seen as intra-family compensatory transfers performing a social function, they also "respond to investment opportunities in the home country as much as to charitable or insurance motives" (IDS 2006, 4).

- Provide incentives for collective transfers to be spent on small business ventures rather than just on social infrastructure.
- Encourage successful expatriate entrepreneurs to invest more of their funds in commercial ventures in the home country.

Research evidence suggests, however, that the three categories of family, collective, and entrepreneurial remittances may not be quite as fungible as is sometimes imagined. That is, the degree to which remittances intended for one purpose can be leveraged to provide funds for another purpose may be structurally constrained by the senders' underlying objectives and values. Many policy makers take for granted a flexibility that may in practice be extremely limited.

Understanding this policy issue requires a reexamination of some assumptions that underpin the current thinking on remittances and their development potential. It is necessary to disaggregate remittances, to consider the logic that drives and sustains them, and to be aware of contextual constraints that might impose severe limits on the possibility of scaling up their development impact.

Family Remittances: Surviving and Thriving

Studies consistently show that remittances figure prominently in the household budgets of migrants' families back home. In the words of one author, they represent "the human face of globalization" (Terry 2005, 6). In Ecuador, for example, some 14 percent of the adult population receives remittance payments (Hall 2005). Families have become increasingly dependent on international cash transfers to meet their basic needs. In Latin America these transfers constitute up to half or more of the average income of benefited households.

Surveys show that, on average, about 85–90 percent of remittances are spent on necessities such as food, clothing, consumer items, education and health services, and utilities. The remainder is invested in savings and property or used to make debt repayments (Terry 2005). Unlike much foreign aid, remittances generally reach beneficiaries directly and quickly, even those in remote areas. The flow of cash tends to be stable in response to household requirements rather than responding to market fluctuations or political factors. Furthermore, transfers are often countercyclical during times of economic hardship, channeling funds precisely when they are most needed and acting as a form of insurance or safety net.

Yet a note of caution is needed regarding the image, conveyed in much of the literature, of remittances as ubiquitous and invariably beneficial. For a start, not all families of migrants receive transfers, nor is their distribution necessarily even. Overall, in Latin America and the Caribbean, the IDB estimates that around 65 percent of expatriate workers send money home on a regular basis, typically US$100–US$300 a month. In Mexico, 870,000 households, about 4 percent of the total population, receive such transfers, but some 3 million—over three-quarters of the households that have sent migrants—do not (Zárate-Hoyos 2005). In Ecuador, half of all migrants' families receive no payments from their relatives working overseas. It was also found in Ecuador that wives lose out when husbands choose to send remittances to their own parents as a way of avoiding conflicts where more than one partner or household is competing for resources. Children thus may not benefit at all unless cash is channeled through paternal grandparents (Zárate-Hoyos 2005). Just as emigrants are often not the poorest citizens, so remittances do not necessarily flow to the poorest households.

Moreover, remittance flows tend to diminish over time, as more migrants' sojourns abroad become permanent rather than constituting an emergency response to crisis, and as parents who have migrated send for their children to join them. Under these circumstances, livelihoods are constructed increasingly in the countries of destination. Even when flows continue, there may be moral hazard or negative demonstration effects in which cash is spent on high-status consumer goods such as satellite dishes and designer clothes rather than on basic necessities. According to some critics, remittances may even create a disincentive to seek work locally as young people, in particular, aspire to move overseas (Orozco and Wilson 2005, 377).

Little is known so far about the impact of international remittances either on the share of the population living below the poverty line (the level of poverty) or on the proportion of average incomes below the poverty line (the depth of poverty). Evidence from one World Bank study is somewhat encouraging in this regard, concluding that a 10 percent increase in the share of international migrants in a country's population will lead to a 1.9 percent decrease in the level of poverty. Similarly, a 10 percent increase in the share of remittances in GDP will result in a 1.6 percent reduction in the level of poverty and a 2 percent reduction in the depth of poverty. Thus, although notable, the poverty impact of migration appears to be relatively small (Adams and Page 2005; Docquier and Rapoport 2006). Furthermore, extreme poverty is unaffected, apparently because very poor families often cannot afford to send family members abroad and therefore do not benefit from remittances. Research on the impacts of remittances and migration on inequality in the home country has provided mixed results. Conclusions seem to be situation-specific, with some nations exhibiting worsening income distribution and others the opposite trend (López-Córdova and Olmedo 2006).

While the impact on income poverty may be variable, the process of migration and associated remittances has clearly had other beneficial livelihood impacts, for example by strengthening human capital and compensating for welfare deficits. In Mexico, literacy among children ages 6–14 was found to improve significantly among families that received higher levels of remittances, while school attendance levels improved for those ages 13–15, especially among girls (López-Córdova and Olmedo 2006). In El Salvador, even modest remittances drastically reduced the likelihood of a family's children dropping out of school (IDS 2006). Remittances are also critical in funding out-of-pocket health care expenses, which account for 75–90 percent of total health costs incurred by individuals in Latin America (compared with less than 40 percent in industrial countries). Expenditure on health funded by remittances as well as the knowledge acquired through migration were found to reduce infant mortality rates and improve birth weight among Mexican children. In addition, the extra income allows some mothers to stay at home and care for their children rather than having to work outside the home (López-Córdova and Olmedo 2006).

By their very nature, remittances are private transfers outside the control of government regulation. In many cases, remittances substitute for wages and are a key to family maintenance, accounting for half or more of household income. When families spend remittances, therefore, immediate survival needs take priority, with some concern for medium-term human capital investment in education and health care. If we include amounts spent on real estate, consumer goods, and debt repayments, it is questionable how much money is actually left over for more "productive" activities. This might amount to 5 percent of the total at most. Thus, even as early as the mid-1990s, "there was relative consensus around the conclusions that family remittances represented income that was spent largely on recurrent costs, that there was little left over to save or invest, and that there might be structural limits that created disincentives for investment" (Goldring 2004, 833).

Some observers believe that this need not lead to pessimistic conclusions regarding the productive use of remittances. Orozco (2005, 171) notes that "the fungible nature of remittances can make it difficult to distinguish consumption expenditures from other broadly productive uses to which these funds could be put." Household studies show that in practice, it is not easy to separate consumption from production decisions. What initially appears to be a consumer item (such as a sewing machine, for example) might be put to productive use by making clothes and selling them to friends and neighbors. The economic potential of consumption goods could therefore be greater than is generally imagined.

Yet the fungibility issue is one not simply of percentages but also of underlying principles. It might well be the case that, in theory at least, a certain (even if relatively small) proportion of family or worker remittances could be diverted from funding recurrent costs into productive development projects. However, in practice, the cultural and social role of family transfers is as important as their economic purpose. Such remittances "have social meaning that involves expressions or claims of membership in a family or social network. People send money as part of a social obligation and to affirm their ongoing role as members of a family or social network" (Goldring 2004, 820). In other words, the sociocultural role of remittances is inextricably embedded within their economic function as major sources of income and livelihood. This "social determinism" calls into question the extent to which family remittances could be reclassified or switched into other projects.

Undaunted, many observers remain upbeat about the general development potential of migrant remittances. Much attention is now being focused on lowering transfer costs and thus making available a greater share of gross earnings to migrants and their families. Transfer costs have long been considered both excessive and regressive. The typical small monthly payments made by migrants incur disproportionately high flat-rate charges, a situation attributed to market inefficiencies caused by lack of competition and inadequate means of transferring money. Benefits can be achieved, it is argued, by reducing transaction costs for migrants and enhancing access to formal financial institutions ("banking the unbanked") for both senders and receivers. Multilaterals are at the forefront of this move, especially the Inter-American Development Bank and the World Bank.[4]

The situation has improved markedly in recent years. Transfer costs to Latin America have been halved from an average of 15 percent of their value, releasing an extra US$3 billion (Terry 2005, 11). In Mexico, the federal government has taken steps to improve migrants' access to financial institutions such as banks and credit unions as an alternative to more expensive commercial money transfer companies such as Western Union and MoneyGram. As a result, transaction costs have fallen significantly in recent years along the U.S.-Mexico corridor (Hernández-Coss 2005).

Ecuadorian migrants, in contrast, must rely on the private sector since the government has no policy for providing such institutional support. The Quito-based Banco Solidario, for example, has discovered that dealing with migrant remittances can be good business. Just 4 percent of its 65,000 clients are migrants, yet they account for 20 percent of the bank's US$20 million in savings accounts. Banco Solidario has linked up with financial institutions in Spain (the major destination for Ecuadorian emigrants) and provides a range of services to facilitate savings and investments, travel, and cash transfers (Hall 2005). Growing use of ATMs and bank cards along with digitalized bank transfers will undoubtedly improve efficiency in the transfer of remittances.

Questions remain over the extent to which family remittances can be harnessed for community-focused or business purposes. Clearly, in some instances so-called basic needs transfers will be invested in family enterprises and self-employment. On balance, however, research evidence suggests that its prime function is overwhelmingly as a form of social insurance or protection to reduce vulnerability to shocks and build a degree of security. A small portion (perhaps 10 percent) of such remittances may be spent on purchasing land and houses as an investment in the future, but it is debatable how much long-term development can be generated in this way. Migrants view such strategies as a form of personal insurance, a way of inflation-proofing their hard-earned money and providing for the family's housing needs. Some evidence from Mexico suggests that remittances to more egalitarian communities such as *ejidos* (settlements on communal lands) tend to be spent on more productive ends (Docquier and Rapoport 2006). However, it remains to be seen whether family funds can be reallocated on any significant scale into small business enterprises.

Collective Remittances: Serving the Community

A second type of cash transfer consists of donations from organized groups of migrants to finance investments back home in social infrastructure such as health and education facilities, refurbishment of public buildings such as the local church, and special events such as patron saint festivals. These are distinct from the first category in that they are designed to benefit not particular individuals or households but the community as a whole.

Collective remittances are typically channeled through informal clubs and hometown associations (HTAs) organized in the countries where migrants live. HTAs comprise members from the same village, town, or state who either individually or collectively fund social and economic works in the country of origin. Such organizations grow in importance as migrants become better established and financially stronger in their adopted countries. By definition, however, their distribution is highly uneven and depends on the pattern and duration of migration from a given locality. Areas with longer traditions of migration have benefited considerably, but zones of more recent exit may not have enough migrants living together overseas to form strong organizations.

In Latin America, Mexico has the longest established tradition of HTA sponsorship, going back to the 1950s. In recent years, HTAs have also become increasingly prominent among migrants from Guatemala, El Salvador, and the Dominican Republic. They fund public infrastructure such as roads, donate ambulances and medical equipment, and promote education through school construction, donations of supplies, and scholarships. The associations thus help to bridge welfare gaps by supplying vital funding for basic services that the state cannot provide.

A relatively small proportion of transfers is sent as collective remittances for building community-based social infrastructure. The affective and symbolic importance of these transfers is, however, disproportionately large for the migrants involved. HTAs allow individuals to maintain their cultural identity and ties to their communities of origin, build a sense of community among fellow migrants in the destination country, and reaffirm their personal status and newfound importance by supporting high-profile local projects. Another important function of HTAs is to transmit the home culture and values to the second generation, that is, to migrants' children born abroad.

Estimates of the total number of hometown associations in the United States vary considerably. For example, the Global Commission on International Migration puts the figure for Mexican HTAs at just 600 in 30 U.S. cities (GCIM 2005, 29). Another study suggests that 2,000 of the estimated 3,000 immigrant HTAs in the United States are Mexican, but this total includes informal clubs as well as formally registered organizations. About 70 percent of Mexican associations are affiliated with the states of Guerrero, Guanajuato, Jalisco, and Zacatecas, and half of all transfers are concentrated in just 460 of Mexico's 2,443 municipalities. Mexican consulates in the United States have stimulated the formation of HTAs through the Program for Mexican Communities Overseas (Programa de Atención a las Comunidades Mexicanas en el Extranjero). In 2002, Los Angeles had the highest number of HTAs registered at Mexican consulates (188), followed by Chicago (82), Dallas (41), and New York (15) (Zárate-Hoyos 2005).

A distinctive feature of the Mexican case is the active role played by federal and state governments in encouraging local investment by migrant associations. In Zacatecas, the state government matches funds sent by emigrants for community projects in the state under the "2-for-1" and "3-for-1" programs (box 9.1). Such cost-sharing schemes have now expanded to 22 Mexican states. Michoacan adopted the scheme in 2002 and set up 64 projects

BOX 9.1
Hometown Associations Assist Zacatecas, Mexico

The state of Zacatecas has a century-old tradition of migration to the United States and the highest proportion of its population living abroad of any Mexican state. From 1993 to 2004, Zacatecan hometown associations spent a total of US$165 million on 1,500 community projects, matched by US$483 million in official funds under the "2-for-1" and "3-for-1" schemes (IDS 2006). In 2005 alone, 320 community projects were funded with own and matching resources of US$20 million. Many of these initiatives have built upon existing community traditions and social networks.

Although the Tres por Uno (3-for-1) program has to some extent improved the quality of life of Zacatecans, migration and development experts believe that it has not effectively reduced poverty in the region. Jobs remain scarce. For this reason, in the past few years Zacatecans abroad have also embarked on business ventures in their home state. For example, a group of 15 Zacatecans pooled their personal savings and invested in a mescal distillery (mescal is a colorless spirit distilled from the juice and pulp of the *agave* plant). Another group invested in the building of the first luxury hotel in the state, the Quinta Real, while still others put their money into small businesses processing foods such as dried chilis, tortillas, and marmalades.

These productive investments have enabled Zacatecans living abroad to strengthen their political clout at home. Mexican politicians are aware of this, and as a result, they spend considerable time visiting Mexican immigrants in the United States and nurturing relationships with them. This is especially true now that a law has been passed allowing Mexicans living abroad to vote in Mexican elections (in the past, Mexican migrants could do little more than persuade their families to vote for their chosen candidates). Governor Amalia García Medina was elected largely due to the massive support of Zacatecan immigrants in the United States.

Source: Federación de Clubes Zacatecanos del Sur de California, http://www.federacionzacatecana.org.

in the first year, over 80 percent of which were for social infrastructure and recreation projects (de la Garza and Cortina 2005).

State governments have also fostered the creation of associations such as the Federation of Zacatecan Clubs of Southern California, set up in 1965. In several states, including Guanajuato and Zacatecas, state governments have established special migrant affairs offices that cooperate with the Ministry of Foreign Relations and consulates overseas. They have actively promoted programs to attract remittances for local investment purposes. One such program, Mi Casa in Guanajuato, has facilitated the setting up of 12 maquiladora factories employing 500 people, with plans to build several more. The state pays up to three months' wages during the start-up period and makes low-cost loans available (IDS 2006).

In El Salvador, following the Mexican model, the government has set up a special office for dealing with migrant affairs, the Dirección General de Atención a la Comunidad en el Exterior (DGACE). The government works closely with hometown associations on rural development projects through its local development fund (Fondo de Inversión Social para el Desarrollo Local, FISDL) in partnership with mayors, the church, the private sector, and nongovernmental organizations. The FISDL and DGACE have developed a program, Unidos por la Solidaridad (United in Solidarity), under which HTAs compete for matching funds from the central government for development projects. Since 2004, the FISDL has jointly sponsored 45 social infrastructure projects costing a total of US$11.45 million, of which 45 percent came from HTAs in the United States and the remainder from central and municipal governments. HTA contributions range from 1 percent to 57 percent of project costs. In a separately funded scheme, another 29 projects costing US$7.6 million have been supported since 2002 with a 61 percent contribution from Salvadoran HTAs.[5]

International aid organizations have become increasingly active in funding research and stimulating debate on the phenomenon of international migration and the rapid growth of remittances. Yet they have been slow to get off the ground in terms of developing specific policies and supporting appropriate projects and programs to encourage remittance-funded local development. An early initiative came from the IDB, which set up the Multilateral Investment Fund (MIF) in 2000. Its subprogram on Remittances as a Development Tool supports studies, surveys, conferences, and projects in the LAC region. By 2005, the MIF was supporting 10 regionwide and national technical assistance projects to promote the development impact of migrant transfers, with several others in the pipeline. These are aimed at easing the flow and lowering the costs of transferring money, mobilizing savings through formal financial institutions, and linking remittances to local entrepreneurship and economic development projects.[6] A notable example is the IDB/MIF-funded regional project to facilitate the financing of microenterprises through formal credit institutions (box 9.2).

The International Fund for Agricultural Development (IFAD) has been co-financing development projects with HTAs in El Salvador. Together with the World Bank, IFAD has been working with Salvadoran associations to identify appropriate projects and provide technical and financial support. Many of these initiatives form part of IFAD's Rural Reconstruction and Mod-

BOX 9.2
Financing for Micro, Small, and Medium Enterprises through Formal Financial Intermediaries

The IDB's Multilateral Investment Fund is supporting a US$2.4 million project in partnership with ACCION Internacional, a nongovernmental organization, to link remittances sent from the United States with micro-finance institutions (MFI) in Latin America and the Caribbean. The project will promote the participation of MFIs in the delivery of remittances as a way to reduce transfer costs and increase the access of recipient households to financial services. The project will forge links between remittance senders and ACCION's partner MFIs in Haiti (SogeSol), Colombia (Banco Caja Social), Bolivia (BancoSol), Nicaragua (FAMA), and Peru (Mibanco).

This project responds to a growing interest in promoting the participation of microfinance institutions in the delivery of remittances as a way to reduce transfer costs and increase the access of recipient households to financial services that can help leverage the economic impact of these funds. Access to savings and credit products tailored to low-income families can help families receiving remittances channel these funds toward future investments such as housing, education, or microenterprises. The long-term goal of this project is to develop linked banking services that serve both immigrants in the United States and their families back home. In order to achieve this, the project will develop partner relationships between MFIs in Latin America and banks in the United States that share the objective of helping low-income immigrants and their families gain greater access to mainstream financial services.

Source: IDB, ACCION International

ernization Program, which encourages migrant associations to invest in community social and income-generating projects in their home countries on a matching-fund basis.[7]

One initiative, co-financed by IFAD and El Salvador's Ministry of Agriculture, is the Rural Development Project for the Central Region (PRODAP-II). A local association in the community of La Labor identified school construction as a priority and worked with three Salvadoran HTAs in the United States, which together provided almost half of the US$55,000 project cost. The government also provided technical assistance and agreed to pay for teachers and school materials (Vargas-Lundius 2004).

In contrast to Mexicans and Salvadorans, Guatemalan migrants have had little support from their government and have had to depend instead on civil society. The U.S. Conference of Catholic Bishops, for example, has worked in collaboration with Mayan HTAs to set up an organization called Pastoral Maya that links Mayan communities in the United States. At its third annual meeting in 2004, Pastoral Maya discussed strategies for helping migrants assist their home communities in Guatemala (see chapter 10 in this volume).

As already noted, some policy makers are optimistic about the potential for mobilizing community investment funds to promote local economic development rather than just building social infrastructure. There is growing pressure to encourage HTAs to become more active in the area of economic investments with support from the private sector. An example is the role of First Data Corporation, owner of Western Union, in Mexico. In 2005, the company pledged US$1.25 million to the official 3-for-1 program to help Mexican HTAs in the United States co-fund development projects. Based on initial experiences with projects in Zacatecas and Michoacan, plans are being made by company officials for consultations with hometown associations in California, Texas, and Illinois.

Yet, as with the case of family remittances, collective transfers have their own distinctive identity and role within the overall process of migration, and this may place serious limits on such flexibility. Collective remittances, unlike family transfers, are designed to directly assist whole communities. Everyone in the community can enjoy the goods made available in this way. Such projects are not private businesses, and there is no allowance for "individual appropriation of the project or of profits, rents or other benefits" (Goldring 2004, 824).

Furthermore, providing for health, education, transport, and communications as well as social insurance becomes an exercise in "social citizenship" in circumstances where the state has left a gap in provision. By visibly substituting for the financial role of the state in serving the public good, civil society organizations such as HTAs and their leaders can accumulate significant social and even political capital. Thus, the kinds of sentiment that underpin community-based investments in the public interest may not be compatible with commercial ventures designed to benefit individuals and small groups.

Based on this logic, it is unsurprising that the vast bulk of projects funded through collective remittances have not been productive in the conventional sense. Of course, social and welfare investments build human capital and thus help form a more productive labor force, while having a multiplier effect on the local economy. However, their whole raison d'être is to serve the community rather than individual interests. Any suggestion or suspicion that a community project is likely to profit individuals or a small group of people at the expense of others is likely to seriously undermine its credibility and cause major problems.

Transparency, together with local participation in planning and implementation, is a major ingredient in successful community projects. Any deviation from this norm has to be understood and accepted from the outset. As noted in the case of Zacatecas, for example, the few production-based projects supported by the 2-for-1 and 3-for-1 schemes, normally reserved for social investments, succeeded precisely because they were recognized from the outset not as community projects but as special entrepreneurial ventures (Goldring 2004).

Furthermore, there are undisputed risks associated with establishing and running small businesses. These relate to access to markets and credit as well as managerial-administrative capacity, and include the high transaction costs of dealing with government agencies. Such risks are likely to make commercial investments relatively unattractive to organizations such as HTAs.

Potential problems also extend to the political arena. As noted in one survey, relations between HTAs and governments are not neutral, but tend to be politicized. Thus, "If the municipal government is of a different political party than the leadership of the HTA, tensions may arise and the municipal government may decide not to provide its support. In some cases, the municipal government may even attempt to block efforts by the HTA to implement projects in the community" (Vargas-Lundius 2004, 11). In addition, fear of corruption and the complexities of dealing with government bureaucracy may dissuade many potential investors.

Entrepreneurial Remittances: Private Enterprise, Profits, and Development

This third category of monetary transfer is very different from the first (family) and somewhat distinct from the second (collective). Entrepreneurial remittances are transfers from successful expatriates who are well-established citizens or permanent residents in the destination country. Such transfers are derived not from current income but from accumulated capital and savings. This is seen by policy makers as a potential source of investment capital, but it is also one from which expatriates will be seeking to profit personally. In Latin American and the Caribbean, this form of "migrant capital" is gradually becoming a more significant component of state and federal government outreach programs, although it is still very much in its infancy as a transfer category (Goldring 2004). Projects tapping these transfers tend to be public–private partnerships supported by state and international organizations.

The newest way of linking emigration with economic development has been to encourage successful expatriates to invest in employment- and profit-generating enterprises in their home country. In Latin America, Mexico leads the way in this field. The National Development Bank (Nacional Financiera, NAFIN) runs a US$2.2 million fund called "Invest in Mexico," supported by the Multilateral Investment Fund of the IDB. It appeals to Mexicans in the United States to "support the development of your community" by making productive investments in businesses such as pharmacies, gas stations, shops, communications, *tortillerias,* cafés, restaurants and many others. It offers technical assistance and credit advice and encourages "all Mexican or Mexican-American entrepreneurs . . . to contribute their entrepreneurial capacity and resources for the development of productive and profitable projects in their place of origin" (Goldring 2004, 830).[8]

Such initiatives appeal to the investor's emotional attachment to the home country, as well as to the profit motive and to market logic. Their aim is to attract investments in small enterprises in areas of high out-migration in order to generate employment. The government tends to negotiate with individuals or small groups of businessmen rather than with HTAs or federations. Depending on the perceived market potential, these investments may or may not be in the investors' own areas of origin. This kind of program can only get off the ground in areas with a long tradition of migration and consolidated, economically successful expatriate communities.

The true potential for generating jobs and stimulating local development through such investments has been the subject of some discussion. Many commentators are encouraged by the possibility of tapping into expatriates' business acumen and financial capital if appropriate incentives are provided through public-private partnerships, such as through extensions of the cost-sharing schemes in Mexico described above. For example, at its 2004 summit, the Group of Eight made a powerful statement on harnessing the potential of remittances to support families and small businesses by reducing transactions costs. The G8 Action Plan called for encouraging "the creation, where appropriate, of market-oriented local development funds and credit unions that give remittance-receiving families more options and incentives for productively investing remittance flows" (Group of Eight 2004).

A major question faced by those advocating greater use of remittances for business purposes is how to mobilize resources on an economically viable scale. One proposal would have migrants pool their resources to make productive investments in a "grassroots venture capital" approach. The New Horizon Investment Club, for example, comprises some 100 Afro-Caribbean Honduran immigrants to the United States. It both pools members' funds and raises additional capital for ventures in real estate, the stock market, and the tourism industry in both the United States and Honduras. A somewhat similar effort known as Indigo proposes to develop a micro–private equity fund financed by profits from a remittance service initially serving the Mexican diaspora. Inspired by the company Working Assets, the Indigo fund aims to facilitate migrants' investments in microfinance institutions as well as small and medium enterprises in their countries of origin.[9]

Not everyone is convinced, though, that such investments have a large development potential. One critique is that the kinds of employment generated are invariably "low-wage jobs that are unlikely to satisfy people with family members working in the U.S., or those with social networks to get them to the other side of the border" (Goldring 2004, 831). The implication is that the investments will do little to stem further emigration. One study set in Mexico concludes

> [I]n terms of development impacts to date, the experience of investor remittances in producing sustainable business has been limited. . . . It is not clear where the current array of programs will lead or, in particular, how successful migrants will allocate their capital, given that the risk of investing for profit is probably higher for them in Mexico than in the U.S. (Goldring 2004, 831–32).

Policy makers, therefore, should be careful not to exaggerate the potential for investing remittances in local economic development. This strategy is as yet barely tested, and more research is needed to understand the feasibility of such enterprises on a significant scale and their likely impacts on local investment, employment, and savings. It may well be the case that such trends take longer to mature than is generally imagined. After all, emigrants' priorities so far have been overwhelmingly in the areas of family and community support. Putting money into profitable enterprises has not, so far, been a major preoccupation.

In cases of long-established migration patterns, however, there is some evidence to suggest that entrepreneurial investments gain in relative importance as migrant communities mature. A study of Jamaica, with its 50-year history of migration to the United States and the United Kingdom, revealed that remittances from returnees contributed some 40 percent of the start-up capital for the small businesses sampled (Kirton 2005). A survey of 6,000 small Mexican firms found that almost 20 percent of the capital invested in urban microenterprises was derived from migrant remittances (Woodruff and Zenteno 2001). Similar findings were reported for the Dominican Republic and for Tunisia, where many small businesses have been established and maintained with the help of remittances from family and friends (Portes 2000; Mesnard and Ravallion 2001).

Conclusions and Policy Implications

"People move north by the millions, while money moves south by the billions," notes the IDB's Donald Terry (2005). In the debate on harnessing remittances to fund economic development, we should be clear that family and collective cash transfers are already doing much to support both the macro economy and local development by increasing consumption of goods and services and by building of social and human capital. Remittances have substantial indirect multiplier effects at the local, regional, and national levels that cannot be ignored.

Figure 9.3 illustrates such linkages at the community level. In the case of Mexico, for example, it was calculated that the production multiplier is

FIGURE 9.3
Effect of Remittances on Community Income

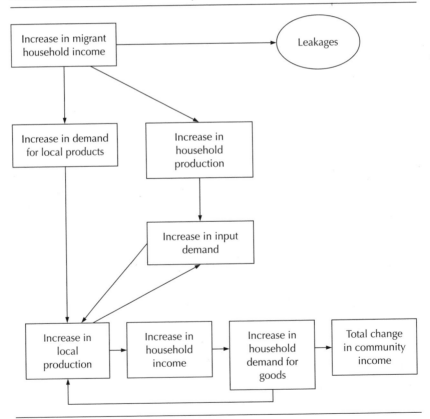

Source: Zárate-Hoyos 2005.

between 1.5 and 2.1 per dollar sent home. Furthermore, although Mexican small farmers and laborers benefited in particular, the agribusiness sector also profited indirectly through increased demand for agricultural inputs (Zárate-Hoyos 2005). In Central America, major new demands for goods and services are provided by nationals returning as tourists, a group that accounts for up to one-third of overseas visitors in the case of El Salvador, for example (Orozco 2005).[10]

Nonetheless, great expectations surround the perceived potential to leverage a larger portion of family and collective remittances as well as expatriate entrepreneurial capital to finance productive development more directly. These hopes seem likely to grow in the future in tandem with the increasing volume of transfers themselves. Remittances, one author notes, could well become the "new development mantra" (Kapur 2005).

In the search for effective interventions, a major source of policy confusion lies in the fact that remittances tend to be regarded as a unitary fund. They are lumped together, with little or no distinction made between the different categories of cash transfers in terms of their role and potential uses. Such assumptions should be carefully reconsidered in the light of the complex nature of remittances and their different economic, social, and sometimes political functions. One of the first tasks of planners in this field should therefore be to recognize the distinctive nature and function of each category of remittance. At the same time, it has to be understood that there is some fungibility and complementarity among family, collective, and entrepreneurial transfers. In particular, consumption-based transfers might have a greater development impact than is indicated by current data. Further research will shed light on this potential

The principal export of several Latin American countries, especially those in Central America and the Caribbean, is now their labor, with remittances exceeding the value even of agro-exports.[11] Desperate people use all means at their disposal to escape poverty and find opportunity. As noted in the opening paragraphs of this chapter, the sheer lengths to which emigrants go and the risks they take bear witness to their single-minded determination to improve their life chances. This logic is underlined by the findings of a research study on how the Mexican government's cash transfers to poor households under the Progresa/Oportunidades program have affected labor migration patterns. The study found that in the case of unconditional cash payments (those not requiring beneficiaries to remain physically present, for example, to attend clinics and schools), the extra money pocketed actually encourages emigration. This is especially true for poorer families with no previous history of working in the United States, who save the extra monthly income to finance otherwise unaffordable international travel (Angelucci 2004).[12]

It may indeed be possible to set aside a greater proportion of collective remittances, moving away from supporting only social infrastructure and public works and toward investing more directly in productive activities. Yet this potential, attractive though it may appear to policy makers, should not be romanticized or exaggerated. Community-based transfers play strong cultural, symbolic, and political roles in the evolving globalized livelihoods of migrants. They do not easily lend themselves to application in commercial ventures unless the terms and conditions are clearly understood from the outset by all parties involved. Governments need to create a policy environment that is conducive to channeling remittances into productive uses, providing appropriate institutional arrangements and incentives for migrants and their families.

Toward this end, policy makers should develop guidelines and take steps in four main areas:

- *Transfer costs.* Actions to reduce transaction costs will benefit families, especially those of poorer migrants who pay disproportionately high charges to send money home.
- *Incentives.* Investment incentives should be targeted at better-established and economically stronger migrant groups that are more likely to allocate their capital to productive ventures. The regional and cultural context of the home country should be taken into account so as to direct initiatives to areas with a greater investment potential.
- *Stakeholder participation.* The successful application of collective and entrepreneurial remittances for productive investments would be facilitated by an open planning process that allows for the effective participation of all stakeholders, including government, HTAs and other migrant clubs and associations, communities, and nongovernmental organizations. Such transparency could help build trust and ease the political tensions that sometimes arise between migrant communities and local government authorities.
- *The policy environment.* In order to persuade migrants to allocate a substantially greater portion of their accumulated savings to promoting local development, major changes will be necessary in all the LAC countries to generate a more attractive development climate that provides greater incentives to invest. The list of what is needed is familiar by now but should be underlined once more: (a) technical support to identify investment opportunities with commercial potential; (b) cost-sharing arrangements with government such those pioneered under Mexico's 2-

for-1 and 3-for-1 schemes; (c) access to microcredit to encourage small entrepreneurs; (d) management training and administrative capacity building; and (e) advertising and marketing support.

Finally, more research on the nature of the ever-larger remittance flows is needed as a basis for considering their potential applications. As we have seen, while remittance use might in principle be fairly compartmentalized, there is in practice a blurring of boundaries. Micro-level research at the household and community levels can help illuminate the links and complementarities among family, community, and entrepreneurial remittances. This includes asking whether seemingly "unproductive" resources might in practice be generating productive activities that are unrecorded, going beyond meeting basic needs and building infrastructure. An understanding of both economic and social conditioning factors behind remittance patterns and decisions about their use is essential. As migration flows become more firmly established and international transfers more ubiquitous, the need for decision makers to make informed policy choices will make such information even more critical.

Notes

1. Notably, the U.S. Congress engaged in heated debates during 2006 over the proposed construction (and subsequent approval) of a 700-mile fence along sections of America's 2,000-mile border with Mexico. See *The Economist* (2006).
2. Even for countries with an established flow of elite emigration, economic crisis may drive a new wave of migrants seeking an emergency income flow, as in the case of Ecuador after 2000 (Hall 2005; Jokisch and Pribilsky 2002). Crisis-driven migration may then settle into a more permanent pattern generating long-standing remittance flows, as happened in Guatemala, Honduras, and El Salvador (Suro 2005).
3. For individual countries the figures can be far higher: for example, Ecuador (9 percent), Guatemala and Nicaragua (10 percent), El Salvador (15 percent), Honduras (13 percent), Jamaica (15 percent), and Haiti (21 percent). Remittance amounts per capita (of the total population) range from US$6 in the case of Argentina to US$131 for Mexico and US$480 for Jamaica.
4. On the IDB's role, see Terry and Wilson (2005); on the World Bank's role, see Maimbo and Ratha (2005). At its annual meeting of governors in Lima, Peru in June 2004, the IDB called on institutions involved in the international migration process to enhance the development impact of remittances. The recommendations focused on reducing transfer costs from the United States to Latin American and the Caribbean and increasing the flow of remittances through the formal financial system. Civil society in particular was urged to strengthen the development impact of transfers by promoting local productive activities.

5. These projects included a health center, road paving, electricity and water supplies, a football pitch, and a town square. See Viceministerio de Relaciones Exteriores (2006).
6. For more information, see the Remittances program Web site at http://www.iadb.org/mif/remittances/index.cfm.
7. In April 2004, a joint program was set up with funds from the IDB (US$4 million), IFAD (US$2 million), and local counterparts (US$1.6 million) to fund special savings and investment projects in rural areas of LAC.
8. For details, see the NAFIN Web site at http://www.nafin.com/portalnf/.
9. See the Indigo Web site at http://www.indigofinanciera.com.
10. Returning Salvadorans spend over two weeks in the country and US$50 per day on average.
11. From 1980 to 1990, for example, the value of transfers to Guatemala, El Salvador, and Honduras increased by over 100 times from US$55 million to US$649 million, while the number of migrants living in the United States grew by 400 percent.
12. However, further studies of *Progresa* have suggested that conditional cash transfers (which do oblige beneficiaries to remain *in situ* as an income conditionality) may have the effect of reducing migration to the United States. See Stecklov et al. (2005).

References

Adams, R. H., and J. Page. 2005. "The Impact of International Migration and Remittances on Poverty." In Maimbo and Ratha 2005, 277–306.

Angelucci, M. 2004. "Aid and Migration: An Analysis of Progresa on the Timing and Size of Labour Migration." Discussion Paper 1187, Institute for the Study of Labour (IZA), Bonn.

Baldwin, T. 2006. "Immigrants Barred by Triple Fences and Double Standards." *Sunday Times* (London), February 27.

Böhning, W. R. 1975. "Some Thoughts on Emigration from the Mediterranean Basin." *International Labour Review* 111 (3): 251–77.

de la Garza, R., and J. Cortina. 2005. "Redefining National Boundaries: Changing Relations Between Diasporas and Latin American States." ARI 16/2005, Real Instituto de Estudios Internacionales y Estratégicos, Madrid.

Docquier, F., and H. Rapoport. 2006. "The Economics of Migrants' Remittances." In *Handbook of the Economics of Giving, Altruism and Reciprocity*, vol. 2, *Applications*, ed. S. C. Kolm and J. Mercier Ythier, chap. 17. New York: Elsevier.

GCIM (Global Commission on International Migration). 2005. *Migration in an Interconnected World: New Directions for Action*. Geneva: GCIM.

Goldring, L. 2004. "Family and Collective Remittances to Mexico: A Multi-dimensional Typology." *Development and Change* 35 (4): 799–840.

Group of Eight. 2004. *G8 Action Plan: Applying the Power of Entrepreneurship to the Eradication of Poverty*. Sea Island, GA, June 9.

Hall, A. 2005. "International Migration and Challenges for Social Policy: The Case of Ecuador." Paper presented at conference on "New Frontiers of Social Policy: Development in a Globalizing World," Arusha, Tanzania, December 12–15.

Hernández-Coss, R. 2005. *The U.S.-Mexico Remittance Corridor: Lessons on Shifting from Informal to Formal Transfer Systems.* Washington, DC: World Bank.

IDB (Inter-American Development Bank). 2004. "Remittance Flows to Latin America and the Caribbean (LAC), 2004." http://www.iadb.org/mif/remittances/markets/index.cfm?language=En&parid=1.

———. 2005. "Remittances to Select LAC Countries in 2005." http://www.iadb.org/mif/remittances/index.cfm.

IDS (Institute of Development Studies). 2006. "Sending Money Home: Can Remittances Reduce Poverty?" *Insights* 60 (January).

IOM (International Organization for Migration). 2005. *World Migration 2005: Costs and Benefits of International Migration.* Geneva: IOM.

Jokisch, B., and J. Pribilsky. 2002. "The Panic to Leave: Economic Crisis and the 'New Emigration' from Ecuador." *International Migration* 40 (4): 75–102.

Kapur, D. 2005. "Remittances: The New Development Mantra?" In Maimbo and Ratha 2005, 331–60.

Kirton, C. D. 2005. "Remittances: The Experience of the English-Speaking Caribbean." In Terry and Wilson 2005, 261–94.

López-Córdova, E., and A. Olmedo. 2006. "International Remittances and Development: Existing Evidence, Policies and Recommendations." INTAL/ITD Occasional Paper 41, Inter-American Development Bank, Washington, DC.

Maimbo, S. M., and D. Ratha, eds. 2005. *Remittances: Development Impact and Future Prospects.* Washington, DC: World Bank.

McKenzie, D. J. 2005. "Beyond Remittances: The Effects of Migration on Mexican Households." In *International Migration, Remittances and the Brain Drain,* ed. Ç. Özden and M. Schiff, 123–47. Washington, DC: World Bank.

Mesnard, A., and M. Ravallion. 2001. "Wealth Distribution and Self-Employment in a Developing Country." CEPR Discussion Paper DP3026, Centre for Economic Policy Research, London.

Mora, J., and J. E. Taylor. 2005. "Determinants of Migration, Destination and Sector Choice: Disentangling Individual, Household and Community Effects." In *International Migration, Remittances and the Brain Drain,* ed. Ç. Özden and M. Schiff, 21–51. Washington, DC: World Bank.

Orozco, M. 2005. "Migration, Money and Markets: The New Realities for Central America." In Terry and Wilson 2005, 193–217.

Orozco, M., and M. R. Wilson. 2005. "Making Migrant Remittances Count." In Terry and Wilson 2005, 375–94.

Passell, J. S. 2006. "Size and Characteristics of the Unauthorized Migrant Population in the U.S.: Estimates Based on the March 2005 Current Population Survey." Pew Hispanic Center, Washington, DC.

Portes, A. 2000. "Globalization from Below: The Rise of Transnational Communities." In *The Ends of Globalization: Bringing Society Back In,* ed. D. Kalb, M. van der Land, R. Staring, B. van Steenbergen, and N. Wilterdink, 253–70. Boulder, CO: Rowman and Littlefield.

Scoones, I. 1998. "Sustainable Rural Livelihoods: A Framework for Analysis." Working Paper 72, Institute of Development Studies, University of Sussex, Brighton, UK.

Stecklov, G., P. Winters, M. Stampini, and B. Davis. 2005. "Do Conditional Cash Transfers Influence Migration? A Study Using Experimental Data from the Mexican PROGRESA Program." *Demography* 42 (4): 769–90.

Suro, R. 2005. "A Survey of Remittance Senders and Receivers." In Terry and Wilson 2005, 21–40.

Terry, D. F. 2005. "Remittances as a Development Tool." In Terry and Wilson 2005, 3–19.

Terry, D. F., and S. R. Wilson, eds. 2005. *Beyond Small Change: Making Migrant Remittances Count.* Washington, DC: Inter-American Development Bank.

The Economist. 2006. "Don't Fence Us Out." April 1.

Vargas-Lundius, R. 2004. "Remittances and Rural Development." Latin America and Caribbean Division, International Fund for Agricultural Development. Paper presented at 27th session of IFAD's Governing Council, Rome, February 18–19.

Viceministerio de Relaciones Exteriores para los Salvadoreños en el Exterior. 2006. "Experiencia FISDL Integrado al Desarrollo Local las Remesas Comunitarias de la Diaspora Salvadoreña: Programa Unidos por la Solidaridad, 2006." San Salvador.

Woodruff, C., and R. Zenteno. 2001. "Remittances and Microenterprises in Mexico." Working Paper, Graduate School of International Relations and Pacific Studies, University of California, San Diego.

Zárate-Hoyos, G. 2005. "The Development Impact of Migrant Remittances in Mexico." In Terry and Wilson 2005, 159–91.

10

Migration, Remittances, and Ethnic Identity: The Experience of Guatemalan Maya in the United States

Shelton H. Davis

Economists, sociologists, and international development agencies are increasingly aware of the role of international migration and remittances in helping people in the developing world improve their living standards. Households in Latin America and the Caribbean have been particularly dependent upon these flows. Migrants from this region sent more than US$45 billion to their countries of origin in 2004. With each immigrant worker sending home an average of US$235 monthly, these remittances are a critical source of support for about 20 million families in the region (Terry 2005). Given the size of these flows, there is growing interest in the possibility that remittances to Latin American countries not only can assist families that receive the funds but also can help promote economic and social development in the communities where these families live.

Within this regional picture, the Guatemalan case is of particular interest. Although Guatemala is one of the largest economies in Central America and is considered a middle-income country, it has one of the highest income poverty rates and lowest human development indices in Latin America. It also has an unusually large indigenous, mainly Mayan, population. Over 41 percent of Guatemala's 11.2 million people speak one of 23 indigenous languages, 21 of which belong to the Mayan language family.[1] The indigenous population is exceedingly poor, accounting for almost three-quarters of the country's population in poverty.

The past two and a half decades have seen a major outflow of Guatemalans to the north. There are currently an estimated 1.3 million Guatemalan migrants in the United States, concentrated in the states of Arizona, California,

Delaware, Florida, Georgia, Illinois, North Carolina, and Texas. In recent years many indigenous Mayan-speaking Guatemalans have joined the exodus.

Annual remittances from Guatemalan migrants have increased steadily, reaching an estimated US$3 billion by 2005 (Orozco 2005b). International reports on remittances tend to present data by country and seldom disaggregate country data by ethnicity. Nonetheless, recent reports indicate sizeable remittance flows from Mayan-speaking immigrants in the United States to their families in Guatemala, especially in the Western Highlands region. A recent survey by the Guatemalan office of the International Organization for Migration found 139,702 Mayan immigrants in the United States who were sending remittances. They include sizeable populations of K'iche' (48,872 migrants), Mam (34,671), Kaqchiquel (17, 870), Q'anjob'al (11,333), and Q'eqchi' (10,363). The Akateco and the Ixil are present in smaller numbers (IOM 2004; see also Dardon 2005).

The IOM study found that over 600,000 Maya in Guatemala were receiving remittances—approximately 15 percent of the Mayan-speaking population of Guatemala, as identified in the 2002 national census. Of the US$2.6 billion in remittances to Guatemala from the United States in 2004, the study estimated, US$546 million was sent to Mayan-speaking families in the Western Highlands. It was estimated, based on this data, that each municipality in the Western Highlands received an average of US$1.9 million per year in family remittances. This amount was significantly higher than the US$0.9 million per year on average that the government allocated to each municipality in this region for public works.

This chapter notes several of the historical and socioeconomic conditions that have led to increasing migration of indigenous Maya from Guatemala to the United States. It then looks briefly at the experiences of Mayan migrants in U.S. communities, especially at the importance of ethnic identity and ethnic organizations. It highlights the potential role of migrant hometown associations in promoting the economic and social development of Mayan-speaking communities in Guatemala—a potential that can be enhanced, I contend, by forging development partnerships with these associations. Finally, the chapter touches on the implications of U.S. immigration policies, not only for the migrants themselves but also for their families and communities in Guatemala.

Reasons for the Mayan Migration

Several structural features of the contemporary Guatemalan economy and society underlie the continuing high emigration of Mayan Guatemalans. Political violence was initially an important factor, as many indigenous Guatemalans sought refuge outside the country during the civil strife of the late 1970s and early 1980s. Although the violence abated with the peace accords of the 1990s, high levels of poverty and a low level of human development, especially among indigenous Guatemalans, have continued to spur a large out-migration. Structural reasons for these poverty trends include a continuing agrarian crisis and a rising rate of both rural and urban unemployment.

Political violence

The war between the Guatemalan military and left-wing guerrilla movements that began in the early 1960s culminated in a period of intense violence in the early 1980s. According to the Historical Clarification Commission, which assessed the causes and effects of the violence, over 200,000 people were killed during the peak period of civil strife between 1980 and 1984. The vast majority of them were indigenous people living in the Northern and Western Highlands. An estimated 1 million people were displaced from their traditional villages; approximately 120,000 of them sought refuge in Mexico and later in the United States (Davis and Hodson 1982; Carmack 1988).

According to the Historical Clarification Commission, 93 percent of the acts of violence were carried out by the Guatemalan military and its allied paramilitary groups. According to the Commission coordinator, violence targeted specifically against the Maya reached the level of genocide: "Within the framework of the counterinsurgency operations carried out between 1981 and 1983, in certain regions of the country agents of the Guatemalan state committed acts of genocide against groups of the Mayan people."[2]

The war also led to the militarization of indigenous and other rural communities. The Guatemalan army created a network of local "civil patrols" as a front line of attack against the guerrilla movement and as a way of testing the allegiance of the indigenous populations living in areas believed to be occupied by the guerrillas. This militarization and the continuing violence disrupted the social, economic, and political organization of Mayan communities, which had formed some of the first local credit and agricultural cooperatives in rural Guatemala. Although the Guatemalan constitution of 1985 and the peace accords of 1996 ended the war, the devastation of the rural areas set the stage for a continuing exodus of indigenous people from the country.

Poverty trends in contemporary Guatemala

In the year 2000 approximately 6 million Guatemalans, more than half the national population, lived in conditions of "general poverty." This meant an income of less than Q389.30 (US$50.56) per person per month. More than a quarter of the country's population, 2.8 million people, lived in "extreme poverty," earning less than Q194.70 per month. These extremely poor families are unable to afford a basic food basket and thus suffer hunger and childhood malnutrition, according to the Guatemalan office of the United Nations Development Programme (UNDP 2001).

The UNDP report also laid bare the stark regional and ethnic differences in poverty rates. General poverty is nearly three times greater in rural than in urban areas of Guatemala. Furthermore, poverty rates are significantly higher in mainly indigenous communities than in mainly nonindigenous ones. In the Guatemala City metropolitan area, UNDP found a general poverty rate of 18.9 percent. By contrast, the percentages in poverty were 81.7 and 77.8 percent respectively in the northern and northwestern regions of the country, where most of the Mayan-speaking communities are located. These indigenous areas also lack access to adequate housing and basic human services such as potable water, sanitation facilities, schools, and health clinics.[3]

A more recent study by the World Bank (2004) also affirms that poverty is deeper and more severe among indigenous Guatemalans than among the nonindigenous or "ladino" population. Although the indigenous represent about 43 percent of the national population, they account for 58 percent of the poor and 72 percent of the extreme poor. Over three-quarters of indigenous Guatemalans live in poverty, as compared with 41 percent of the nonindigenous population. This study also found important differences between indigenous groups, with Mam and Q'eqchi' speakers having the highest poverty rates.[4]

The agrarian crisis

One of the key causes of these poverty trends is inequality in land possession between the indigenous and nonindigenous populations. In the late 19th century, a new national government passed a series of liberal agrarian laws calling for the private expropriation and ownership of public lands and the individual or municipal titling of indigenous communal lands. This agrarian legislation was related to a new era of export-oriented production based upon the creation of large, often foreign-owned, plantations. Large areas of the most productive lands in the lowland and coastal regions were claimed for coffee, bananas, and other cash crops. Indigenous communal lands, which had traditionally been used as natural forests or for subsistence farming of corn, beans, and squash, were expropriated and privatized.

This opening up of Guatemala to plantation agriculture and exports also led to the forced mobilization of indigenous labor from the Northern and

Western Highlands, especially for coffee harvesting. It changed the agrarian structure of the country and led to the increasing exploitation and impoverishment of indigenous farmers and their communities. This process was briefly countered by a short-lived radical agrarian reform program in the early 1950s. Since then, trends of demographic growth, land fragmentation, and land scarcity have continued apace.[5]

The resulting agrarian structure is an unbalanced patchwork of "minifundia" and "latifundia." An agrarian census in 1979 showed that almost 95 percent of farms in the seven departments of the Western Highlands region, mainly occupied by Mayan-speaking indigenous families, were less than seven hectares in size—too tiny even to provide subsistence for a family. They contrasted sharply with the few large farms, mainly owned by nonindigenous people, which controlled over 58 percent of the farmland in the Western Highlands.[6]

More recently, the 2003 agrarian census showed that the number of farms throughout the country had increased by nearly 56 percent since 1979 as a result of demographic growth, land fragmentation, and the settlement of some formerly remote areas such as the northeastern Petén region. But the land area possessed by these farms decreased by 9.5 percent during this period. At the same time, the proportion of landless in Guatemala's rural population increased from 22 percent in 1979 to 33 percent in 2003. These trends toward ever-smaller farms and landlessness in the Mayan areas persisted even though the 1985 Guatemalan constitution called on the national government to "provide state lands to the indigenous communities that need them for their development," and the peace accords of the 1990s called for special land rights and programs for indigenous peoples.[7]

Unemployment and low wages

Recent years have seen a significant decline in the agricultural export economy of Guatemala and rising unemployment in both the rural and urban sectors. According to the Guatemalan Institute of Social Security, the number of jobs in the agricultural export sector fell from 279,234 in 1990 to 184,292 in 1999. This resulted in part from the crisis in the international coffee and cotton markets that affected Guatemala and a number of other Central and South American countries in the 1980s and 1990s.[8] At the same time, the urban labor market in Guatemala, as in numerous other Latin American countries, has also shown a decline. An estimated 6,400 formal sector jobs were lost each year during the 1990s (World Bank 2004).

Those who can find jobs face depressed wages, especially in the rural agricultural sector and the urban informal sector. Furthermore, according to the World Bank (2004), "wage discrimination is high for indigenous groups," with an average wage gap between indigenous and nonindigenous workers of 50 percent, even when their educational backgrounds are similar.

It is hardly surprising, then, that growing numbers of rural indigenous people have sought new employment opportunities in the United States. Those leaving in recent decades for economic reasons have been able to make use of their social contacts with Guatemalan Mayan migrants already in the United States, especially those who migrated in the early 1980s to escape political violence and social disruption.

Guatemalan Maya in California and Florida: A Difficult Adjustment

The Guatemalan Maya seeking refuge from the political violence in their home country and communities headed first for the state of Chiapas in southern Mexico and then beyond, to various cities and towns in the United States. Many of the early migrants concentrated in Los Angeles, California. This was especially true of people who lived in the northern department of Huehuetenango and spoke a Mayan language called Q'anjob'al. The Q'anjob'al Maya, from communities such as San Miguel Acatán, Santa Eulalia, Santa Cruz Barillas, San Rafael La Independencia, and San Pedro Soloma, were particularly affected by the violence of the early 1980s and migrated in large numbers. According to some sources, over 2,000 people from the community of San Miguel Acatán alone sought refuge outside Guatemala in 1980.

By 1990 there were an estimated 4,000 Mayan-speaking Guatemalans living in Los Angeles. The majority of them were Q'anjob'al speakers, but there were also Chuj speakers from the communities of San Sebastián Coatán and San Mateo Ixtatán in northern Huehuetenango and K'iche' speakers from the departments of El Quiche and Totonicapán.[9]

Many Mayan refugees from Guatemala also settled in Florida during this period. They gravitated in particular to a community called Indiantown in southern Florida. In the early 19th century, this community had provided refuge for Seminole Indians who had been displaced from their native territory in the state of Georgia. By the mid-20th century, the growth of the agricultural economy in this part of Florida drew rural workers from the Caribbean, Mexico, and eventually Guatemala to Indiantown and its surrounding areas. The Mayan-speaking population of Indiantown consisted mainly of Q'anjob'al-speaking refugees from Huehuetenango, many of whom had previously lived in Mexico or Los Angeles. From an estimated 400 to 500 people in the mid-

1980s, this migrant community grew to an estimated 4,000 to 5,000 people in 1990 and 1991 (Burns 1993; Wellmeier 1998).

Early Mayan migrants faced high costs and endured many hardships in reaching the United States. They had to pay large sums of money to those who helped them travel through Mexico, cross the border (usually without documentation) into Arizona and New Mexico, and then make their way to their final destinations in California, Florida, and other parts of the United States. To pay the *coyotes*, or refugee smugglers, many Maya had to sell their ancestral lands in Guatemala. Some also borrowed money from friends and relatives already in the United States.

Once at their destinations, the migrants faced serious problems in obtaining rental housing and maintaining stable employment. Those who came with their families or whose families joined them later struggled to earn enough income to cover food, health care, and schooling for their children. Many were monolingual in a Mayan language, and they now had to learn enough Spanish and English to survive in their new environment. Urban neighborhoods in California presented an array of unaccustomed hazards, from heavy automobile traffic to teenage gangs. In rural places such as Indiantown, some local people were becoming antagonistic to the growing presence of Afro-Caribbean and indigenous Guatemalan and Mexican residents in their communities.[10]

Moreover, throughout the 1980s the migrants had to contend with the U.S. government's changing positions in relation to both Central American refugees and migrant workers. At the height of the political violence in Guatemala, in 1983 and 1984, Mayan refugees found themselves increasingly pursued by agents of the U.S. Immigration and Naturalization Service (INS) seeking to apprehend and deport "illegal aliens." In Florida, for example, the number of border patrol agents increased from 27 to 90 during 1983 and the apprehensions of migrants rose from an estimated 400 to 800 persons per month. In January of that year, agents raided an apartment building in Indiantown and took seven Mayan men and one Mayan woman to an INS detention center in Miami. A Catholic priest who had incorporated the Indiantown Maya into his parish helped obtain a lawyer for the detained migrants, and in March a federal immigration judge freed them on their own recognizance. Together with 120 other Guatemalan Mayan refugees living in Florida, they then applied to the INS for political asylum (Davis 1983).

Guatemalan immigrants in Los Angeles faced similar problems. In September 1984, the *Los Angeles Times* reported that INS authorities in Los Angeles had sent more than 1,000 Guatemalans, including several Q'anjob'al refugees from San Miguel Acatán, back to their country during the previous year. The agency had approved only two of the 318 political asylum applications filed by Guatemalan refugees in Los Angeles in the first half of 1984. An INS official told the newspaper that while the agency would judge political asylum requests on a case-by-case basis, "in general the State Department feels that there is no merit in the Guatemalans' statements that they fear persecution" (Hernandez 1984).

In 1986 the U.S. Congress approved the Immigration Reform and Control Act (IRCA), whose main objective was to halt the flow of undocumented migrants to the United States. On one hand, the law imposed penalties on employers who hired undocumented workers and boosted resources for border control, especially in the southwestern United States. On the other hand, it also set legal standards for providing permanent residency status to some categories of recent migrants. These included those who had been living in the United States since January 1982 or had been working as agricultural laborers for at least 90 days in 1986.[11]

Despite these social, economic, and legal difficulties, many of the early Mayan migrants managed to settle into productive lives in their new communities. As they did, they increasingly formed local Mayan organizations that provided immigrants with practical assistance and sociability. These ethnic associations, often called hometown associations (HTAs), generally brought together migrants from the same home community or group of communities. They enabled the transplanted Maya to maintain their ethnic identities, support new migrants from their hometowns, and assist the families and communities they left behind in Guatemala.

The Role of Hometown Associations

In the early 1980s, a group of Q'anjob'al Maya in Los Angeles, with help from a North American Catholic priest who had worked in Guatemala, formed an organization called IXIM, the Mayan word for corn. Members of IXIM helped Mayan migrants adapt to their new living conditions and work situations in Los Angeles, organizing workshops on workers' rights, physical and mental health, drugs, and gangs. They provided advice to new migrants on legal matters related to immigration, such as political asylum and amnesty. The group also raised emergency financial assistance for migrants and their families, collected documentation on social and political conditions in Guatemala, and hosted language and literacy classes in English, Spanish, and Q'anjob'al.

An important purpose of IXIM was to promote the solidarity and development of the Mayan migrant community in Los Angeles and to affirm their cultural heritage and ethnic identity. The group organized cultural events, including annual religious festivals celebrated on the same dates as in their home communities in Guatemala. "With a view toward preserving our own cultural heritage," one of the IXIM leaders wrote in the group's bulletin, *El Vocero de Ixim*, "we have always tried to promote our folklore, our native dances, our traditional handicrafts, the publication of our myths and folktales, and our marimba group, now comprised of young people" (November 1989). In an interview with the *Los Angeles Times*, one of the group's founders, Samuel Simon, said, "Sometimes modernization changes the roots of a culture. It would be similar to us forgetting our culture. But with IXIM, it's different because we practice our culture like it was before. We change nothing. It's important that we conserve the Mayan and Kanjobal culture so that we people can know it" (Baxter 1990).

Beginning in 1989, IXIM undertook four main projects to assist its members and their children. These included a recreation center in the Pico-Union neighborhood of Los Angeles, a program for preserving Mayan cultural and artistic values and transmitting them to new generations, a program for preserving the Q'anjob'al language by means of *El Vocero de Ixim* and other publications, and a project for training young people in computer skills. The organization also helped members acquire sewing machines so that they could learn the needle trades and gain employment in the garment industry, where most early Mayan migrants to Los Angeles worked. Sewing machine training was also directed at increasing the production of traditional dance costumes for use in festivals and other cultural events. IXIM worked to promote more sporting events, especially in soccer and basketball, for Mayan young people in Los Angeles.

Numerous other Mayan migrant associations, including one called the Corn Maya Project in Indiantown, Florida, emerged in cities around the country where Maya had settled. Like IXIM, almost all focused on assisting Mayan young people, women, and children, who were coming to represent an increasing proportion of the indigenous migrants arriving from Guatemala. These associations also shared an emphasis on promoting the cultural heritage and ethnic identities of the migrants by encouraging the continued use of their native languages and by organizing religious festivals that featured traditional dress, traditional musical instruments such as the marimba, and traditional modes of dancing and food preparation (Loucky and Moors 2000; Burns 1993; Wellmeier 1998).

As the Mayan organizations became more firmly established in the 1990s, some began to give more consideration to ways they could help their local communities in Guatemala. IXIM, for example, sought donations to buy land for a soccer field in San Miguel Acatán, one of the major hometown communities of the organization's members.

From the beginning, the Catholic Church played an important role in helping Mayan migrants create ethnic organizations and stay in touch with their hometowns. In 1991, for example, the Church helped a group of Q'anjob'al-speaking Maya from the community of Santa Eulalia in Hue-huetenango form a new hometown association in Los Angeles called the Asociación Q'anjob'al Ewulense. Its initial purpose was to assist with the reconstruction of the Catholic church in Santa Eulalia, which had suffered severe damage as the result of a fire. Throughout the 1990s the members of the association maintained contact with the Catholic priest in Santa Eulalia, who was also of Mayan descent, and helped him by providing funds for the rehabilitation of the community's historic church.

In 1998, with the assistance of a linguistics professor who had done research in Guatemala and spoke Q'anjob'al, this Mayan HTA obtained nonprofit status and began to provide support for other projects in its home community. It helped with the financing of a new community hospital in Santa Eulalia, provided a vehicle to serve as an ambulance for the hospital, and assisted with the purchase of hospital equipment such as an x-ray machine. In addition, the Q'anjob'al HTA began to hold an annual festival in Los Angeles every February to honor Santa Eulalia, the patron saint of their hometown. The HTA would collect donations from participants at the Los Angeles festival each year and send them to Santa Eulalia to support local community development projects, including several having to do with protection of the community's cultural patrimony and support for its growing number of primary and secondary schools.[12]

As the number of Mayan migrant associations grew, the Catholic Church became interested in helping the different associations work together. In the late 1990s the U.S. Conference of Catholic Bishops, in collaboration with Mayan migrant associations, established the Pastoral Maya project. Its purpose has been to help cement more formal links between different Mayan organizations in the United States and to facilitate a relationship between these organizations and communities in Guatemala.[13]

At the project's annual national meetings, representatives of Mayan migrant associations throughout the United States come together to exchange experiences, develop strategies for assisting their members, and seek ways of working together to help their hometowns in Guatemala. The 2004 annual meeting included a talk by the director of El Fondo de Desarrollo Indígena de Guatemala (FODIGUA), a Guatemalan government agency set up following the peace accords to promote local development in the country's indigenous communities. The FODIGUA director's presence indirectly signaled the Guatemalan government's growing awareness of the potential for migrant associations to play a development role.

As the hometown associations have grown they have gradually enlarged their sphere of interest, going beyond social service and material aid to attempt to influence the policies and programs of the Guatemalan government. In September 2004 the First Encounter of Mayan Organizations in Los Angeles brought together 12 Mayan associations based in Southern California. The participating groups included IXIM and another Santa Eulalia organization called Asociación Cultural Jolom Conob, as well as Maya Vision, which works to "preserve the best traditions of the thousands of members of the Mayan ethnic groups in California" (Morales Almada 2004).

The meeting issued a press release that expressed concern about the continuing insecurity and the high levels of crime and violence that continue to affect the poor and indigenous populations of Guatemala. It called upon the Guatemalan government to "defend the human rights of the families in the interior of the country" and "comply with the Peace Accords signed in 1996." The encounter participants also called for steps to create a more inclusive multiethnic society in Guatemala. "As Mayan residents of the United States of America," the press release stated, "we request that the government promote laws and public policies of inclusion in order to protect, develop and promote the identity and the culture of the Maya people." Participants at the encounter emphasized the increasingly important role that migrant remittances are playing in the national economy of Guatemala. They requested that Guatemalan consulates provide appropriate services to migrants and take steps to defend their rights in both the transit country (Mexico) and the destination country (the United States).

Helping Migrants Help Their Homelands: Opportunities for Social and Economic Development in Mayan Communities

By 2000, the Guatemalan newspaper *Prensa Libre* estimated that there were 300 Guatemalan migrant organizations—not necessarily all ethnic Mayan—in the United States (Rodríguez 2000). Los Angeles alone had 50, according to the Guatemalan consulate in that city. The same article noted the presence of two umbrella organizations: the Coalition of Guatemalan Immigrants (CONGUATE) and the National Congress of Guatemalan Organizations in the United States (GUATENET). CONGUATE, with 25 member organizations in 2004, was founded "to promote the advancement of Guatemalans in the United States, and to support the social and economic development of Guatemala," according to its website. Thus the dual purpose of migrant organizations—to serve migrants in the United States and assist their home communities in Guatemala—was becoming more explicit.

International development agencies such as the Inter-American Development Bank and the World Bank recognize that the billions of dollars in remittances sent home by international migrants are an important source of support for many poor families in the developing world. There is ongoing debate, however, regarding the potential for these transfers to promote broader economic development and poverty reduction in the communities where these families live (see chapter 9 in this volume). Some agencies question whether remittances have the capacity to promote local economic development without major changes in the national economic policies of the countries receiving remittances (Williams 2006). For example, a recent World Bank study of remittances to Latin America finds that their impact on poverty and growth in the region has been positive but is in most cases quite modest (Fajnzylber and López 2007).

With respect to Guatemala, World Bank researchers found in 2004 that remittances from both internal (rural-to-urban) and external (international) migrants had reduced "the level, depth, and severity of poverty in Guatemala," but that the impact was greater on the severity than on the level of poverty (R. H. Adams 2004). According to this study, the "squared poverty gap" fell by 18.5 percent when internal remittances are included in household income statistics and by 20.4 percent when international remittances are included in such income. Despite this, the study found, remittances had little or no effect on income inequality in Guatemala.[14]

Although there are as yet no definitive answers to these questions, there is rising interest in finding public policy interventions that could enhance the development impact of remittances in Guatemala and throughout Latin America. Two potential avenues stand out. One is to lower the cost of transferring remittances and increase the access of migrants and their families to formal financial services such as banks, credit unions, and microfinance institutions. The other is for international development agencies, Latin American governments, and nongovernmental organizations (NGOs) to partner with migrant associations to promote the economic and social development and cultural integrity of the migrants' home communities.

Lower the cost of transfers

Migrant remittances have traditionally been handled mainly by commercial cash-transfer companies, which charge high fees. A number of researchers and international organizations have argued that governments can increase the impact of remittances on the welfare of the recipients by working to lower the costs of sending remittances and by demanding more competition among institutions that transfer such monies (Task Force on Remittances 2004; Bair 2005; Orozco and Wilson 2005).

The most important task for governments and nongovernmental agencies, states the Washington-based Inter-American Dialogue, is to help both senders and recipients of remittances gain access to formal financial institutions. This can reduce costs and increase the security of remittance transfers. In addition, bringing migrants and their families into the banking system can spur them to take advantage of saving accounts, household mortgages, and other credit and investment services. These traditionally have only been available to elite groups in most Latin American countries and, because of legal documentation problems, have not often been made available to recent migrants in the United States. The Inter-American Dialogue concludes, "By opening and using accounts in banks and other financial institutions, migrants and their family members back home gain economic citizenship" (Task Force on Remittances 2004, 8–14).

One institution that has taken steps to lower the costs of remittance transfers and provide receivers with access to financial services is the World Council of Credit Unions (WOCCU), which has affiliated credit unions throughout the United States. In 1999 WOCCU created an International Remittance Network (IRNet). A year later it formed a partnership with Vigo Remittance Corporation to transfer remittances through the IRNet from immigrant workers and credit unions in the United States to remittance receivers and credit unions in over 40 countries in Latin America and other parts of the world.

To better serve the burgeoning Guatemalan migrant community, WOCCU affiliated with the Guatemala-based Federación Nacional de Cooperativas de Ahorro y Crédito (FENACOAC). This enabled WOCCU to link its IRNet with 25 credit unions in Guatemala, most of which are members of FENACOAC. By the end of 2004 these credit unions had 563,446 members and were located in numerous departments and municipalities throughout the country, including in several indigenous regions. The number of remittance transactions handled by these Guatemalan credit unions increased from 53,893 in 2002 to 497,504 in 2004, and the value of their transactions through the IRNet rose sharply as well, from US$26.6 million in 2002 to US$178.8 million in 2004 (Grace 2005).

A study by WOCCU found that by the end of 2004 the 25 local credit unions affiliated with FENACOAC still controlled only 6.7 percent of the market for remittance transfers from the United States to Guatemala. However, the study also found that both members and nonmembers of these credit unions who had their remittances processed through the credit unions and the IRNet did so at much lower cost than had been the case with the traditional cash transfer companies. In a more detailed look at five of the credit unions, 40 percent of the receivers said that the main reason they had joined the credit union was because of the remittance services it offered. They particularly appreciated the credit unions' rural locations and their speedy delivery of funds sent from the United States (WOCCU 2005).

Moreover, Guatemalans who used the credit unions to receive remittances were able to access other financial opportunities as well. Over 65 percent of the people surveyed, many of whom were rural indigenous women, said they were willing to deposit an average of 22 percent of the remittances they received into their new credit union savings accounts. These new members of Guatemalan credit unions were also able for the first time to draw on credit to cover payment of outstanding loans and to invest in new activities to improve the income and welfare of their families.

By supporting such local credit unions, the Guatemalan government and international development institutions could contribute to lowering the costs of remittance transfers. This in turn would increase the social welfare impacts of remittances on Mayan and other poor families. These institutions could also help by partnering with Mayan hometown associations—and perhaps also with religious organizations such as Pastoral Maya—to inform Mayan migrants in the United States and their families in Guatemala about the services provided by such organizations as WOCCU and FENACOAC.

Forge development partnerships with migrant associations

The government of Guatemala and international development and migration agencies are exploring various opportunities to collaborate with Guatemalan hometown associations to promote local economic development in Guatemala. These include, among others, partnerships aimed at directing remittances to local development, support for Mayan cultural tourism projects, and marketing of traditional products made by indigenous agricultural and artisan groups.

The International Organization for Migration has announced a National Community Fund Program for Guatemala. This program, which is in an early stage of development, will "harness the productive potential of remittances to the development needs of Guatemalan communities" by promoting joint investment ventures to benefit the migrants' hometowns (Orozco 2005a).

Agencies in Guatemala are attempting to promote local community development through the support of cultural tourism initiatives in Mayan communities in the Western Highlands. The Multilateral Investment Fund of the Inter-American Development Bank has provided a US$1.6 million grant to the Guatemalan Chamber of Tourism to "strengthen the capacity of Mayan communities to design, organize, and market ethnic tourism products in a sustainable manner." Among other things, the project includes the development of tourism products, the organization of ethnic tourism networks, technical assistance for Mayan organizations and communities interested in promoting cultural tourism, and improvements in the marketing of cultural tourism by these organizations and communities (IDB 2005).

There appears to be ample potential for Mayan associations in the United States to become involved in cultural tourism in Guatemala by providing both cultural and financial support. Q'anjob'al Mayan migrant leaders with whom I talked in Los Angeles in February 2006 indicated strong interest in such a possibility. Promotion of cultural tourism would enable them to maintain their cultural heritage and identity while supporting projects to increase the income and development of their hometowns. This may be one of the principal areas for future collaboration between Mayan migrants in the United States and Mayan communities in Guatemala.

Finally, Guatemalan migrant associations interested in supporting local economic and social development could also benefit from contacts with several new NGOs in Guatemala that are seeking international markets for indigenous products. The Corn Maya Project in Indiantown, for instance, has been working with organic coffee producers in the indigenous community of Jacaltenango in the state of Huehuetenango to help them market their products in Florida and other parts of the southern United States.

Other potential partners include indigenous agricultural cooperatives such as Manos Campesinas (Peasant Hands), an association of small coffee producers. When the association was created in 1997, it comprised 620 farmers belonging to six cooperatives that produced coffee on traditional indigenous lands. Today it has 1,073 members organized in eight cooperatives located in the heavily indigenous departments of San Marcos, Quetzaltenango, Retalhuleu, and Sololá. Manos Campesinas provides its farmers with technical assistance to increase the quantity and quality of their coffee harvests. It has formed fair trade agreements with a number of international coffee purchasers, including Starbucks, that are interested in purchasing organic coffee.[15]

Another indigenous organization in Guatemala that markets its products abroad is Mayan Hands. Established in 1989, it works with approximately

200 weavers, organized in groups of 12 to 50 women, living in 11 different communities around the Western and Northern Highlands. The organization provides the weavers with quality raw materials and helps them develop products whose design and colors suit the international market. It then purchases the products from the women at fair prices and markets them in the United States and Europe. Although most of the women artisans are still quite poor, members of this organization can now count on a modest but regular income.[16] A major opportunity exists for linking up Mayan hometown associations in the United States with these and other Mayan NGOs in Guatemala for purposes of economic development and trade. It is likely that the Internet can play a key role in facilitating these connections.

In sum, there are many possibilities for Mayan migrant associations in the United States to send assistance to their hometowns, collaborate with credit unions and NGOs, and eventually cooperate with governmental and international agencies to promote local economic and social development in their communities of origin. All, however, depend on the migrants' ability to remain in the United States and earn adequate income. This in turn hinges in large part on the U.S. government's immigration policies and practices, especially in relation to the large proportion of Guatemalan immigrants who are undocumented and whose future in the United States is far from secure.

Impact of U.S. Immigration Policy

Of the estimated 1.3 million Guatemalan migrants in the United States, approximately 60 percent are believed to be undocumented. Like millions of other undocumented immigrants from Latin America and other regions, they have a fragile foothold in their adopted country. U.S. immigration policies are increasingly geared toward criminalizing and eventually deporting such "illegal" migrants, as well as stemming the tide of new entrants. This stands as an enormous obstacle to the migrants' efforts to assist not only their own families but also entire communities in their countries of origin.

The Guatemalan government has emphasized the critical importance of migration and remittances to the country's poor and rural communities. In October 2005, Hurricane Stan raked the Western Highlands, killing 1,500 people and leaving rural villages devastated. Following the precedent set after Hurricane Mitch, which hit Honduras and Nicaragua in the late 1990s, the Guatemalan government asked the U.S. government to grant temporary work permits to about 300,000 Guatemalans who were living and working in the

United States but lacked legal documentation. Guatemalan officials feared that if large numbers of migrants were forced to return to Guatemala, they would be unable to find productive employment in the hurricane-ravaged economy. Equally important, U.S.-based migrants and hometown associations were sending valuable financial support to the communities damaged by the hurricane. Deportation of undocumented migrants would sever that lifeline (Aizenman 2006).

The U.S. government refused to respond to the Guatemalan government's request for the work permits. At the same time, the U.S. Congress began to discuss legislation that would crack down on unauthorized immigrants in the country. Approved by the House of Representatives in December 2005, the bill sparked protests among immigrant groups, labor organizations, and religious groups. It also drew an anguished response from inside Guatemala. Representatives of over 80 community organizations in mainly rural and indigenous areas of the country sent a letter to the U.S. Senate, asking senators not to approve the proposed law. The letter, written in English, Spanish, and Maya K'iche', stated,

> Should legislation such as H.R. 4437 pass, Central America will enter a period of economic and political instability. . . . We ask that you consider a collaborative and comprehensive solution to immigration issues, one that *looks carefully at the long-term development and stability of migrants' communities of origin* as well as their destinations in the United States [emphasis added].

Although the bill was not enacted, efforts to restrict and deport undocumented migrants redoubled at both the state and federal levels. Immigration and Customs Enforcement, successor to the INS, introduced a nationwide program to conduct raids on workplaces and deport undocumented workers. More than 18,000 Guatemalans were sent back to their native country in 2006. Border security funding doubled between 2001 and 2007, to US$10.4 billion, and the number of border patrol agents increased by 63 percent, even as discussions on new immigration legislation began.

Criminalizing aliens and attempting to seal the country's borders is not in the United States' interests, for at least three reasons. One, such efforts are costly and ineffective. Two, they are counterproductive in relation to the U.S. economy: these workers fill an important gap in the U.S. labor force. And three, the favorable spillover effects from migration contribute to higher living standards, stability, and democracy "in the neighborhood." In light of these factors, U.S. immigration policy needs to be more innovative, providing migrants with a clear path to legal residency and work permits—and eventually citizenship—so that they can contribute to their new communities while continuing to assist their communities of origin.

In the 21st century, immigration is a key aspect of the struggle to reduce poverty and inequality and promote sustainable development. Immigration policy and international development programs must work hand in hand. This is particularly true in relation to indigenous migrants, who make up a significant proportion of those from Latin America. The large Mayan-speaking population of Guatemala suffers much higher rates of poverty than the country's non-indigenous population. Mayan migrants in the United States are providing critical help to their families and home communities, especially through their ethnic migrant associations. If undocumented Mayan immigrants continue to be forced to repatriate against their wishes, poverty in rural Guatemala is likely to increase. But if indigenous immigrants are provided with more secure rights of residency, employment, and social protection in the United States, they could become one of the most important forces helping the Guatemalan government create a more socially inclusive, equitable, and multicultural democracy and society.

Notes

1. These figures come from the 2002 national census. Two non-Mayan indigenous languages, spoken by smaller groups of people, are Xinca and Garífuna. For background on the Maya and other indigenous groups in Guatemala, see Tovar (2001) and Shapiro (2006).
2. The findings of the Historical Clarification Commission are described by Susanne Jonas (2000) in her book on the Guatemalan peace process. The Commission's charge of genocide is reported in a detailed article in the *New York Times* (Navarro 1999) that also contains a special section by Christian Tomuschat, coordinator of the Historical Clarification Commission, titled "The Atrocity Findings: The Historic Facts Must be Recognized."
3. Guatemalan academic and social researchers have carried out some important studies of poverty issues, especially as they relate to the country's large rural and indigenous populations. See, for example, von Hoegen and Palma (1999), Lopez Rivera (1999), and Alvarez Aragon (2003).
4. Chapter 2 and annex 4 of the 2004 World Bank study provide more detailed data on rural and indigenous poverty rates in Guatemala. However, besides the IOM 2004 survey already noted and some data in the 2000 Encuesta Nacional de Condiciones de Vida (ENCOVI), which was the basis of the 2004 World Bank study cited here, relatively limited household survey research has been done on the relations between poverty, ethnicity, and migration in Guatemala.

5. For background studies on these changes in agrarian structures and their effects on indigenous communities, see the works of the Guatemalan historian Julio Castellanos Cambranes (1986, 1992). Also see the Spanish translation of my 1970 doctoral dissertation on the history of indigenous land tenure in the Q'anjob'al-speaking community of Santa Eulalia in the department of Huehuetenango (Davis 1997). A major study of minifundia/latifundia agrarian structure in Guatemala was conducted by the Inter-American Committee of Agricultural Development under the direction of the well-known agricultural economist Solon Barraclough in the early 1960s (CIDA 1971).

6. For a detailed analysis of the findings of the 1979 national agrarian census and the changes in land use in rural Guatemala in the 1980s and early 1990s, see World Bank (1995).

7. The National Indigenous and Campesino Coordinating Committee (CONIC), a Guatemalan nongovernmental organization, has attempted to pressure successive Guatemalan governments to implement the sections of the 1985 Guatemalan constitution and the peace accords that call for protection of the land and natural resource rights of indigenous and other rural Guatemalans. Despite enormous repression, CONIC has highlighted the need for the national government to address problems of unequal land tenure.

8. For background on these changes in the rural export and labor economies of Guatemala and their impact on migration in the 1990s, see Gutiérrez Echeverria (2004) and Gálvez Borrell and Gellert (2000).

9. For background on the early experiences of Mayan Indian refugees in Los Angeles, see Loucky (2000) and Popkin (1999).

10. On the experiences of Q'anjob'al Mayan migrants in Los Angeles in the 1980s, see Peñalosa (1985) and Arriola (1987). On the Indiantown migrant community, see Wellmeier (1998) and Burns (1993). In addition, an interesting series of articles titled "Indiantown's Guatemalans" appeared in the December 12, 1988 edition of the *Palm Beach Post*. One of these articles, "Guatemalans Divide Indiantown," describes conflicts between the Mayan migrants and some sectors of the host community who opposed the presence of the newcomers.

11. Hagan (1994) provides an interesting account of how IRCA affected one Mayan migrant community, a group of K'iche' speakers from the department of Totonicapán that settled in Houston, Texas in the 1980s and early 1990s.

12. Background on the history and current activities of the Asociación Q'anjob'al Ewulense is available on the organization's website at http://www.ewulenseusa.org.

13. The Pastoral Maya project has worked closely with the faculty of Kennesaw State University in Georgia, which has provided facilities for the annual meetings. On the objectives and activities of the project, see LeBaron (2006).

14. With a Gini coefficient of 58.3 in 2000, Guatemala continues, along with Brazil, to be among the countries with the highest income inequality measures in Latin America (see de Ferranti et al. 2004 and R. N. Adams 2002).

15. For background on Manos Campesinas, see http://www.manoscampesinas.org.

16. For background on Mayan Hands, see http://www.mayanhands.org.

References

Adams, R. H. Jr. 2004. "Remittances and Poverty in Guatemala." Policy Research Working Paper 3418, World Bank, Washington, DC.

Adams, R. N. 2002. *Etnicidad e igualidad en Guatemala*. Serie Políticas Sociales 107. Santiago, Chile: Economic Commission for Latin America and the Caribbean.

Aizenman, N. C. 2006. "For Guatemalan, Deportation Would Be 'Disaster.'" *Washington Post*, February 2, A15.

Alvarez Aragon, V., ed. 2003. *El rostro indígena de la pobreza*. Guatemala City: FLACSO.

Arriola, L. 1987. "Instrumental Acculturation: The Experience of Kanjobal Amerindians in Los Angeles." Hampshire College, Amherst, MA.

Bair, S. C. 2005. "Improving the Access of Recent Latin American Migrants to the U.S. Banking System." In Terry and Wilson 2005, 95–131.

Baxter, K. 1990. "Mayan Culture Finds a Haven." *Los Angeles Times*, August 30, E10.

Burns, A. F. 1993. *Maya in Exile: Guatemalans in Florida*. Philadelphia: Temple University Press.

Carmack, R. M., ed. 1988. *Harvest of Violence: The Maya Indians and the Guatemalan Crisis*. Norman: University of Oklahoma Press.

Castellanos Cambranes, J. 1986. *Introducción a la historia agraria de Guatemala: 1500–1900*. Guatemala City: Serviprensa Centroamericana.

———. 1992. *500 años de lucha por la tierra: Estudios sobre propiedad rural y reforma agraria en Guatemala*. Guatemala City: FLACSO.

CIDA (Comite Interamericano de Desarrollo Agrícola). 1971. *Tenencia de la tierra y desarrollo socio-económica del sector agrícola en Guatemala*. Guatemala City: Editorial Universitaria.

Dardon, J. 2005. "Pueblos indígenas y la migración internacional en Guatemala: De las comunidades en resistencia hacia las comunidades transnacionales." Paper presented at conference on "Migración: Pueblos Indígenas y Afroamericanos," organized by the Universidad Nacional Autónoma de México, Universidad Iberoamericana de Puebla, and the Instituto de Ciencias Juridicas A.C., Mexico, November 15–19.

Davis, S. 1983. "Guatemala's Uprooted Indians: The Case for Political Asylum." *Global Reporter: A Journal of Peoples, Resources and the World* (Anthropology Resource Center) 1 (3).

———. 1997. *La tierra de nuestros antepasados: Estudio de la herencia y la tenencia de la tierra en el altiplano de Guatemala*. Antigua, Guatemala: Centro de Investigaciones Regionales de Mesoamérica; South Woodstock, VT: Plumstock Mesoamerican Studies.

Davis, S., and J. Hodson. 1982. *Witnesses to Political Violence in Guatemala: The Suppression of a Rural Development Movement*. Boston: Oxfam America.

de Ferranti, D., G. Perry, F. Ferreira, and M. Walton. 2004. *Inequality in Latin America: Breaking with History?* Washington, DC: World Bank.

Fajnzylber, P., and H. López. 2007. *Close to Home: The Development Impact of Remittances in Latin America*. Washington, DC: World Bank.

Gálvez Borrell, V., and G. Gellert. 2000. "Las migraciones como estrategias de sobrevivencia de los excluidos y sus determinantes territoriales." In *Guatemala: Exclusion social y estrategias para enfrentarla*, 175–343. Guatemala City: FLACSO.

Migration, Remittances, and Ethnic Identity: Guatemalan Maya **353**

Grace, D. C. 2005. "Exploring the Credit Union Experience with Remittances in the Latin American Market." In *Remittances: Development Impact and Future Prospects,* ed. S. M. Maimbo and D. Ratha, 158–73. Washington, DC: World Bank.

Gutiérrez Echeverria, M. 2004. "Enfermedad holandesa y migración internacional: El caso de Guatemala." In *Después de Nuestro Señor, Estados Unidos: Perspectivas de análisis del comportamiento e implicaciones de la migración internacional en Guatemala,* ed. S. I. Palma C., 207–26. Guatemala City: FLACSO.

Hagan, J. M. 1994. *Deciding to Be Legal: A Maya Community in Houston.* Philadelphia: Temple University Press.

Hernandez, M. 1984. "Kanjobal Indians: Guatemala to L.A.: Bid for Survival." *Los Angeles Times,* September 24, 1.

IDB (Inter-American Development Bank). 2005. "Guatemala: Competitive Development of Cultural Tourism with Indigenous Communities." Donors memorandum GU-M1005. Multilateral Investment Fund, Inter-American Development Bank, Washington, DC.

IOM (International Organization for Migration). 2004. *Encuesta sobre impacto de remesas familiares en los hogares guatemaltecos: Año 2004.* Cuadernos de Trabajo Sobre Migración 19. Guatemala City: IOM.

Jonas, S. 2000. *Of Centaurs and Doves: Guatemala's Peace Process.* Boulder, CO: Westview.

LeBaron, A., ed. 2006. *Maya Pastoral: National Conferences and Essays on the Maya Immigrants: 2004 and 2005.* Kennesaw, GA: Kennesaw State University Press.

López Rivera, O. A. 1999. *Guatemala: Intimidades de la pobreza.* Guatemala City: Instituto de Investigaciones Económicas y Sociales, Universidad Rafael Landívar.

Loucky, J. 2000. "Maya in a Modern Metropolis: Establishing New Lives and Livelihoods in Los Angeles." In Loucky and Moors 2000, 214–22.

Loucky, J., and M. M. Moors. 2000. *The Maya Diaspora: Guatemalan Roots, New American Lives.* Philadelphia: Temple University Press.

Morales Almada, J. 2004. "Al rescate de la cultura Maya." *La Opinión* (Los Angeles), May 16.

Orozco, M. 2005a. "Migrant Hometown Associations (HTAs): The Human Face of Globalization." In *World Migration 2005: Costs and Benefits of International Migration,* 279–85. Geneva: International Organization for Migration.

———. 2005b. "Migration, Money and Markets: The New Realities for Central America." In Terry and Wilson 2005, 193–217.

Orozco, M., and S. R. Wilson. 2005. " Making Migrant Remittances Count." In Terry and Wilson 2005, 375–94.

Peñalosa, F. 1985. "La situación sociolinguistica de los Kanjobales en Los Angeles, California." Paper presented at VII Taller Maya, Antigua, Guatemala, June 17–25.

Popkin, E. 1999. "Guatemalan Mayan Migration to Los Angeles: Constructing Transnational Linkages in the Context of the Settlement Process." *Ethnic and Racial Studies* 22 (2): 267–89.

Rodríguez, L. F. 2000. "Nuestra gente en Los Estados Unidos." *Prensa Libre,* October 18. Available at http://www.prensalibre.com/especiales/ME/chapines/default.htm.

Shapiro, J. 2006. "Guatemala." In *Indigenous Peoples, Poverty and Human Development in Latin America,* ed. G. Hall and H. A. Patrinos, 106–49. New York: Palgrave Macmillan.

Task Force on Remittances. 2004. *All in the Family: Latin America's Most Important International Financial Flow*. Washington, DC: Inter-American Dialogue.

Terry, D. F. 2005. "Remittances as a Development Tool." In Terry and Wilson 2005, 3–19.

Terry, D. F., and S. R. Wilson, eds. 2005. *Beyond Small Change: Making Migrant Remittances Count*. Washington, DC: Inter-American Development Bank.

Tovar, M. 2001. *Perfil de los pueblos: Maya, Garífuna y Xinka de Guatemala*. Guatemala City: Regional Unit for Technical Assistance (RUTA), World Bank, and Guatemalan Ministry of Culture and Sports.

UNDP (United Nations Development Programme). 2001. *Guatemala: El financiamiento del desarrollo humano*. Cuarto informe nacional de desarrollo humano. Guatemala City: United Nations.

von Hoegen, M., and D. Palma. 1999. *Los pobres explican la pobreza: El caso de Guatemala*. Guatemala City: Instituto de Investigaciones Económicas y Sociales, Universidad Rafael Landívar.

Wellmeier, N. J. 1998. *Ritual, Identity, and the Mayan Diaspora*. New York: Garland.

Williams, K. 2006. "Immigrants Sending US$45 Billion Home." *Washington Post*, October 19, A9.

World Bank. 1995. *Guatemala: Land Tenure and Natural Resources Management*. Washington, DC: World Bank.

———. 2004. *Poverty in Guatemala*. Washington, DC: World Bank.

WOCCU (World Council of Credit Unions). 2005. *Credit Union Remittance Services in Guatemala: Expanding the Access of Low-Income Remittance Recipients to Financial Institutions*. AMAP Microreport 24. Washington, DC: U.S. Agency for International Development.

Index

STs. *See* scheduled tribes
subprotective welfare state, 138
Survey of Labour and Income Dynamics
(SLID), 129, 130–131, 131*f*
SUSENAS. *See* National Socioeconomic
Survey (SUSENAS)
Sweden
income mobility, 137–138, 150–151,
154, 155*t*, 156, 157–158*t*, 159–160
Level of Living Survey, 128, 137–138,
154, 155*t*, 156, 157–158*t*,
159–160
poverty persistence, 1991-2000, 143,
143*f*, 144
poverty persistence by social origin,
1991-2000, 145, 145*f*, 146
poverty rate and persistence by sex
and social class, 1991-2000, 144,
144*f*, 145
welfare regime, 139
symmetric income movement, 5

T
Tanzania
datasets used in research, 117*t*
Kagera Health and Development Study,
106–107, 107*t*
Targeted Public Distribution System
(TPDS), 200–201
Thimmegowda, T., 209, 214–215
Three Worlds of Welfare Capitalism, 138
time dependence, 5
TPDS. *See* Targeted Public Distribution
System (TPDS)
transfer costs, 316, 321*b*, 328, 344–346
transient poor, 80–81, 82–83*t*
Tres por Uno program, 319*b*, 322–323
Tunisia
entrepreneurial remittances, 325

U
Uganda
attrition in panel surveys, 103*t*
datasets used in research, 117*t*
poverty trends, 176
Stages of Progress study, 165, 168
UNDP. *See* United Nations Development
Programme (UNDP)
Unidos por la Solidaridad, 320
United in Solidarity, 320

United Kingdom
Cross-National Equivalent Files,
135–136, 136*f*
measuring poverty dynamics, 146,
146*t*, 147
poverty rates and poverty persistence
over six or eight years, 135–136,
136*f*, 154*t*
relation between income stability
and individual characteristics,
143, 150
welfare regime, 139, 151
United Nations
Commission on Human Rights, 299
Human Development Index, 135
Millennium Development Goal, 200
United Nations Development
Programme (UNDP)
Guatemalan report, 336
Human Development Index, 2
United States
Cross-National Equivalent Files,
135–136, 136*f*
Guatemalan migrants, 333–334,
338–348
hometown associations, 318–319,
319*b*, 320–323, 340–343
United States—*Cont.*
impact of Guatemalan migrants on
immigration policy, 348–350
measuring poverty dynamics, 146,
146*t*, 147
migration into, 308
Panel Study of Income Dynamics,
104, 128, 130–131, 131*f*, 132,
134–135
poverty dynamics, 150
poverty rates, exit rates, and poverty
persistence, 1993-95, 130–131,
131*f*, 132, 134–135, 152–153*t*
poverty rates and poverty persistence
over six or eight years, 135–136,
136*f*, 154*t*
relation between income stability
and individual characteristics,
142–143
Stages of Progress study, 168
welfare regime, 139–141
U.S. Conference of Catholic Bishops,
322, 342

ECO-AUDIT
Environmental Benefits Statement

The World Bank is committed to preserving endangered forests and natural resources. We have chosen to print *Moving Out of Poverty (vol. 1): Cross-Disciplinary Perspectives on Mobility* on 50-pound New Life Opaque, a recycled paper with 30% post-consumer waste. The Office of the Publisher has agreed to follow the recommended standards for paper usage set by the Green Press Initiative, a nonprofit program supporting publishers in using fiber that is not sourced from endangered forests. For more information, visit www.greenpressinitiative.org.

Saved:

• 15 trees

• **10 million** BTUs of total energy

• **1,296** pounds of net greenhouse gases

• **5,381** gallons of waste water

• **691** pounds of solid waste